MW01078266

Celebration Bar Review

Multistate Bar Review Book 2

This book is provided for the exclusive use of

This Registered Celebration Bar Review Student

And may not be used by any other person without written permission of Celebration Bar Review. No Resale Permitted.

TABLE OF CONTENTS

CONTRACTS & SALES

This outline follows the outline provided by the National Conference of Bar Examiners (NCBE) which spells out the testable areas of the law. For the Multistate Bar Examination, examinees are to assume that Articles 1 and 2 of the Uniform Commercial Code have been adopted and are applicable when appropriate. According to the NCBE, approximately 60% of the Contracts questions for each MBE will be based on categories I, VII, and VIII (Formation, Conditions, and Remedies). All of the major topics (designated by Roman numerals) will be represented in each examination, but not necessarily all of the subtopics. Approximately 25% of the Contracts questions for each MBE will be based on provisions of the Uniform Commercial Code, Articles 1 and 2.

Applicability of Article 2

Where Article 2 of the U.C.C. applies, and where it contains provisions in conflict with the common law of contract, the U.C.C. is the applicable law. Article 2 applies whenever there is a sale of goods, even if the sale is between nonmerchants. Therefore, if A, a lawyer, sells her computer to B, a consultant, the transaction is covered by Article 2.

Some of the rules of Article 2 change depending upon whether the parties (or at least one of the parties) is a merchant, but all sales of goods are covered.

In a few areas, there is some question as to whether Article 2 is applicable. A troublesome situation is where the transaction is primarily a service contract, for example, a treatment provided by a beauty shop or by a barber. In many of these cases there is a transfer of some good (hair shampoo), and the question is whether the Code applies to all or part of the transaction. Another questionable transaction is that which involves a sale of goods along with the sale of the goodwill of a business. In all of these cases, it appears that the trend is to apply the U.C.C. either directly or by analogy, but there is no uniformity among the decisions. See Barco Auto Leasing Corp. v. PSI Cosmetics, Inc., 125 Misc.2d 68, 478 N.Y.S.2d 505 (1984).

Article 2 of the Code is perhaps best understood if it is remembered that its many provisions "fill in the gaps" left by the agreement of the parties. Freedom of contract pervades this article, and most of its provisions take effect only if the parties fail to agree.

When Article 2 of the U.C.C. applies, and when it contains provisions in conflict with the common law of contract, the U.C.C. is the applicable law. Article 2 states that it applies to "transactions in goods," except secured transactions. U.C.C. §2-102. It does not apply to sales of realty.

A **sale** is basically a **transaction wherein the seller transfers ownership of goods to the buyer for a price.** The primary obligations of the **seller** are:

1) to **transfer title** to the goods; and
2) to **deliver possession** of the goods.

The primary obligations of the **buyer** are:

1) to **accept ownership** of the goods; and
2) to **pay the price.**

The Code specifically provides that the service of food by a restaurant is a contract for the sale of goods under Article 2, at least for the purpose of the implied warranty of merchantability. U.C.C. §2-314. Additional examples will be provided throughout these materials.

I. FORMATION OF CONTRACTS

The most common definition of a contract is "a promise that the law will enforce." Most contracts consist of mutual promises between two or more parties. In general, the requirements of a contract may be listed as follows:

1) **Mutual assent**, i.e., offer, and an acceptance of that offer;
2) **Consideration**;
3) Two or more parties having **legal capacity** to contract; and
4) An object of the agreement that is **not prohibited by law**.

A. MUTUAL ASSENT

The first requirement of a contract is that the parties mutually assent to the terms of the agreement. Manifestation of assent is sometimes called a **"meeting of the minds." Objective manifestation of assent is essential**. It is immaterial what the parties secretly or subjectively intended.

A manifestation of assent may be made by written or spoken words, by acts, or by a failure to act. For conduct to be effective as a manifestation of assent, the party must

1) **intend** to engage in the conduct, and
2) know or have reason to know that the **other party may infer his consent** from his conduct.

The mutual assent necessary for the formation of a contract generally takes the form of an **offer by one party and an acceptance of that offer by the other party**. An intent to adopt a written memorial of an agreement later does not in and of itself prevent the formation of a contract once an offer has been accepted. A contract concluded by preliminary agreements is, however, modified by a subsequent written memorial of the contract that changes the terms, pursuant to the parol evidence rule.

1. Offer and Acceptance

a. The Law and Rules of "Offer"

An offer is defined as **a communication which gives the recipient of the communication the power to conclude a contract by accepting**. The test of when a communication amounts to an offer is whether the recipient could reasonably believe that the one communicating intended to give him **the power to conclude a contract**. Whether it is reasonable for the recipient to believe that an offer has been made is determined from the words and actions of the person making the alleged offer, and the circumstances surrounding the making of the communication.

The use of the word "quote" in general indicates that no offer is intended, while the use of the word "offer" indicates that an offer is intended. However, the use of either word **does not necessarily control** whether the communication will be construed as an offer. The law recognizes that these words, or similar words, may be used interchangeably in business without intending to give them their technical effect.

> For example, in the case of Fairmount Glass Works v. Cruden-Martin Woodenware Co., 106 Ky. 659, 51 S.W. 196 (Ky. App. 1899), the language, "We quote you Mason fruit jars . . .pints, $4.50; quarts, $5.00; half gallons, $6.50 per gross, for immediate acceptance, and shipment not later than May 15, 1895 . . ." was held to be an offer to sell. The reasons – *(1)* the terms of the proposal were spelled out in considerable detail – even the time for acceptance of the offer ("for immediate acceptance"), and the time for delivery, were specified – and *(2)* the "quote" was in response to an inquiry made by the potential buyer.

Inquiries, invitations for offers and simple statements of intent are not offers. Therefore, the statement, "I want to sell my car for $10,000; are you interested?" is not an offer. Nor would the following communication be an offer: "I need 200 widgets and will pay up to $400 for them. Can you deliver them by January 15th?"

Although an answer to an inquiry is not always an offer, there is a tendency to hold that less specific language is required to create a contract when the communication is sent in response to an inquiry.

It may be important in a given fact situation **whether the communication is sent to one or to many people.**

> For example, a flyer sent out by a real estate company to all past customers advertising a reduced price on a house would not be construed as an offer, if it was clear from the body of the letter that the flyer was sent to more than one person.

An offer may, however, create a power of acceptance in more than one person.

> For example: A, the purveyor of a medical preparation, says that he will pay $100 to anyone who contracts a certain disease after using the preparation as directed. B, C, and D use it as directed. Each has made a contract independent of the others, and is entitled to the $100 if he later contracts the disease.

Advertisements in newspapers, on television, or by direct mail are **not generally considered to constitute offers**. They are merely "invitations to make an offer." The reason for this rule probably combines a policy decision favoring the right of a merchant to make known what he has for sale without exposing himself to liability in the event that many people wish to purchase his product, with a determination by the court that the language used in advertisements generally is not such as to indicate that the advertiser is giving to the public the power to conclude a contract.

Multistate Bar Review Book 2

An advertisement may be held to be an offer where it is definite, limits quantity, and states something indicating an intent to be an offer. For example, if a store advertised, "One fur coat, $500 value for $1 - one only, first come, first served," this would be an offer.

A promise to pay a reward in the event that something is found or a criminal is captured does constitute an offer. These cases are different from the normal commercial advertisement in that in the case of a reward only one person (or at least only a very few people) will have the opportunity to accept.

At **auctions**, generally the **auctioneer invites offers** from successive bidders which he may accept or reject. However, **where the auction is without reserve, the auctioneer makes an offer to sell at the highest price bid**. After the auctioneer calls for bids, the goods cannot be withdrawn unless there is no bid within a reasonable time. A bidder may always withdraw his bid until the auctioneer announces completion of a sale, even if the auction is without reserve. Such a retraction does not revive any previous bid.

When a statement which could be construed as an offer is made **in anger or in jest, and the person to whom it is made knows this or should have known it**, then no offer is made. For example, where A is unhappy with her car, which is worth $5,000, and says, "I'll sell this thing to the first person who pays me $100," if a reasonable person would conclude that she is simply saying this as a joke or because she is angry, there would be no offer.

b. How Long Does the Offer Last?

Assuming that an offer has been made, **the offeree's power of acceptance arises on completion of the offeror's manifestation of assent, and continues until terminated**. Once an offer is terminated, it can no longer be accepted. An offer may be terminated in any one of the following ways:

1) **When the offer specifies a particular time during which the offeree may accept, the offer expires automatically upon the passage of that period of time. Courts tend to construe strictly provisions stating when an offer will terminate.** Where the time is specified as a certain number of days, e.g., "This offer expires in five days," the time starts to run from the time the offer is received by the offeree. If a certain day is set for expiration of the offer, e.g., "This offer expires on January 5th," the acceptance must be before midnight of the day stated.

2) **When there is no time specified in the offer for its termination, it automatically terminates after the passage of a reasonable period of time. Even offers which state that they may be accepted "at any time" are construed to mean "within a reasonable time."** The **basic test** of what constitutes a "reasonable period of time" is the time that would be thought satisfactory to the offeror by a reasonable person in the position of the offeree. This depends upon the circumstances of the case and the nature of the offer. Where the parties are dealing face to face or on the telephone, the time for acceptance does not extend beyond the end of the conversation, unless a contrary intent is indicated.

3) **An offer sent by mail clearly is seasonably accepted if the acceptance is mailed any time before midnight on the day the offer is received. A longer time may be reasonable.** For example: A makes B an offer by mail to sell goods. B receives the offer at the close of business hours. His prompt acceptance by letter the next morning is timely.

Multistate Bar Review Book 2

4) **Trade custom or language in the offer may expressly or impliedly extend the time for accepting.** Since the need for a limit on the time for acceptance of an offer is based on the need to limit the offeror's risk of commitment during the period for communication of acceptance, when the offer is for the purchase or sale of goods or property subject to rapid fluctuation in value, the time for acceptance may be very short.

5) **In the case of an offer for a reward, it has been held that the reasonable period of time can be as long as is necessary for the criminal to be captured and convicted.** On the other hand, if the reward is prompted by a temporary emergency, then the offer terminates as soon as the emergency is over.

6) **Once the offeree rejects the offer, the offer is terminated.** There must, however, be a rejection of the offer and not a mere inquiry. For example: If there is an offer to sell goods for $500, and the offeree says: "Can't you lower the price to $400?" this does not constitute a rejection, and the offer is not terminated.

A rejection is not effective until it is brought to the attention of the offeror. Thus, when a rejection is sent by mail, the offeree can still "overtake the rejection" and accept by a telephone call made prior to the time that the letter is received by the offeror.

An attempted acceptance which changes the terms of the offer operates as a rejection and terminates the offer. Thus, if the offeror offers to sell Blackacre for $200,000, and the offeree states that he will buy the property but pay only $185,000, this amounts to a rejection of the offer and it cannot be later accepted. **The communication by the offeree would be a "counteroffer,"** i.e., an offer by the offeree to the offeror relating to the same matter as the original offer and proposing a substitute bargain different from that proposed by the original offer. The counteroffer can be accepted by the original offeror.

Similar to the rule governing rejections, **an inquiry or request for different terms does not constitute a counteroffer**. Thus, if the offeree, in response to the original offer, said: "I don't think I can pay $200,000, but would you consider $185,000?" this would not constitute a counteroffer, and would not terminate the original offer to sell for $50,000.

Uniform Commercial Code Section 2-207 often alters the rules of counteroffers. Under this section, **a purported acceptance which changes the terms of the offer often operates as an acceptance**. (This section is discussed in more detail later.)

c.   Revocation of the Offer

Unless the offer is "irrevocable" or a "firm offer," the offeror retains the power to revoke it at any time, even if the offer states that it will be held open for a specified period of time. Thus, even if an offer states, "I will hold this offer open until January 23rd," the offer can be revoked prior to January 23rd, unless some rule makes it irrevocable. Use of any words that clearly indicate that the offeror no longer wishes to enter into the deal are sufficient; use of the word "revoke" is not necessary.

General offers (those made to a large number of unnamed people, such as by advertisement in a newspaper), **can only be revoked by a notice given publicity equal to that given the offer**. If better means of notification are available, publication alone may not be effective to revoke the offer.

> For example: A, a newspaper, publishes an offer of prizes to the persons procuring the largest number of subscriptions as evidenced

> by cash or checks received by a specific time. B submits an entry blank with his name and address, which is received by A. Thereafter, during the contest, A publishes a notice that personal checks will not be counted; B does not see the notice. B is not bound by the notice of revocation, since A could have given B personal notice. However, as to anyone who has actual knowledge of the intent to revoke, a revocation is good.

A divisible offer may be revoked so that no future contracts will be created, even though some contracts have already been formed. An offer is divisible if it contemplates a series of independent contracts created by separate acceptances.

> For example: A offers to sell B a ton of cotton daily and tenders one ton at once. B accepts the tender. The same amount is furnished daily for a number of days. A notifies B that he revokes the offer and will furnish no more cotton. A contract is formed each day that cotton was furnished, but the revocation prevents the formation of any contracts thereafter.

A revocation is effective as of the time it is received by the offeree. Thus, if A sends an offer to B by mail, and later mails a revocation, a contract is formed if B accepts after receiving the offer but before receiving the revocation. However, if A, after mailing the offer, calls B before B has accepted, informing him that A is revoking, B cannot thereafter accept.

Where the offeree becomes aware of facts which clearly show that the offeror no longer wishes to enter into the deal, the offer is also revoked. This is called **indirect revocation**. In most cases, revocation is accomplished by the offeror's giving notice to the offeree that he or she wishes to revoke the offer.

> Example: if A offers to sell her violin to B, and promises to keep the offer open for 10 days, the offer is nonetheless revoked if B learns from a reliable source that A has sold her violin to C during the 10-day period.

Brokers' listing agreements may be terminated without notice, direct or indirect, to the offeree (the broker) of the revocation. Where an owner has listed his house for sale with a broker, this amounts to an offer, with the owner promising to pay a commission in the event that the broker procures a buyer ready, willing, and able to purchase on the terms specified by the owner. If the owner privately sells the house, or sells it through another broker, this amounts to a revocation of the offer, even though the broker is not informed of the sale and even if he knows nothing about it.

d.   Limitations on Revocation

There are three situations in which an offeror does not have the power to revoke his offer:

1) where there is a promise not to revoke and that promise is enforceable;
2) where the acceptance consists of an act by the offeree and the offeree has begun to perform; and
3) where U.C.C. §2-205 makes the offer irrevocable.

Multistate Bar Review Book 2

If the offeror promises to keep the offer open for a specified period of time, and the offeree pays him for this promise to keep the offer open, the offer is irrevocable during that period of time. This is called an **option contract.**

> Example: If A says, "I will sell you Blackacre for $200,000, and I will keep this offer open for 30 days," and if B, the offeree, pays A $100 in return for A's promise to keep the offer open, the offer cannot be revoked by A. There is good consideration for the promise to keep the offer open, and that promise is in itself an enforceable contract. The offeror is considered to have lost or bargained away the *power* to revoke, and an acceptance of the offer by B after an attempted revocation by A operates to form a contract for the sale of Blackacre.

In some circumstances a promise to keep the offer open can be implied, and that the doctrine of promissory estoppel will operate to make enforceable the implied promise to keep the offer open.

> Example: If a general contractor asked for bids on parts of a job, and a subcontractor agreed to do the paving work required in the general contract for a specified price, it was held that the subcontractor could not revoke his bid (offer) once the general contractor had used the subcontractor's figure in preparing his own bid. The court found an implied promise to keep the offer open for a reasonable time after the general contractor won the job, and that this promise was enforceable because the general contractor had relied to its detriment on the subcontractor's offer.

When the offeror requires that his offer be accepted by the performance of some act (an offer for a unilateral contract), and the offeree performs part of the act, there is no acceptance because an acceptance occurs only when all of the act is performed. However, it would be unjust to allow the offeror to revoke once there has been any substantial performance by the offeree.

Section 45 of the Restatement therefore, provides that once there has been the beginning of performance or tender of performance by the offeree, a contract is formed, and the offeror must perform when the offeree completes his or her performance. In effect, this makes the offer irrevocable **as soon as there is substantial part performance.**

A distinction is made between **"part performance"** and **"mere preparations;"** the offer does not become irrevocable if the act done by the offeree is merely in preparation for doing what was asked.

> Example: If A says to B, "I will pay you $5,000 if you paint my house," once B has started to paint the house, A can no longer revoke her offer. If B had merely purchased the paint or brought his equipment to A's house, the offer would not become irrevocable.

UCC Section 2-205 provides that offers to buy or sell goods become irrevocable under the following circumstances:

1) when there is an **assurance** that the offer to buy or sell goods will not be revoked;
2) the assurance is in a **writing signed** by the offeror; and
3) the offeror is a **merchant.**

The period of irrevocability cannot exceed three months under this section. **No consideration is necessary** to support the promise or assurance that the offer will be kept open.

e. Termination of the Offer

The general rule is that the **death or insanity of the offeror automatically terminates the offer, even if the offeree does not know of the offeror's death or insanity.** The death or insanity of the **offeree** also effectively terminates an offer, because there is no one who has the power to accept.

Where performance by one of the parties becomes illegal prior to acceptance by the offeree, the offer is considered automatically terminated even though performance was legal at the time the offer is made.

> For example, A offers to sell B 10 AK45 weapons. After the making of the offer, but before its acceptance, a law is passed prohibiting the sale of such weapons. The offer is terminated.

If the offer contemplates the sale or lease of specific property, its destruction before acceptance terminates the offer.

The terms of the offer may specify certain conditions of acceptance which must be complied with for the offer to be accepted. Such a condition may be express, implied, or constructive. For example: Since by common understanding, an offer of a reward can ordinarily be accepted only once, the first acceptance terminates the power of acceptance by others. Also, a bid at an auction terminates the power of the auctioneer to accept a prior, lower bid.

After an offer has terminated, it can be revived by the offeror. This usually occurs when the termination is caused by a rejection or a counteroffer. Thus, if A makes an offer to B to sell B his car for $1,000 and B rejects, but A then says, "Well, why don't you think it over for a couple of days?" the offer is revived and B has a couple of days in which to accept.

f.   Acceptance at Common Law

An acceptance is **the assent by the offeree to the proposal made by the offeror.** In effect, it is the exercise of the power to conclude a contract which the offeror gave to the offeree. The requirements of an acceptance are as follows:

1) it must be made by a party to whom the offer is addressed;
2) it must be in the terms of the offer;
3) the offeree must know of the offer at the time he accepts; and
4) the acceptance must be communicated to the offeror to be effective.

Party to Whom an Offer Is Made. Offers may be made to particular individuals or to groups of persons. When the offer is made to a number of individuals, the offer is called a "general offer." An offer to pay a reward for the capture of a criminal or for the return of a lost item are typical examples of "general offers." Anyone within the general class of individuals addressed may accept a general offer.

The power to accept an offer is not transferable. When one or several individuals are addressed specifically in the offer, then only they are eligible to accept. If A makes an offer to B, B cannot transfer the right to accept to C. Thus, if A offers to purchase goods from the XYZ Company and the XYZ Company allows the Acme Corporation to fill the order, the filling of the order by Acme does not constitute an acceptance or a contract, but merely an offer by Acme to A to provide goods.

However, an option is transferable. Also, if the person to whom the offer is made accepts, he can usually assign his rights and delegate his duties under the contract. These rules are supplemented by the rules of agency. If there is no indication to the contrary, it is assumed that any necessary act, including an acceptance, may be performed on behalf of a contracting party by an agent. Thus, the agent of an offeree may accept for her.

Acceptance Must Be in Terms of Offer. An offeror is in complete control of his offer, and the acceptance must be on the terms of the offeror. This means that:

1) the acceptance cannot vary the terms of the offer;
2) unilateral offers must be accepted by the doing of an act; bilateral offers generally must be accepted by a promise, but can sometimes be accepted by performance; and
3) if the offeror specifies any particular manner of acceptance, this must be followed by the offeree.

If, however, the offeror does not specify a form of acceptance, the offeree may accept by any reasonable means of acceptance.

Traditional contract law takes the position that any change in the terms of the offer made by the offeree in her attempted acceptance prevents the formation of a contract. This is still the majority view in cases not governed by Article 2 of the U.C.C.

> Example, if A offers to sell B Blackacre, "The closing to be on December 15," and B responds, "I accept, closing to be held on December 10," no contract results because B did not accept A's offer on the terms stated by A. B has made a "counteroffer" which operates to reject A's offer and to make a new offer from B to A.

However, when the offeree attempts to add **terms which would be implied by the law even if not stated**, an acceptance does occur and a contract results.

> Example: If A agrees to sell Blackacre to B, and does not mention the type of title to be conveyed, a response by B that she accepts, "provided marketable title is tendered," would form a contract because the law would require A to provide marketable title.

Also, when the original offer leaves details of the bargain unstated, the filling in of these details by the offeree, provided they are reasonable, does not make her response a counteroffer.

> Example: If the offer did not state the place of closing for a real estate contract, and the offeree provided in her acceptance that, "closing will be at your office," a contract would be formed.

Likewise, the **fact that the offeree inquires as to whether the offeror would consider changing terms does not constitute a rejection and counteroffer**.

> Example: If the offeror offers to sell at $1,500, and the offeree responds "Would you consider selling for $1,400?" and the offeror says no, the offeree can still accept the offer to sell at $1,500. This is to be contrasted with the case where the offeree responds, "I will purchase for $1,400." This is more than an inquiry; it states a new term. Therefore, it is a counteroffer and a rejection.

A conditional return promise by the offeree does not make the acceptance itself conditional.

> Example: A makes a written offer to sell B a patent in exchange for B's promise to pay $15,000, and there is language in the offer that B's acceptance will be considered conditioned upon "B's advisor (X) approving the purchase." B signs the writing in a space labeled "Accepted" and returns the writing to A. B has made a conditional promise but an unconditional acceptance. There is a contract, but B's duty to perform the contract is conditioned on X's approval.

Contracts formed by offers which call for a promise are called "bilateral contracts" because, upon formation, both parties are bound by enforceable promises. **Contracts formed by offers which call for an act are called "unilateral contracts" because, upon formation, only the original offeror has any remaining obligation.** When an offer calls for an act, the doing of the act constitutes the acceptance, and it must be done before the contract is formed.

Unless the offer specifies, the offer can be accepted by either promise or performance. In this case, part performance or the tender of performance is an acceptance and at the same time is a promise to complete the performance. If the offer requires any specified method of acceptance, this must be followed in order for the acceptance to be valid. The mere **suggestion** of the time, place, or manner of acceptance does not necessarily preclude another method of acceptance.

> Example: A offers to sell a bicycle to B for $250, and states that no acceptance will be honored other than the mailing of B's personal check for exactly $250. B personally tenders $250 in cash, or mails a personal check for $275. There is no contract.

Offeree's Knowledge of Offer at Time of Acceptance. **Performance of an act requested by an offer made before the offeree has knowledge of the offer does not create a contract**. However, where the offeree has only partially completed performance, completion of the requested performance with knowledge of the offer acts as an acceptance of the offer.

> Examples: A offers a reward for the apprehension and delivery of a certain criminal. B apprehends the criminal before he knows of the

> offer, but then delivers the criminal to the police after learning of the reward. B is entitled to the reward. Or A, an employer, posts a notice offering a certain bonus to any employee who continues to work for A for four months. B, an employee, learns of the offer one month after the notice was posted, and continues to work three more months. B is entitled to the bonus.

Where identical offers are made, A to B and B to A, and these cross in the mails, no contract is formed under traditional contract law, even though there is mutuality of assent in fact. This is because neither A nor B knew of the other's intent to contract.

Communication of Acceptance. The general rules relating to the need for communication of acceptance to the offeror are:

1) where the acceptance is by **performance** of an act (unilateral contract), **no notification** of acceptance is necessary, unless the offer requests it; but
2) where acceptance is made by a **promise** (bilateral contract), the offeree generally **must notify** the offeror of his acceptance.

The rule that no communication is required for acceptance by performance of an act is subject to the qualification that notice is required where the performance is not likely to come to the attention of the offeror. Technically, the offeror's contractual duty arises as soon as the offeree completes the act, but it is discharged if the offeree does not use reasonable diligence in notifying the offeror.

The majority rule in contracts concluded by correspondence is that the acceptance takes effect as soon as it is put out of the possession of the offeree. This rule generally applies to correspondence by mail or telegram. Thus, an offeree accepts as soon as he posts his letter of acceptance. This is often called the **mailbox rule**. Adams v. Lindsell, 1 B. & Ald. 681 (K.B. 1818). However, an acceptance delivered by an employee or agent of the offeree is not effective until it is received by the offeror. The agent-employee's possession is held to be the same as the offeree's.

Since the offeror is in control of the offer, he may vary these rules if he wishes. He may, for example, dispense with the requirement of notice of the acceptance, even though he is entitled to it. On the other hand, he may provide that no acceptance is valid until he actually receives notification of it.

When contracts are concluded by correspondence, the traditional rule is that the offeree must respond by the same means in which the offer was made. In other words, if the offer is by mail, the acceptance must be by mail. The **modern trend,** however, is away from this strict rule and toward a rule which provides that **any reasonable means of communicating the acceptance is valid.** Article 2 of the U.C.C. provides that acceptance can be "by any medium reasonable under the circumstances," unless a specific medium is required by the offer. U.C.C. §2-206.

The means used in giving notice of acceptance is usually important only in those cases where the acceptance never reaches the offeror or arrives late. If the offeror, in fact, receives the notice of acceptance within the time allowed for acceptance, the acceptance operates to conclude a contract, no matter how it is communicated.

> Example: If A communicates an offer to B in which A states, "I must receive your acceptance by return mail," an acceptance sent within a reasonable time by some other means which reaches A as soon as return mail would have, creates a contract on arrival, because the offer will be interpreted as simply requiring an answer within the time it takes for return mail to arrive. The offeror, however, has full control and if he *specifically* requires that the acceptance must be made in a particular manner, then no attempted acceptance is valid unless the manner specified in the offer is followed.

Normally, silence does not constitute acceptance. Thus, if an offer includes the provision, "Unless I hear from you within five days, I will assume that you have accepted my offer," the offeree will not be bound if he or she remains silent for the five-day period.

Silence will constitute acceptance only in the following situations:

1) where the **offeree takes the benefit of offered services** with a reasonable opportunity to reject them, and with reason to know that they were offered with the expectation of compensation;

2) where the **offeror has stated or given the offeree reason to understand that assent may be manifested by silence or inaction**, and the offeree by his silence or inaction intends to accept; or

3) where, due to **previous dealings** or otherwise, **it is reasonable that the offeree should notify the offeror if he does not intend to accept**.

> Example: A salesman visits businesses soliciting offers for his company. If over a period of time, his company has consistently accepted all offers made by the businesses he visits, then silence constitutes an acceptance of orders given by the businesses.

> Example: A gives a number of piano lessons to B's child, intending to give the child a course of twenty lessons, and to charge B the price. B never requested A to give this instruction, but silently allows the lessons to continue, having reason to know A's intention. B is bound to pay the price of the course.

> Example: A offers by mail to sell to B a cow already in B's possession for $250, saying: "I am so sure that you will accept that you need not trouble to write me. Your silence alone will operate as acceptance." B makes no reply, *intending to accept* the offer. The cow belongs to B. B owes A $250.

Conduct on the part of the offeree may also be construed as assent to the proposition made by the offeror. Thus, the retention of an insurance policy may be tantamount to a promise to pay premiums and constitute an acceptance of an offer to insure.

g. Acceptance under the Uniform Commercial Code

Article 2 makes contracts somewhat easier to form. **Under §2-204(1), a contract for the sale of goods may be made in any manner sufficient to show agreement, including conduct by both parties which recognizes the existence of a contract.**

U.C.C. Section 2-207 changes the counteroffer rule with regard to contracts for the sale of goods. Section 2-207, as **unamended (see callout box below)** provides:

(1)   A **definite and seasonable expression of acceptance** or a written confirmation which is sent within a reasonable time operates as an acceptance, even though it states terms additional to or different from those offered or agreed upon, unless acceptance is expressly made conditional on assent to the additional or different terms.

(2)   The **additional terms are to be construed as proposals** for addition to the contract. Between **merchants, such terms become part of the contract unless**:
   (a)   the offer expressly limits acceptance to the terms of the offer;
   (b)   they materially alter it; or
   (c)   notification of objection to them has already been given within a reasonable time after notice of them is received.

(3)   Conduct by both parties that recognizes the existence of a contract is sufficient to establish a contract for sale, although the writings of the parties do not otherwise establish a contract. In such cases, the terms of the particular contract consist of those terms on which the writings of the parties agree, together with any supplementary terms incorporated under any other provisions of this Act.

Under §2-207(1), a contract is formed whenever there is a **"definite and seasonable expression of acceptance"** or a **"written confirmation,"** unless acceptance is expressly made conditional on assent to the additional or different terms. The extent to which the terms of the acceptance vary or add to the offer does not seem to be relevant, except that the changes may bear upon whether the writing can be construed to be a **"definite"** acceptance or confirmation. It is only where the acceptance is **expressly** conditioned upon the offeror's assent to the new or different terms that a contract is not formed.

However, where the "expression of acceptance" deviates substantially from the offer, courts are reluctant to find that a contract is formed. There is a tendency to treat the response of the offeree as something other than an "acceptance," and to hold that the response is a counteroffer. Whether a contract ultimately results depends on whether the original offeror accepts the counteroffer. This approach is a throwback to the common law.

Assuming that a contract has been formed even though the acceptance contains terms additional to or different from the offer, the question arises whether these additional or different terms become a part of the contract formed.

If **both** parties are merchants, **additional or different** terms **do** become a part of the contract, **unless**:

   1)   they materially alter the offer, **or**
   2)   they are objected to by the offeror in advance of the acceptance, **or**

3) they are objected to by the offeror within a reasonable time after the offeror obtains notice of them.

The U.C.C., by its terms, treats different and additional terms differently. Under the plain wording of the U.C.C., different terms (those that vary or contradict a term of the offer) never become part of the contract. However, courts have either ignored or avoided this rule, presumably viewing it as too harsh and impractical. Thus, the rule applied on the bar exam is that different terms are incorporated into a contract if they meet the criteria stated above.

U.C.C Section 2-207(3) provides for the formation of a contract by virtue of the **conduct of the parties**. If the conduct includes some written expression of the parties' agreement, then the terms of the contract include whatever terms the parties agreed to in writing. As to other terms, those implied by the Code in the absence of agreement apply. For example, if the writings of the parties agreed only to the description and quantity of the goods, the Code would supply the price term, the place of delivery, warranties, and so on.

> Note that UCC 2-207 has been recently amended, and probably not for the better. Basically, the unamended 2-207 states above that a contract is formed whenever there is a "definite and seasonable expression of acceptance" or a written confirmation (even if the terms are different) unless acceptance is expressly made conditional on those additional or different terms. Between merchants, those different terms become part of the contract unless the offer expressly limits acceptance to the terms of the offer, they materially alter it, or notification of the objection to the new terms is timely given. UCC 2-207(3) provides that a contract is formed by virtue of the parties' conduct, including what is in their writing and the UCC would fill in terms that are not in writing (i.e. place of delivery). Pre-amended 2-207 deals with the offer and acceptance, whereas the amended version now applies to all contracts and is only concerned about the terms that constitute the contract, namely, those terms that appear in the records of *both* parties to which they both agree. So, for 2-207 to even apply there must be a contract and then it is a question of sorting through the parties' correspondence to determine what the terms of the contract are. The text of new 2-207 reads as follows:
>
> Subject to Section 2-202, if (i) conduct by both parties recognizes the existence of a contract although their records do not otherwise establish a contract, (ii) a contract is formed by an offer and acceptance, or (iii) a contract formed in any manner is confirmed by a record that contains terms additional to or different from those in the contract being confirmed, the terms of the contract are:
> (a) terms that appear in the records of both parties;
> (b) terms, whether in a record or not, to which both parties agree; and
> (c) terms supplied or incorporated under any provision of this Act.
>
> Please keep in mind that this section is quite vague. Even the new comment points this out by stating that its intent may be to give courts more discretion to determine what contract terms have been

> agreed to (i.e. inviting litigation). There is much uncertainty and debate with the new 2-207, so, although you may want to be aware of the new provision, it is probably not necessary to fully understand its application.

Under §2-206 of the Uniform Commercial Code, an offer to buy or sell goods may be accepted in any reasonable manner. The U.C.C. does not subscribe to the common law distinction between bilateral and unilateral contracts. The section specifically says that an order for goods may be accepted either by shipping the goods, or by promising to ship them. The shipment of defective, nonconforming goods is an acceptance, and a contract is formed unless the seller notifies the buyer that they are not meant to fill the order. The buyer may reject them and sue for any damages resulting from the seller's failure to deliver conforming goods, or if the buyer accepts the goods, he may have a remedy for any damages resulting from the nonconformity.

2. Mistake, Misunderstanding, Misrepresentation, Nondisclosure, Confidential Relationships, Fraud, Undue Influence, and Duress

Mistake in General. The law of mistake involves situations where one or more parties to an agreement were **mistaken about a material fact at the time of the agreement.** Mistake can be raised either as a defense by a party seeking to avoid liability under a contract or affirmatively by a party seeking cancellation, rescission or reformation.

Often parties enter into a contract with the knowledge that they may be mistaken about a material fact. **If a party consciously assumes the risk** that a fact may be different from what that party thinks, and it later develops that the party was in fact "mistaken," **the law provides no relief** for that party.

> Example: A sells a gem to B, both believing that the gem is probably topaz, but both also are aware that it might be a diamond, which is far more valuable. If after the sale the gem is determined to be a diamond, A cannot claim "mistake" and obtain rescission of the contract.

> Example: B purchases an annuity from the C Insurance Company whereby B pays C $100,000 in return for C's promise to pay B $10,000 a year for the remainder of B's life. B has a life expectancy of 12 years. If B dies a month after the contract is executed, B's estate cannot claim "mistake" in an attempt to recover the $100,000 from C. In this case, B has assumed the risk that he would die before he recouped his investment, and C has assumed the risk that B might live for 25 more years

Generally, courts have divided mistake into **two categories - mutual and unilateral.** Courts use the distinction in determining whether the mistake is one for which the law provides relief.

Mutual Mistake. If **both parties to a contract are mistaken about a basic assumption** on which the contract was made, the contract is voidable by the person adversely affected by the mistake, **if the mistake has a material effect on the bargain.**

> Example: A and B contract to sell and buy Whiteacre, both believing it is covered by timber. Before the agreement was reached, the timber had been destroyed by fire. If the value of the land depends primarily on the existence of the timber, the contract can be avoided by the purchaser.

> Example: A and B contract to sell and buy Greenacre, both believing that it contains 100 acres, whereas it actually contains 90 acres. The price is not calculated from the acreage, but rather is a lump sum. The purchaser is entitled to relief if the total acreage was a material element of the agreement.

> Example: A agrees to sell a cow, "Rose," to B. Both parties believe the cow to be barren, good only for its value as beef, but in fact the cow is fertile, and capable of being bred. The contract is avoidable by A if there is a material difference in value between a barren and a fertile cow. Sherwood v. Walker, 66 Mich. 568, 33 N.W. 919 (1887).

> Example: In the classic case of Raffles v. Wichelhaus, 2 H & C. 906 (1864), the parties contracted for the purchase and sale of cargo, to be shipped by the vessel Peerless sailing from Bombay. Neither party was aware that there were two ships named Peerless, both sailing at different times, and each had a different Peerless in mind. The court held that there was a mutual mistake, and that there was no contract because there was not a meeting of the minds.

Unilateral Mistake and Misunderstanding. A unilateral mistake occurs when only one of the two parties to a contract was mistaken about a material fact which was a basic assumption upon which the contract was made. The general rule, in the case of unilateral mistake, relief will not be afforded the mistaken party unless the other party knew or should have known of the mistake, or unless the other party had a duty to disclose the fact as to which the other party was mistaken.

Consider the following examples:

> Example: A sends B a letter offering to sell B 1,000 pairs of shoes at $7.05 per pair. A intended to write that the price was $7.50 per pair. B accepts the offer. A contract is formed despite A's mistake. Note, however, that if B knew or should have known of the error – for example, if A's letter offered the shoes for $.75 per pair, clearly too low a price – B will not be allowed to "snap up" the bargain.

> Example: Similarly, A may intend to say to B, "I'll sell you my horse for $100," but, because of a slip of the tongue, A actually says "I'll sell you my cow for $100." If B accepts, a contract is formed for the sale of A's cow unless B knows or should have known of A's mistake.

The modern tendency in cases of unilateral mistake is for courts to be more lenient in allowing the mistaken party to avoid the contract. Today, avoidance is generally allowed if:

1) enforcement of the contract against the mistaken party would be **oppressive or result in an unconscionably unequal exchange of values**; and

2) rescission would pose **no substantial hardship** on the other.

The most common application of this doctrine involves a mistaken bid by a subcontractor, either because of a computational error or a misconstruction or misunderstanding of the invitation to bid.

> Example: A submits a bid to B to do certain work for $150,000. A believes this to be the correct total, but has inadvertently omitted a $50,000 item. B, having no reason to know of A's mistake, accepts A's bid. A is bound by the contract at common law. The Restatement (Second) of Contracts §153 (a) and the modern tendency suggests that A might be able to avoid the contract if the result were unconscionable, such as A's having to incur a $30,000 loss rather than a $20,000 profit.

Mistake in Transmission of Offer. Where an intermediary is used to transmit an offer and a mistake is made in the transmission, the majority rule is that **a contract is formed on the terms that are actually transmitted, unless the offeree has reason to suspect that a mistake has been made**. This is akin to the traditional "unilateral mistake" reasoning. Some courts reason that the intermediary is the agent of the offeror and the offeror is therefore bound. Other courts have ignored the agency theory, but have held the party who chose the method of transmission liable, most often the offeror.

Some courts have held that no contract exists because the transmitter is an agent that has exceeded the bounds of his agency. Still others have held that the intermediary is an independent contractor, and, neither party being bound by his actions, no contract has been formed because there was no "meeting of the minds."

Misrepresentation. If a person makes a fraudulent statement or misrepresents a fact, he may be liable in an action sounding in tort for damages resulting from the misrepresentation. In contract law, a misrepresentation made in connection with an agreement between parties may prevent the formation of a contract or make a contract voidable.

In general, **a misrepresentation is an assertion that is not in accord with the facts**. If the misrepresentation is **made knowingly (with scienter), it is fraudulent**. Under the Restatement (Second) of Contracts §162, it is also fraudulent if the person either:

1) does not have confidence in the truth of his assertion, or

2) knows that he does not have a basis for his assertion.

Multistate Bar Review Book 2

Nondisclosure. **In general, nondisclosure is not actionable**. However, a person's **nondisclosure** of a fact known to him is equivalent to an assertion that the fact does not exist (i.e., equivalent to an affirmative misrepresentation **only if:**

1) he knows that disclosure is necessary to prevent some **previous assertion** from being fraudulent;
2) he knows that disclosure would correct a mistake of the other party as to a **basic assumption,** and nondisclosure would amount to lack of good faith and fair dealing;
3) he knows that disclosure would correct a mistake of the other party as to the **contents or effect of a writing** evidencing or embodying their agreement; or
4) the other person is entitled to know the fact because of a **confidential or fiduciary relationship** between them. Restatement (Second) of Contracts §161.

Fraud in the Factum. Fraud in the factum, or as it is also called, fraud in the execution, **occurs when the fraudulent misrepresentation prevents a party from knowing the character or essential terms of the transaction.** In such cases, no contract is formed, i.e., the apparent contract is void. Where, however, the person could have discovered with the exercise of reasonable diligence the character or essential terms of the transaction, he is estopped from asserting that the contract is void. (However, the contract would probably be voidable under the rule applying to fraud in the inducement, discussed infra.)

> Example: Where the wife signed a separation agreement on the representation that it was a property division for income tax purposes, this was held to be fraud in the factum, and a void transaction. Curtis v. Curtis, 248 P.2d 683 (N.M. 1952).

In most cases, whether the contract is void or voidable is immaterial because the person has a defense in both cases. The distinction is more important when the rights of third parties are involved. A voidable contract can be ratified after the fraud is discovered, but a void one may not be.

Fraud in the inducement occurs when the misrepresentation is used to induce someone to enter into a contract. A contract thus entered into is voidable by the aggrieved party.

> Example: A, to induce B to purchase Blackacre from him, tells B that it contains 500 acres, when A knows that it contains only 400 acres. Under the more modern view, B has a right to avoid the contract even if A believed but did not actually know that Blackacre contained 400 acres. The rationale of the modern theory is that a contract is voidable whenever the misrepresentation is material, regardless of fraudulent intent.

Generally, **any wrongful act or threat which deprives a party of meaningful choice constitutes duress.** When a party's agreement is the result of physical duress, e.g., a strong person taking the other's hand and compelling him to sign a contract, the contract is void. When the duress is in the nature of a threat, then the contract is voidable. However, not all threats are improper. For example, a "threat" that one "will never talk to the person again" if he refuses to enter into a contract is not duress. Like fraud, duress can result in either a void or voidable contract.

Multistate Bar Review Book 2

Undue influence occurs when one party uses his **dominant psychologic position** or **position of trust and confidence** to induce the subservient party to consent to an agreement to which he would otherwise have not consented. A prima facie case of undue influence requires four elements:

1) Facts showing **susceptibility of the party influenced**. Mental and physical weakness and psychological dependency go to show susceptibility;
2) Evidence of the **opportunity to exercise undue influence**. The existence of a confidential relationship such as husband-wife, physician-patient, pastor-parishioner, guardian-ward, parent-child, or fiancee-fiancee is strong evidence of such an opportunity;
3) Evidence of a **disposition to exercise undue influence**; and
4) Evidence of the **unnatural nature of the transaction**, whether via inadequacy of consideration or the neglect of the natural objects of one's bounty.

3.   Problems of communication and 'battle of the forms'

The "battle of the forms" refers to the problem of the drafter of a contract gaining the advantage in the transaction. UCC Section 2-207 attempts to do away with the battle of the forms. (See discussion under "Acceptance under the Uniform Commercial Code," infra.)

4.   Indefiniteness or absence of terms

The more definite the communication is, the more likely it is to be held to be an offer. In other words, where the alleged offer spells out such terms as quantity, quality, price, time of delivery, etc., a court will have less difficulty finding an intent to make an offer. For example: If A and B promise that clearly specified services shall be mutually rendered by them "immediately," "at once," "promptly," "as soon as possible," or "in about one month," offers have been made. On the other hand, if the communication simply says, "I have some widgets for sale," this looks like a mere invitation to make an offer.

For a communication to operate as an offer, it must be **sufficiently certain to allow the court to determine when a breach of the promise occurs, and also to permit the court to fashion a remedy for that breach.** Thus, if it is impossible to tell from the communication what is being promised, no contract can result even if the recipient attempts to "accept."

Section 2-204(3) of the Uniform Commercial Code specifically permits the parties to a contract for the sale of goods to **postpone agreement on certain terms** until sometime after the contract is formed. Thus, the parties can leave "open" terms that have not been agreed upon.

Where one or more terms are left open, then, under the Code, a contract is formed if:

1) the parties intended to make a contract, and
2) there is a reasonable and certain basis for giving an appropriate remedy.

If the open term is omitted from the contract, the Code will often fill the gap. For example, if there is no price term noted in the contract and the parties have not otherwise agreed to a price, the Code states that the price is a *"reasonable price."* U.C.C. §2-305.

B. CAPACITY TO CONTRACT

Kinds of Incapacity. In order to have a contract, the parties must have the legal capacity to incur at least voidable contractual duties. **Incapacity** arises from the following causes:

1) infancy;
2) mental illness or defect;
3) intoxication;
4) guardianship; and
5) corporate incapacity.

In addition, the civil powers of convicts, including the power to contract, may be suspended during imprisonment.

Liability for Necessaries. Persons with no capacity or a limited capacity to enter into a contract may be held liable for **necessaries** furnished. Liability, however, is based upon a quasi-contract theory and the person furnishing the necessaries can recover only their reasonable value and not the contract price.

1. Infancy

The traditional rule is that a natural person has the capacity to incur only **voidable** contractual duties until the beginning of the day before his **twenty-first birthday**. Virtually all jurisdictions have reduced this age to **eighteen**. Parties may have full capacity to contract when married, even if under the age of majority. If sued on a contract, the infant may defend on grounds of infancy.

Who May Avoid Contract. **Only the infant** has the right to avoid the contract, and if he elects to stand upon it, the other party is bound and must perform.

When Avoidance Must Occur. An infant need not take any action to disaffirm a contract until he comes of age. If the infant does not avoid the contract within a reasonable period of time after he reaches majority, he has ratified it and is liable on it. **Ratification** may be by any positive act signifying assent to the contract made after the infant reaches majority, or it may simply be by inaction. The right to avoid a contract is **personal to the infant,** and may not be exercised by a trustee in bankruptcy or other third party other than his guardian.

Requirement of Restitution. If the contract has been executed or partially executed, and the infant has reaped some gain from it, he must **return anything** that he still possesses when he elects to disaffirm. If he has used, lost, or otherwise disposed of the goods, he may still disaffirm and there is no requirement that he make restitution, or in any way pay for the use of the goods.

Necessaries. Infants **may avoid** contracts made for **"necessaries,"** but the law does require **payment of the fair market value** of those necessaries which are not returned. Technically, the recovery here is in quasi contract, as the law allows the infant to avoid his contract, but implies a promise to pay the fair value of the goods received.

2.   Mental Illness Or Defect

When a person is under guardianship because of mental incapacity, the general rule is that his or her contracts are **void** and thus unenforceable. A person not under guardianship incurs only **voidable** contractual duties if, by reason of mental illness or defect, he is:

a) unable to understand in a reasonable manner the nature and consequences of the transaction; or
b) unable to act in a reasonable manner in relation to the transaction, and the other party has reason to know of this condition.

When a contract is made on fair terms and the other party is without knowledge of the mental illness or defect, the power of avoidance of the mentally ill party terminates to the extent that the contract has been performed in whole or in part, or when the circumstances have so changed that avoidance would be inequitable. In such a case, a court may grant relief on such equitable terms as the situation requires.

> For example: A, an incompetent married woman not under guardianship, mortgages her land on fair terms to B, a bank which has no knowledge or reason to know of her incompetency, for a loan of $2,000. At her request, the money is paid to her husband, C, who absconds with it. The contract is not voidable.

Policy Considerations. Two conflicting policy interests must be reconciled in this area:

a) protection of justifiable expectations and of the security of transactions; and
b) protection of persons unable to protect themselves against imposition.

The law recognizes a wide variety of degree and types of mental incompetency, including: congenital deficiency in intelligence; mental deterioration from old age; brain damage by organic disease; and mental illnesses evidenced by such symptoms as delusions, hallucinations, delirium, confusion, and depression.

Burden of Proof. With **no adjudication** of incompetency, **the burden of proof is on the party asserting mental incompetency**. Almost any conduct of the party may be relevant to such proof. Proof of irrational, unintelligent behavior is essential. If a person has some understanding of a transaction, the controlling consideration is whether the transaction in its result is one which a reasonable, competent person might have made.

3.   Intoxication

A person incurs only **voidable** contractual duties by entering into a transaction **if the other party has reason to know** that by reason of intoxication, he is:

a) unable to understand in a reasonable manner the nature and consequences of the transaction; or
b) unable to act in a reasonable manner in relation to the transaction.

When a contract is voidable on the ground of intoxication, the party must **act promptly** to disaffirm when he becomes sober and learns of the contract. He must offer to restore any consideration received. Restitution is excused if the consideration was dissipated during the period of intoxication.

If the party has some understanding of the transaction despite intoxication, the controlling consideration is whether the transaction is one which any reasonable, competent person might have made. If so, the contract cannot be avoided, even though it is entirely executory. Few cases have actually allowed avoidance on the grounds of drunkenness. Even where drunkenness is a good defense, it is generally held that the party claiming it as a defense is liable on a quasi-contractual theory for the fair value of any goods or services rendered.

4. Guardianship

A person has **no capacity to incur contractual duties if his property is under guardianship** by reason of an adjudication of mental illness or defect, habitual intoxication, narcotics addiction, or because the person is a spendthrift, aged, or a convict. The policy of appointing a guardian is to preserve the property from squandering or improvident use. The guardianship proceedings are treated as giving public notice of the incapacity of the ward. Property under guardianship may be reached to satisfy the torts or quasi-contractual obligations of the ward.

It is important to distinguish between a guardianship of property, and the situation where a party is merely confined to a hospital.

> Example: Shortly after commitment to a hospital for the insane and while still confined, A conveys land to B, taking back a purchase money mortgage. Subsequently, C is appointed guardian of A's property. On A's behalf, C ratifies the conveyance, and sues to enforce the mortgage by foreclosure. B has no defense. Since A was not under guardianship, the conveyance and mortgage were voidable, not void.

5. Corporate Incapacity

Traditionally, corporations had capacity to contract only with regard to certain subject matters, usually outlined by government or corporate charter. Thus, any contract not contemplated by the charter was ultra vires and voidable at the election of the corporation. The modern tendency is to restrict the defense of ultra vires, and to give corporations full capacity to contract through duly authorized agents.

C. ILLEGALITY, UNCONSCIONABILITY, AND PUBLIC POLICY

1. Illegality

The law will not enforce a bargain that is in violation of any statute, court decision, or administrative ruling. Under this general rule, whenever an agreement requires one or more of the parties to perform an illegal act, the law will refuse to enforce the contract. Usually, this means that no relief will be given whether the action is brought on the contract, or in a count in restitution.

> For example: A enters into a gambling contract with B in a state where gambling is illegal. If A wins the bet, he cannot enforce his rights

> against B. On the other hand, if B voluntarily pays A, she will have no right to recover the money from A.

The same rule applies where a person renders valuable performance under the contract.

> For example: If the sale of tobacco were illegal under a state law, and X, under a contract of sale, delivered $1,000 worth of tobacco to Y, X would have no right to recover damages from Y either on the contract or in a count in restitution.

If a bargain that is legal when made becomes illegal before performance, the doctrine of impossibility provides that neither party is bound. If the reverse occurs, and a bargain that is illegal at the time it is made becomes legal, the general rule is that the bargain remains unenforceable unless the statute making the transaction legal is specifically retroactive.

The basic rule that illegal agreements are not enforced is, however, subject to a number of exceptions discussed below.

Divisible Contracts. When the performance of one of the parties is divisible, with part being legal and part illegal, the courts will generally enforce the part which is legal if the other party has performed.

> Example: A agreed to paint B's house in return for B's promise to pay $100 (legal), and also to smuggle goods into the country (illegal). Upon painting the house, A could recover the $100 promised by B, but could not recover any damages for B's refusal to bring goods into the country illegally.

If the illegal part of the bargain is particularly offensive - for example, involves killing someone - the court will probably refuse to enforce even the part of the deal that is legal.

Intended Illegal Use of Performance. In some transactions, the performance promised by one party can be used by the other party in either a legal or illegal way.

> Example: If A agrees to sell roulette tables to B in a state where gambling is prohibited, these may be used illegally in a gambling house, but they also can be used legally by a club or association if no money is being exchanged by those playing. Assuming that the sale of roulette tables is not itself illegal, A can recover the price of the tables when they have been delivered (or damages if B refuses to accept the tables), even if A knows that B intends to use them illegally. However, if A participates in the illegality, then A cannot recover. Thus, if A supervised the tables while they were being used illegally, he could not recover.

Pari Delicto. Where the parties are not in pari delicto (i.e., one of the parties is "less guilty" than the other) courts have allowed the "less guilty" party recovery when he has performed. Generally, this doctrine is applied where the statute being violated is designed to protect a class of persons of which the party seeking recovery is a member.

Multistate Bar Review Book 2

> Example, it has been held that a person can recover money paid to a professional bookmaker, and that a borrower is allowed to recover interest paid a lender in excess of the legal interest rate.

Locus Poenitentiae - Repudiation. The doctrine of locus poenitentiae applies in situations where one of the parties has **repudiated the agreement in time to prevent the illegal act**. In such cases, the repudiating party is generally allowed to recover for any performance rendered up until the time of repudiation. In most cases, the repudiation must occur prior to the performance of any illegal act. Most jurisdictions, however, refuse to apply the doctrine in cases where the illegal act would have involved moral turpitude.

Malum Prohibitum Acts. Although the general rule is that **all** illegal contracts are unenforceable, the argument has been raised in a number of cases that a contract should be enforced if the illegal act was only malum prohibitum and not malum in se. Although this argument is generally rejected, it is sometimes accepted in conjunction with a finding that there was no legislative intent to render contracts involving the statutory violation void.

Generally, contracts will be interpreted as **not** requiring an illegal act where this is reasonable. For example, one court held that a promise by the female plaintiff to "stay" with the deceased, a male, did not necessarily imply illegal cohabitation.

Licensing Statutes. Many statutes require individuals to obtain a license if they wish to engage in a particular trade, profession, or enterprise. Failure to procure the license is illegal, but not all contracts made by unlicensed persons are unenforceable. The basic rule is that the contract will not be enforced if the purpose of the statute is regulatory; however, if the purpose of the licensing requirement is to raise revenue, the contract will be enforced.

2. Unconscionability Under Article 2

Even if the contract is valid with respect to the above criteria, the court may refuse to enforce the contract in whole or in part on the ground of unconscionability.

UCC Section 2-302 states:

1) If the court as a matter of law finds the contract or any clause of the contract to have been unconscionable at the time it was made, the court may refuse to enforce the contract, or it may enforce the remainder of the contract without the unconscionable clause, or it may so limit the application of any unconscionable clause as to avoid any unconscionable result.

2) When it is claimed or appears to the court that the contract or any clause thereof may be unconscionable, the parties shall be afforded a reasonable opportunity to present evidence as to its commercial setting, purpose, and effect to aid the court in making the determination.

This section may be broken down into its important provisions as follows.

Question of Law. The section requires that the court find "as a matter of law" that the provision is unconscionable. Courts of equity, at least, have given specific recognition to the concept of

Multistate Bar Review Book 2

"unconscionable" contracts to prevent oppression and unfair surprise. In addition, many cases have given a strained interpretation to contract language in order to avoid harsh results. This section gives express approval to the equitable doctrine, and extends its application to cases at law involving contracts for the sale of goods.

Time Factor. The contract or clause must be offensive "at the time it was made," and facts subsequent to the moment of agreement have no bearing on the applicability of the section.

Divisibility. Under §2-302, the court may invalidate all or part of the contract.

Procedural and Substantive Unconscionability. Unconscionability can take two forms: procedural or substantive. **Procedural unconscionability** occurs when a clause of a contract is so worded as to make it confusing to the other party, or when the clause is hidden in a maze of other terms, on the back of the document, in small print, etc.

Substantive unconscionability occurs where the provision is so one-sided as to give an unfair (unconscionable) advantage to one party. In other words, substantive unconscionability involves overly harsh terms, while procedural unconscionability occurs when there is an attempt to "sneak" a provision into a contract without full awareness of the other party. **Williams v. Walker-Thomas Furniture Co.**, 350 F.2d 445 (D.C. Cir. 1965).

Unequal Bargaining Position of Parties. Although unconscionability is not confined by §2-302 to situations where one of the parties is in a superior bargaining position, e.g., a large corporation selling to an individual consumer, it is far more likely to be applied in such situations, particularly when there is a showing both of the seller's guile and of the consumer's ignorance, e.g., lack of ability to read the language of the contract.

Commercial Setting. Parties are permitted to introduce evidence of the "commercial setting, purpose, and effect" of the clause as relevant to its unconscionability. Courts are not receptive to claims of unconscionability raised by one merchant against another.

Examples. Comment 1 to the section cites the following examples of unconscionability and limitations imposed by courts on the application of such clauses:

(a)   The arbitrary right of a buyer to reject farm produce offered by seller, a farmer, under an entire output contract, coupled with the right to refuse seller permission to sell the rejected goods elsewhere, would be unconscionable.

(b)   A clause limiting time for complaints would be held inapplicable to latent defects which could be discovered only by microscopic analysis.

(c)   A general disclaimer of warranty clause would be held applicable only to express warranties, thus letting in an implied warranty.

(d)   A clause permitting the seller, upon the buyer's failure to supply shipping instructions, to postpone the delivery date indefinitely 30 days at a time, would be held not to postpone indefinitely the date of measuring damages for the buyer's breach.

(e)   Under a similar clause in a rising market, the court would permit the buyer to measure his damages for nondelivery at the end of only one 30-day postponement.

(f)   A clause limiting the buyer's remedy to return would be held to be applicable only if the seller had delivered a machine which reasonably met the contract description.

(g)   An express warranty by description would override a clause reading, "with all faults and defects," where adulterated meat below the contract description was delivered.

Whether inadequacy of consideration is sufficient to make a contract unconscionable is not clear. The official comments to the section indicate that it is not, but several cases have given the doctrine of unconscionability as a reason for holding a contract for sale invalid where the buyer had agreed to pay an unreasonable sum. American Home Improvement, Inc. v. MacIver, 105 N.H. 435, 201 A.2d 886 (1964); Jones v. Star Credit Corp., 59 Misc.2d 189, 298 N.Y.S.2d 264 (1969).

D.   IMPLIED-IN-FACT CONTRACT AND QUASI-CONTRACT

Conduct may indicate assent or agreement.

> Example: Thus, if one takes a pack of cigarettes from the counter of a drug store, this conduct indicates his intent to purchase the cigarettes. When the agreement is formed by virtue of conduct rather than expressed words, this gives rise to what is called an "implied contract."

In certain cases the terms of a contract are determined both by the expressed words of the parties and by conduct on their part. Whether the contract is express or implied does not affect the legal relationship between the parties or the rules of law that apply to this relationship.

"Quasi contracts," or, as they are sometimes called, **"contracts implied in law,"** are not true contracts at all. They do not depend upon assent between the parties, nor is recovery based upon a promise. In a quasi contract, the law imposes an obligation because it appears just.

Since the defendant has not made a promise in cases seeking quasi contractual recovery, the law cannot "enforce the promise" as it does in contract actions. Rather, **the law implies a promise (establishes a duty) that the defendant must make restitution to the plaintiff of any benefit that the plaintiff has conferred upon the defendant**. This is accomplished by awarding the plaintiff money **damages in the amount of the value of the benefit**. Thus, the theory of the action is restitutionary in nature; the law will restore the plaintiff to the position he or she was in prior to the transaction or event.

Although the theoretical distinction between contracts implied in fact and quasi contracts is clear, the differences sometimes fade and even appear entirely nonexistent in certain fact situations. For example: In a contract for services where no price term is agreed upon, the recipient of the services is obligated to pay the reasonable market value of the services. In such a case, it is difficult to determine whether the law finds this obligation because it assumes that the parties **implicitly agreed** on the fair market value as the price for the services, or because it believes that **it is just** to impose the obligation as a matter of law.

        Multistate Bar Review Book 2

E. 'PRE-CONTRACT' OBLIGATIONS BASED ON DETRIMENTAL RELIANCE

Although the common law rule is that an offer may be withdrawn prior to acceptance, an increasing number of courts are holding that **an offer may be rendered irrevocable on the basis of promissory estoppel where the offeree has relied to its detriment on the offer**.

> Example: A general contractor receives a low bid from a subcontractor and uses that low bid in preparing his own bid on a project. The majority of courts which have considered this issue have held that justifiable injurious reliance on the offer will render it irrevocable. See Restatement, Second, Contracts, § 87. However, if the subcontractor's bid is so low as to indicate it is based on a mistake, reliance is not justified.

F. EXPRESS AND IMPLIED WARRANTIES IN SALE-OF-GOODS CONTRACTS

The basic function of the warranty sections of the Code is to define what goods are sold, i.e., to spell out the kind and quality of the goods that must be delivered by the seller if she is to meet her delivery obligations. The warranty sections, along with negligence and strict liability theories, have also been used as a basis for products liability actions. Here, we are concerned primarily with warranties as the means of determining what goods must be delivered.

Comment 4 to §2-313 succinctly explains the role that warranties play in the Code: "The whole purpose of the law of warranty is to determine what it is that the seller has in essence agreed to sell."

The seller in a sales transaction has the obligation to transfer and deliver goods of the proper kind and quality. The kind and quality of goods that the seller must tender depend upon the representations the seller has made as to the goods she is offering for sale (express warranties), and upon any implied warranties imposed by the Code.

The initial source of evidence of kind and quality is the description of the goods in the contract. Such evidence also comes from all the representations and affirmations by word or conduct made by the seller to induce the buyer to enter into the transaction. These are classified by the Code as express warranties.

In addition to the objective manifestations of kind and quality made by the seller, **the law imposes upon her the obligation to tender goods meeting a minimum standard**. This is called the **implied warranty of merchantability.**

The Code also imposes a further duty on the seller whenever she has reason to know the particular purpose for which the goods were purchased. This is termed the implied **warranty of fitness for a particular purpose.**

1. Express Warranties

Express warranties consist of all **affirmations of fact and promises** made by the seller that relate to the goods, and are a part of the basis of the bargain. These may include, among other things:

1) Oral representations;
2) Written representations - in the written contract, or in advertisements and brochures;
3) Description of the goods;
4) Any sample or model shown;
5) Plans or blueprints of the item;
6) Technical specifications;
7) Reference to a market or official standard;
8) Quality of goods sent to the buyer in the past.

Thus, practically any objective manifestation made by the seller which relates to the goods may constitute an express warranty.

An essential requirement is that the representation became a part of the basis of the bargain. In other words, did it become a reason for the buyer's assent to the contract? No showing of reliance is required; rather, **it is assumed that the statement became a part of the basis of the bargain unless there is clear, affirmative proof to the contrary.**

The Code does not, however, destroy the principle that some statements made by a seller are mere seller's talk or "puffing." A statement purporting to be simply the seller's opinion is not an express warranty, nor is a simple affirmation of the value of the goods.

Express warranties can be made subsequent to the contract for sale. The subsequent promise or representation operates as a modification of the agreement, and under §2-209, no consideration is necessary to make it enforceable.

2. Disclaimers

Under §2-316(1), affirmations tending to establish an express warranty and disclaimer clauses are to be construed as consistent wherever possible. But if it is impossible to construe them as consistent, then the disclaimer clause is ignored.

In effect, the section says that when there is a positive affirmation, by word or conduct, which constitutes a warranty, a clause in the contract stating that there are no express warranties has no effect. Since the description of the goods constitutes a warranty, as does the use of any model or sample, §2-316(1) makes it difficult to imagine a contract in which no warranties are given.

3. Implied Warranty of Merchantability

When Given. A warranty of merchantability is given by **all sellers who are merchants**. Section 2-314(2) sets out the substance of the warranty of merchantability. It states:

Goods to be merchantable must be at least such as:

a) pass without objection in the trade under the contract description; and

b) in the case of fungible goods, are of fair average quality within the description; and

c) are fit for the ordinary purposes for which such goods are used; and

d) run, within the variations permitted by the agreement, of even kind, quality, and quantity within each unit and among all units involved; and

e) are adequately contained, packaged, and labeled as the agreement may require; and

f) conform to the promises or affirmations of fact made on the container or label, if any.

Basic Test. The basic test for the warranty of merchantability is **whether the goods would pass without objection in the trade** under the contract description, and whether they **are fit for the ordinary purpose for which such goods are used,** but each of the other requirements of the section must also must be met. Plaintiff must not only show a breach, but also that it was present at the time of the sale. This may be proved by inference.

Disclaimers. Under §2-316, the warranty of merchantability can be disclaimed (1) if the disclaimer uses the word "merchantability," and (2) if in writing, the language of the disclaimer is "conspicuous." An oral disclaimer of the warranty of merchantability is effective, but the word "merchantability" must be used.

"Conspicuous" is defined in §1-201 in the following way:

A term or clause is "conspicuous" when it is so written that a reasonable person against whom it is to operate ought to have noticed it. A printed heading in capitals (as: NONNEGOTIABLE BILL OF LADING) is conspicuous. Language in the body of a form is "conspicuous" if it is in larger or other contrasting type or color. But in a telegram, any stated term is "conspicuous." Whether a term or clause is "conspicuous" or not is for decision by the court.

4. Warranty of Fitness for a Particular Purpose

When Given. Under §2-315, a warranty of fitness for a particular purpose arises whenever the seller has reason to know:

1) of any particular purpose for which the goods are required; and

2) that the buyer is relying upon the seller's skill to select suitable goods.

There is no specific requirement that the buyer make the purpose known to the seller. It is enough if the seller has reason to know of the purpose and of the buyer's reliance, no matter what the source of this knowledge. Comment 5 to the section indicates that if the buyer asks for a trade name or patented product, this may indicate that he is not relying upon the seller's skill. Comment 4 to the section makes it clear that any seller, whether merchant or not, producer or not, makes this warranty under the proper circumstances.

Requirements of Warranty. When the warranty of fitness for a particular purpose is given, the goods must be fit for whatever the particular purpose is.

Disclaimer. Unlike a disclaimer of the warranty of merchantability, **the warranty of fitness cannot be excluded orally. It must be disclaimed in writing.** No specific language is required, however, and the section explicitly states that a clause reading "there are no warranties which extend beyond the description on the face hereof," is sufficient. The language must be "conspicuous."

5. Disclaimer of All Implied Warranties

Section 2-316(3) provides that:

(a) Unless the circumstances indicate otherwise, all implied warranties are excluded by expressions like **"as is,"** **"with all faults,"** or other language which in common understanding calls the buyer's attention to the exclusion of warranties and makes plain that there is no implied warranty; and

(b) When the buyer, before entering into the contract, has examined the goods or the sample or model as fully as he desired, or has refused to examine the goods, there is no implied warranty with regard to defects which an examination ought in the circumstances to have revealed to him; and

(c) An implied warranty can also be excluded or modified by course of dealing or course of performance or usage of trade.

"As Is," Etc. From subsection (a) of §2-316(3) it appears that a simple way in which to disclaim all implied warranties of quality is to state in the contract that the goods are sold "as is" or "with all faults." The catch is that the subsection begins with the words "unless the circumstances indicate otherwise."

Comments 6 and 7 to the section indicate that **an "as is" disclaimer may be effective only if it is reasonable to expect that the buyer will understand that there are no warranties** under the circumstances of the transaction. Under the wording of the section and the Comments, it would not be difficult for a court to refuse enforcement of the "as is" disclaimer where a form contract is used and the buyer is not a merchant.

Examination. Although subsection (b) provides that examination of a sample by the buyer will exclude certain warranties, it must be noted that it operates only as to defects that should have been revealed by a careful examination. Also, the exclusion of warranties applies only where there has been an actual examination, or a refusal to examine. "Refusal" means something more than simply an opportunity to examine which was not taken. There must be a demand by the seller that is refused by the buyer.

6. Limitations on Right to Modify Warranties as to Consumers

There is a trend, both through legislative enactment and court decisions, to prohibit limitation of warranty liability in consumer transactions. Thus, Alternative C of §2-318 (see infra under Privity) and some states prohibit the disclaimer of warranties in consumer sales. Also, cases have relied heavily upon the unconscionability section of the Code (§2-302) to hold disclaimers invalid where there is unequal bargaining power between the parties, or where the disclaimer is in fine print.

7. Applicability of Parol Evidence Rule

Section 2-316(1) specifically makes the provisions of the **parol evidence rule applicable to warranties.** However, a provision in the contract merely indicating that the writing is a complete integration of the parties' agreement would probably not have the effect of barring proof of any express warranties made before or at the time the writing was signed, since the Code provides that express warranties must be disclaimed specifically and obviously. Also, the requirement of good faith and the doctrine of unconscionability would probably prevent a seller from disclaiming express warranties by a nonspecific merger clause, at least as against a consumer. A merger clause would also not affect implied warranties, because implied warranties arise by operation of law.

8.   Cumulation and Conflict of Warranties

Under §2-317, **warranties, whether express or implied, are cumulative**. Thus, if an express warranty is made, this does not negate any implied warranty unless the implied warranty is inconsistent therewith. Comment 2 to the section states that the seller may be estopped from denying any inconsistency which in fact exists if she has led the buyer to believe that all of the warranties could be performed.

If the warranties do in fact conflict, then the **intention of the parties** determines which is dominant. The section provides three rules for ascertaining this intent:

1) Exact or technical specifications displace an inconsistent sample or model or general language of description;
2) A sample from an existing bulk displaces inconsistent general language of description; and
3) Express warranties displace inconsistent, implied warranties other than an implied warranty of fitness for a particular purpose.

9.   Privity of Contract and Warranty

The Official Text of the Uniform Commercial Code §2-318 has three alternative sections regarding the necessity of privity in a warranty action, with no recommendation as to which one a particular state should select. These alternatives are as follows:

ALTERNATIVE A

A seller's warranty whether express or implied extends to any natural person who is in the family or household of his buyer or who is a guest in his home if it is reasonable to expect that such person may use, consume, or be affected by the goods and who is injured in person by breach of the warranty. A seller may not exclude or limit the operation of this section.

ALTERNATIVE B

A seller's warranty whether express or implied extends to any natural person who may reasonably be expected to use, consume, or be affected by the goods and who is injured in person by breach of the warranty. A seller may not exclude or limit the operation of this section.

ALTERNATIVE C

A seller's warranty whether express or implied extends to any person who may reasonably be expected to use, consume, or be affected by the goods and who is injured by breach of the warranty. A seller may not exclude or limit the operation of this section with respect to injury to the person of an individual to whom the warranty extends.

Most states have accepted the position of **Alternative B** by case decision, or by a separate, non-Code statute. Thus, there is a clear trend toward abolition of the privity requirement.

Multistate Bar Review Book 2

II. CONSIDERATION

Most promises are enforced because they are supported by consideration. Consideration is generally defined as "bargained-for legal detriment." Thus, there are two elements of consideration:

1) **legal detriment** (what is given for the promise); and
2) **bargain** (the process by which the legal detriment was obtained by the promisor).

A.   BARGAIN AND EXCHANGE

The person furnishing the consideration (the promisee) must **do something or promise to do something that he does not legally have to do,** or he must **promise to forbear or actually forbear** from doing something that he has the legal right to do. The emphasis is on the word **"legal."** Thus, a promise to refrain from smoking would furnish perfectly good consideration, because everyone has the right to smoke, even though the forbearance may in fact be of benefit to the person promising it.

It is not necessary that the person attempting to enforce the contract be the one who furnished the consideration.

> Examples: If A says to B, "I will give you $1,000 if you will promise to write a book for C," and B makes this promise to C, then C can enforce the promise. The benefits of the bargain may go to the third party, rather than to the promisor. Thus, if A promises B that A will guarantee payment if B sells goods to C, the selling of the goods to C is good consideration for A's promise. Also, where A promises to pay $1,000 to a seller in exchange for the seller's delivery of a car to B, the delivery of the car to B is good consideration for A's promise.

Illusory Promises. Some statements which appear to be promises really promise nothing at all. Thus, if A says, "I promise to sell you my car next week **if I want to,"** this is in reality no promise, and it will not furnish good consideration for a return promise by someone else. Such promises are generally called "illusory promises." A common example of this is found where a definite promise is made but the promisor reserves the right to cancel.

> Thus, if A promises B to act as B's agent for two years from a future date, and B agrees to hire A but reserves the power to cancel the agreement at any time, then B's agreement is not consideration, since it involves no promise by him.

Alternative Promises. Whenever a promisor promises alternative performances reserving to himself the right to choose between them, there is consideration if each of the promised alternatives would be sufficient consideration in and of itself. Alternative promises constitute consideration if they offer at least the possibility of detriment over which the promisee has no control. A promise is not consideration if it involves alternatives over which the promise has control or freedom of choice, and one of the alternatives is non detrimental to the promisee.

Multistate Bar Review Book 2

> For example: A offers to deliver to B at $3 per bushel as many bushels of corn, not exceeding 4,000, as B may want within the next 60 days, if B will promise to order at least 1,000 bushels within that time. B accepts. B's promise is consideration, since B must order at least 1,000 bushels.

In addition to the requirement that there must be legal detriment, the concept of consideration also contains the requirement of bargained-for exchange. The performance or return promise of the promisee must be bargained for.

Conditional Gifts. There is a fine line between bargain and conditional gifts in some situations. When A says to B, "If you will come to my office, I will be glad to give you that book you have wanted," this is quite clearly a promise to make a gift and unenforceable, unless A has some reason for wanting to have B come to his office. There is no bargained-for exchange involved, so the requirement of consideration is not fulfilled.

Nominal Consideration. Confusion has arisen when a party attempts to transform a gift into a legally binding obligation by the use of nominal consideration. Assume Father wishes Daughter to have Blackacre, which is worth $25,000 on the open market. In order to make the promise to transfer Blackacre to Daughter binding, Father agrees in writing to sell Blackacre to Daughter for $1. Two contracts principles conflict: on the one hand, the law does not look into the adequacy of consideration in determining the validity of a contract. On the other hand, Father and Daughter have not "bargained" here, but merely attempted to disguise a gift as a contract.

Although there is authority to the contrary, the general view, as well as the Restatement (Second) of Contracts position (see §79, comment d, on "pretended exchange"), is that a contract such as the one described above is unenforceable. This situation is distinguished from an option to purchase land, where an owner is foregoing the legal right to sell his land for a specified period of time in return for a would-be purchaser's payment of a bargained-for sum.

> For example, if A paid $10 for a thirty-day option to purchase Blackacre for $10,000, the $10 is consideration for the collateral agreement to keep the offer open for thirty days.

Where an obligation is barred by the running of the statute of limitations, **a new promise to perform the obligation is enforceable,** even though it is not supported by consideration. Also, where there has been part payment of the debt after the statute has run, the part payment itself operates to revive the debt, and no new promise to pay the debt is necessary.

> For example, A owes B a $500 debt barred by the statute of limitations. A sends B a check for $300. If A states, or the facts suggest, that the check is sent as part payment of the debt, the delivery operates as a new promise to pay the debt. If there are no such facts or statements referable to the larger debt, it does not operate as a new promise.

Multistate Bar Review Book 2

B.   'ADEQUACY' OF CONSIDERATION: MUTUALITY OF OBLIGATION, IMPLIED PROMISES, AND DISPROPORTIONATE CHANGES

As a general rule, courts will not look into the adequacy of consideration. In other words, they will not attempt to determine whether the promises or performances exchanged are of comparable value, or are of any value at all. Equity courts, however, have refused to grant specific performance on the basis of inadequacy of consideration; and §2-302 of the Uniform Commercial Code may render unconscionable contracts unenforceable. Courts have also had some difficulty where the consideration, although bargained for by the promisor, is totally worthless.

Thus, if A promised to pay $1,000 for a stock certificate that was worthless, a question would be raised whether there was any consideration for A's promise. Gross inadequacy of consideration may raise issues of capacity to enter the contract and of fraud.

It is not necessary that the promisor derive any benefit from the promise or the act given as consideration. Thus, courts enforce promises where the promisor agrees to pay a sum of money if the promisee will take a trip to Europe or name a child after the promisor. A promise to attend the promisor's funeral has been held to be good consideration; and a leading case held that a promise not to drink, swear, use tobacco, or play cards or billiards for money before reaching age 21 was sufficient consideration. Hamer v. Sidway, 124 N.Y. 538, 27 N.E. 256 (1891).

Output and Requirements Contracts. A promise to purchase all of the buyer's requirements for particular goods from a particular seller (called a "requirements contract"), or a promise by a seller to sell his entire output to a particular buyer (called an "output contract"), is **specifically enforceable under §2-306 of the Uniform Commercial Code**. The consideration in the requirements contract is the buyer's implicit promise not to purchase from another; in the output contract, it is the seller's promise not to sell to anyone else.

Under the U.C.C., an output or requirements contract is enforceable to the quantity of goods produced by the seller or required by the buyer, respectively, in good faith, as long as that quantity is not unreasonably disproportionate to any estimates given or the prior practices of the parties. In fact, under a requirements contract, a purchaser who legitimately ceases to need the subject goods may cancel the contract. At common law, such a promise might be found illusory if interpreted to mean that the promisor would sell or buy only so much as he desired, reserving the right to sell or buy elsewhere.

Promises Implied by Court. In some situations, the formal contract between two parties does not spell out any specific obligations for one of them. In a leading case, A, a woman of some renown, entered into an agreement with B, wherein it was provided that B was to have the exclusive right to market A's name to dress manufacturers. The agreement between A and B did not specify any obligations on B's part. The court, however, held that B was obligated to use his best efforts in marketing A's name. Wood v. Lucy, Lady Duff-Gordon, 222 N.Y. 88, 118 N.E. 214 (1917).

Forbearance from Suing on a Claim. A promise not to prosecute a cause of action is **good consideration**, as is the actual forbearance from prosecuting a claim. Difficulty arises only where the claim itself is invalid. The general rule is that if the person with the claim (or defense) **honestly believes** that he has a right to enforce (or assert) it, or if the claim is **doubtful** because of uncertainty as to fact or law, then forbearance (or a promise to forbear) is sufficient consideration.

The policy behind this rule is to **favor compromises of disputed claims** in order to reduce the volume of litigation. Clearly, when one threatens to sue, knowing that he has **no** claim whatsoever against the other, his promise not to sue cannot furnish good consideration for a return promise.

> For example, suppose A, knowing that he has no legal basis, often complains to B, his father, that B's other children have received more gifts from B than A has. B promises that if A will cease complaining, B will forgive a debt owed to B by A. A's forbearance to assert his claim of discrimination is not consideration for B's promise.

Execution of a written instrument surrendering a claim or defense by one under no duty to execute it is consideration if execution of the written instrument is bargained for, even though the party is not asserting a claim or defense and believes that no valid claim or defense exists. Typically, such an instrument may be a release or a quitclaim deed. The assurance that a claim will not be asserted may be useful to the party bargaining for it.

Voidable and Unenforceable Promises. A promise may be made in exchange for a promise which is voidable or unenforceable. If A makes a promise in exchange for a return promise by B, The fact that the contract is voidable by A because of his own infancy or because of B's fraud does not prevent A's promise from being consideration for B's promise. Similarly, the fact that A's promise is unenforceable under the local Statute of Frauds does not prevent it from being consideration for B's promise. The rationale is that the value of a promise does not necessarily depend on the availability of a legal remedy for its breach.

Conditional Promises. A conditional promise is **not** consideration if the promisor knows at the time of making the promise that the condition cannot exist or occur.

> For example: A promises to pay B $5,000 if B's ship, now at sea, is lost, not knowing whether or not the ship has been lost. A's promise is consideration even though A has reason to know that the ship has not been lost. However, if A actually knows it is not lost, then A's promise is not consideration.

A promise may be conditional on the happening of a future event - an **aleatory** promise.

> A common example is where A promises to convey to B immediately a patent owned by A, while B promises to pay A $5,000 when pending litigation is terminated and the patent is held valid. B's promise is consideration for A's promise.

Multiple Exchanges. The fact that part of what is bargained for would not have been consideration if that part alone had been bargained for does not prevent the whole from being consideration.

> For example: A owes B $5. B promises to give A book if A will pay the $5 and $1 in addition. A pays the $6. B's promise is binding, although A's payment of the $5 he owed would not of itself have been consideration for the promise to convey the book.

Recitals of Consideration. Often a written contract contains a clause such as, "For $1.00 and other good and sufficient consideration, receipt of which is hereby acknowledged." Such a recital of consideration is simply evidence that consideration has been given, and contrary evidence can be introduced without violating the parol evidence rule. If it is shown that the $1.00 was not in fact paid, and that the other "good and sufficient" consideration has not been given, there is no consideration, and the promise is not enforceable. Some courts, however, will interpret a recital of consideration clause as a promise to pay the recited amount, and hold that the promise is sufficient consideration.

C. MODERN SUBSTITUTES FOR BARGAIN: "MORAL OBLIGATION," DETRIMENTAL RELIANCE, AND STATUTORY SUBSTITUTES

Consider the following fact pattern: A sees that B is in danger of being hit by something falling from a building, and A pushes B out of the way. B, thankful for A's actions, promises to pay A $1,000 at the end of the year. Is B's promise enforceable? Clearly, there was legal detriment, i.e., A's pushing B out of the way. Just as clearly, however, the legal detriment was not used to bargain for B's promise to pay $1,000, as the act was done before the promise was made.

The traditional view is that because the bargain element of consideration is missing, B's promise is not enforceable. A few states do enforce promises made under these circumstances, on the theory that B had a moral duty to compensate A, and that this is a substitute for consideration. **Webb v. McGowin**, 27 Ala. App. 82, 168 So. 196 (1935). The Restatement (Second) §86 recognizes such promises as binding "to the extent necessary to prevent injustice."

1. Seal

At common law, if a contract was under seal, the seal served as a substitute for consideration. Today, most states have abolished any difference between sealed and unsealed contracts. Therefore, **in most jurisdictions, lack of consideration is a defense to an action on a contract under seal**. A seal does not substitute for consideration in contracts for the sale of goods or commercial paper.

Where the seal is still a substitute for consideration, what is recognized as a seal varies from state to state. Examples of what may be held to operate as a seal are: a recital in a contract that the contract is sealed, or that it is the intention of the parties that it operate as a sealed instrument; a private seal; a scroll; the letters "L.S.;" any scrawl or mark intended as a seal; and every contract in writing.

2. Promissory Estoppel

A promise which the promisor should reasonably expect to induce action or forbearance on the part of the promisee or a third party, and which does induce such action or forbearance, is binding if injustice can be avoided only by its enforcement. Restatement (Second) of Contracts §90. This is known as the doctrine of **promissory estoppel**, and allows for the enforcement of promises which are not supported by consideration. In effect, it provides that a promise is enforceable if the promisee justifiably relied upon the promise to his detriment. Since legal detriment is still required, the basic theory of promissory estoppel is to **substitute "reliance" for "bargain."**

Initially, the doctrine was applied in charitable subscription cases, and a promise to make a gift was held enforceable if the charitable donee changed its position in reliance upon the promise. Barnes v. Perine, 12 N.Y. 18 (1854). In recent years, the doctrine of promissory estoppel has been applied to fact situations other than those involving gifts.

There has been considerable litigation over whether a bid by a subcontractor made to a general contractor can be revoked after the general contractor uses the subcontractor's bid in his own bid, but before the general contractor has accepted the subcontractor's bid. In most of the modern cases, courts have refused to permit the subcontractor to revoke, on the ground that he made a subsidiary promise, express or implied, to hold his offer open until the general contractor had a reasonable opportunity to accept, and that this subsidiary promise, although not supported by consideration, was enforceable under the doctrine of promissory estoppel because the general contractor foreseeably relied upon it. Drennan v. Star Paving Co., 51 Cal.2d 409, 333 P.2d 757 (1958).

Under the doctrine of promissory estoppel, the remedy for breach of a promise may be limited as justice requires. Thus, a promise may be only partially enforced, or only reliance damages may be given.

D.   MODIFICATION OF CONTRACTS: PREEXISTING DUTIES

1.   Pre-existing Duty

An act promised or performed as consideration must be something that the person furnishing it does not otherwise have a legal duty to do. If he is already under a **legal duty** to do the act, it does not constitute good consideration.

> Thus, if A says to B: "I will give you $100 if you do not walk across my land for a month," B's forbearance from walking across A's land will not constitute good consideration, as B is already under an obligation not to trespass.

Payment of Debt with Lesser Amount. A common example of the pre-existing duty rule is found when a debtor bargains for a full release from his creditor in return for paying less than the full amount of the debt. Even if the creditor promises a full discharge, his promise is unenforceable, because the debtor is already under an obligation to pay the full amount of the debt, and his new promise to pay part of it or his act of paying part of it does not constitute legal detriment.

Of course, if there is some **change in the terms of the obligation,** then there is consideration.

> For example: if the debtor is obligated to pay $1,000 on October 30th, and he agrees to pay $750 in full satisfaction of the debt on October 1st, the change in the date of payment will constitute sufficient consideration for the release.

Payment of less than the full amount actually owed will also be good consideration if there is a **good faith dispute** about the existence of the debt or its amount.

Performance of Similar Duty. Performance similar to that owed under a legal duty is consideration if it differs from what was required by the duty.

> For example: A offers a reward for evidence leading to the arrest and conviction of the murderer of B. C, a police officer, produces the evidence in the course of his official duty. This is not consideration for A's promise. If C's duties as a police officer are limited to State D, however, and while on vacation he gathers evidence on the crime, which was committed in State E, this is valid consideration.

2. Modification

New Obligation Required. The pre-existing duty rule arises in connection with attempts to modify existing contracts where one of the parties undertakes no new obligations by virtue of the attempted modification. For example, assume A promises to construct a house for B and B promises to pay him $120,000. If A, after he has commenced work, refuses to continue unless B will increase his payment to $125,000, the pre-existing duty rule would prevent A from collecting the additional $5,000, even if B promises to pay it and A completes the work. The theory for refusing to enforce the new promise is that the contractor was already obligated to construct the house, and that he or she gave up nothing in return for the promise by B to pay the additional $5,000.

Exceptions. In modification cases, the courts often avoid the pre-existing duty rule and enforce the modification on one of the following theories:

1) that there has been a **rescission of the old contract and the formation of a new contract by the parties**. This involves interpreting the parties' acts at the time they agreed to the modification as constituting first a mutual agreement to rescind the old contract, leaving the parties without any contract at all, followed by their agreement to the new bargain at the increased price.
2) that **something in addition** was promised or done by the person receiving the additional consideration. For example, in the hypothetical given above, it might be found from a close examination of the facts that the builder agreed to do something more than he was obligated to do under the original contract, e.g., install a different kind of storm windows, or that he agreed to finish the job sooner.
3) that there was some **unforeseen hardship** that made it difficult for the person to complete the job. For example, the undersurface was granite instead of soil, making it much more costly to excavate for the basement.

3. Modification of Contracts for the Sale of Goods

Consideration. Section 2-209 of the Uniform Commercial Code **eliminates the requirement of consideration for modifications of sale of goods contracts**. However, it imposes a test of good faith. Comment 2 to the section states:

> **Modifications ... must meet the test of good faith imposed by this Act**. The effective use of bad faith to escape performance on the original contract terms is barred, and the extortion of a "modification" without legitimate commercial reason is ineffective as a violation of the duty of good faith. Nor can a mere technical consideration support a modification made in bad faith.

The test of "good faith" between merchants or as against merchants includes "observance of reasonable commercial standards of fair dealing in the trade" [Section 2-103], and may in some situations require an objectively demonstrable reason for seeking a modification. But such matters as a market shift which makes performance come to involve a loss may provide such a reason even though there is no such unforeseen difficulty as would make out a legal excuse from performance under Sections 2-615 and 2-616.

No consideration is needed for modification, but the modification must be in good faith. Modification presents no parol evidence problem, because the parol evidence rule applies only to statements prior to or contemporaneous with the signing of the contract.

Statute of Frauds. Subsections 2-209(2) and (3) deal with the question of whether a modification must be in writing. Subsection (3) makes the **Statute of Frauds (§2-201) applicable to modifications. Hence, if the price of the goods under the contract as modified equals or exceeds $500**, there must be a writing (or "record" under amended U.C.C.) evidencing the contract. However, the writing may consist of a mere "memorandum" of the contract which, under §2-201, may be incomplete. Also, the exceptions to the Statute of Frauds are applicable to modifications. **Note that the $500 amount has recently been amended and is now $5,000. Many states, however, have yet to adopt this amendment in their state commercial code.**

Subsection (2) permits inclusion in the original sales agreement of a provision that modifications must be in writing. However, if at least one of the parties is not a merchant, and a form contract is used, a provision requiring a modification to be in writing is ineffective against the non merchant unless it is separately signed by him.

Extra Compensation Promised by Third Party. Courts have had difficulty with cases where a third party promises something to one of the parties to a contract if the person performs the contract. For example, assume that A, a famous basketball player, has agreed to perform at Madison Square Garden, and B has agreed to promote the event. C, who has the right to the concession stands, promises B that he will pay her $1,000 if B assiduously promotes the event. Since B is already under this obligation because of her contract with A, there is no legal detriment to B in exchange for C's promise. In such a case, traditional contract law would refuse to enforce C's promise because of the preexisting duty rule, and this is still the majority rule. The more modern approach, represented by the Restatement (Second) of Contracts, would enforce the promise on the theory that the benefit to C is sufficient as a substitute for legal detriment.

A similar but distinguishable case involves a promise by the third party to both parties to the contract. Assume, for example, that C promises to pay $500 to both A and B if the basketball performance is held as scheduled. Since A and B had the right to agree to rescind their original performance, their giving up of this right constitutes legal detriment, and there is consideration. Hence, C's promise is enforceable.

E.   COMPROMISE AND SETTLEMENT OF CLAIMS

Accord and Satisfaction. The parties to a contract may subsequently make an agreement which they intend as a substitute for the original contract. The substitute agreement is called an **"accord"** and the performance of the agreement is called the **"satisfaction."** Traditionally and also under the Restatement (Second), an accord does not discharge the original duty until it is performed.

The accord is distinguished from a **"substitute contract,"** under which a **promise** of substituted performance is accepted in satisfaction of the original duty, and an immediate discharge is effected. Under an accord, the original duty is merely suspended until performance of the accord. If the accord is breached, the obligee may enforce either the original duty or any duty under the accord. Restatement (Second) of Contracts §281. Breach of a substituted contract does not give the obligee a right to enforce the original duty. Restatement (Second) of Contracts §279.

Consideration for an executory accord exists if there is a bona fide dispute as to the amount owed. (See supra). If a drawer of a check tenders a check "in full satisfaction" of an obligation, there is an offer of an accord and satisfaction as to the compromise amount. If the payee endorses the check she may be bound by the accord and satisfaction and may not sue for the remainder of the disputed amount, even if the payee scratches out the drawer's "in full satisfaction" memo or the payee writes "with reservation of rights" or the like on the check. U.C.C. §1-207(2).

Release. At common law, a contractual obligation could be discharged by a sealed writing not necessarily supported by consideration. Under the Uniform Commercial Code §1-107, a claim arising out of an alleged breach of contract can be discharged without consideration by a written waiver or renunciation signed and delivered by the aggrieved party.

If the seal no longer is a substitute for consideration in the jurisdiction and if the transaction does not fall under the Uniform Commercial Code, then a writing that purports to discharge a person's obligation is invalid unless supported by consideration. However, a release or other form of discharge generally need not be in writing since even a contract originally executed in writing and purporting to allow only written modifications may be modified or discharged by an oral transaction. The Restatement (Second) §284 recognizes the release as a formal written document delivered to the obligor, similar to the Restatement's rule on renunciation, i.e., a formal writing substitutes for consideration.

Arbitration And Award; Judgment. The parties may, voluntarily or pursuant to a mandatory clause in the contract, submit a controversy to an arbitrator. The decision of the arbitrator is called an award. The parties' prior contractual duties are **merged** into the award. Similarly, if a party obtains a judgment against the other for breach of contract, the contractual duties are discharged by merger into the judgment.

III. THIRD-PARTY BENEFICIARY CONTRACTS

In most contracts cases, the plaintiff is the person to whom the promise was made (the promisee), and the defendant is the person who made the promise (the promisor). In some cases, however, one of the parties bargains for a promise which is for the benefit of some third person who is not a party to the contract. Initially, courts held that such a third-party beneficiary could not bring an action on the contract because he was not in privity with the promisor, but that rule has changed in all states.

The leading case, **Lawrence v. Fox,** 20 N.Y. 268 (1859), involved a situation in which A owed $300 to C. A then loaned $300 to B in return for B's promise to pay $300 to C. When B refused to pay C, C sued B for the $300. The court allowed recovery.

Throughout this section we will be referring to three parties:

A - The Original Promisee who contracts with **B - The Original Promisor** who promises to deliver a performance to - -	Parties to the Original Contract
C - The Third Party Beneficiary	Not a Party to the Original Contract

Three primary issues arise in litigation involving third-party beneficiary contracts:

1)   which types of people who would benefit from a contract to which they are not a party have a right to sue on the contract;
2)   when do the rights of parties who can sue "vest"; and
3)   to what extent are they subject to defenses raised by the promisor?

The Multistate examiners test the law of third-party beneficiary contracts as set forth in the Restatement (Second) of Contracts.

A.   INTENDED BENEFICIARIES

Under the first Restatement of Contracts, beneficiaries who could sue to enforce a contract made for their benefit were classified as either **donee** or **creditor** beneficiaries, depending on whether the promisee's purpose in making the contract was to make a gift or to satisfy an actual or supposed or asserted duty of the promisee to the beneficiary. Restatement of Contracts §133(1)(a), (b). The Restatement (Second) eliminates the terms "donee" and "creditor," calling them both **"intended"** beneficiaries, but the distinctions are not entirely eliminated.

Under §302(1) of the Restatement (Second), a right to performance will be recognized in the beneficiary if:

1) the performance of the promise will **satisfy an obligation** of the promisee to pay money to the beneficiary; or
2) the circumstances indicate that the promisee **intends** to give the beneficiary the benefit of the promised performance.

Under the Restatement (Second), if the performance owed by the promisee to the beneficiary is other than for the payment of money, or if the obligation is only "supposed or asserted" rather than "actual," the beneficiary is not a beneficiary of a "promise to pay the promisee's debt" under §302(1)(a) but may still be an intended beneficiary of a "gift promise" under §302(1)(b). The promisee under §302(1) becomes a surety for the promisor, even if the promisee's duty was voidable or unenforceable by reason of the statute of limitations, the Statute of Frauds, or a discharge in bankruptcy. See Restatement (Second) of Contracts §302, comment b.

A "gift promise" under §302(1)(b) includes the promise of an insurance company to pay benefits upon the insured's death to the beneficiary named in the policy.

Rights Against the Promisor. An intended beneficiary acquires a right to sue the promisor under the third-party beneficiary contract.

Rights Against the Promisee. A third-party beneficiary contract between the promisor and promisee creates no new contractual obligations for the promisee. Thus, if the purpose of the contract was to confer a gift on the third-party beneficiary, the beneficiary may not sue the promisee to collect the gift.

However, the third-party beneficiary contract does not discharge any pre-existing duty or debt the promisee owed to the third-party beneficiary, who can elect to sue either the promisee on the prior obligation or the promisor on the third-party beneficiary contract, or both, but can obtain only one full satisfaction. Restatement (Second) of Contracts §310. The beneficiary need not first seek recourse against the promisor.

B.   INCIDENTAL BENEFICIARIES

Incidental beneficiaries gain no rights under the contract. Incidental beneficiaries are all those who are not intended beneficiaries.

> Examples: A enters a contract with B whereby B is to erect a house on A's land. C owns land next to A's, and the value of C's land will be enhanced by the building. C is an incidental beneficiary of B's promise to construct the house, and C has no rights under the contract.
>
> B contracts to purchase a "Floyd" automobile from A. "Floyd" autos are made by the "Floyd" company. The "Floyd" company is an incidental beneficiary of the contract between A and B.

It is the **intent of the promisee** which governs. In neither of the two immediately preceding examples did the promisee, A, intend to confer a benefit on the third party, C.

Multistate Bar Review Book 2

C. IMPAIRMENT OR EXTINGUISHMENT OF THIRD-PARTY RIGHTS BY CONTRACT MODIFICATION OF MUTUAL RESCISSION

After the contract is made, the original parties may wish to modify the contract in some way. Also, the parties may wish to rescind their agreement, or one of the parties may wish to release the other from all or part of his promise. The question is whether the parties to the contract can do this without the permission of the third-party beneficiary. **After vesting has occurred, the beneficiary must consent to any subsequent agreement that would modify or discharge the promisor's duty to the beneficiary**.

The promisor and promisee may modify or rescind their contract without the beneficiary's consent **before the beneficiary's rights have vested**. Under the Restatement Second, §311(3), **vesting** occurs as to an intended beneficiary:

1) when the beneficiary changes her position in justifiable reliance on the promise; or
2) brings suit on it; or
3) manifests assent to the contract at the request of the promisor or promisee.

The promisor and promisee can provide in the contract for when the rights of the beneficiary will vest. For example, a life insurance policy will often reserve a right in the promisee to change the beneficiary. Rights do not vest in such a beneficiary until the designation becomes irrevocable, such as upon the death of the insured. However, to avoid being taxed as the owner of the policy, the insured might make the designation of the beneficiary irrevocable, thus giving the beneficiary vested rights.

D. ENFORCEMENT BY THE PROMISEE

The promisee also has a right of action against the promisor if performance is not rendered to the intended beneficiary. If the promisee's intent was to make a gift of the performance to the beneficiary, then the promisee will ordinarily have suffered no economic loss from the nonperformance of the promisor and may recover only nominal damages. Therefore, courts may consider the damage remedy inadequate and grant specific performance. Drewen v. Bank of Manhattan Co., 31 N.J. 110, 155 A.2d 529 (1959).

If the promisee owed the promised performance to the beneficiary, the promisor's failure to perform may cause substantial damages to the promisee. However, the recovery of damages by the promisee may expose the promisor to double liability since the promisor is also liable to the beneficiary. Some courts refuse to allow the promisee to recover damages unless the promisee has already made payment to the beneficiary to cover the default. See White v. Upton, 255 Ky. 562, 74 S.W.2d 924 (1934).

The Restatement (Second) §310(2) provides that the promisee has a right of reimbursement from the promisor to the extent that the claim of an intended beneficiary is satisfied from assets of the promisee. Once the beneficiary's claim is satisfied in full, the promisee is entitled as subrogee to assert the beneficiary's claim against the promisor. Alternatively, the promisee (A) may seek specific performance of his right as a surety to compel the principal (B) to pay the creditor (C). McFey–

Fansher Co. v. Rowen, 232 Iowa 660, 5 N.W.2d 911 (1942); see Restatement (Second) of Contracts §307, comment c.

Defenses Of The Promisor. The promisor (B) can raise any defenses against the beneficiary that the promisor would have against the promisee on the contract if it were not a third-party beneficiary contract. For example, the promisor (B) can raise against the third party (C) the defenses of lack or failure of consideration for the contract; lack of offer and acceptance forming the contract; the Statute of Frauds; the statute of limitations; and fraud, duress, illegality, etc. The promisor (B) can also raise as a defense against the third-party beneficiary (C) that a condition to B's obligation to perform was not fulfilled.

The promisor may not, however, assert defenses that the promisee would have had against the third-party beneficiary. For example, if the statute of limitations had run on the debt that the promisee owed the third party, this could not be raised by the promisor. Nor may the promisor raise any defenses based on separate transactions with the promisee, unless the third-party beneficiary contract subjects the rights of the beneficiary to such claims. Restatement (Second) of Contracts, §309, comment c.

IV. ASSIGNMENT OF RIGHTS AND DELEGATION OF DUTIES

An "assignment" is a transfer of a right, while a "delegation" is a transaction whereby someone having an obligation gets someone else to perform it. For example, assume that A has entered into a contract with B under which A is to paint B's house in return for the payment of $500 to A by B as soon as the job is completed. This is a typical "bilateral contract" and, as soon as the contract is made, A has a right to receive $500. This right is conditional, i.e., the house must be painted before B has to pay, but it is a right nonetheless. A also has a duty or obligation as soon as the contract is signed: he must paint the house, and if he does not, he can be sued for any damages resulting from his failure to fulfill his contract obligation.

A can "assign" his right to the $500. If he does, the assignment is basically a transfer similar to a sale of personal or real property. A is the assignor, B is the obligor, and C is the assignee.

A can also "delegate" his obligation to paint the house by getting someone else to do the job for him. A is the obligor/delegator, B is the obligee, and C is the delegatee.

A.   ASSIGNMENT OF RIGHTS

Formalities. There is no formality required in the assignment of rights, and no "magic words" which must be used. It is essential, however, that the words show a **present intent to assign,** and that no subsequent act be required. Hence, the statement, "I will assign you 10% of the royalties I will obtain," is not an assignment, as it expresses only an intent to assign in the future.

Oral assignments are valid unless a specific statute provides otherwise.

An **"order"** is not an assignment. The most common example of this is the check, which, under both common law and the U.C.C., does not operate as an assignment of the drawer's rights against the bank.

Partial Assignments. A partial assignment is valid. Hence, there can be an assignment of a fraction of the assignor's rights. When suit is brought, however, all of the persons owning rights after the assignment must be joined in the action, unless joinder is not feasible and it is equitable to proceed without joinder.

What Rights Are Assignable. The general rule is that **all rights are assignable**. The **exceptions** to this general follow:

The right is not assignable if the assignment would materially change the risk or obligations of the other party to the contract. For example, if A agrees for consideration to support B during the rest of B's life, B cannot assign the right to C so as to require A to support C for C's life. However, if A were to breach the contract to support B, B could assign the right to damages. Also, B could assign whatever he would receive from A's promise to support him.

Under U.C.C. §2-210(2), rights of either the seller or the buyer in a contract for the sale of goods can be assigned unless the assignment would materially change the duty of the other party, materially increase his burden or risk under the contract, or materially impair his chance of obtaining return performance.

A right may be considered too "personal" to transfer, or public policy may preclude a transfer. For example, claims for negligence are not assignable unless a judgment has been obtained against the tortfeasor.

> Hence, if A, a physician, negligently treats B, B cannot assign the cause of action to C, but, if B obtains a judgment, the rights under the judgment can be assigned.

Generally, states have restrictions on the right to assign wages, and there are specific statutes which prevent assignment of certain other rights.

Provisions in contracts prohibiting assignments are valid but are strictly construed. The trend has been **to limit or invalidate the prohibition**. The following rules are the present law:

1) **Unless the contract specifically states that an assignment is "void," a prohibition against assignments at most gives a right of action against the assignor, and does not invalidate the assignment**. Hence, if the contract between A and B provides that B may not assign his rights, but he does in fact assign them to C, the assignment is **valid**; but A can sue B for any damages resulting from the assignment.

2) A provision in the contract that simply prohibits **"assignment of the contract"** does not bar assignment, but rather bars only delegation. Hence, if the contract between A and B states "This contract shall not be assigned," the language is read as allowing either A or B to assign, but as prohibiting delegation by either.

3) A provision in the contract prohibiting the **"assignment of rights"** under the contract is read as prohibiting assignment, **but** it does not apply to rights arising because of the breach of the contract. Hence, a party to the contract would be liable for damages if he assigned rights under the contract, but not if he assigned a right to damages after breach of the contract. Also, such a provision is held to be for the sole benefit of the other party to the contract, so that the assignor cannot raise this provision against the assignee as a ground for invalidating an assignment.

4) Under the **Uniform Commercial Code §2-210(3),** prohibitions against assignment "of the contract" in **contracts for the sale of goods** will be construed as barring only the delegation of the assignor's performance. A right to damages for breach of the whole contract or a right arising out of the assignor's performance of his entire obligation can be assigned despite agreement to the contrary. U.C.C. §2-210(2).

5) **An offer cannot be assigned.** Hence, if A has offered to sell a car to B, B cannot assign this offer to C. However, an option is assignable, and hence if A has agreed to sell land to B and B has paid consideration to keep the offer open for six months, B can assign the option to C.

6) Rights under a **contract to be formed** cannot be assigned. For example, if A expects to enter into a contract with B for the sale of Blackacre, A cannot transfer the right to the proceeds of the sale to C. However, if the future right is attempted to be assigned, it operates as an assignment at the time that A does enter into the contract with B.

7) The right of a **partner** to share in the management of the partnership is not assignable, but the right to profits and to the partner's share in a dissolution is assignable.

Gratuitous Assignments: Valid Against Obligor. An assignment for no consideration is a perfectly valid transfer of rights, and the obligor cannot raise as a defense against the assignee the fact that no consideration was given to the assignor for the assignment.

Between Assignor and Assignee. Between the assignor and the assignee, the law of gifts governs the question of whether the assignor can revoke the assignment. A gift requires that there be **donative intent and delivery.** Because the assignment is a transfer of a chose in action, it is impossible to deliver physically the intangible right, but delivery of something representative or symbolic of the right is held to be sufficient to meet the delivery requirement.

> Thus, if a bankbook is delivered to the assignee with the intent of assigning the rights represented by the bankbook, this is a completed gift and cannot be revoked. The fact that the assignment itself is in writing does not make it irrevocable. Thus, if A states in a writing that she assigns her rights to her account in the B Bank to C, and delivers this writing to C, the assignment is still revocable; but if A also delivers to C her bankbook, it is irrevocable.

Even if there is no delivery, the assignment becomes irrevocable once payment of the obligation has been made to the assignee. Also, the assignor will be estopped from revoking the assignment if the assignee acts to his detriment in reliance upon the assignment.

Rights of the Assignee Against the Obligor. The basic rule is that **an assignee gets whatever rights to the contract his assignor had.** The assignee also takes subject to whatever defenses the other party could have raised against the assignor.

> Thus, if A agrees to paint B's house for $500, and A assigns his right to the $500 to C, B can raise any defense against C that B had against A. If, for example, A failed to paint the house, B would have the defense of failure of consideration in a suit by C. Other defenses such as fraud, lack of capacity, duress, the Statute of Frauds, etc., can also be raised by B against C.

Multistate Bar Review Book 2

Payment to Assignor. If the obligor (B) pays the assignor (A), this is also a defense which can be raised against the assignee (C), provided that payment was made before notice was given to the obligor. Once notice of the assignment is given, payment to the assignor is no defense. If the obligor doubts whether the assignment was in fact made, he can pay the money into court and interplead the assignor and assignee.

Set-offs and Counterclaims. If the obligor has a right of set-off which could be raised against the assignor, it can always be raised against the assignee if the alleged set-off arises out of the same transaction.

> Thus, if A sells goods to B and B accepts the goods, and A has assigned his rights to C, B would be liable for the price to C as the assignee, but B could set off any damages resulting from a breach of warranty by A.

If, however, the set-off arises out of a separate transaction, it is available against the assignee only if the transaction giving rise to the set-off arose before notice of the assignment was given to the obligor.

> For example: A contracts to sell goods to B for $500. A then assigns to C her right to the $500 due from B. When C sues B, B wishes to set off against C's claim a $300 debt which A owes B. B can do this only if the transaction giving rise to his $300 right against A arose before B received notice of A's assignment to C.

The obligor and the assignor may agree to an adjustment of their rights without consent of the assignee up until the time that the assignee has given notice of the assignment to the obligor.

> Thus, if A and B have contracted and A has assigned his rights to C, A and B may agree that B will receive a discharge if he pays half of what is owed a week early. This compromise will be valid as to C so long as it was reached prior to the time that B received notice of the assignment.

Waiver of Defenses. If one of the original parties to the contract agrees that he will not raise defenses against an assignee in the event that the rights are assigned, the waiver is enforceable with **two limitations**:

1) Even when there is such an agreement, defenses which are in the nature of "real defenses" under Article 3 of the U.C.C. can be raised. These defenses include infancy, other incapacity which voids a contract, fraud in the execution, duress (when it removes the parties' capacity to contract), discharge in bankruptcy, and any other discharge of which the assignee has reason to know.

2) The agreement not to assert defenses is not valid if the obligor who signed the waiver was the buyer or lessee of **consumer goods.**

Rights of Assignee Against Assignor. Unless a contrary intention is manifested, one who assigns or purports to assign a right for value warrants to the assignee:

1) that he will do nothing to defeat or impair the value of the assignment, and has no knowledge of any fact which would do so;

2) that the right as assigned actually exists and is subject to no limitations or defenses good against the assignor, other than those stated or apparent at the time of the assignment; and

3) that any writing evidencing the right which is delivered to the assignee or exhibited to him to induce him to accept the assignment is genuine.

An assignment does not of itself operate as a warranty that the obligor is solvent, nor that he will perform his obligation.

Rights Among Successive Assignees. The problem of rights among successive assignees arises in the following situation: A, who is owed $100 by B, assigns his right to the $100 to C, the first assignee. A later assigns the same right to D, the second assignee. Both C and D attempt to collect from B, the obligor. A is liable for assigning the same right twice, but if A is bankrupt or cannot be found, the question is whether B is liable to C or D.

The majority rule is that the **first assignee prevails** - C in the above example. There are various **exceptions** to this rule in different jurisdictions. The Restatement position (§342) is that the second assignee, D, who has **paid value and takes the assignment in good faith,** will prevail in the following situations:

1) the second assignee obtains payment from the obligor; or
2) the second assignee recovers a judgment on the debt; or
3) the second assignee enters into a new contract with the obligor; or
4) the second assignee receives delivery of a tangible token or writing from the assignor, the surrender of which is required by the obligor's contract.

B. DELEGATION OF DUTIES

Delegation is a transaction whereby a party who has a contractual obligation gets someone else to perform the obligation, usually for a consideration. Unlike an assignment of rights, it is not a "transfer" in any sense.

Rights of Obligee Against the Delegator. A delegation does not relieve the delegating party from his obligations under the contract.

> For example, assume that B has agreed to pay A $500 in return for A's promise to paint B's house, and that A has engaged C to paint the house. The delegation to C does not relieve A of the obligation to paint the house; if C fails to paint it, B can bring an action for damages against A. Similarly, if C paints the house, but does it improperly, A will be liable for any damages caused by the defective performance of C.

Novation. If there is a novation, the delegating party is relieved from the obligations under the contract, but this requires **a clear promise by the obligee** to release the delegator in return for the liability of the delegatee.

> Thus, if in the example above, A went to B and asked B to give him a release in return for the liability of C, and B agreed, then there would be a novation and A would no longer be liable on the contract. Simple assent to the delegation, however, is not enough to effectuate a novation; there must also be a promise to release the delegator.

Rights of Obligor or Obligee Against the Delegatee. When the delegatee has agreed to perform the delegator's contract obligations, he is clearly liable to the delegator if he does not do so. Under the third-party beneficiary theory, he is also liable to the obligee, because the obligee is an intended beneficiary of the promise made to the delegator.

> This can be demonstrated from the example used above. When C promised A that he would paint the house, the purpose of the promise was to discharge the duty that A owed to B. Hence, B is a third-party beneficiary of that promise.

What Duties Can Be Delegated. The general rule is that **all obligations can be delegated**. The **exceptions** fall into the following categories:

1) When a party agrees to perform the service **"personally."** For example, in a sale of storm windows, the seller agrees that he will personally install them on the buyer's house.
2) When the contract calls for the exercise of **personal skill or discretion**. For example, teachers, writers, artists, singers, etc., cannot delegate their obligations under a contract.
3) When the **contract prohibits delegation**. Unlike prohibitions against assignments, contract provisions forbidding delegation are fully enforceable.

An attempted delegation of a nondelegable duty operates as an immediate breach of the contract, and gives the other party an immediate right to sue. Thus, if there is a clause in the contract between A and B forbidding A from delegating his obligation to paint the house, and A attempts to delegate, B does not have to wait to see if the performance of C will be satisfactory; rather, B may sue immediately for breach.

Under the Uniform Commercial Code §2-210(5), any delegation of performance may be treated by the other party as creating **reasonable grounds for insecurity**. The other party has a right to demand assurances from the assignee without prejudicing his rights against the assignor.

V. STATUTES OF FRAUDS

The Statute of Frauds provides that certain contracts are enforceable only if they are evidenced by a written memorandum. American statutes have generally followed the English Statute of Frauds, enacted in 1677. Some classes of contracts which were traditionally subject to the Statute of Frauds are now governed by the Statute of Frauds provisions of the Uniform Commercial Code.

A contract may fall within more than one of the provisions of the Statute of Frauds. Generally, a contract subject to the Statute of Frauds is unenforceable if the requirements of the Statute are not satisfied, but the Statute does not necessarily bar the remedy of restitution. **Partial performance** or **action in reliance** on an unenforceable contract may, in some situations, make a contract enforceable.

A. THE MEMORANDUM

Unless additional requirements are prescribed by the particular statute, a contract within the Statute of Frauds is enforceable if it **is evidenced by any writing, signed by or on behalf of the party to be charged**, which:

1) reasonably **identifies the subject matter** of the contract;
2) is sufficient to indicate that **a contract has been made** between the parties, and
3) states with **reasonable certainty the essential terms and conditions** of the unperformed promises in the contract.

The "party to be charged" is the person against whom enforcement of the contract is sought in the action, i.e. the defendant. Local statutes may specifically require that "the contract" be in writing, meaning that a mere memorandum will not suffice. A statement of consideration may also be specifically required.

When a memorandum of a contract within the Statute is signed by fewer than all of the parties to the contract, the contract is enforceable against the signers but not against the others.

The Writing. A writing sufficient for a statutory memorandum includes any intentional reduction to tangible form. Neither delivery nor communication is essential. Sufficient memoranda include a written contract, a will, a notation on a check, a receipt, a pleading, and an informal letter. The loss or destruction of a memorandum does not deprive it of effect under the Statute.

Several Writings. The memorandum may consist of several writings if the writings clearly indicate that they relate to the same transaction. At least one of the writings must be signed by the party to be charged.

> For example: A and B make an oral contract within the Statute. A writes and signs a letter to B which is a sufficient memorandum, except that it does not identify B. The deficiency may be supplied by the name and address on the envelope in which the letter arrives. Of course, the memorandum would only bind A, as B has not signed it.

Informal Writings. The Statute may be satisfied by a signed writing not made as a memorandum of a contract, such as a letter. A signed writing may be a sufficient memorandum of a contract even though it repudiates or attempts to cancel the contract.

© 1995-2018 Celebration Bar Review, LLC   **Multistate Bar Review Book 2**

Signature. The signature to a memorandum may be any symbol made or adopted by the signer with an intention, actual or apparent, to authenticate the writing as that of the signer. Sufficient signatures include initials, a thumbprint, an arbitrary code sign, a rubber stamp, or a signature in pencil, typed, printed, or impressed into the paper. In a number of cases, an "unsigned" writing on letterhead paper has been held sufficient, on the theory that the letterhead is a signature.

Time of Memorandum. A memorandum sufficient to satisfy the Statute may be made or signed at any time after the formation of the contract. The memorandum may even be made after breach or repudiation of the contract. A memorandum written prior to formation of the contract - for example, during the preliminary negotiations - does **not** satisfy the Statute. However, a written offer that is accepted does operate as a memorandum.

B.   CONTRACTS WITHIN THE STATUTE OF FRAUDS

Statutes of Frauds based upon the English statute require written memoranda of the following contracts:

1.   Contract of an Executor or Administrator

A contract of an executor or administrator to **answer personally for a duty of his decedent** is within the Statute of Frauds if a similar contract to answer for the duty of a living person would be within the Statute as a contract to answer for the duty of another. If there was no obligation before the death of the decedent, the promise is not within this provision, because it is not a promise to perform an obligation of the decedent. The Executor-Administrator Provision is subject to the same exceptions as the Suretyship Provision, infra.

2.   Contract of Suretyship

A contract of suretyship is one whereby **one party promises to be answerable for a debt or duty of another party**. Such a contract is within the Statute of Frauds if:

1) the promisee is an obligee of a third person's duty;
2) the promisor is a surety for the third person; and
3) the promisee knows or has reason to know of the suretyship relationship.

There must be a **liability or duty of a third person which is guaranteed**. Duty includes all duties recognized by law, whether contractual or not, already incurred or to be incurred in the future. The duty may be conditional, voidable, or unenforceable. The person owing the duty is the principal debtor or obligor.

> For example: D, an infant, obtains goods on credit from C, who is induced to part with them by S's oral guaranty that D will pay the price as agreed. The goods are not necessaries, but D is subject to a duty, although it is voidable, and S's promise is within the Statute of Frauds. Where there is no duty, the Statute does not apply, since such a promise does not create a suretyship contract. Another example: In consideration of the delivery of goods by C to X at S's request, S orally promises to pay the price of them. S's promise is not within the Statute of Frauds, since X is under no duty to C.

Promise to Obligee-Promisee. The promise must be **made to the obligee-promisee** (i.e., the creditor) for it to be within the Statute.

> For example: S, for consideration, orally promises E to pay a debt of E's son, D, to C, if D fails to pay it at maturity. S's promise is not within the Statute of Frauds because it was made to E, not to the creditor C, and E can enforce the promise. This is true even though C also may be able to enforce the promise as a third-party beneficiary.

Joint Promises. Where promises of the same performance are made by two persons for a consideration which inures to the benefit of only one of them, the promise of the person receiving no benefit is within the Statute of Frauds as a contract to answer for the duty of another. This is true whether or not the promise is in terms conditional on default by the one to whose benefit the consideration inures, unless:

1) the promisee neither knows nor has reason to know that the consideration does not inure to the benefit of both promisors; or
2) the promises are in terms joint, and create neither several duties nor joint and several duties.

When the promises of the surety and the principal debtor impose joint and only joint liability, there is no requirement of a writing. The rationale for this is that a joint obligation gives rise to only one debt and the surety, even though he received no benefit himself, is a principal debtor. If, however, the obligation is several or joint and several, then the promise of the surety must be in writing. Most promises give rise to joint and several liabilities.

The Main Purpose Rule. A contract is not within the Statute of Frauds as a contract to answer for the duty of another **if the consideration for the promise is in fact or apparently desired by the promisor mainly for his own economic advantage**, rather than for the benefit of the third person. Thus, such a promise is enforceable even though oral. The expected advantage must justify the conclusion that the surety's main purpose is to advance his own interests. Slight and indirect possible advantage to the promisor is insufficient for application of this rule. The benefit may be supplied to the promisor by the promisee, by the principal obligor, or by some other person.

> For example: D owes C $1,000. C is about to levy an attachment on D's factory. S, who is also a creditor of D's, fearing that the attachment will ruin D's business and thereby destroy his own chance of collecting his claim, orally promises C that if C will forbear from taking legal proceedings against D for three months, S will pay D's debt if D fails to do so. S's promise is enforceable, because under the main purpose rule, it is not within the Statute of Frauds.

Indemnity Contracts. An indemnity contract is one in which one person promises to reimburse another if the other suffers any loss or liability. A promise to indemnify is not within the Statute of Frauds as a contract to answer for the duty of another. For example: T promises to indemnify S if he will guarantee T's obligation to C. T's promise is not within the Statute of Frauds; however, S's promise is.

Independent Duty. Where the promisor, if he keeps his promise, will be doing no more than he is bound to do by reason of a duty other than that imposed by the promise, the promise is not within the Statute of Frauds. The independent duty of the promisor may exist when the promise is made, or may arise subsequently.

> For example: D pays $100 to S in trust to apply it to whatever judgment C may recover against D in an action then pending. S orally promises C to pay the judgment in full. C recovers judgment for $125. C has an enforceable right against S for $100, because S was under an independent duty, by virtue of the trust agreement, to pay that amount. However, C may not recover the full $125.

Novation. A contract that is itself accepted in satisfaction of a previously existing duty of a third person to the promisee is not within the Statute of Frauds as a contract to answer for the duty of another. The reason is that the original duty has been extinguished by the novation. It makes no difference whether the new promisor promises the same performance or a different performance from that formerly due from the first obligor.

Promise to Sign a Written Contract of Suretyship. A promise to sign a written contract as a surety for the performance of a duty owed to the promisee, or to sign a negotiable instrument for the accommodation of a person other than the promisee, is within the Statute of Frauds. For example: In consideration of a loan by C to D, S orally promises C to execute a written instrument guaranteeing the debt. S's promise is within the Statute, and unenforceable.

Contract of Assignor or Agent. A promise by the assignor of a right that the obligor of the assigned right will perform his duty is not within the Statute of Frauds as a contract to answer for the duty of another. A contract by an agent with his principal that a purchaser of the principal's goods through the agent will pay their price to the principal is not within the Suretyship Provision of the Statute of Frauds.

Contract to Buy a Right from the Obligee. A contract to purchase a right which the promisee has or may acquire against a third person is not within the Statute of Frauds as a contract to answer for the duty of another. For example: D owes C $1,000 on open account. S, who specializes in the purchase of slow accounts, orally promises to buy C's right against D for $800 if assignment is made within three months. At the end of three months, C tenders S an assignment of the account. S's promise is not within the Suretyship Provision of the Statute of Frauds. The distinction between a contract to buy and a contract of a surety lies in the reality of the transaction - whether under all the circumstances the promisor is acquiring a right or protecting a creditor against a default.

Consideration. Problems of consideration are often interwoven with problems involving this provision of the Statute of Frauds. It should be remembered that consideration is always necessary to make a promise enforceable, and even if the Statute of Frauds does not apply, the promise of the surety will be unenforceable unless there is consideration.

Part Performance. Part performance in no way takes promises to answer for the debt of another out of the Statute of Frauds.

3. Contracts in Consideration of Marriage

A promise for which all or part of the consideration is either marriage or a promise to marry is within the Statute of Frauds, except in the case of an agreement which consists only of the mutual promises of two persons to marry each other.

> For example: In consideration of A's promise to marry B, B orally promises to marry A and to settle Blackacre upon A. B's promise to settle Blackacre upon A is within the Statute of Frauds.

The Statute does not apply, however, to agreements which are conditional upon marriage. For example: If a man and woman agreed that after they were married, they would hold all of their personal property as joint tenants, this agreement would not offend against this provision of the Statute of Frauds. Marriage is a condition to the promise, but the promise was not made in consideration of marriage.

An oral contract between prospective spouses made in consideration of marriage does not become enforceable merely because the marriage has taken place in reliance upon it.

4. Contracts Related to an Interest in Land

An interest in land within the meaning of the Statute is any right, privilege, power or immunity, or combination thereof which is an interest in land under the law of property, and is not "goods" within the Uniform Commercial Code. Interests in land include:

1) leaseholds;
2) interest of mortgagor and mortgagee or vendor and purchaser under a specifically enforceable contract;
3) present and future interests - both legal and equitable;
4) easements and profits;
5) contracts between owners of adjoining tracts of land fixing a dividing boundary;
6) contracts by joint tenants or tenants in common to partition land into separate tracts for each tenant; and
7) interests created by restrictive covenants.

Licenses, however, are not subject to the Statute of Frauds.

The provision applies to **any executory promise to transfer an interest in land**. Transfer includes creation or extinguishing of an interest, with the effect of giving another an interest she did not previously have.

> For example: A owes B $1,000. In consideration of B's promise to extend the time of payment three months, A promises orally that he will sell Blackacre and apply the proceeds as far as necessary to pay the debt. A's promise to sell the land is within the Statute of Frauds. A promise to transfer includes an option contract, but does not apply to a promise to refrain from making a transfer. For example: A promises his daughter, B, that he will die intestate so that B will inherit a share of Blackacre. A's promise is not within the Statute of Frauds. The contemplated transfer to B is a transfer by operation of law, not a transfer by virtue of the contract. Many states, however, have added a special provision to the Statute of Frauds for contracts to make or not to make a will.

Real Estate Brokers' Contracts. A contract to employ a real estate broker and to pay him a commission is not within the Statute of Frauds under the Land Contract Provision, unless the commission is to take the form of an interest in land. Again, some states have added a special provision to the Statute of Frauds applicable to brokers' contracts.

Part Performance Doctrine. A contract for the transfer of an interest in land may be enforced, notwithstanding failure to comply with the Statute of Frauds, if it is established that the party seeking enforcement, in reasonable reliance on the contract and on the continuing assent of the party against whom enforcement is sought, has so changed his position that injustice can be avoided only by specific enforcement.

Under the part performance rule, once the vendor deeds the land to the purchaser, the purchaser must pay the price agreed upon even if the contract is oral. On the other hand, when the purchaser is trying to enforce the contract, payment by the purchaser alone is not sufficient to take the contract out of the Statute. In some jurisdictions, payment by the purchaser plus occupancy of the land is sufficient, while other states require more, such as improving the land.

The part performance doctrine is limited to equitable relief. When a contract is specifically enforceable under this rule, other provisions of the Statute, such as the One-Year Provision, do not operate to prevent enforcement.

5. Contracts Which Cannot Be Performed Within One Year

The One-Year Provision covers only contracts whose performance **cannot possibly be completed within a year**.

> For example: A orally promises to work for B, and B promises to employ A during A's life at a stated salary. The promises are not within the One-Year Provision of the Statute, since A's life may terminate within a year.

Excuse from Performance Distinguished. The possibility of performance within a year makes the Statute of Frauds inapplicable. However, an excuse for nonperformance within one year will not take the contract out of the Statute of Frauds. The possibility that a contract may be discharged by a subsequent agreement of the parties within a year is not a possibility that the contract will be "performed" within a year.

> For example: A orally promises to work for B, and B promises to employ A for three years at a stated salary. The agreement is within the Statute. Here, if A dies within a year, there is an excuse for nonperformance, but no possibility of performance.

When Period Begins. The period of a year begins when the agreement is complete - ordinarily, when the offer is accepted. (A subsequent restatement of the terms will, however, start the period again.) The one-year period ends at midnight of the anniversary of the day on which the contract was made, regardless of what hour of the day the contract was entered into. Thus, if A orally agrees to work for B for ten months, the employment to commence three months after the agreement is made, then the contract is within the Statute and is not enforceable. Although the term of employment is only ten months, the contract cannot be performed within one year of the date of the agreement.

Part Performance. Part performance not amounting to full performance on one side does not take a contract out of the One-Year Provision, but restitution is available in such cases.

Set-offs and Counterclaims. Where a contract within the Statute of Frauds is not enforceable against the party to be charged by an action against him, it is not enforceable by way of a set-off or counterclaim to an action brought by him, or as a defense to a claim made by him.

Estoppel. A promise which the promisor should reasonably expect to **induce action or forbearance** on the part of the promisee or a third person, and which does induce the action or forbearance, may be enforceable notwithstanding the Statute of Frauds **if** injustice can be avoided **only** by enforcement of the promise. The remedy granted for breach is to be limited as justice requires.

In determining whether injustice can be avoided only by enforcement of the promise, the following circumstances are influential:

1) the availability and adequacy of other remedies, particularly cancellation and restitution;
2) the definite and substantial character of the action or forbearance in relation to the remedy sought;
3) the extent to which the action or forbearance corroborates evidence of the making and terms of the promise, or the promise and its terms are otherwise established by clear and convincing evidence; and
4) the reasonableness of the action or forbearance and the misleading character of the promise.

Full Performance. Where the promises in a contract have been fully performed by both parties, the Statute of Frauds does not affect their legal relations.

Priorities. Where a transfer of property or a contract to transfer property was unenforceable against the transferor under the Statute of Frauds but subsequently becomes enforceable, the transfer or contract has the same priority it would have had aside from the Statute of Frauds over an intervening contract by the transferor to transfer the same property to a third person.

> For example: A orally contracts to sell Blackacre to B. Later a creditor of A's attaches Blackacre. Thereafter, A signs a memorandum of the contract. B can enforce the contract specifically against A and the creditor. However, if the third person obtains title to the property by an enforceable transaction before the prior contract becomes enforceable, the prior contract is unenforceable against him and does not affect his title.

Contract of Rescission. Notwithstanding the Statute of Frauds, all unperformed duties under an enforceable contract may be discharged by an oral rescission. The Statute, however, applies to a contract to rescind a transfer of real property; hence, the rescission must be in writing.

Modification of Statute of Frauds by Contract. It is generally held that a provision in a contract providing that no modification of the contract may be made except in writing is not effective. Thus, oral modifications of contracts with such a provision are valid if they meet the other requirements of a modification. The rule is just the opposite, however, where the contract is for the sale of goods. U.C.C. §2-209 provides that such clauses are enforceable.

6. Sale of Goods

A contract for the sale of goods where the price is **$500 or more** is not enforceable unless there is a **written memorandum** of the transaction **signed by the party to be charged**, or unless one of the stated exceptions discussed below applies. U.C.C. §2-201. (Note that the most recent revision of UCC §2-201 increases this triggering amount to $5,000, but as of 2006 no U.S. state has adopted revised Section 201.) If a number of items are sold, the Statute of Frauds will be applicable to the total amount, unless the sale is determined to involve several separate contracts. If the price involved in one contract is $500 or more and the writing requirement is not met, the entire contract is unenforceable.

Sufficiency of Memorandum. The Code has "liberalized" the requirements for a memorandum. A writing is sufficient as a memo if:

1) it **indicates that a contract has been made** between the parties;
2) it contains the **quantity** of goods sold, and
3) it is **signed** by the party to be charged.

The writing need not state all the material terms of the contract. Even though the memo has incorrect terms, or omits terms, it is sufficient if it meets the tests above. For example, the price term may be omitted from the writing and be supplied orally. If the quantity term is incorrect, however, the contract can be enforced only up to the quantity mentioned in the memo.

Failure to Respond to Memo. Where both of the parties are merchants, and a memo, sufficient against the sender, is sent to the other party to the contract, and the party receiving it has reason to know its contents, then the memo is sufficient not only against the person who signed and sent it, but also against the recipient, unless the recipient gives **written** notice of objection within 10 days.

Exceptions to Sale of Goods Statute of Frauds. The Code makes the following exceptions to the Statute of Frauds provision (no writing is needed in the following cases):

1) where the goods are **specifically manufactured** for the buyer and are **not suitable for sale to others** in the ordinary course of the seller's business, and the seller has **begun to perform** or made a commitment for procurement of the goods.
2) where the goods have been **received and accepted.** (Note: Applicable only if the goods are actually received and accepted or paid for, and not to any part of the contract which is still executory.)
3) **where payment has been made and accepted for the goods.** (Note: Applicable only if the goods are actually received and accepted or paid for, and not to any part of the contract which is still executory.)
4) **where the party to be charged admits** in his pleadings, testimony, or otherwise in court that a contract for sale has been made; but here again the exception goes only to the quantity admitted.

VI. PAROL EVIDENCE AND INTERPRETATION

When a contract is in writing, and the parties intend that the writing be a **complete and final expression** of the rights and duties they have undertaken, the parol evidence rule excludes any evidence (oral or written) of statements made by either of the parties **prior to or contemporaneous with** the signing of the contract which **vary or contradict** the writing.

This is a substantive rule of law, for it involves a choice by the law that the written document is representative of the agreement between the parties, rather than other statements made by either or both of them. Since the rule applies only where the parties have intended that the writing be a complete and final expression of their agreement, the rule furthers the intent of the parties.

A. THE WRITING AS FINAL EXPRESSION OF AGREEMENT

Before applying the parol evidence rule, the court must first find that the parties intended that the writing be the final expression of their agreement. Although this is a fact question, it is reserved for the judge and does not go to the jury.

If there is a writing, it may be:

1) simply a **memorandum** of the transaction, with the parties having no intent that their agreement be integrated into the writing; or
2) a complete and final expression of the parties' agreement if they intended the writing to represent the total agreement **(full integration);** or
3) a document that expresses the agreement of the parties on those points covered by the agreement, but the parties did not intend that it cover all of their agreement **(partial integration).**

"Merger clauses" are often included in contracts as an expression of the parties' intent that the writing be a final and complete expression of their agreement. A typical merger clause reads as follows:

> "The parties agree that this writing shall be a complete and final expression
> of their agreement, and no evidence of oral or other written promises shall be
> binding."

Although such a merger clause is strong evidence that the parties intended to integrate their agreement in the writing, it is **not conclusive**; and where the merger clause is in fine print or on the back of a document, the court may find that there was no real assent to it.

Procedure. When there is an objection to testimony or other evidence on the ground that it is parol evidence, the judge will normally allow the offering party to make a preliminary presentation of his evidence out of the presence of the jury. The judge will then consider whether the document was intended by the parties to cover material such as that presented by the parol evidence. If he finds that the parties did intend the writing to be a final expression of their agreement on the point, he will exclude the evidence and it will never get to the jury.

On the other hand, if the judge holds that the writing does not cover the area, he will then allow the attorney to present the evidence to the jury. As a general rule, the more complete and formal the writing, the greater the likelihood that a court will find that the contract is integrated, and that the parol evidence is to be excluded. Of course, if the parol evidence is admitted, it is totally within the province of the jury to determine whether the evidence should be believed.

B. EXCEPTIONS

Subsequent Oral Agreements. Subsequent oral agreements are not covered by the parol evidence rule. In other words, if the parties orally agree to something after the writing is signed, the parol evidence rule does not bar introduction of this agreement.

Defenses to Contract. Parol evidence is always admissible to show that **no contract** was in fact made, or that some **defense** exists to the enforceability of the contract. Thus, fraud, mistake, duress, incapacity, or illegality may be shown through parol evidence in all cases.

Condition Precedent. A condition precedent to the existence of a contract may also be shown by parol evidence. For example, if A and B agree to the sale of B's house to A for a set price and express this in writing, it may be shown that they also agreed orally that the written agreement would have no effect unless some fact occurred. This does not change the terms of the writing, but shows that no binding effect was to be given to the contract terms unless the fact occurred.

Ambiguity; Custom and Usage. Parol evidence is admissible where there is an **ambiguity** in the written agreement. It is not always easy to determine whether an ambiguity exists, but generally courts will admit the parol evidence if the writing is not clear on its face. **Custom and usage** may also be introduced to show that the parties intended that a word or expression have a particular meaning.

Collateral Agreements. Parol evidence of collateral agreements is admissible. Parties may, at the same time, enter into two or more agreements, only one of which is in writing. The **separate agreement** may be proved by parol evidence, since it was not intended to be integrated into the writing.

> For example: If A agrees to sell his house to B, and at the same time
> agrees to sell his power mower to B as a separate transaction, the

> parol evidence rule will not exclude proof of the transaction involving the lawnmower, even though it is not included within the written agreement to sell the house.

Facts Not in Accord with Writing. A recital of facts in the writing may be shown not to be true. Thus, if the document reads "for consideration received," it may be shown that no consideration was actually given. Also, it could be shown that the actual consideration was something different from a specific consideration stated in the writing.

C. PAROL EVIDENCE RULE UNDER THE UNIFORM COMMERCIAL CODE

Section 2-202 of the Code provides a parol evidence rule applicable to contracts for sales. The following rules, which are incorporated in the section, do not significantly change the general law:

Intent of Parties Controls. In order for the parol evidence rule to operate, the parties must have **intended** the writing to be a final expression of their agreement. There can be a **partial integration** under the Code, if the parties intend that the agreement be their final expression of the items contained in the writing, but some items of their agreement are left out or not covered by the writing.

There is no "test" by which the parties' intent can be absolutely ascertained. **Evidence of intent** would include the formality of the writing, its completeness, and any merger clauses whereby the parties in the writing agree that the writing contains all of their agreement.

Explanation or Supplementation of Terms. The Code distinguishes between parol evidence that **contradicts** the writing, and parol evidence that **explains or supplements** the writing. If the intent of the parties is for the writing to be the final expression of their agreement, then **no evidence to contradict the writing** is admissible.

However, even where there is an intent to make the writing final, the writing may be **explained or supplemented** by:

1) course of dealing, trade usage, or course of performance; **and** by
2) evidence of **consistent additional terms unless** the court finds that the writing is intended as a **complete and exclusive** statement of the terms of the agreement.

UCC Section 1-105 provides that the law of the forum is to be applied to a transaction involving more than one jurisdiction whenever the transaction bears **an appropriate relationship** to the law of the forum. The relationship need not be the **most** appropriate. Often, the transaction bears an appropriate relationship to more than one jurisdiction. In such cases, the law of the forum will govern.

Parties are free under the Code to choose the law that will govern their rights and obligations by a provision in the contract. They must, however, choose the law of a jurisdiction which bears a **reasonable** relationship to the transaction. Thus, if the transaction is between parties in Virginia and New Jersey, the parties could not agree that the law of New Mexico should govern.

VII. CONDITIONS

A.   EXPRESS

In some contracts, the obligation to perform is **expressly** conditioned upon some event or some action by the other party. For example: The obligation of an insurance company to pay a claim is generally conditioned upon the filing of notice of the claim. An express condition prevents recovery on the contract unless the condition has been fulfilled.

The law has traditionally distinguished between **"conditions precedent"** and **"conditions subsequent."** The difference between the two is procedural, and goes only to the question of burden of proof. If the condition is classified as a condition **precedent,** then the **promisee** has the burden of proving that it occurred before he can recover. However, if the condition is labeled a condition **subsequent,** then the **promisor** must prove the condition was not met, or else be held liable.

Restatement Definitions. Under §250 of the first Restatement of Contracts, a condition precedent was defined as one which "must exist or occur before a duty of immediate performance of a promise arises." The Restatement defined a condition subsequent as one which "will extinguish a duty to make compensation for breach of contract after the breach has occurred."

The Restatement (Second) §224 abandons the terminology of "conditions precedent" and "conditions subsequent." **Conditions precedent** are now merely referred to as "conditions," defined as **"an event, not certain to occur, which must occur, unless its non-occurrence is excused, before performance under a contract becomes due."** Conditions subsequent are dealt with by the Second Restatement in conjunction with the rules on discharge of contracts. Under Restatement (Second) §230, "if under the terms of the contract the occurrence of an event is to terminate an obligor's duty of immediate performance or one to pay damages for breach, that duty is discharged if the event occurs."

Under the Restatement (Second) definition, a provision in an insurance policy that the insurer's duty to pay a properly presented claim is "discharged if the insured fails to commence an action within one year" would not be a condition but merely an event whose failure to occur will discharge the duty after it has arisen. A requirement that the insured file proof of loss forms with the insurer within 60 days after suffering a fire loss might be worded as either a condition to the duty or as an event discharging the duty. A court might decide the case based merely on the wording used, under the Second Restatement rule.

However, a better result might be reached by analyzing the burden of proof issue on its own terms, allocating the burden to the party most capable of bearing it. In insurance cases, courts generally express a preference for placing the burden of proof on the insurer and in the past would arbitrarily classify most such conditions in an insurance contract as "conditions subsequent" to achieve this result. Such policy considerations continue to influence most courts.

Satisfaction As A Condition. In some contracts, performance by one party is expressly conditioned upon his or her "full satisfaction" with the performance of the other party. Such conditions require the court to determine what is meant by "full satisfaction" or similar language. This could mean either that the condition is met whenever a reasonable person would be satisfied with the proffered performance; or that the actual, subjective satisfaction of the promisee is required.

The primary determinant as to which type of satisfaction is required is the kind of performance called for by the contract. If the promised performance involves **personal taste,** then courts require that the promisee **actually be satisfied,** but if the promised performance is something which can be judged **objectively** by a reasonable standard, then the **reasonableness test** is applied.

Even when a subjective standard is applied, **good faith** must be used in making the decision.

> For example: If A agreed to paint a portrait for B "to B's full and complete satisfaction," B would be entitled to reject the portrait even if it was considered to be an excellent painting by any objective artistic standard. However, B would have to exercise good faith in rejection. If he rejected simply because he had changed his mind and no longer wanted his portrait painted, this would be wrongful and he would be liable for the contract price. Gibson v. Cranage, 39 Mich. 49, 33 Am. Rep. 351 (1878).

Third Party Satisfaction or Certificate. A similar type of case involves the requirement that a certificate be obtained from some third party before the promisor becomes liable. The most common case of this is the requirement that the builder obtain an architect's certificate before the landowner is obligated to pay for the construction. In such cases, courts have held that there is no recovery on the contract until the certificate is procured, in the absence of fraud by the architect in refusing to give it or such gross mistake that bad faith or failure to exercise honest judgment is implied. Thus, even if the architect's reasons for refusal are unreasonable, there can be no recovery on the contract. George S. Chatfield v. O'Neill, 89 Conn. 172, 93 A. 133 (1915). There may, however, be recovery in quantum meruit. Courts also excuse the procurement of the certificate when this is rendered impossible (e.g., when the architect has died), or when the architect's refusal is due to the intervention of the owner.

B.   CONSTRUCTIVE

1.   Conditions of exchange: excuse or suspension by material breach

Bilateral Contracts. In the typical bilateral contract, where A promises some performance in return for a performance by B, A cannot recover from B until A has himself performed, and conversely, B cannot recover from A unless B has performed. Thus, A's performance is a condition to A's recovery, and B's performance is a condition to B's recovery. These conditions are called **"constructive conditions of exchange."** This is simply a common sense doctrine which recognizes that A is in fact bargaining for B's performance, and that A should not be required to render his promised performance unless he gets what he bargained for.

Partial Performance. This doctrine works very well so long as there is no problem of "partial performance." This problem arises when A has partially performed and for some reason cannot or does not complete his performance. There may be injustice in refusing to allow him to recover anything from B, on the basis that he has not fulfilled the condition to his right to recover.

This problem of partial performance has resulted in two theories which will be discussed separately: the doctrine of **substantial performance** and the **divisibility** of contracts.

Precedent and Concurrent Constructive Conditions of Exchange. Constructive conditions of exchange may be either precedent or concurrent. For example, in a contract for sale where payment and delivery are to be at the same time, the conditions are concurrent; but where payment is to be made thirty days after delivery of the goods, delivery is a condition precedent to the right to payment.

2.   Immaterial breach and substantial performance

The doctrine of substantial performance provides that **where one party to a bilateral contract has "substantially performed," he may recover from the other party on the contract even though he has not completely performed**, and therefore has not completely fulfilled the constructive condition to his right to recover.

Thus, if A agrees to build a house for B in return for B's payment to him of $200,000, the doctrine of substantial performance would hold that once A has "substantially performed," he may recover on the contract from B. Of course, there is an allowance for that part of the performance which has not been completed.

Damages for Promisee. The measure of recovery in substantial performance cases is the promised price minus any amount it will cost B to complete the house as A promised to complete it. If, however, completion of the house as promised would result in **economic waste,** the court will grant a recovery of the difference in the value of the house as A left it, and the value it would have had if it had been completed as promised.

Intentional Breaches by Promisor. There can be no recovery, either in contract or quasi-contract, for an **intentional** breach. "Intentional" connotes more than just knowledge; it means some kind of unfair dealing.

3.   Independent covenants

A covenant or promise is independent if it is unqualified or if nothing but the lapse of time is necessary to make the promise presently enforceable. Independent covenants or promises are rare except in those instances where one party by the terms of the contract must perform before the other.

A lease may be looked an as an example of independent covenants. In a lease, the lessee's obligation to pay rent is independent of the landlord's duty to make repairs, although there are exceptions to this rule both by statute in may jurisdictions and under various theories such as constructive eviction.

4. Constructive conditions of non-prevention, non-hindrance, and affirmative cooperation

A subspecies of the duty of good faith is the duty implied into every contract that the party will not hinder the other party's performance and, where legitimately required, will cooperate with the other party. See U.C.C. §2-311(3). This is sometimes called a duty of non-prevention or non-hindrance.

C. OBLIGATIONS OF GOOD FAITH AND FAIR DEALING IN PERFORMANCE AND ENFORCEMENT OF CONTRACTS

A duty of good faith is implied into all contracts. Restatement (2d) Contracts, §205; U.C.C. §1-203. Good faith does not require that the party be nice or particularly accommodating; it only requires that the party's conduct not be unreasonable or unfair.

The U.C.C. defines "good faith" as **"honesty in fact"** for laypersons, §1-201, and **"honesty in fact and the observance of reasonable commercial standards of fair dealing in the trade"** for merchants, §2-103.

This duty of good faith can be enforced affirmatively (e.g., by forcing an exclusive agent to use his or her best efforts to accomplish the principal's desired result). However, it is more often raised as a defense where a party will claim that it is excused from performance under the contract by the other party's failure to act in good faith.

Also, the duty of good faith and fair dealing can be raised only in regard to the performance of the contract. A failure to deal fairly in negotiating the contract can be raised only as an issue of unconscionability or fraud.

D. SUSPENSION OR EXCUSE OF CONDITIONS BY WAIVER, ELECTION, OR ESTOPPEL

The concepts of waiver, election and estoppel arise in many contexts in the fabric of the law. Here we are concerned with these concepts only as they relate to excuse of contractual conditions. We also briefly consider here the topic of renunciation of a right to damages for partial or total breach.

Estoppel. The doctrine being discussed here is **equitable estoppel which is also known as estoppel *in pais***. It is a progenitor of the doctrine of promissory estoppel discussed above. In its traditional form the doctrine of equitable estoppel states that a party:

1) who is guilty of a misrepresentation of existing fact including concealment;
2) upon which the other party justifiably relies;
3) to his injury,

is estopped from denying his utterances or acts to the detriment of the other party.

Generally, not only must the representation be false but that the party to be estopped must be shown to have known that the representation was false. In addition, under this view it must be shown that the party to be estopped must have intended that the representation be acted upon or at least must so act that the party asserting the estoppel has a right to believe that it was so intended.

Contrary to the traditional view of equitable estoppel some of the more modern cases are stating that a misrepresentation of fact is not necessary for the doctrine to apply. A promise is sufficient to form the basis of an equitable estoppel. Under this view actual fraud, bad faith or intent to deceive is not essential.

Once it is decided that a promise may be the basis of an equitable estoppel it becomes more difficult to distinguish equitable estoppel from promissory estoppel.

> For example, if a party promised before breach to accept a late payment he would be estopped from asserting the lateness of the payment unless the promise was withdrawn in time.

Here a promise is being enforced even though there is no consideration for it. This is a type of promissory estoppel except that the term promissory estoppel is ordinarily used in reference to the formation of a contract and not to the performance of a contract. The ultimate point being made is that this promise is effective upon a theory of estoppel whether it be denominated equitable or promissory.

It is often stated that **equitable estoppel is an affirmative defense that must be established by clear and convincing evidence** and that its existence is ordinarily a question of fact.

Waiver and Election. A waiver is defined as a **voluntary and intentional relinquishment of a known right.** The general notion is that the party waiving must have actual knowledge of the facts giving rise to the right he waives. Here we are talking about the waiver of the right to enforce the constructive condition.

If it is a **waiver after failure of condition it is referred to as an election**. Waiver is also ordinarily a question of fact. A waiver may be express or implied.

E.   PROSPECTIVE INABILITY TO PERFORM: EFFECT ON OTHER PARTY

Prospective inability, or unwillingness to perform may be manifested:

1) by word or by conduct;
2) destruction of the subject matter;
3) death or illness of a person whose performance is essential under the contract;
4) encumbrance or lack of the title in a contract vendor at the time of the making of the contract, or a sale of the property by him subsequent to the making of the contract;
5) existing or supervening illegality of a promised performance;
6) insolvency of a party; and
7) under the Uniform Commercial Code defective performances rendered under other contracts between the parties or even a contract with third parties.

When the First Restatement discusses this topic it seems clear that it is concerned with inability or unwillingness which arises before the party who is unable or unwilling to perform is obliged to perform. In such a situation what the other party may do depends upon how serious the prospective inability or unwillingness is.

First Restatement Position. Under some circumstances where there is prospective non-performance **the other party may be justified only in suspending his performance; at other times he may be justified in regarding the contract as cancelled or in changing his position.** The course which may be taken ultimately depends upon whether there is reasonable probability that a party will not or cannot substantially perform. If substantial performance is still possible the most that the other party can do is suspend his performance.

The Restatement Second has rejected the approach of the First Restatement and has adopted a view essentially the same as that adopted by the UCC, discussed below.

In other words under the Second Restatement **the insecure party may no longer, for example, change his position. He must proceed by way of a demand for assurances.** The insecure party may, if he wishes, still resort to the responses previously discussed. The Restatement Second also gives the insecure party the choice of treating a failure to provide assurances as a repudiation or as a material breach.

Prospective Inability To Perform Under Article 2. Between the time a contract is made and the time for performance, each party should enjoy a reasonable expectation that performance will be forthcoming when due. A party's expectations of performance may be diminished by the occurrence of some event after the contract was made. A common example of this is a credit sale, when the buyer becomes insolvent prior to the time the goods are delivered.

Such cases have generally been classified as examples of prospective inability to perform. The law is less settled in the area of prospective inability to perform than it is in cases of anticipatory repudiation; and in general, there is a reluctance to excuse a party from performing solely on the ground that he does not expect counter-performance to be given.

Buyer's Insolvency. Section 2-702(1) allows the seller in a credit sale to demand cash before delivery if she discovers that the buyer is insolvent. If the goods are in the possession of a carrier, the seller may exercise her right of **stoppage in transit**. Under §1-201, a person is insolvent in any one of three separate situations:

1) he cannot pay his debts as they become due; or
2) he has ceased to pay his debts in the ordinary course of his business; or
3) his liabilities exceed his assets.

Reasonable Grounds for Insecurity. Other instances of a party's inability to perform are not delineated by the Code. Instead, §2-609 provides that whenever a party has **reasonable grounds for insecurity,** he **may demand, in writing, "assurance"** from the other party. Until the assurance is given, he **may suspend performance**.

Insecurity. What constitutes reasonable grounds for insecurity is vague. Between merchants, commercial standards are to apply. Comment 3 to §2-609 indicates that the grounds for insecurity need not necessarily be directly related to the contract for sale, giving the following examples:

1) a buyer falls behind in his account with the seller, even though the items involved concern separate contracts;
2) a seller of precision parts delivers defective goods to a customer with needs similar to the buyer's; and

3) a manufacturer breaches an exclusive dealing provision in a franchise agreement, although not defaulting in orders, deliveries, or payments.

Even a false rumor of insecurity may provide sufficient ground to demand assurances if the report came from apparently reliable sources.

Assurances. Section 2-609(2) provides that the adequacy of any assurance is to be determined according to commercial standards. Comment 4 to the section states that:

> What constitutes "adequate" assurance of due performance is subject to the same test of factual conditions [as the question of when they may be demanded]. For example, where the buyer can make use of a defective delivery, a mere promise by a seller of good repute that he is giving the matter his attention and that the defect will not repeated, is normally sufficient. Under the same circumstances, however, a similar statement by a known corner-cutter might well be considered insufficient without the posting of a guaranty or, if so demanded by the buyer, a speedy replacement of the delivery involved. By the same token, where a delivery has defects, even though easily curable, which interfere with easy use by the buyer, no verbal assurance can be deemed adequate which is not accompanied by replacement, repair, money-allowance, or other commercially reasonable cure.

As assurance, the demanding party may insist upon more than mere compliance with prior contractual obligations; he may demand greater security than he was originally entitled to under the contract, subject to the limits of good faith and commercial reasonableness.

No assurance is required unless **demanded in writing** by the party having reasonable grounds for assurances. When demand is made, the other party has a reasonable time, not exceeding 30 days, in which to provide the assurance. If no assurance is given, the contract is breached by repudiation and the party demanding the assurance has all of the usual remedies under the Code.

VIII. REMEDIES

A. TOTAL AND PARTIAL BREACH OF CONTRACT

The doctrine of **"divisible contracts"** also has had an ameliorating effect upon the doctrine of constructive conditions of exchange. In effect, this doctrine holds that where the parties intended that the contract be "divisible," performance of one part of the contract entitles the performing party to recover from the other that part of the other's performance that was set against what the performing party has completed. Thus, in a sense at least, full performance of all of the obligations under the contract is not a condition to recovery.

It is usually easy to tell whether a contract is divisible. Generally, when part of the performance by one party is set against a part of the performance by the other party, there is a divisible contract.

Examples. A typical divisible contract would be one in which the plaintiff agreed to work for the defendant for one year, and the defendant agreed to pay him a certain salary each week. Unless there were unusual circumstances, this would be a divisible contract, and the plaintiff would be entitled to recover his wages from the defendant at the end of each week, even though obviously he had not worked for the entire year. In such a contract, the plaintiff-employee would be entitled to recover for a week's work which had been completed, even though at the end of the week he refused to work for the defendant-employer any longer.

> If A agreed to construct a house for B, and B agreed to pay him a certain amount after the foundation was in, another amount after the siding was up, a third amount when the house was closed in, etc., this would not be a divisible contract. Here, the owner was contracting for a completed house, and not for the individual parts of it. Where, however, A agreed to paint three of B's houses and B agreed to pay him a certain amount as soon as each house was completed, this would be a divisible contract.

Effect of Divisibility. Where there is a divisible contract, each part of the contract is treated independently for the purposes of constructive conditions of exchange.

> For example: If A agrees to paint three of B's houses and B agrees to pay him $1,000 upon completion of each house, A has a right to recover for the first house as soon as he finishes painting it. If he does not complete it or only substantially performs, then the doctrine of constructive conditions of exchange applies to that house, as does the doctrine of substantial performance. However, even though A's performance on the first house is so defective as to prevent him from recovering anything for that part of the contract, this will generally not affect his right to paint the second house and recover for his work. This is because the contract is "divisible," and the agreement as to each house is treated separately for this purpose. However, if the breach as to the first house destroys the value of the total contract to B, then this would constitute a breach of the entire contract, and A would have no right to paint or to recover for painting the second or third house.

B.   ANTICIPATORY REPUDIATION

Whenever a promisor fails to perform his promise at the time performance is due there is a breach of contract, giving the promisee a right to recover damages, or in some cases, the right to specific performance. The doctrine of anticipatory breach is applicable when a promisor **repudiates his promise before the time for performance arises.** A repudiation sent by mail or telegram becomes effective at the time the letter or telegram is sent, and the law of the place where it is sent governs.

Theoretically, such a repudiation is not a breach because the promisor has not yet failed to do what he promised. For example, if A promises to purchase B's land for $1,000 on June 15th, he cannot **fail to perform** that promise until June 15th. However, in all jurisdictions except Massachusetts, if A repudiates his promise prior to June 15th, the repudiation may be treated as a breach by B, and B may sue A immediately.

Promisee's Rights Upon Repudiation. When there is a repudiation by a promisor, the promisee has the option to **immediately treat the repudiation as a breach** and resort to any remedies available for the breach. Hence, the promisee may:

1) **cancel the contract**, thereby terminating all obligations of either party under the contract; **or**
2) the promisee may immediately **bring an action** for damages (or, in a proper case, for specific performance).

The promisee need not commence his action immediately, but may wait until the time for performance occurs, or for that matter, may wait until just before the statute of limitations expires.

> For example, if A agrees to purchase B's house on June 15th and A repudiates the contract on June 10th, B can sell the house to C on June 11th and still sue A. Even though B could not have performed the condition to A's obligation, i.e., tender of the house, he can show that he would not have sold to C and would have been able to tender performance on June 15th if A had not repudiated.

Right to Ignore Repudiation. In most cases a promisee also can ignore the repudiation. Hence, in the above example, B could have paid no attention to A's repudiation and tendered the house on June 15th, hoping that A would have changed his mind by that time. However, where there is some continuing performance required by the non-repudiating party under the contract, most cases have held that the promisee cannot ignore the repudiation and continue to perform if this will increase the damages of the promisor who repudiated.

Promisee's Obligations upon Repudiation. The promisee is also relieved of any obligations that he has under the contract, and **need not perform any conditions precedent** to the promisor's obligation. He must, however, be able to prove that he would have been **"ready, willing, and able"** to perform if the repudiation had not occurred.

What Constitutes A Repudiation: Repudiation Must Be Definite. A repudiation by a promisor must be "clear and unequivocal." McCloskey & Co. v. Minweld Steel Co., 220 F.2d 101 (3rd Cir. 1955). Thus, if the promisor says, "I don't see how I can perform unless the price is increased," this is not a repudiation, but simply a request for renegotiation of the contract.

The repudiation may be by acts instead of words. Hence, if A contracts to sell his house to B and then transfers title to C before the time for him to close with B, this would constitute a repudiation. Also, it is generally held that the bankruptcy of the promisor, if it makes performance of the contract impossible for him, constitutes a repudiation.

When Liability Is in Dispute. When the promisor denies in good faith that he is bound by the contract to perform all or part of it, courts have generally held that the **doctrine of anticipatory breach does not apply**, and that the promisee must wait until the time for performance before bringing an action. Thus, if A contracts to build a house for B and A denies that he is also obligated to build a garage under the contract, this would not give rise to a repudiation, and B could not sue until the time for performance arose.

Retraction Of Repudiation. A promisor who repudiates has the right to retract the repudiation until the promisee:

1) **acts in reliance** on the repudiation;

2) positively **accepts the repudiation** by so signifying to the promisor; or

3) **commences an action** for breach of the contract.

Thus, if the promisor repudiates and the promisee does nothing, the promisor may change his mind and decide to perform the contract. If the promisor does retract the repudiation, and gives the promisee notice of his retraction sufficient to permit the promisee to perform his part of the contract, it is just as though there was no repudiation. See, United States v. Seacoast Gas Co., 204 F.2d 709 (5th Cir. 1953).

Anticipatory Repudiation And Unilateral Contracts. It is generally held that the doctrine of anticipatory repudiation does not apply to unilateral contracts, nor to contracts where the promisee has nothing further to do under the contract. Thus, if A sells his house to B, title being transferred on April 15th and payment to be made on May 15th, if B repudiates his obligation to pay on May 1st, after the title has been transferred to him, this would not give A an immediate right of action for the price. A would have to wait until May 15th before he could bring an action.

Anticipatory Repudiation Under Article 2. The Code continues the general pattern of the common law of most jurisdictions in the area of anticipatory breach. Under §2-610, a repudiation occurs when a party **unequivocally** states his unwillingness to perform his obligations under the contract. Repudiation occurs automatically when a party creating reasonable grounds for insecurity fails to provide adequate assurance within 30 days of demand, as described above. Otherwise, a demand for greater performance than agreed upon is not a repudiation unless "under a fair reading of the contract it amounts to a statement of intention not to perform except on conditions which go beyond the contract." Comment 2. If there is a repudiation of only part of a party's duty, whether this constitutes an actionable breach depends upon whether the prospective loss to the aggrieved party will **substantially impair the value of the contract** to him.

Effect of Repudiation Under Article 2. When a repudiation occurs, the aggrieved party may await performance for a commercially reasonable time, or he may immediately resort to any remedy given by the Code or the contract for breach. The aggrieved party is excused from his own performance in either case, but he may proceed to identify goods to the contract or to salvage unfinished goods.

Retraction of Repudiation Under Article 2. Under §2-611, the repudiating party may retract his repudiation until the aggrieved party has either canceled the contract, materially changed his position, or otherwise indicated that he considers the repudiation final. If the repudiation resulted from a failure to provide assurances, then the retraction must include any assurance that was justifiably demanded under §2-609.

Seller's Right to Stop Goods in Transit. When the seller has shipped goods to the buyer under the contract and the goods are in transit, the Code gives the seller the right to order the carrier not to deliver the goods to the buyer in two instances:

1) When the buyer is **insolvent**; and
2) When, if the goods are shipped in carload lots, the buyer **repudiates or otherwise breaches** the contract; as for example, by refusing to make a payment that was due before delivery.

A seller **loses her right to stop goods in transit** when any one of the following occurs:

1) the buyer has received the goods;
2) the carrier has acknowledged the buyer's rights to the goods either as a warehouseman or by reshipping the goods;
3) a bailee other than a carrier (e.g., a warehouseman) has acknowledged the buyer's rights to the goods; or
4) a negotiable document of title has been negotiated to the buyer.

Procedure. Section 2-705(3) provides the procedure for effectuating stoppage in transit. It states:

1) To stop delivery, the seller must so notify as to enable the bailee by reasonable diligence to prevent delivery of the goods.
2) After such notification, the bailee must hold and deliver the goods according to the directions of the seller, but the seller is liable to the bailee for any ensuing charges or damages.
3) If a negotiable document of title has been issued for goods, the bailee is not obligated to obey a notification to stop until surrender of the document.
4) A carrier who has issued a nonnegotiable bill of lading is not obliged to obey a notification to stop received from a person other than the consignor.

It should also be noted that a carrier is not obligated to stop delivery of less than carload lots, except where the seller's right to stoppage is predicated upon the buyer's insolvency.

C. ELECTION OF SUBSTANTIVE RIGHTS AND REMEDIES

As a general rule, a plaintiff may not have both a restitution and damages for breach of the contract. At some stage, he must elect his remedies.

Under the UCC, however, a buyer may exercise the remedy of restitution and recover damages as well. For example, a purchaser of goods may revoke his acceptance upon discovery of a breach of warranty, offer to return the goods, and recover the purchase price plus damages measured by his expectation and reliance interests.

D. SPECIFIC PERFORMANCE; INJUNCTION AGAINST BREACH; DECLARATORY JUDGMENT

1. Specific Performance

When damages are an inadequate remedy, equity will order specific performance of the contract. If the equity decree is not observed, the breaching party is in contempt and may be fined or imprisoned.

Factors. In determining whether damages are adequate, the Restatement (Second) of Contracts §360 provides that the following factors should be taken into consideration:

1) the difficulty of proving damages with reasonable certainty (e.g., the difficulty may be posed by sentimental associations and aesthetic interests, not measurable in money, which would be affected by breach);
2) the difficulty of procuring a suitable substitute performance by means of money awarded as damages; and
3) the likelihood that an award of damages could not be collected.

Because **every parcel of real property is considered unique,** contracts involving the transfer of an interest in real property may be enforced by an order of specific performance.

Even if the remedy of damages is inadequate, specific performance will not be granted where the **court cannot supervise enforcement.** Thus, courts do not grant specific enforcement of contracts for personal services, although they may restrain the breaching party from working for another. For example, if a performer agrees to sing in a particular theater, the court will not grant a decree ordering the person to sing at that theater, but it will grant a decree restraining the performer from appearing at competing theaters. Lumley v. Wagner, 42 Eng. Rep. 687 (1852).

Also, courts will usually refuse to grant specific performance in an action where the act or forbearance will occur outside the jurisdiction of the court. Thus, if A agrees to sell land to B, and both A and the land are located outside the jurisdiction of the court, the court will usually not grant a decree of specific performance upon A's refusal to deed the land.

Since a decree of specific performance is an equitable remedy, the usual rules for seeking equitable relief apply, e.g., the clean hands doctrine. Whether the court will grant the relief requested is always within the discretion of the court.

Specific Performance Under the U.C.C.. In sale of goods cases, §2-716 of the Uniform Commercial Code provides that specific performance may be granted where the goods are unique or in other proper circumstances, such as for breach of a requirements contract where there is not another convenient supplier.

2. Injunction Against Breach

A party, such as a landlord, may apply to the court for it to grant an injunction against a tenant in respect of a breach or anticipated breach of a tenancy agreement. Often the tenant is engaging in conduct causing annoyance or nuisance or allowing or encouraging others to engage in such conduct. Thus, the court may issue an injunction against this kind of anticipatory breach.

3. Declaratory Judgment

A declaratory judgment declares the rights of the parties or expresses the opinion of the court on an issue of law, but does not order anything to be done.

As long as there is an actual controversy, an interested party may petition a court for a declaratory judgment regarding unclear rights or duties in respect to the government, other persons or property, or the validity and interpretation of an ambiguous contract or other written document, statute or ordinance.

The court may choose to deny declaratory relief if the judgment would not terminate the controversy. However, the court is not required to deny declaratory relief simply because there is some other legal relief available (e.g., an action for damages).

If the right to jury trial has not been waived, issues of fact may be submitted to a jury for determination as in other actions at law.

Along with a declaratory judgment, the petitioner may seek other relief (including damages and injunctions). The appropriate relief can be awarded by the court even if no declaratory judgment is entered.

A declaratory judgment is binding on the parties in any subsequent litigation, but will not prevent the parties from later seeking other relief.

E. RESCISSION AND REFORMATION

1. Rescission

If A and B enter into an executory bilateral contract, they are free to rescind the agreement by a mutual agreement. The surrender of rights under the original agreement by each party is the consideration for the mutual agreement of rescission. Formerly, a sealed instrument could be discharged by a subsequent agreement only if the later agreement was also under seal. Today, however, the prevailing view in jurisdictions which have retained the seal is that an agreement under seal may be modified, rescinded or substituted by an oral agreement or an unsealed written agreement.

Where Contract Provides for No Rescission. Sometimes a contract provides that it cannot be rescinded except in a writing signed by the contracting party. As a common law proposition such a provision is **ineffective** as the parties cannot restrain their future ability to contract with each other in the future. However, the U.C.C. and some state statutes of general applicability give efficacy to such provisions.

Part Performance. If the original agreement has been performed in part by one of the parties before the agreement of mutual rescission, the question frequently presented is whether the performance which has been rendered should be paid for. The question is one of the intention of the parties. Very often, however, the parties have expressed no intention on the matter, expressing themselves in broad terms such as "Let's call the whole deal off."

Some courts have ruled that in such a case a promise to pay for the performances rendered should be implied. Others have indulged in the presumption that unless an affirmative agreement to the contrary appears the parties intended that payment need not be made for services rendered prior to rescission.

It is a general rule that **an attempt to discharge a duty that has arisen by complete or substantial performance requires consideration.** If one of the parties has fully performed under a bilateral contract or as offeree of a unilateral contract, a mutual agreement to put the contract to an end is ineffective as the party whose duties remain executory has incurred no detriment and therefore the promise of the party who has performed is not supported by consideration.

Under some circumstances this purported rescission may be effective as a "release." But generally speaking, as we have seen, if a party who has completely performed his part of the contract promises to surrender or purports to surrender his rights under the contract in the absence of consideration or of a statute providing otherwise or in the absence of a completed gift, the transaction is ineffective.

A similar problem arises where a party cancels the contract because of a material breach. Uniform Commercial Code Section 2-720 provides that:

> Unless the contrary intention clearly appears, expressions of 'cancellation' or 'rescission' of the contract or the like shall not be construed as a renunciation or discharge of any claim in damages for an antecedent breach.

The Code language and comment make it clear that this provision applies after a breach and is designed to avoid an involuntary loss of a remedy for breach by the use of language by the aggrieved party to the effect that the contract is called off. The Code takes cognizance of the fact that the term "rescission" is often used by lawyers, courts and businessmen in many different senses; for example, termination of a contract by virtue of an option to terminate in the agreement, cancellation for breach and avoidance on the grounds of infancy or fraud.

Under the UCC. "Rescission" is utilized as a term of art to refer to a mutual agreement to discharge contractual duties. "Termination" refers to the discharge of duties by the exercise of a power granted by the agreements "Cancellation" refers to the putting an end to the contract by reason of a breach by the other party. Section 2-720, however, takes into account that the parties do not necessarily use these terms in this way.

Rescission also occurs where the parties enter into a new contract which is substituted for the original contract. The old agreement is discharged but the parties are still bound contractually. At times new terms are added to an existing contract. The manner of distinguishing among these situations has not been authoritatively answered and it may be that the variation in factual settings is so extensive that no test can be formulated, yet a good attempt has been made by one court: **"An alteration of details of the contract which leaves undisturbed its general purpose constitutes a modification rather than a rescission of the contract."**

Although rescissions are ordinarily expressed in words there are a good number of cases involving implied rescissions. For example, a mutual failure of the parties to cooperate in the performance of a contract or concurrent breaches by both parties may be deemed an implied rescission. Where the parties are in dispute as to the mechanics of implementing their contract the failure of one party to reply to the other's offer to rescind may give rise to an implied rescissions.

2.   Reformation

Reformation is the remedy by which writings are rectified to conform to the actual agreement of the parties. At the simplest level it is the mechanism for the correction of typographical and other similar inadvertent errors in reducing an agreement to writing. There was no common law writ for such redress and reformation was developed as an equitable remedy, although now in a merged court it is sometimes available at law.

Reformation is available on grounds of **mistake** or **misunderstanding** as well as **duress** and related misconduct. The substantive requisites vary with the basis. Reformation is not available except on **clear and convincing evidence**, a higher standard of proof than is normal in civil cases.

Contracts are not reformed for mistake; writings are. The distinction is crucial. With rare exceptions, courts have been tenacious in refusing to remake a bargain entered into because of mistake. They will, however, rewrite a writing which does not express the bargain. Stated another way, courts give effect to the **expressed wills of the parties; they will not second-guess what the parties would have agreed to if they had known the facts**.

> Example: Suppose X owns Blackacre, including 100% of the mineral interests therein, but mistakenly believes that he owns but 50% of the mineral interests. He informs a prospective purchaser that he has a 50% mineral interest and that he will convey his entire interest with the land. Acting under this mutual mistake as to the extent of his ownership, he conveys Blackacre together with all his mineral rights in Blackacre to the purchaser. Upon discovery of the mistake, may he have reformation? Was the agreement to convey his entire interest or to convey a 50% mineral interest in Blackacre? Courts have reached contradictory results in cases such as this, some being of the opinion that the mistake was one which induced the bargain and others that the mistake is in articulating the bargain.

The **requisites for reformation** on grounds of mistake are three:

1) There must have been an agreement between the parties;
2) There must have been an agreement to put the agreement into writing; and
3) There is a variance between the prior agreement and the writing.

Some courts add that the mistake be mutual. However, except in cases of fraud, every variance between the prior agreement and the writing is deemed to constitute a mutual mistake. Consequently the fourth element is included in the third.

When courts speak of mutuality of the mistake, they usually have in mind that a mistaken belief by one party alone that the writing will contain a given provision is not a ground for reformations This, however, is encompassed in the requisite that there be a prior agreement that the provision be included in the writing. Thus, the mutual-unilateral mistake dichotomy adds nothing to the analysis of reformation problems.

Privity is not a requirement. A third party beneficiary may obtain reformation even under circumstances where he is mistakenly excluded from the writing.

When reformation of the contract is available to cure a mistake, neither party can avoid the contract.

> For example, assume that A agrees to sell Redacre to B, with B agreeing to pay $50,000 and to "assume a mortgage in the amount of $100,000." If the parties fail to include a provision regarding the assumption of the $100,000 mortgage, A can obtain reformation of the agreement to reflect B's promise. A has no right to avoid the contract because reformation adequately remedies the mistake in drafting the written agreement.

F. MEASURE OF DAMAGES IN MAJOR TYPES OF CONTRACT AND BREACH

The primary objective of contract damages is to put the non breaching party in the same position that he would have been in **had the contract been performed.** Thus, it is sometimes said that the plaintiff in a contract action is entitled to the **"benefit of his bargain"** or his **"expectancy damages."**

Although "expectancy damages" are the normal means of determining damages in a contract case, two alternative types of damages are recognized: **"restitution damages"** and **"reliance damages."** In both of these the plaintiff is not to be put in the position that he would have been in had the contract been performed, but rather to be put in the position he was in **at the time the contract was made.**

In addition, a plaintiff may have suffered damages that go beyond loss of the benefit of his bargain. These are classified as **"consequential damages."**

1. Expectancy Damages

Expectancy damages are normally measured by a formula that looks at the value of the performance of the breaching party and the consideration promised for that performance. The general formula is the **market value of the promised performance less the consideration promised** by the nonbreaching party.

> For example, assume a contract were for the sale of a used car and the seller breached. The damages would be the buyer's cost to purchase the same used car from another source less the original contract price. Thus, if the contract price for the sale of a 1995 Honda Prelude was $13,500 and the buyer, after the seller's breach, purchased a 1995 Honda Prelude in similar condition for $15,000, the buyer's damages would be $1,500. This $1,500 damages from the seller puts the buyer in the position he would have been in had the contract been performed – he has his car at a total cost of $13,500.
>
> Conversely, assume that the buyer had breached in the example above, and the best price the seller could get for his car thereafter was $12,500. His damages would be $1,000. Again, the seller would be put in the same position he would have been in had the contract been performed.

Even if no second contract is entered into by which to measure damages, the same basic formula exists: **Seller's damages are contract price minus market value** of the goods, and **Buyer's damages are market value minus contract price.**

The same basic formula applies in contracts for services; compare the difference between the value of the services to be performed under the contract with the price that was promised for those services. If Contractor agrees to paint Homeowner's house for $5,000, and the fair market value of the job is $6,000, Homeowner can recover $1,000 if Contractor defaults, but Contractor can recover nothing if Homeowner defaults before performance.

Partial Performance. If one of the parties has partially performed at the time of the breach of the other party, the performing party can recover for work done at the contract rate plus "expectancy damages" for the work not yet performed.

> Thus, assume a contractor agreed to paint O's house for $10,000, with $9,000 representing the cost of performance and $1,000 representing the contractor's profit. If O breaches when Contractor is half finished, having thus far incurred $4,500 in costs, Contractor could recover the $4,500 and the $1,000 in anticipated profit, for a total of $5,500. He could not recover the remaining $4,500, which represents the costs not incurred by not yet finishing the contract.

2. Nominal Damages

Damages are not an essential element in a cause of action for breach of contract. If no damages are alleged or none are proved, the plaintiff is still entitled to a judgment for "nominal" damages: usually $1.

G. CONSEQUENTIAL DAMAGES: CAUSATION, CERTAINTY, AND FORESEEABILITY

A breach of contract may result in damages to the nonbreaching party that go beyond the difference between the value of the nonbreaching party's performance and what the nonbreaching party would have received had there been no breach. For example, if a contract calls for the construction of a motel and the builder fails to perform, the basic measure of damages would be the difference between the contract price and the amount that it cost the owner to have someone else construct the building.

However, the failure to construct the building may cause additional damages to the owner in the way of lost profits because of delay, or by causing him to breach contracts he may have made with third parties for the use of the building. If such damages can be proven by the plaintiff and were foreseeable by the breaching party at the time of the contract, consequential damages are recoverable.

Foreseeability and the Rule of Hadley v. Baxendale. The leading case on consequential damages is Hadley v. Baxendale, 9 Exch. 341 (1854), which involved an action by the owner of a factory against a carrier. The owner had contracted to have a shaft needed to run machinery in the factory transported to a third party, who was to use it as a model for the manufacture of a new one. The shipment was delayed by the defendant-carrier, and the plaintiff asked damages to compensate for the loss resulting from the stoppage of work in the factory during the delay.

The court held that the damages recoverable in a contract action are those which "may fairly and reasonably be considered either arising naturally, i.e., according to the usual course of things, from such breach of contract itself, or such as may reasonably be supposed to have been in the contemplation of both parties at the time the contract was made, as the probable result of the breach of it."

Thus, the rule under Hadley v. Baxendale is that damages are recoverable if they were the **"natural and probable consequences," or** if they were **"in the contemplation of the parties at the time the contract was made."** In other words, the damages must be **"foreseeable."**

Thus, in the motel hypothetical above, if the builder did not complete construction on time, the owner would be able to recover damages representing the ordinary profit that he would have made during the period of the delay, and perhaps any additional costs he incurred in arranging financing because his capital would be tied up longer than anticipated. A contractor could foresee these consequences of his delay.

However, if the owner had entered into a particular contract that would have netted him an unusual profit (for example, if he had a contract to rent the entire motel to a convention group for the week after it was supposed to open), he could recover the loss on that contract due to the delay only if the builder knew of the contract with the third party at the time the contract was made.

Certainty of Damages. In order to recover damages, a plaintiff must prove the dollar amount of the damages with reasonable certainty. To put this in the negative: the damages **must not be speculative**. The Restatement (Second) of Contracts §352 requires that the evidence of the amount of damage must afford "a sufficient basis for estimating their amount with reasonable certainty." This does not mean that the plaintiff can recover nothing if part of the damages he attempts to prove fails to meet the requirement of certainty; those damages that were proved with sufficient certainty can be recovered, although others may not be allowed.

The Restatement gives the following examples, among others, of the application of this rule:

1) A and B contract to form a partnership and to continue it for a specified period. B dissolves the partnership prior to the time specified. A could recover damages for lost profits by proving what the profits were during the life of the partnership.
2) A contracts to allow B to operate his established coal mine and to pay B $25 per ton for coal produced. A breaches the contract by refusing B entry to the land. If the mine has been operating for an extended period of time and the veins are well established, B can recover damages by showing the cost of producing the coal, the amount that could have been produced during the contract period, and the market price at which it could have been sold.

Courts are hesitant to award damages for lost profits because they are, in the eyes of most courts, too speculative. This is particularly true in a new or relatively young enterprise. For example, if a plaintiff is suing to recover lost profits because of the defendant's failure to deliver a boiler necessary for plaintiff's new factory, a court may award the plaintiff the rental value of his factory during the time it was inoperative, but will not grant an award on the presumption that the new enterprise would have made a profit.

H.   LIQUIDATED DAMAGES AND PENALTIES

Parties to a contract may fix the amount of damages that will be recoverable in the event of breach; however, a party may not be "penalized" for his breach of contract. Therefore, **penalty clauses in a contract are unenforceable.**

A provision for liquidated damages will be enforced, and not construed as a penalty, if the amount of damages stipulated in the contract is **reasonable in relation to either the actual damages suffered, or the damages that might be anticipated** at the time the contract was made. If a particular stipulated damage provision in a contract fails to meet this test, it will be deemed a "penalty" and therefore unenforceable.

I.   RESTITUTIONARY AND RELIANCE RECOVERIES

If the plaintiff wishes, he may seek restitution rather than regular damages. This means is that the plaintiff may seek to recover from the defendant whatever benefit the plaintiff has conferred on the defendant up until the time that the defendant breached the contract. In essence, **the remedy of restitution returns the parties to their original position** prior to the time of the contract.

Thus, if the buyer under a contract to purchase a house has paid $1,000 down and the seller refuses to convey title, the buyer may sue for the return of the $1,000 only. The remedy of restitution, therefore, is available where it is impossible to prove that the buyer would have made a profit on the house had the sale gone through. Indeed, the general rule is that the buyer can recover the $1,000 even if the seller can prove that had the sale gone through the buyer would have suffered a loss as a result of the transaction because the house was worth far less than the buyer had agreed to pay for it under the contract.

Restitution is an available remedy in all contracts cases no matter what the subject matter of the contract, and it may be combined with expectancy damages. Restitution is also available in quasi contract cases.

Reliance damages may be sought when a **nonbreaching party has incurred some expense** in relation to a contract which is later breached. Reliance damages do not require that the breaching party receive the benefit of any expenditure by the nonbreaching party.

The classic case involved a contract for the sale and purchase of machinery. Prior to the time the machinery was to be delivered to the buyer, the buyer constructed a concrete pad upon which the machinery was to be installed. When the seller failed to deliver the machinery, the buyer was allowed to recover the cost of the concrete pad.

J.   REMEDIAL RIGHTS OF DEFAULTING PARTIES

In an action at law, whenever there has been a failure of express condition to the defendant's obligation or a material breach by the plaintiff, there can be no successful action for breach of contract although quasi-contractual relief is available in some jurisdictions. Generally, the same rule prevails in equity.

There is, however, a different rule with respect to the plaintiff's readiness, willingness and ability to perform. In an action at law, plaintiff must prove that he would have been **ready, willing and able**

Multistate Bar Review Book 2

to perform but for the defendant's breach. In an action for specific performance, the plaintiff must instead show that he was ready, willing and able to perform at the time of the breach and continues to be ready, willing and able.

There is one other major difference in the treatment of conditions in law and equity. The difference is expressed by the maxim **"equity abhors a forfeiture."** The main application of the maxim has been in contracts for the sale of land where a plaintiff in default has made substantial payments toward the purchase price. Such a plaintiff may obtain specific performance on condition that future payments are well secured to the satisfaction of the court and on condition that damages be paid to the defendant.

In a number of jurisdictions where the practice of selling real property for installment payments is ingrained, statutes have been enacted to regulate the matter. Another application of the doctrine has been in the area of options to renew or to purchase ancillary to a lease. Courts have permitted late acceptance of such options where the tenants would otherwise forfeit fixtures, and good will built up during the leasehold period.

K.   AVOIDABLE CONSEQUENCES AND MITIGATION OF DAMAGES

A party to a contract has the obligation of **avoiding or mitigating damages to the extent possible by taking such steps as do not involve undue risk, expense, or inconvenience.** The nonbreaching party is held to a standard of **reasonable conduct** in preventing loss. Thus, the plaintiff in a contract action cannot recover damages which were foreseeable by him, and which he could have avoided by the expenditure of reasonable effort.

> For example: A contracts to manage B's farm for a year. Several weeks before the planting season, A quits. If B could have found another manager by the exercise of reasonable effort, B cannot recover for damages resulting from the fact that no crops were planted.

L.   BUYER'S REMEDIES UNDER ARTICLE 2

Breach By The Seller. When the time for the seller's tender of goods arrives, the seller may make a conforming tender, thereby performing her obligations under the contract, and bringing into play the buyer's obligations, discussed, infra.

Alternatively, the seller may breach the contract by not making any tender at all; or the seller may make a tender, but still breach the contract, either because the tender is improper (e.g., at the wrong place), or because the goods fail to conform to the warranties. In either case, it is said that the seller has made a "nonconforming tender," and the rules are the same whether the tender itself is nonconforming or the goods are nonconforming.

1.   Buyer's Remedies When Seller Fails To Make A Tender

If the seller fails to make any tender at all, the buyer has **three remedies**:

1) He can attempt to force the seller to perform by seeking a decree of **specific performance** or by bringing an action for **replevin.** As will be seen, the situations in which these remedies may be obtained are limited.
2) He may seek **damages**.
3) He may **"cover"** by purchasing similar goods elsewhere and then recover damages.

Specific Performance. Section 2-716 says that **specific performance may be decreed where "the goods are unique" and "in other proper circumstances."** The concept of "uniqueness" may be somewhat broader than that in the law of equity generally. Comment 2 to §2-716 indicates that inability to cover may be strong evidence that specific performance would be appropriate. The section also provides that a decree for specific performance may give complete relief by including whatever terms and conditions regarding payment of the price, damages, or otherwise the court may deem just.

Buyer's Right to Replevin. Section 2-716(3) gives the buyer a right to replevin "for goods identified to the contract if after reasonable effort he is unable to effect cover" or if "the circumstances reasonably indicate" that efforts to cover will be unavailing. Goods are "identified to the contract" for purposes of this section just as in determining impracticability.

A buyer who has paid part or all of the price of goods in which he has a "special property" may, on making tender of any unpaid portion of their price, recover them from the seller if the seller becomes insolvent within ten days after receipt of the first installment on their price. U.C.C. §2-502.

Damages for Nondelivery. Another remedy of the buyer is to sue for damages under §2-713. Damages are measured by the difference between the market price and the contract price **(Market Price minus Contract Price).** The applicable market price is that existing at the place tender was to be made under the contract, and as of the time the buyer learned of the breach. Reports of market quotations in official publications, trade journals, newspapers, and periodicals of general circulation may be introduced as evidence of the market price under §2-724.

Section 2-713 is essentially a statutory liquidated damages clause, not requiring a showing of the plaintiff's actual damages. This remedy applies only when or to the extent that the buyer has not covered, as described below. Comment 5.

Cover. Essentially, the right to cover means that **the buyer may go into the marketplace and purchase substitute goods**, the difference between what he pays and the contract price then becoming the **absolute measure of his damages**. Under §2-712(1), the repurchase must be made in good faith, and without unreasonable delay or upon unreasonable terms. The measure of damages is **Cover Price minus Contract Price.**

Incidental and Consequential Damages. Whether the buyer elects damages after he has effectuated "cover" or damages for nondelivery, the Code also allows him to recover incidental and consequential damages. The Code defines these terms in §2-715:

Incidental damages resulting from the seller's breach include expenses reasonably incurred in inspection, receipt, transportation, and care and custody of goods rightfully rejected, any commercially reasonable charges, expenses, or commissions in connection with effectuating cover and any other reasonable expense incident to the delay or other breach.

Consequential damages resulting from the seller's breach include:

1) any loss resulting from general or particular requirements and needs of which the seller at the time of contracting had reason to know and which could not reasonably be prevented by cover or otherwise; and

2) injury to person or property proximately resulting from any breach of warranty.

This section may be varied by agreement, with the following limitation imposed by §2-719(3):

Consequential damages may be limited or excluded unless the limitation or exclusion is unconscionable. Limitation of consequential damages for injury to the person in the case of consumer goods is prima facie unconscionable, but limitation of damages where the loss is commercial is not.

"Consumer goods" are defined in §9-109 as goods used or bought for use primarily for personal, family, or household purposes.

Buyer's Right to Cancel and Recover Payments Made. An additional remedy of the buyer is to cancel the contract. If this is done, the buyer retains the right to recover any damages caused by the seller's breach under the above theories, and the buyer has the right to recover any payments made in advance to the seller.

Buyer's Right to Goods. Generally, where the buyer has a right to damages, his right to reach the goods covered by the contract for sale to satisfy a judgment will be equal to that of all general creditors of the seller. The buyer will have to obtain judgment and execute on the goods or attach them prior to judgment. However, if the seller becomes insolvent within ten days after the buyer has paid the first installment of the price, the buyer may, upon making and keeping good a tender of any unpaid portion of the price, recover the goods if they have been identified to the contract.

Liquidated Damages. A clause in the contract fixing damages at a certain amount - a liquidated damages clause - is valid under the Code if the amount stated as damages bears a reasonable relationship to either the amount of actual damages suffered, or an amount which could have been anticipated by the parties when they entered into the contract.

2. Buyer's Remedies When Tender Or Goods Are Nonconforming

Requirement of Strict Performance. The contract doctrine of substantial performance does not apply in contracts for the sale of goods, and the seller is required to perform her obligations under the contract in all respects. Thus, if the delivery is a day late, if the quantity is different from that called for by the contract, or if the goods have even a minor defect, the tender is nonconforming, and the seller has breached. However, this **"perfect tender"** rule is not applicable in installment contracts, and the seller generally has a right to cure a defective tender (see below).

Remedies In General. When the seller makes a tender but the tender itself or the goods are nonconforming, **the seller has breached the contract** just as though she had made no tender at all. However, when a nonconforming tender is made, **the buyer can, if he wishes, accept the goods despite the nonconformity.** U.C.C. §2-601. Since the buyer's remedies will differ considerably depending upon whether he accepts or rejects, it must first be determined which course of action the buyer has in fact pursued.

Acceptance: Inspection. The buyer's duty to accept the goods is influenced by his right to inspect the goods. Under §2-513, **the buyer always has a right to inspect before he accepts**. In the absence of a contrary provision in the contract for sale, the buyer may inspect the goods at any reasonable time and place. Generally, inspection will be made when the goods are tendered. It may, however, be made before shipment, or it may be postponed until a reasonable time after the goods have been received.

Under §2-513, the buyer has a right to inspect the goods in any reasonable manner. It is not incumbent upon the buyer to choose the most convenient place, and the reasonableness of the time and place will be determined by trade usage, past practices between the parties, and the circumstances of the case.

Section 2-513(2) provides that the buyer must pay the costs of inspection, but that these costs may be recovered from the seller if the goods are rightfully rejected for nonconformity.

What Constitutes Acceptance. In some cases, the buyer will expressly acknowledge his assent to become owner of the goods, but in many cases acceptance is inferred from the actions of the buyer. Thus, a resale of the goods after they have been received from the seller is clearly an acceptance unless they are being sold for the benefit of the seller.

Section 2-606 defines the acts which constitute acceptance. It states:

(1)   Acceptance of the goods occurs when the buyer:

    (a)   after a reasonable opportunity to inspect the goods signifies to the seller that the goods are conforming or that he will take or retain them in spite of their nonconformity; or

    (b)   fails to make an effective rejection (subsection (1) of Section 2-602), but such acceptance does not occur until the buyer has had a reasonable opportunity to inspect them; or

    (c)   does any act inconsistent with the seller's ownership; but if such act is wrongful as against the seller, it is an acceptance only if ratified by him.

(2)   Acceptance of a part of any commercial unit is acceptance of that entire unit.

Acceptance of Part of Shipment Permitted. Section 2-601 permits the buyer to accept "any commercial unit or units and reject the rest." The use of the term "commercial unit" is designed to require that good faith and commercial reasonableness be used by the buyer to avoid undue impairment of the value of the portion rejected. Thus, if the goods have greater value as a whole than the total value of the individual components, they must be accepted as a whole or rejected entirely.

Revocation of Acceptance. The buyer may, in some situations, elect to revoke his acceptance. If the buyer has the right to revoke acceptance and does so, it is just as though he had rejected in the first place. Under §2-608, the buyer may revoke his acceptance of goods, if the nonconformity substantially impairs the value of the goods, and if he has accepted either:

    1)   on the reasonable assumption that its nonconformity would be cured, and it has not been seasonably cured; or

    2)   without discovery of such nonconformity, if his acceptance was reasonably induced either by the difficulty of discovery before acceptance or by the seller's assurances.

        Multistate Bar Review Book 2

If revocation is permitted, it must be made within a reasonable time after the defect or nonconformity has been or should have been discovered. The goods must be returned in substantially the same shape in which they were tendered, except for damage caused by the defect. Notice must be given to the seller, and the revocation is not effective until such notice has been given. When the buyer properly revokes, he has all the rights and obligations of one who has not accepted the goods.

Buyer's Rights and Remedies When Nonconforming Tender Is Accepted. When there is a nonconforming tender by the seller, the buyer has a right to reject the goods. He may, however, intentionally agree to accept them despite the nonconformity, or he may unintentionally accept them by failing to make a proper rejection. If the buyer does in fact accept them, he still has a right to recover from the seller any damages caused by the seller's breach.

Notice Requirement. Although acceptance does not impair any remedy that the buyer has other than his right to reject the goods, the buyer must give notice to the seller of any breach within a reasonable time after he discovers or should have discovered the breach. Failure to give notice bars the buyer from all remedies. U.C.C. §2-607(2).

Damages Recoverable.

1) **Breach of Warranty.** When the goods are nonconforming, this amounts to a **breach of warranty** by the seller. The measure of damages in such cases is the difference (at the time and place of acceptance) between the value the goods would have had if they had been as warranted, and their actual value with the defect.
2) **Breach of Tender Obligations.** When the nonconformity results from the seller's failure to perform one of her tender obligations (e.g., where the delivery is late), the buyer may recover all loss that results from the breach in the ordinary course of events, as determined in any manner that is reasonable. In effect, all damages that are proximately occasioned by the breach are recoverable.
3) **Incidental and Consequential Damages.** Incidental and consequential damages are also recoverable by the buyer in either instance. U.C.C. §2-714.

Rejection. Section 2-606(1)(b), supra, on acceptance by failure to reject, requires reference to §2-602(1), which states:

Rejection of goods must be within a reasonable time after their delivery or tender. It is ineffective unless the buyer seasonably notifies the seller.

Thus, when a tender of goods is made by the seller, positive action is required by the buyer in order to avoid acceptance. He must act within a reasonable time, which time will depend upon the facts of the individual case, especially upon the contract terms relating to inspection and the physical ease or difficulty of making an inspection of the goods. If the contract permits him to inspect within a definite time after receipt of the goods, this determines the period during which a rejection can be made.

Notice of Rejection. Section 2-602(1) requires the buyer to notify the seller that he has rejected the goods. What constitutes notice is defined in §1-201(26):

A person "notifies" or "gives" a notice or notification to another by taking such steps as may be reasonably required to inform the other in ordinary course, whether or not such other actually comes to know of it.

Section 2-602(1) does not prescribe the form of notice to be given. It does not require the buyer to state the grounds of his objection. However, note should be taken of §2-605(1), which does require particularization of the grounds in certain instances. Section 2-605(1) provides:

The buyer's failure to state in connection with rejection a particular defect which is ascertainable by reasonable inspection precludes him from relying on the unstated defect to justify rejection or to establish breach:

a)   where the seller could have cured it if stated seasonably; or
b)   between merchants when the seller has after rejection made a request in writing for a full and final written statement of all defects on which the buyer proposes to rely.

Buyer's Obligations Regarding Goods Upon Rejection. If the buyer has received the goods prior to his rejection, or if he has revoked his acceptance, he will have possession of the goods. The Code imposes certain obligations upon the buyer with respect to the goods in such cases. In the first place, he cannot exercise any ownership over the goods. If he does, this is wrongful against the seller and may be treated by the seller as an acceptance.

The buyer also has the positive obligation to hold the goods for a reasonable time to permit the seller to remove them. If the seller has no agent at the place of business or market of rejection, the buyer must await instructions from the seller and follow any reasonable instructions given by him. Where the goods are perishable and the seller has no local agent, the buyer must sell the goods for the account of the seller if no instructions are forthcoming.

If the goods are not perishable and the seller has no agent at the place of rejection, in the absence of instructions from the seller, the buyer may either store the rejected goods for the seller's account, reship them to the seller, or sell them for the seller's account. Such action is neither acceptance nor conversion.

If the seller who has no agent in the place of rejection gives instructions to the buyer, the instructions are deemed unreasonable if the seller refuses to give indemnity for the buyer's expenses incurred in carrying out the instructions. If the buyer sells the goods for the seller, he is entitled to reimbursement out of the proceeds for reasonable expenses for caring for the goods and for selling them, including a seller's commission equal to that which is usual in the trade, or to a reasonable sum not to exceed ten percent.

The buyer may alternatively retain possession of the goods as security for any payments made on the price, and any expenses incurred in their inspection, care, or transportation. U.C.C. §2-711(3).

Buyer's Remedies When Buyer Rejects Nonconforming Tender. When the goods are rejected by the buyer because they (or the tender) were nonconforming, **the buyer's remedies are the same as though no tender was made at all**. Thus, the buyer has a right to damages (Market Price minus Contract Price), or to cover and cover damages (Cover Price minus Contract Price), or, in some instances, the right to specific performance or replevin. However, the seller may have the right to cure the defect.

Multistate Bar Review Book 2

Seller's Right to Cure. **If the seller makes a nonconforming tender before his time for performance has expired**, §2-508(1) provides that upon rejection of the tender by the buyer, **the seller may give seasonable notice of his intent to cure the shipment.** If he does give notice, he has a right to make a conforming delivery under the contract. The "cure" must be completed by the last date for delivery under the contract, unless the time for cure is extended.

Section 2-508(2) provides that:

Where the buyer rejects a nonconforming tender which the seller had reasonable grounds to believe would be acceptable with or without money allowance the seller may if he seasonably notifies the buyer have a further reasonable time to substitute a conforming tender.

This subsection assumes that the seller's time for performance has expired, and it therefore extends the seller's right to cure. Section 2-508(2) is sharply limited, however, by the requirement that the seller have "reasonable grounds to believe" that the tender would be accepted despite the nonconformity. If time of delivery is specifically made essential in the contract, or the contract expressly provides that no replacements will be allowed, the seller cannot have grounds to believe that a nonconforming tender will be accepted, and the subsection is inapplicable.

Effect of Cure. When a cure is properly made under these provisions, it is **just as if the seller had properly performed in the first place**. Thus, when a buyer rightfully rejects a nonconforming tender, he has the same remedies that are available where no tender is made, unless there is a cure by the seller. In the event of cure, the seller has fully performed and the buyer has no right or remedies because he got what he bargained for.

M.   SELLER'S REMEDIES UNDER ARTICLE 2

When the seller makes a tender of goods that conform to the contract, the buyer is obligated to accept. In actual fact, however, the buyer may accept or reject. If the buyer does accept, then he has performed one of his obligations under the contract. If the buyer rejects, however, the rejection is wrongful and the buyer has breached the contract.

1.   Seller's Remedies When Buyer Wrongfully Rejects

If the buyer breaches the contract by wrongfully rejecting the goods, the seller has three possible remedies:

1) Sue for **damages** (normally, Contract Price minus Market Price);
2) **Resell** the goods to a third party and **sue for the difference** between the contract price and the resale price (Contract Price minus Resale Price); or
3) **Sue for the price if the goods** are not salable in the seller's ordinary course of business.

Seller's Suit for Damages for Non-acceptance. Section 2-708 provides two alternative measures of damages for a wrongful rejection by the buyer. It states:

1) Subject to subsection (2) and to the provisions of this Article with respect to proof of market price [Section 2-723], the measure of damages for non-acceptance or repudiation by the buyer is the difference between the market price at the time and place for tender and the unpaid contract price, together with any incidental damages

provided in this Article [Section 2-710], but less expenses saved in consequence of the buyer's breach.

2) If the measure of damages provided in subsection (1) is inadequate to put the seller in as good a position as performance would have done then the measure of damages is the profit [including reasonable overhead] which the seller would have made from full performance by the buyer, together with any incidental damages provided in this Article [Section 2-710], due allowance for costs reasonably incurred and due credit for payments or proceeds of resale.

Incidental Damages. The seller's incidental damages are described in §2-710 as including: [A]ny commercially reasonable charges, expenses or commissions incurred in stopping delivery, in the transportation, care, and custody of goods after the buyer's breach, in connection with return or resale of the goods or otherwise resulting from the breach.

Resale of the Goods. A second remedy of the seller, which is really an alternate method of measuring damages, is to resell goods that have been identified to the contract. After the resale, the seller is entitled to the difference between what was realized on the resale and the contract price. In addition, the seller has a right to any incidental damages caused by the breach.

Section 2-706 of the Code provides for the seller's right to resell and recover damages. Under this section, when a resale is made for less than the contract price, the difference between the resale price and the original price is the actual measure of damages, and not just evidence thereof. If the seller makes a resale for more than the contract price, she is not accountable to the buyer for any profit she makes on the new transaction.

Method of Resale. Subsections 2-706(2), (3), and (4) govern the manner in which a resale must be made. Unless otherwise agreed upon, the **sale may be public or private**. One or more contracts may be made, and the seller is allowed to use the goods to fulfill a contract already made with another customer. The method, manner, time, place, and terms of the sale must be **commercially reasonable,** and the sale may be of all the goods as a unit or of portions thereof. There must be some identification of the transaction as a resale of goods originally sold under the broken contract. If the resale is to be a private sale, the seller must give the buyer reasonable notification of his intent to resell.

If the sale is a public sale, there are several additional rules:

1) Only identified goods can be sold unless there is a recognized market for a public sale of futures in goods of the kind; and

2) The sale must be made at a usual place or market for public sale if one is reasonably available, and except in the case of goods which are perishable or threaten to decline in value speedily, the seller must give the buyer reasonable notice of the time and place of the resale; and

3) If the goods are not to be within the view of those attending the sale, the notification of sale must state the place where the goods are located and provide for their reasonable inspection by prospective bidders; and

4) The seller may buy.

Goods Must Be Identified. Unless there is a recognized futures market in the goods, only goods that have been identified to the contract may be resold under §2-706. However, under §2-704(1)(a), a seller may proceed to identify conforming goods to the contract if the goods were in her possession or control at the time she learned of the breach. This section is important because it allows the seller

Multistate Bar Review Book 2

to identify so that she may resell under §2-706, or in some cases, to sue for the price under §2-709. Section 2-704(1)(b) allows the seller to resell goods which have been demonstrably intended for the contract even though the goods are not finished. Unfinished goods are covered in §2-704(2), which states:

> Where the goods are unfinished, an aggrieved seller may in the exercise of reasonable commercial judgment, for the purpose of avoiding loss and of effective realization, either complete the manufacture and wholly identify the goods to the contract, or cease manufacture and resell for scrap or salvage value or proceed in any other reasonable manner.

Seller's Right to the Price After the Buyer Has Wrongfully Rejected. The third possible remedy of the seller is to recover the price. This remedy, which is similar to the buyer's right of specific performance, is allowed only where the goods have been identified to the contract and the seller is unable to sell them at a reasonable price after a reasonable effort, or if the circumstances reasonably indicate that such effort will be unavailing. §2-709(1).

If the seller sues for the price, she must tender the goods to the buyer. If the court refuses to allow recovery of the price, judgment is still to be given for damages as discussed above.

Cancellation. Another right given to the seller is to cancel the contract. When a seller "cancels," she retains her right to sue for any damages resulting from breach of the entire contract or for any unperformed balance. "Cancellation" therefore does not put an end to the buyer's obligation to pay damages. Comment to §2-703 rejects any idea that election of remedies is to be a fundamental policy of the Code, and states that the remedies set forth in the section are cumulative.

Right to Retain Deposits. If the seller has possession of the goods and the buyer has paid a deposit, one of the easiest ways to settle damages upon the buyer's breach or default is for the seller to retain the deposit and forego suing. However, if the deposit far exceeds the actual or expected damages, retention can be tantamount to a penalty. Section 2-718(2) provides for the return of the deposit to the buyer in the following manner:

> Where the seller justifiably withholds delivery of goods because of the buyer's breach, the buyer is entitled to restitution of any amount by which the sum of his payments exceeds:
>
> a) the amount to which the seller is entitled by virtue of terms liquidating the seller's damages . . . [see below], or
> b) in the absence of such terms, 20% of the value of the total performance for which the buyer is obligated under the contract or $500, whichever is smaller.

If the buyer brings suit for restitution under this section, the actual damages resulting from his breach may be offset by the seller.

Liquidated Damages. A liquidated damages clause in a contract for sale is enforceable if the amount of damages bears a reasonable relationship either to actual damages or to those which could have been anticipated at the time the contract was made.

2. Seller's Right to Payment of the Price

The second obligation of the buyer, after the obligation to accept a conforming tender, is to pay the price for the goods. This is a distinct obligation from the duty to accept the goods. When the buyer accepts a tender of the goods, the seller is entitled to recover the price as established by the contract and the U.C.C.

Amount of Price. In the vast majority of contracts for sale, the price is set by the parties in the contract itself. In some cases, however, the parties may leave the price open. Section 2-204(3) expressly permits the parties to contract even though some of the terms of the contract are not yet settled. Section 2-305 augments this principle in connection with the price term. It states:

(1)   The parties if they so intend can conclude a contract for sale even though the price is not settled. In such a case the price is a reasonable price at the time for delivery if:
    (a)   nothing is said as to price; or
    (b)   the price is left to be agreed by the parties and they fail to agree; or
    (c)   the price is to be fixed in terms of some agreed market or other standard as set or recorded by a third person or agency, and it is not so set or recorded.

(2)   A price to be fixed by the seller or by the buyer means a price for him to fix in good faith.

(3)   When a price left to be fixed otherwise than by agreement of the parties fails to be fixed through fault of one party, the other may at his option treat the contract as canceled or himself fix a reasonable price.

(4)   Where, however, the parties intend not to be bound unless the price is fixed or agreed and it is not fixed or agreed, there is no contract. In such a case the buyer must return any goods already received or if unable to do so must pay their reasonable value at the time of delivery and the seller must return any portion of the price paid on account.

The section is basically the same as what might be expected under general contract principles, but three points should be emphasized:

1)   the parties may "agree to agree" in the future to a price;
2)   the parties may agree that one of them will unilaterally set the price; and
3)   if the price depends upon an external market standard or is to be decided by a third party and the price is not so set, then the contract remains enforceable and the price is a reasonable one unless the parties intend otherwise.

Price Term Omitted. If there is no mention of price in the contract for sale and the parties do not agree upon the price, the Code provides that **the sale is valid** and that the **buyer must pay a reasonable price.** The Code gives no hint of how a reasonable price is to be determined, but it would seem that the market price would normally be accepted as a reasonable price.

Where there is no market price, an independent appraisal might establish a reasonable price. If there is no way of ascertaining a reasonable price, then the contract would necessarily fail under §2-204(3) as it would be impossible to give adequate relief to the seller.

Price to Be Agreed Upon by Parties. If the contract provides that the parties will agree to a price in the future, then it is clearly enforceable if they do in fact agree. **If they cannot agree, then a reasonable price is supplied by the Code if they intended that a reasonable price should govern in absence of agreement.** This is clearly a question of fact, and may often be difficult to resolve in the absence of some expression of intent by the parties.

     Multistate Bar Review Book 2

Payment by Check. Under §2-511, the buyer has a right to pay in any manner current in the ordinary course of business unless the seller demands payment in legal tender. If the seller does demand legal tender, the buyer must be given additional time to procure it.

Price Payable in Goods, Realty, or Otherwise. Section 2-304 provides that the price may be payable in money, goods, realty, services, or otherwise. Where the goods are paid for in part or entirely by an exchange of other goods, each party is a seller as to those goods he transfers, and each is a buyer as to those he receives. Where realty is all or part of the price, then the Code applies to the transfer of the goods but not to the transfer of the realty.

Time and Place of Payment in General. Section 2-310 restates the general rule that if the parties do not provide a definite time for payment in the contract for sale, **payment is due when the goods are delivered** to the buyer. Thus, generally the time for payment is when the buyer receives the goods. If the seller is to transport the goods to the buyer, no right to payment exists until they are tendered at the place of destination, whether the contract is one of "shipment" or "destination."

Right to Inspect Before Payment. In most cases, the buyer's obligation to pay does not arise immediately upon receipt of the goods because the buyer has a right to inspect the goods before paying, and inspections are usually made after receipt of the goods. Thus, the payment obligation generally arises after the time for inspection has passed. The contract may provide that payment is to be made before inspection, however, and **in three cases the Code specifically requires payment before inspection**:

1) Where the delivery is C.O.D. (cash on delivery) or on like terms;
2) Where the contract is C.I.F. or C. & F.; and
3) Where the contract provides for payment against documents of title and does not state that such payment is due only after the goods are made available for inspection.

3.   Seller's Right To Reclaim The Goods

When the buyer refuses to pay the price, the seller's remedy is to sue for the price. In two instances, the seller also has some rights in the goods.

Right to Reach Goods Upon Buyer's Insolvency. Once a buyer accepts goods, he becomes their owner and they become assets of his estate. They can be reached by all creditors of the buyer for the purpose of realizing on debts owed by the buyer, unless they are subject to a lien or security interest in favor of a particular creditor. Absent a right to the goods created either by the law or by a consensual agreement, the seller of the goods stands in no better position than the other general creditors of the buyer.

Section 2-702(2) creates a limited security interest in favor of the seller:

Where the seller discovers that the buyer has received goods **on credit while insolvent**, he may reclaim the goods upon a demand made within ten days after the receipt; but if misrepresentation of solvency has been made to the particular seller in writing within three months before delivery, the ten-day limitation does not apply. Except as provided in this subsection, the seller may not base a right to reclaim the goods on the buyer's fraudulent or innocent misrepresentation of solvency or of intent to pay.

Rights of Good Faith Purchaser from Buyer. Section 2-702(3) makes the seller's rights subject to those of a good faith purchaser from the buyer:

> The seller's right to reclaim under subsection (2) is subject to the rights of a buyer in ordinary course or other good faith purchaser under this Article [Section 2-403]. Successful reclamation of goods excludes all other remedies with respect to them.

Right to Reach Goods When Delivery Made Under C.O.D. Contract. Subsection 2-507(2) provides that:

> Where payment is due and demanded on the delivery to the buyer of goods or documents of title, his right as against the seller to retain or dispose of them is conditional upon his making the payment due.

Thus, where a C.O.D. sale has been made, and the seller accepts a check upon delivery, the seller is entitled to reclaim the goods if the check is not paid when presented.

IX. IMPOSSIBILITY OF PERFORMANCE AND FRUSTRATION OF PURPOSE

The doctrines of impossibility of performance and frustration of purpose provide a promisor an excuse for not performing his contractual duties. When applicable, the appropriate doctrine may be raised as a defense in an action brought for breach of contract. The doctrines may also be raised affirmatively as grounds for rescission or cancellation of a contract.

Generally, **impossibility of performance** occurs when the promisor has promised to do something that becomes **objectively impossible without his fault.** **Frustration of purpose** occurs when the **value of the performance** to be obtained by the promisor **becomes useless** to him due to an unforeseen change in circumstances.

A. IMPOSSIBILITY OF PERFORMANCE

Impossibility of performance has traditionally arisen in three types of cases: destruction of subject matter, death or incapacity of one of the parties, and illegality.

Destruction of Subject Matter. If the existence of a specific thing is contemplated by the parties at the time they contract, and the existence of that thing is necessary for performance of the contract, then performance is excused if the thing is destroyed. Thus, if A agrees to sell a specific horse to B, the death of the horse before delivery excuses A from his obligation under the contract. The contract must contemplate the delivery of a **specific** thing. If A's obligation were to deliver **a** horse, the death of the horse that A intended to tender does not excuse him, because he can obtain a different horse and tender it under the contract.

Compare the following two situations: (1) A agrees to purchase 1,000 bushels of wheat from B. B's crop is destroyed. Here, the doctrine does not apply because B can procure the wheat elsewhere. (2) A agrees to purchase 1,000 bushels of wheat "to be grown on B's farm." Here, if the crop were destroyed, B would be excused because it would be impossible to deliver wheat "grown on B's farm."

In a number of cases, the doctrine of impossibility has been raised when a contractor agrees to build a house and the house is destroyed after it has been partially completed. Here, the doctrine does not apply because the contractor can rebuild the house, and has the obligation to do so.

Death or Incapacity. The death or illness of a promisor gives rise to the defense of impossibility **only if the contract requires the personal services of the promisor**. If an artist agrees to paint a picture, he is excused if he dies or becomes incapacitated. However, if the contract is such that the promisor has the right to hire someone else to perform his obligations, neither death nor incapacity operates as an excuse. (The decedent's estate would be liable in the case of death.)

When a corporation is voluntarily dissolved, the general rule is that the doctrine of impossibility does not apply, and the corporation is liable on contracts calling for its performance. In some cases, however, courts have found that the continued existence of the corporation was a condition to its obligations, the condition being implied from the facts of the transaction.

A party may also be excused if a third person who was hired to perform the contract dies or is disabled, but only if the services of another cannot replace that third party. An example would be where A contracts with B to provide C to appear at a concert, and C dies.

Also, if the life, health, or property of one party is seriously threatened by performance, he may be excused. For example: A contracts with B for A to work in a certain county as a salesman, and an epidemic of a dangerous, communicable disease breaks out in that area. A is excused from his performance.

Illegality. If performance is prohibited by a change in statutory law, a constitution, an administrative regulation, a municipal ordinance, or by judicial order, the doctrine of impossibility applies and the promisor is excused from performance.

Performance Must Be Objectively Impossible. Courts distinguish between situations where the performance cannot be done by anyone, and where the promisor cannot do it. The distinction is between "the thing cannot be done," and "I cannot do it," the former being objective impossibility.

> For example: A agrees to sell an electronic calculator to B. The one that he was going to deliver to B is stolen, but others are available on the market. A is not discharged, even though it is impossible for him to obtain another calculator in time to deliver it within the time specified in the contract. On the other hand, if A had agreed to sell a specific calculator to B, its theft would excuse his performance.

The Event Must Be Unforeseeable. The event which makes the contract impossible to perform must have been unforeseeable at the time the contract was made.

Existing and Supervening Impossibility. Generally, the doctrine of impossibility arises in situations where performance was possible at the time the contract was made, but subsequently becomes impossible. The doctrine also applies where performance was impossible when the contract was made.

> For example: A contracts to paint B's vacation home. Unknown to both, B's vacation home had been destroyed by fire a week prior to

the agreement. A is discharged from his obligation to paint and B is discharged from the obligation to pay.

Greater Obligation Can Be Assumed. A contract may contain a provision that damages will be paid in the event that performance becomes illegal.

For example, assume that A is employed as manager of a pulp plant in Alabama, and that he receives an offer from another company to manage a similar plant in Arizona. A and the new company might properly include a provision for liquidated damages for A in the event that Arizona adopted environmental controls forcing pulp plants to abandon operations there.

Temporary Impossibility. Sometimes performance is rendered impossible temporarily. For example, an embargo may be placed upon a port and may make delivery there impossible for a month. In such cases, if performance by the promisor after the embargo was lifted would impose a substantially greater burden on him than there would have been had the impossibility not occurred, then he is excused. Otherwise, he is not.

Part Performance. When the event giving rise to the impossibility occurs after the promisor has partially performed, the promisor may recover the value of his partial performance in quasi contract.

Impracticability of Performance Under Article 2. Destruction of Goods. The seller is excused from performing where the contract for sale calls for specific goods, and the goods are destroyed before the risk of loss has passed to the buyer. Section 2-613 provides for casualty to identified goods in some detail:

Where the contract requires for its performance goods identified when the contract is made, and the goods suffer casualty without fault of either party before the risk of loss passes to the buyer, . . . then:

1) if the loss is total, the contract is avoided; and
2) if the loss is partial or the goods have so deteriorated as no longer to conform to the contract, the buyer may nevertheless demand inspection and at his option either treat the contract as avoided or accept the goods with due allowance from the contract price for the deterioration or the deficiency in quantity but without further right against the seller.

Fault. The section applies only when the loss is without the fault of either party. Comment 1 to the section indicates that "fault" is intended to include negligence as well as willful wrong.

Identified Goods. The seller is excused from performance only if the goods were identified when the contract for sale was made. Identification, in the sense of this section, occurs when the parties agree that **particular goods are the subject of the sale**. For example, if the contract is for ten specific chairs that the seller has shown the buyer, this would meet the requirement of being identified when the contract was made.

Multistate Bar Review Book 2

On the other hand, if the contract were simply for ten chairs of a specific description, and the seller could tender any ten chairs meeting the description, they would not be identified at the time of the contract. Even if they had been identified subsequent to the contract and prior to the loss, the section would not apply.

Partial Loss. If the loss is less than total, the buyer has the option of avoiding the contract totally, or of taking those goods still conforming to the contract at the pro rata price.

Impracticability Under the UCC Caused by Other Events. It has been generally held that when performance by a seller is rendered illegal by state action, e.g., legislation or administrative regulations, the seller is excused. Section 2-615 adopts this position. There is less agreement in decisional law over whether other occurrences which render performance extremely difficult should operate to terminate a party's obligations.

The Code, in §2-615, provides that the seller shall be excused for delay in delivery or nondelivery, if performance "has been made impracticable by the occurrence of a contingency, the non-occurrence of which was a basic assumption on which the contract was made." Although the section speaks only of excusing the seller, the comments to the section indicate that a buyer's obligations may be excused as well.

As when the goods are destroyed, if the impracticability goes only to a part of the party's ability to perform, there must be an apportionment of the performance that can be rendered among those with whom the seller has contracts. Thus, if the seller's operation can produce only half of its normal output, each of the persons with whom the seller has a contract must be tendered half of what was called for under the particular buyer's contract. The buyer may then take what is offered or decide to cancel the contract.

Substituted Performance. In two instances, the Code requires that a party make substitute performance in the event that the agreed method of performance becomes impracticable. In these cases, the other party to the contract must accept the substituted performance. Section 2-614 provides that when an agreed upon **method of transportation** fails or becomes commercially impracticable, the seller must use any **commercially reasonable substitute** that is available.

Thus, if a particular carrier is unavailable because of a strike or a flood, and there is another carrier who can transport the goods satisfactorily and for a reasonable price, the goods must be sent by the available carrier and must be accepted by the buyer. Similarly, if an agreed-upon **method of payment** fails, the buyer must use a commercially reasonable substitute method of payment if one is available, and the seller must accept the substituted method of payment.

Impracticability. While courts have been reluctant to excuse a promisor from performance for any reason other than impossibility, the **Restatement (Second) of Contracts** §261 and the U.C.C. provide that a promisor may be excused if his performance becomes "impracticable" due to unforeseen difficulties or increased costs. Even the courts that have allowed relief due to impracticability have held that increased cost alone is not sufficient as an excuse. The party seeking relief from the contract must show impracticability due to some unforeseen contingency, the risk of which was not assumed by either party, coupled with an increase in the cost of performance far beyond what either party might have anticipated. The most common settings for the commercial impracticability doctrine are war, embargo and crop failure.

B.   FRUSTRATION OF PURPOSE

The doctrine of frustration of purpose applies where the **value of the performance** bargained for by the promisor **is destroyed by a supervening event which was not anticipated when the contract was made**.

> For example, A promises to pay B $1,000 to paint his house. Before performance, A's house is condemned by the state and will be torn down in three months. Here, it is possible for B to paint the house before its destruction, and if A wishes, he can require B to do so. However, if A does not wish to go through with the contract, he has the right to rescind it on the ground that the purpose of the contract – the value of B's performance to him – has been destroyed by the condemnation.

Basic Requirements. Courts have applied the doctrine of frustration of purpose sparingly. Two requirements must be met before the doctrine applies:

1) the value of the contract to the Promisor must have been totally, or almost totally, destroyed; and
2) the event causing the frustration must have been unforeseeable at the time of the contracting.

The classic case involves the 1902 coronation parade in England. Because of the illness of the monarch (Edward VII), the parade was called off. The court refused to enforce a contract by which a person had obtained a license to use rooms to view the parade. Since the license fee was based upon the desirability of the rooms as a viewing point, and they were no longer useful for that purpose, the court held that the purpose of the contract had been frustrated. **Krell v. Henry,** 2 K.B. 740 (1903).

American courts have been very reluctant to apply this doctrine. In a number of cases arising during the Second World War, courts refused to grant a party rescission. In these cases, gas stations, garages, and other businesses which were dependent upon the availability of cars and gasoline tried to avoid leases, on the ground that the property could no longer be used to service automobiles. The courts refused to grant relief, on the ground that the property could be used for other purposes, and that the value of the lease was not totally destroyed. See **Lloyd v. Murphy,** 25 Cal.2d 48, 153 P.2d 47 (1944).

Assumption of the Risk. Before a court will apply the doctrine of frustration of purpose, it must determine that the risk of the supervening event had not been allocated by the parties, or, in other words, that the promisor had not assumed the risk of the supervening event.

> For example, investor A purchases stock in Company X, hoping that its value will go up. Instead, Company X goes bankrupt and the stock becomes worthless. A will still be liable for the purchase price of the stock; it was implicit in the transaction that A assumed the risk that the value of the stock would decrease, even to the extent of becoming worthless.

X. DISCHARGE OF CONTRACTUAL DUTIES

A contractual duty **may be discharged by full performance** or may be discharged in **a variety of ways without full performance**. Some means of discharge are discussed elsewhere, including impossibility or frustration of purpose, failure of the opposing party to perform or other nonoccurrence of a "condition precedent," occurrence of a "condition subsequent," avoidance of a voidable obligation such as by an infant, or a novation. A duty may be discharged in bankruptcy or by the running of the statute of limitations on the claim. Some of the other methods will be discussed here along with issues arising out of actual performance.

A.   OBLIGATIONS OF SELLER UNDER ARTICLE 2

The primary obligations of the seller are to **transfer ownership** and **deliver the goods.** U.C.C. §2-301. Assuming that none of the excuses for nonperformance (e.g., impracticability) has occurred, at some point in time the seller must make a proper tender of goods conforming to the warranties. The seller will usually have to act first in a contract for sale; i.e., the seller must make a tender of the goods to the buyer before the buyer's obligations arise.

The seller may also undertake other substantial obligations in the contract for sale. For example, he may promise that the goods will be packed in a particular manner, that they will be labeled in accordance with the buyer's instructions, or that he will service the goods for a specified period of time. Such undertakings are in a sense collateral to the contract for sale. They are enforceable nonetheless as promises.

Obligation to Transfer Ownership. The seller's obligation to transfer ownership raises relatively few problems. The Code expresses this obligation as a **warranty of title,** and provides for the seller's warranty of title in the following manner:

There is in a contract for sale a warranty by the seller that:

1) the title conveyed shall be good, and its transfer rightful; and
2) the goods shall be delivered free from any security interest or other lien or encumbrance of which the buyer at the time of contracting has no knowledge. §2-312(1).

Quiet Possession. Under the Code, there is no specific warranty of quiet possession, but Comment 1 to §2-312 states that "disturbance of quiet possession . . . is one way, among many, in which the breach of the warranty of title may be established." It should be noted, however, that the statute of limitations provided in §2-725 will begin to run, even as to a disturbance of quiet possession, from the time tender of delivery is made.

Knowledge by Buyer of Encumbrances. Under subsection (1)(b), *supra,* knowledge by the buyer of a security interest or encumbrance on the property will nullify any warranty that there is no lien on the goods. **Actual knowledge of encumbrances is required,** however, and constructive knowledge imposed by the recording requirements of Article 9 of the Code is not sufficient.

Disclaimer of Warranty of Title. A general disclaimer of "all warranties, express and implied," is not sufficient under the Code to negate the existence of the implied warranty of title. Subsection (2) to §2-312 provides the requirements of a disclaimer:

> A warranty [of title] will be excluded or modified only by specific language or by circumstances which give the buyer reason to know that the person selling does not claim title in himself or that he is purporting to sell only such right or title as he or a third person may have.

There is no warranty of title where the sale is by "sheriffs, executors, foreclosing lienors, and persons similarly situated." Comment 5 to §2-312.

Delivery Obligations. An agreement for sale may contain no reference to delivery, or the provisions on delivery may be highly complicated. When the agreement is silent on one or more of the delivery terms, the U.C.C. supplies these terms. The omission of a provision in the contract governing delivery of the goods does not render the agreement too indefinite to be enforceable. If no mention is made of delivery, the Code specifies the duties of the seller as follows:

Time of Delivery	Absent a contrary provision in the contract for sale, the goods must be delivered within a **reasonable time after the contract is made.** U.C.C. §2-309. Comment 3 to this section indicates that "surprise is to be avoided, good faith judgment is to be protected, and notice or negotiation to reduce the uncertainty to certainty is to be favored." The reasonableness of the time depends upon the circumstances of the individual case.
Manner of Delivery	If the contract does not provide whether the goods are to be delivered in one shipment or a number of shipments, §2-307 provides that they are to be tendered in a **single delivery** unless the circumstances give either party the right to make or demand delivery in lots. Comment 3 gives as an example of circumstances which would compel delivery in lots the case of bricks being ordered for construction of a building, where there is obviously insufficient space to store all of the bricks at the site.
Place of Delivery	Under §2-308, if no mention is made of where delivery is to be made, the place for delivery is the **seller's place of business,** or if he has none, his residence, unless the goods are identified and both parties know that they are in some other place. If the parties do know that the goods are not at the seller's place of business, the location of the goods is the place of delivery.

Importance of Place of Delivery and Tender. It is important to know whether the seller has completed his delivery obligation in order to determine whether the buyer's obligations are due, whether the seller has breached, and whether the risk of loss has passed to the buyer. Since the seller's delivery obligations vary in accordance with the place of delivery, the delivery point specified by the contract becomes important. The Code distinguishes among four situations:

1) where the seller's place of business is the delivery point;
2) where the goods are in the hands of a bailee;
3) where the seller is obligated to ship the goods to the buyer **(shipment contract)**;
4) where the seller is obligated to deliver the goods to the buyer at a particular place other than the seller's place of business **(destination contract)**.

The seller must make a valid tender at the delivery point, in accordance with the rules in the following paragraphs, in order to perform his delivery obligations.

Method of Tender. If the goods are to be delivered at the seller's place of business, the seller must place and hold conforming goods at the buyer's disposition for a sufficient time to allow the buyer to take possession of them, and the seller must give the buyer notification of this fact where notice is necessary to enable him to take delivery. The tender must be at a reasonable hour of the day. The buyer must furnish facilities reasonably suited to the receipt of the goods.

Goods in the Hands of Bailee. If the goods are in the possession of a bailee at the time the contract is made and both parties know this, §2-503 provides that the seller must negotiate a negotiable document of title covering the goods, or procure an acknowledgment by the bailee of the buyer's right to possession. However, a nonnegotiable document of title or a written direction to the bailee to deliver will suffice if the buyer does not object.

Goods to Be Transported. If the goods are to be transported, the Code differentiates between "shipment contracts" and "destination contracts." Basically, under a **shipment contract**, the **seller has the duty of arranging for transportation**, and her performance is complete as soon as this is properly done and the goods have been delivered to the carrier. In the **destination contract**, however, the seller's obligation is to **deliver the goods to the buyer at the selected point specified in the contract**. Her obligations are therefore not fulfilled until delivery has been accomplished.

Under the Code, **the shipment contract is the "normal" one**, and the destination contract is the "variant" one. There is, in effect, a presumption in favor of shipment contracts. The distinction is not as to who is to pay the transportation, but rather whether the contract requires the seller to deliver the goods at a particular destination. Thus, a shipment contract arises where the seller is required or authorized to send the goods to the buyer, and the contract does not require him to deliver them at a particular destination. A destination contract exists only where the seller is required to deliver at a particular destination.

Shipment Contracts. If the contract is a shipment contract, the seller must make tender in the following manner:

1) She must put the goods in the possession of the carrier and make such a contract for their transportation as may be reasonable, having regard for the nature of the goods and other circumstances of the case; and
2) Obtain and promptly deliver or tender in due form any document necessary to enable the buyer to obtain possession of the goods; and
3) Promptly notify the buyer of the shipment.

Destination Contracts. Under §2-503, the seller must put and hold the goods at the buyer's disposition at the destination point, and give the buyer notice that they are ready for his receipt. The tender must be at a reasonable hour, and the goods must be kept available for a period reasonably necessary to allow the buyer to take them. The buyer is obligated to furnish any facilities needed to receive the goods.

Under a destination contract, the exact point of delivery will depend on the contract. If the goods are to be delivered "in New York City," tender can be made while the goods are still in the hands of the carrier, and the buyer would be obligated to pick them up at the carrier's terminal. If, however, the goods are to be delivered "to 40 Riverdale Avenue, New York City," then tender can be made only at that point. Unloading is the obligation of the buyer, and any storage charges incurred after a tender has been made are also the buyer's responsibility.

Mercantile Symbols. The use of the mercantile symbols - F.O.B., F.A.S., C.I.F., and C. & F. - is common in signifying obligations of the parties to a contract for sale. Under the Code, the symbols are specifically defined, and the obligations imposed are carefully delineated. **Note that under the amended UCC Article 2 (2-319-2-324), the FOB and CIF shipping terms have been deleted in order to conform more to modern commercial practices.**

F.O.B.	Section 2-319(1) specifies the rights and obligations imposed under an F.O.B. **(free on board)** contract. This section makes three distinctions in regard to the term F.O.B.: (1) F.O.B. shipment point; (2) F.O.B. destination point; and (3) F.O.B. vessel, car, or other vehicle.
F.O.B. Shipment Point	If the symbol is followed by the name of the place from which the goods are to be shipped, the seller is obligated only to put them into the possession of the carrier. All expenses incurred up until that point must be borne by him, and absent a contrary provision in the contract, the seller does not bear the cost of loading them on the carrier, any cost of storage after delivery to the carrier, or the cost of transportation to the buyer. As noted previously, a contract for sale is ordinarily a shipment contract.
F.O.B. Point of Destination	When the symbol is followed by some place other than the point of shipment, the rules as to F.O.B. **place of destination** apply. Here, the parties have entered into a destination contract, and the seller must at her own expense and risk transport the goods to the specified place and tender delivery of them there. If only the name of a city follows the symbol, shipment to that city, with instructions that the buyer will pick up the goods at the carrier's terminal, is sufficient. If, however, a street address is given as the place of delivery, then delivery to that address is necessary for fulfillment of the seller's obligations. Unless otherwise provided, the seller must pay the transportation charges.
F.O.B. Vessel, Car, or Other Vehicle	When the term used is "F.O.B. cars" (or vessel or other carrier), the seller has the responsibility of loading the goods on the carrier's freight cars, ship, truck, etc. Until they are loaded, he has not completed his delivery obligations. The seller must pay whatever charges are incurred in the loading operation.
F.A.S	Under an F.A.S. (free alongside) contract, the seller must deliver the goods alongside a vessel in the named port. She must also tender to the carrier a receipt, which will obligate the carrier to issue a bill of lading for the goods. Under an F.A.S. contract, the seller is not obligated to load the goods onto the vessel.
C.I.F.	C.I.F. (Cost, Insurance, Freight) means that the quoted price includes the cost of the goods, the cost of their transportation to the named destination, and the cost of insuring the goods during transit. Thus, if a contract provides that the goods are sold for "$10,000, C.I.F. New York," this means that the seller is obligated to ship the goods to New York at his own expense and to insure them during transit. The buyer's total obligation will be to accept the goods and pay $10,000.

C. & F.	C. & F. has a similar meaning, except that no insurance is contemplated or provided for in the contract. C.I.F. and C. & F. contracts are "shipment contracts," because they only require the seller to ship the goods to a particular place, and not to deliver them there. Under C.I.F. and C. & F. contracts, tender occurs when the bill of lading is presented to the buyer.

B.   INSTALLMENT CONTRACTS UNDER ARTICLE 2

If the contract for sale does not contain an express provision specifying whether the goods are to be delivered in one lot or in multiple lots, the seller is obligated to deliver in one lot unless circumstances show that the intent of the parties was to provide for multiple deliveries. When the parties do intend that the goods be delivered in separate installments, an "installment contract" results. Section 2-612 defines an installment contract as follows:

An "installment contract" is one which requires or authorizes the delivery of goods in separate lots to be separately accepted, even though the contract contains a clause, "each delivery is a separate contract," or its equivalent.

Payment. Section 2-307 provides that payment is due upon each tender of a part of the goods if the price can be apportioned.

Breach Of One Installment: Effect On That Installment. Under §2-612(2), the buyer may reject any installment which is nonconforming only if it substantially impairs the value of that installment and cannot be cured. But if the nonconformity can be cured and the seller gives adequate assurances of its cure, the shipment must be accepted by the buyer. In effect, this means that when the nonconformity is not substantial and can be cured, the buyer must accept the goods and his only right is to sue for damages.

Breach Of One Installment As A Total Breach. Under §2-612(3), there is a breach of the whole contract - a total breach - only when the nonconformity or default with respect to a particular delivery **"substantially impairs the value of the whole contract."** Comment 6 to the section provides, in part, that:

Whether the nonconformity in any given installment justifies cancellation as to the future depends, not on whether such nonconformity indicates an intent or likelihood that the future deliveries will also be defective, but whether the nonconformity substantially impairs the value of the whole contract. If only the seller's security in regard to future installments is impaired, he has the right to demand adequate assurances of proper future performance but has not an immediate right to cancel the entire contract. It is clear under this Article, however, that defects in prior installments are cumulative in effect, so that acceptance does not wash out the defect "waived."

Thus, only when the breach or cumulative breaches substantially impair the value of the whole contract can the nonbreaching party cancel as to subsequent installments.

C.   RISK OF LOSS AND INSURABLE INTEREST UNDER ARTICLE 2

The Code rules on risk of loss place the risk on the party most likely to have insured against or taken steps to prevent loss, generally the party in actual or constructive possession of the goods.

Risk of Loss. Before a contract for the sale of goods is made, a person must bear any loss of goods or damage to goods that she owns. The owner may have a cause of action against another if the loss or damage was occasioned by the other's fault, or the owner may have a right to recover insurance, but initially the loss is hers. At some point after a contract of sale is signed (or conceivably at the time of its signing), the risk of loss will shift from the seller to the buyer. This time may be determined by agreement of the parties, but if it is not, the Code provides rules establishing when the shift occurs.

Basic Rules.

1) When the seller's place of business is the delivery point, the risk of loss passes a reasonable time after the seller has offered the goods to the buyer if the seller is not a merchant, or at the time the buyer receives the goods if the seller is a merchant.
2) In a shipment contract, it passes when the seller gives possession to the carrier and makes a proper contract for their shipment; in a destination contract, it passes when the seller makes a tender at the destination point. U.C.C. §2-509.
3) If risk of loss is on the seller when the goods are destroyed, the seller must tender a replacement or be liable to the buyer for nondelivery.
4) If that risk of loss has passed to the buyer before destruction of the goods, the buyer will be liable for the price.

Exceptions. When there has been a breach of the contract, the Code provides different and additional rules. A party who is in breach of contract may have to bear the risk of loss in circumstances when he would not otherwise bear that risk. Three distinct situations are covered:

1) **Tender of Nonconforming Goods.** Section 2-510(1) prevents the seller from shifting to the buyer the risk of loss of goods which do not conform to the contract for sale unless the buyer accepts. Therefore, if the seller ships nonconforming goods which would give the buyer a right of rejection and the goods are destroyed in transit, the risk of loss does not pass to the buyer, even though a "shipment" contract was involved.
2) **Revocation of Acceptance.** When the buyer rightfully revokes his acceptance, he may treat the risk of loss as being on the seller to the extent that the buyer's effective insurance does not cover the goods. Thus, if the buyer revokes his acceptance, and the goods are not covered by his insurance when destroyed, the seller must bear the loss. U.C.C. §2-510(2). This provision and the following one are anti-subrogation clauses intended to place the loss on the insurance company of the aggrieved party who is in control of the goods; any deficiency in coverage falls on the contract breaker, but the insurance company is not subrogated to its insured's rights against the contract breaker. Comment 3.

3) **Repudiation or Breach by Buyer.** If the goods have been identified to the contract, and the buyer repudiates or breaches the contract for sale before the risk of loss has passed to him, the seller may treat the risk of loss as being on the buyer for a commercially reasonable time, to the extent that the seller's effective insurance does not cover the goods. U.C.C. §2-510(3).

Sale on Approval or Sale or Return. If delivered goods may be returned by the buyer even though they conform to the contract, the transaction is a "sale on approval" if the goods are delivered primarily for use, and a "sale or return" if the goods are delivered primarily for resale. U.C.C. §2-326. Unless otherwise agreed, under a sale on approval the risk of loss does not pass to the buyer until acceptance. After due notification of election to return, the return is at the seller's risk and expense but a merchant buyer must follow any reasonable instructions. Under a sale or return, the return is at the buyer's risk and expense, unless otherwise agreed. U.C.C. §2-327.

Insurable Interest. In order to insure goods, a person must have an insurable interest in them. In a contract for the sale of goods, the question can arise (if there is a suit against an insurance company based upon a policy covering the goods that are the subject matter of the sale) whether the seller or the buyer, or both, have an insurable interest in the goods that are covered by the policy.

Seller's Insurable Interest. The seller has an insurable interest in the goods so long as she has either title to them or a security interest in them. U.C.C. §2-501(2). The security interest can be one that arises automatically under Article 2, or one that is given to the seller under Article 9.

Buyer's Insurable Interest. The buyer has an insurable interest as soon as the goods are identified to the contract. If the goods are in existence at the time the contract is made, the identification occurs at that time if the specific items which are the subject matter of the sale are designated by the parties. Otherwise, it occurs as soon as the seller decides which goods will be allocated to the buyer under the contract. U.C.C. §2-501(1). The buyer's insurable interest will at times overlap with the seller's, and in such cases, both will have an insurable interest.

D.   TITLE AND GOOD FAITH PURCHASERS UNDER ARTICLE 2

Title. The parties to a contract for the sale of goods may determine by agreement when title to the goods will pass from the seller to the buyer. **Absent a specific agreement, the Code provides that title passes at the time the seller completes her delivery obligations.** U.C.C. §2-401. The passage of title is important because it determines whether the seller still has an insurable interest. It is also important because it will determine, at least initially, whether creditors of the seller or creditors of the buyer can reach the goods to satisfy a judgment.

Entrustment. If the owner of goods gives possession of them to a person in the business of selling goods of the same kind, the person receiving possession has the power to transfer good title to a **buyer in the ordinary course of business**. U.C.C. §2-403. A buyer in ordinary course is defined in §1-201(9) as:

a person who in good faith and without knowledge that the sale to him is in violation of the ownership rights or security interest of a third party in the goods buys in ordinary course from a person in the business of selling goods of that kind, but does not include a pawnbroker. . . . "Buying" may be for cash or by exchange of other property or on secured or unsecured credit and includes receiving goods or documents of title under a pre-existing contract for sale but does not include a transfer in bulk or as security for or in total or partial satisfaction of a money debt.

A typical example of the application of the entrusting provision is where the owner of a watch takes it to a jewelry store to have it repaired and the jewelry store sells it to a third person. Assuming the jewelry store ordinarily sells used watches, the third person will get good title even against the true owner if the third person meets the definition of a buyer in ordinary course.

Voidable Title. A general rule of property law provides that when title to property passes, the transferee has the power to transfer good title to a subpurchaser even if the original transaction is voidable by the original transferor. A person with voidable title has power to transfer a good title to a good faith purchaser for value. When goods have been delivered under a transaction of purchase, the purchaser has such power even though:

1) the transferor was deceived as to the identity of the purchaser; or
2) the delivery was in exchange for a check which is later dishonored; or
3) it was agreed that the transaction was to be a "cash sale;" or
4) the delivery was procured through fraud punishable as larcenous under the criminal law.

TORTS

This outline follows the outline provided by the National Conference of Bar Examiners (NCBE) which spells out the testable areas of the law. The Torts questions should be answered according to principles of general applicability. You are to assume that there is no applicable statute unless otherwise specified; however, survival actions and claims for wrongful death should be assumed to be available where applicable. You should assume that joint and several liability, with comparative negligence, is the relevant rule unless otherwise indicated.

Approximately half of the Torts questions will be drawn from topics under Roman Numeral II (Negligence), and approximately half from topics included under the remainder of the subject matter outline. All of the major topics will be represented in each examination, but not necessarily all of the subtopics.

I.   INTENTIONAL TORTS

A.   HARMS TO THE PERSON: ASSAULT, BATTERY, FALSE IMPRISONMENT, INFLICTION OF MENTAL DISTRESS

1.   Assault

The action for assault lies to redress the intentional invasion of a person's interest in freedom from **apprehension of imminent harmful or offensive contact**. Restatement (Second) of Torts §21.

Intent to Commit Harmful or Offensive Touching or to Create Apprehension of Same. To render the defendant liable in an assault action, the plaintiff must prove that the defendant intended at the time of the act either to commit the harmful or offensive contact, or to instill apprehension of such contact. ·Substantial certainty that such consequences will result satisfies the requirement of intent. There is no liability on an assault theory for **negligently causing apprehension of contact**.

However, there would be liability if the defendant inadvertently put a bystander in fear of harm while intending to threaten another specific victim.

> For example, A threatens B while in a crowded theater by brandishing a bottle of nitroglycerin. C, seated in the theater, is put in apprehension of imminent bodily harm. Both B and C have a cause of action for assault against A. C's recovery in assault is based upon the doctrine of transferred intent.

Apprehension of Imminent Harmful or Offensive Touching. Subjective Mental State. To recover against the defendant for assault, the plaintiff must prove that he was placed in apprehension of imminent harmful or offensive contact. Restatement (Second) of Torts §24. There is a **subjective standard** here. If an act is intended to put another in apprehension of an immediate bodily contact and succeeds in so doing, the actor is subject to liability for an assault, **although his act would not have put a person of ordinary courage in such apprehension.** Restatement (Second) of Torts §27.

On the other hand, even though the defendant intends to cause apprehension, **no assault results if the plaintiff is unaware of the threat**. For example, if the defendant points a pistol at the plaintiff, but because the plaintiff is blind or believes the pistol is a toy he is not placed in apprehension, the defendant has not committed civil assault. Because apprehension is a mental state requiring awareness of imminent contact, a person may not be assaulted while unconscious or asleep. Restatement (Second) of Torts §22.

There is a distinction between apprehension and fright. One may, for example, be apprehensive of an insulting contact (e.g., being spat upon), without being frightened. Or, in the case of an impending blow, the fact that the plaintiff believes that he is easily capable of self-defensive measures (and is therefore not frightened) does not prevent an assault. See Restatement (Second) of Torts §24, comment b.

Imminent Harm. The apprehension required for an assault is of imminent or immediate bodily harm. Thus, threats of future bodily harm, not of an immediate nature, do not constitute an assault, Cucinotti v. Ortmann, 399 Pa. 26, 159 A.2d 216 (1960); (Such threats, if of a serious nature, may suffice, however, for an action for intentional infliction of mental distress. See State Rubbish Collectors Association v. Siliznoff, 38 Cal.2d 330, 240 P.2d 282 (1952)).

Apparent Present Ability. The requirement of apprehension of immediate bodily contact is usually satisfied by the showing of a threatening gesture by the defendant indicating an **apparent present ability** to bring about such a contact. Thus, an assault results when a rifle is aimed at the plaintiff which the plaintiff believes to be loaded, despite the fact that the rifle is in fact unloaded.

Words. Words alone do not make the actor liable for assault unless, together with other acts or circumstances, they put the plaintiff in apprehension of imminent harmful or offensive contact. Restatement (Second) of Torts §31. Sometimes words may negate what might otherwise be an assault by showing that the defendant does not intend imminent offensive or harmful contact.

> Thus, if during a quarrel, A half draws his sword and says: "If we weren't standing right in front of the police station, I would draw and quarter you," such actions do not constitute the tort of assault because A's words indicate that he does not intend to commit any imminent contact. See Tuberville v. Savage, 86 Eng. Rep. 684 (1669).

Conditional Threats. The fact that the defendant makes his threat a conditional one (i.e., the defendant gives the plaintiff the option of avoiding contact by obeying defendant's command) will not prevent an assault if the plaintiff believed, notwithstanding the condition, that he was in danger of immediate bodily harm. Ross v. Michael, 246 Mass. 126, 140 N.E. 292 (1923). Furthermore, the plaintiff is not required to buy his safety by complying with a condition. If, of course, the condition was one which the defendant had a right to impose, and the threatened force was such as was reasonable under the circumstances, the defendant's conduct would be privileged

2.   Battery

The interest redressed in a battery action is the right of a person to be free from **intentional and unpermitted offensive or harmful bodily contact**. Restatement (Second) of Torts §18. In order to establish a prima facie case in battery, the plaintiff must prove the following elements:

1) Intent;
2) A Harmful or Offensive Touching; and
3) Without the Plaintiff's Consent.

Intent to Commit Harmful or Offensive Touching or to Create Apprehension of Same. The intent on the part of the defendant necessary to establish a battery is the same as that for assault; namely, to bring about a touching which is harmful or offensive, or apprehension of such touching. Restatement (Second) of Torts §18(1)(a). Thus, liability in battery **will not exist for a touching which is brought about by negligence or even willful and wanton conduct**. If, however, the defendant knows with substantial certainty that the contact will result from his conduct, the requisite intent for a battery has been satisfied. Garratt v. Dailey, 46 Wash.2d 197, 279 P.2d 1091 (1955).

It is not necessary to show that the defendant entertained a hostile intent toward the plaintiff, or an intent to cause him injury or embarrassment. Vosburg v. Putney, 80 Wis. 523, 50 N.W. 403 (1891). Intent to bring about the unpermitted contact is sufficient. Therefore, a child (Ellis v. D'Angelo, 116 Cal. App.2d 310, 253 P.2d 675 (1953), or an insane person (McGuire v. Almy, 297 Mass. 323, 8 N.E.2d 760 (1937)), may be liable in battery **if he has the mental capacity to entertain, and does in fact entertain, an intent to strike the plaintiff**, despite the absence of knowledge in the defendant of the wrongfulness of the act or his lack of capacity to foresee the consequences of his acts. (Compare a negligence action brought against a child, where the capacity of the child to foresee the reasonable consequences of his acts is critical.)

Motive Distinguished. Furthermore, intent should not be confused with motive; the defendant may be liable in battery for the intentional unpermitted touching **even though his action emanated from a benevolent motive**. Clayton v. New Dreamland Roller Skating Rink, Inc., 14 N.J. Super. 390, 82 A.2d 458 (1951). Thus, a doctor may be held liable under certain circumstances for the unpermitted extension of an operation, even though the doctor's motive in extending the operation may have been benevolent.

Transferred Intent. Although battery will not lie for a negligent touching, where the defendant has the requisite **intent** for the commission of a battery, his **inadvertent touching of a third person in carrying out that intent will nevertheless result in a battery.**

> Thus, for example, if D, intending to strike X, inadvertently strikes P, D is liable to P in battery, although D had no intent to strike P. Restatement (Second) of Torts §20. This is the doctrine of transferred intent. Also, it is not required that the precise injury which was done be the one that was intended. So, if D intends to scare X by throwing something at him, but injures P's, D is liable for injury to P. Alteiri v. Colasso, 362 A.2d 798 (Conn. 1975).

The Touching. In order to establish a battery, the plaintiff must show that there has been a **harmful or offensive touching**. Thus, any touching which is unpermitted by the norms of social custom, even though not harmful in nature, will suffice. Jones v. Fisher, 42 Wis.2d 209, 166 N.W.2d 175 (1969) (removal by the defendant of the plaintiff's false teeth, by force). A bodily contact is offensive if it offends a reasonable sense of personal dignity, Restatement (Second) of Torts §19, as for example, spitting upon or slapping a person.

Of the Person. While the touching in a battery is usually a direct touching of the plaintiff's person, the unpermitted touching of something close to his person (e.g., a hat being worn by the plaintiff) will suffice. Thus, in Fisher v. Carrousel Motor Hotel, Inc., 424 S.W.2d 627 (Tex. 1967), the defendant-restaurant was held liable for the battery committed by its manager in snatching a plate from the hands of a patron. In Crossman v. Thurlow, 336 Mass. 252, 143 N.E.2d 814 (1957), the court upheld a recovery in battery when the defendant intentionally struck the plaintiff's automobile knowing that the plaintiff was inside it.

The touching in a battery need not be brought about by a direct application of force. It is sufficient if the defendant sets something in motion which ultimately produces an unpermitted touching, such as putting a poison or other deleterious ingredient in the plaintiff's food. Commonwealth v. Stratton, 114 Mass. 303 (1873). Finally, a person who orders another (e.g., an employee) to commit an unpermitted touching is likewise liable in battery.

Awareness of Touching Not Required. Since the interest protected in a battery action is bodily integrity rather than mental tranquillity, a person may recover for a battery even though at the time of the unpermitted touching he was asleep or unconscious or otherwise unaware of the touching.

Absence of Consent. For a touching to be actionable as a battery, the plaintiff must establish that he **did not consent** to the touching. This is a part of the plaintiff's prima facie case. Consent may be expressed or implied from conduct. O'Brien v. Cunard S.S. Co., 154 Mass. 272, 28 N.E. 266 (1891) (holding up an arm to a doctor who is vaccinating people in a line). The defendant is entitled to act upon reasonable appearances in inferring consent.

It is not the plaintiff's secret state of mind that controls, but rather **what the defendant may reasonably construe the plaintiff's state of mind to be from his actions**. Kirschbaum v. Lowrey, 174 Minn. 107, 218 N.W. 461 (1928). Consent may also be implied from social custom (e.g., touching someone on the shoulder to get his attention), unless the plaintiff has previously negated consent to such ordinary contact expressly to the defendant. Participation in activities known to include certain types of physical contact implies consent to such contacts.

Effect of Incapacity on Consent. Consent must be given by one who has the capacity to consent. Consent of a minor or mentally deficient person can still be effective if he is capable of appreciating the nature and consequences of the conduct consented to. Restatement (Second) of Torts §892A, comment b. However, it is generally held, in the absence of an emergency, that the consent of a parent is necessary for a doctor to perform surgery or other serious medical treatment upon a minor. Zoski v. Gaines, 271 Mich. 1, 260 N.W. 99 (1935). Statutory exceptions have appeared in recent years, particularly with respect to the treatment of drug dependency and venereal disease. Furthermore, at least with respect to minor operations, some cases have held valid the consent of minors who are close to maturity. Lacey v. Laird, 166 Ohio St. 40, 139 N.E.2d 25 (1956).

Consent obtained by duress or the defendant's fraud or misrepresentation by is ineffective, Restatement (Second) of Torts §892B (2), (3). Furthermore, if a plaintiff's consent is induced by a substantial mistake as to the nature of the invasion of his interests, or the extent of the harm to be expected, and this is known by the defendant, then the consent will not bar a battery action as to the unexpected invasion or harm. Restatement (Second) of Torts §892B(2).

To render the consent ineffective, the fraud, misrepresentation or mistake must relate to the nature or essence of the invasion, or to the extent of the harm to be expected from it (the essence of the touching), and not merely to a collateral matter. Thus, where the defendant, "a magnetic healer," took liberties with a patient's person on the pretense that it was necessary for her cure, a battery was committed. **Bartell v. State**, 106 Wis. 342, 82 N.W. 142 (1900). Such fraud went to the essence of the touching.

Where, on the other hand, the plaintiff consented to have intercourse with the defendant upon his promise to marry the plaintiff, no action for battery was found, even though the plaintiff's consent to the touching was obtained by the defendant's fraud. **Oberlin v. Upson**, 84 Ohio St. 111, 95 N.E. 511 (1911). Such fraud goes to a collateral matter.

With regard to **mistake**, the Restatement (comment e) gives the example of a plaintiff consenting to have sexual intercourse with the defendant, who knows that he has a venereal disease. Defendant is liable to the plaintiff for a battery. If the mistake goes to a matter not affecting the nature of the invasion or the extent of the harm, then no battery results. The Restatement gives the example of a defendant giving the plaintiff counterfeit money to have sexual intercourse with him. Defendant is not liable for battery, even though the plaintiff would not have consented had she known the money was counterfeit.

Consent to Illegal Acts Generally Valid. Generally, the plaintiff in an action for battery cannot disclaim his consent on the ground that the act was illegal and that therefore the consent should be void. There are, however, two possible exceptions to this rule. One exception accepted by some jurisdictions (e.g., **McNeil v. Mullin**, 70 Kan. 634, 79 P. 168 (1905)), is that consent to a breach of the peace, such as fist fighting, is void and thus the combatants may recover from one another in battery. Presumably such an approach is supposed to operate as a deterrent to breaches of the peace.

This view is rejected by the Restatement, which holds that **the mutual consent to engage in fist fighting bars both of the participants**. Restatement (Second) of Torts §892C. However, consent to engage in a fist fight may not operate as consent to a more serious touching, such as being stabbed with a knife. **Teolis v. Moscatelli**, 44 R.I. 494, 119 A. 161 (1923).

Another exception is where the criminal law of the jurisdiction voids the victim's consent for the protection of the victim. Thus, in **Bishop v. Liston**, 112 Neb. 559, 199 N.W. 825 (1924), the Court held that the plaintiff, who because of her age was the victim of a statutory rape, could recover civilly against the defendant for battery. The court held that the legal invalidity of the consent of the minor-female to sexual intercourse under the criminal statute applied also in a civil action for battery.

Exceeding Consent. The actor may be sued in tort for going beyond the act or conduct for which consent was given. Consent, whether express or implied, is generally given to a specific type of conduct or touching or, at most, to conduct and acts of a substantially similar nature. Such cases most commonly arise in medical practice, where a doctor, having obtained the consent of his patient to a particular type of surgery, expands the scope of the surgery upon discovering further internal disorders or upon discovering that his original diagnosis was incorrect.

Emergency Situations. The traditional rule is that a doctor may extend an operation only when an emergency exists in the sense that a failure to extend the operation would endanger the patient's life or health, or where a later operation might unduly endanger the life or health of the patient and it is impracticable to obtain the consent of the patient's family. **Tabor v. Scobee**, 254 S.W.2d 474 (Ky. 1953). This is the Restatement view. Restatement (Second) of Torts §892D. Some jurisdictions have adopted a more liberal view in light of the conditions under which operations are now performed.

The test applied by most courts is whether a reasonable person in the position of the patient would grant consent to the extension if he were able to choose. Thus, in **Kennedy v. Parrott**,

243 N.C. 355, 90 S.E.2d 754 (1956), the Court held that in the absence of proof to the contrary, consent to an operation will be construed as general in nature, and the surgeon may extend the operation to remedy any abnormal or diseased condition in the area of the original incision whenever she, in the exercise of her sound professional judgment, determines that correct surgical procedure dictates and requires such an extension of the operation beyond that originally contemplated.

Lack of Informed Consent - Failure to Disclose the Relevant Risks in Full. The area of medical malpractice involving the extension of an operation without the patient's consent (where the action sounds in battery because absence of consent makes the touching unpermitted), should be compared with the type of medical malpractice wherein plaintiff claims that his or her consent to the medical treatment was obtained by the doctor's withholding of material information concerning the risks of such treatment (i.e., the doctor failed to obtain the patient's informed consent).

These latter cases originally were treated as battery actions, on the theory that if the plaintiff's consent was so obtained, it was not a valid consent, and the touching was therefore unpermitted. However, most jurisdictions today treat the "informed consent" cases as negligence actions, the critical issue being whether the doctor unreasonably failed to disclose material information to the patient concerning the risks of the medical treatment, and the availability of other types of treatment. See Miller v. Kennedy, 11 Wash. App. 272, 522 P.2d 852 (1974), aff'd, 85 Wash.2d 151, 530 P.2d 334 (1975).

3.　　False Imprisonment

The interest protected by an action for false imprisonment is an individual's right to **freedom from confinement** (Restatement (Second) of Torts §35), or **freedom from restraint of movement**. (Prosser, §11). In order to recover for false imprisonment, the plaintiff must establish:

1) Intent;
2) Confinement;
3) Consciousness of Confinement; and
4) Absence of Consent

Intent. As with other actions of trespass to person, **false imprisonment is an intentional tort**. There is no such tort as negligent false imprisonment. As with the action for battery, a distinction must be made between intent and motive. Absent a privilege, if the defendant intentionally confined the plaintiff without his consent, the plaintiff may recover even though the defendant may have acted with the best of motives.

Confinement. The plaintiff must establish that the defendant imposed **a restraint upon his freedom of movement**. An action will not lie for false imprisonment where the defendant merely impedes the plaintiff's progress in one particular direction, or confines him within an area from which there is a reasonable exit which is apparent. Bird v. Jones, 7 Q.B. 742, 115 Eng. Rep. 668 (1845). The restraint sufficient for false imprisonment may be imposed by force, threats of force, or threats of personal difficulty.

> Examples: If at closing time a store owner locks all but one door, there is no confinement even though plaintiff preferred to exit through another door. Restatement (Second) of Torts §36, comment a. A

> person may be unlawfully imprisoned upon a yacht, Whittaker v. Sanford, 110 Me. 77, 85 A. 399 (1912), or a moving automobile.

Confinement sufficient for false imprisonment may result by taking a person into custody under an asserted **lawful authority which is in fact unlawful**, Restatement (Second) of Torts §41; and no force or threat of force is necessary. Suppose a police officer standing on the sidewalk calls to the operator of a moving automobile: "Stop - You're under arrest." If the operator stops the automobile and submits to the arrest, a confinement results, even though the operator could have escaped by driving on. See Restatement (Second) of Torts §41, comment b.

In Martin v. Houck, 141 N.C. 317, 54 S.E. 291 (1906), defendant, a policeman, went to plaintiff's house at night and, although having no warrant, told plaintiff he was under arrest and to come to the police station the next morning. Plaintiff did so. The court held defendant liable for false imprisonment. However, false imprisonment from the assertion of lawful authority can result only if the authority was unlawfully exercised.

Consciousness of Confinement. The Restatement (Second) of Torts, §42, takes the position that there can be no liability for false imprisonment **unless the person confined is aware of his confinement**. One exception to this approach adopted by the Restatement is where harm results from the confinement, as for example where the plaintiff, although unconscious during the confinement, incurs illness as a result of it.

Absence of Consent. Many false imprisonment actions today involve shopkeepers who have restrained persons upon suspicion of theft. The cases recognize a privilege to protect one's property. (See infra.) However, before the issue of privilege is reached, the factual question arises whether the plaintiff consented to the confinement voluntarily to establish his innocence, or whether the plaintiff was coerced by force, threats of force, or threats of inconvenience. Where the plaintiff, having been informed that she is suspected of theft, allows herself to be detained and searched, without, however, any force or threats of force by the defendant, it is generally held that the plaintiff has consented to the restraint of her liberty, and no action for false imprisonment will lie. Lester v. Albers Super Markets, Inc., 94 Ohio App. 313, 114 N.E.2d 529 (1952). However, some courts have found a moral coercion sufficient to vitiate consent. Jacques v. Childs Dining Hall, Inc., 244 Mass. 438, 138 N.E. 843 (1923).

4. Infliction Of Mental Distress

"One who, by extreme and outrageous conduct, intentionally or recklessly causes severe emotional distress to another, is subject to liability for such emotional distress, and if bodily harm results from it, for such bodily harm." Restatement (Second) of Torts §46.

Intent. Liability for the tort of intentional infliction of mental or emotional distress may be founded not only on subjective intent or substantial certainty of the result, but also on reckless disregard of the probable consequences of the defendant's behavior.

Severity of Emotional Distress. It is insufficient to show conduct which, although calculated to cause embarrassment or humiliation, is inadequate to cause severe emotional distress. Wallace v. Shoreham Hotel Corp., 49 A.2d 81 (D.C. 1946). A mere showing of bad manners is insufficient. Gelhaus v. Eastern Air Lines, 194 F.2d 774 (5th Cir. 1952). Thus, while a plaintiff in an assault action may recover for the mental distress involved in being placed in apprehension of immediate harmful or offensive contact, without reference to the degree of mental distress, the hallmark of the tort of intentional infliction of mental distress is severity.

Conduct which would not be deemed outrageous by average standards may be actionable under the tort of intentional infliction of mental distress if performed with knowledge by the defendant of a peculiar weakness or sensitivity of the plaintiff to such conduct, and is thus calculated to feed upon such sensitivity. **Nickerson v. Hodges**, 146 La. 735, 84 So. 37 (1920). Recovery for intentional infliction of mental distress includes damages for such emotional distress and for bodily harm resulting from it. **State Rubbish Collectors Association v. Siliznoff**, 38 Cal.2d 330, 240 P.2d 282 (1952).

Special Relationships. Because of the special relationships involved, most courts allow recovery against common carriers, innkeepers, and public utilities for mental distress to patrons resulting from gross insults of a highly offensive nature. **Lipman v. Atlantic Coast Line R.R. Co.**, 108 S.C. 151, 93 S.E. 714 (1917); **Restatement (Second) of Torts** §48. Liability for such insulting language has not, however, been extended to owners of all places of business open to the public. **Slocum v. Food Fair Stores of Florida**, 100 So.2d 396 (Fla. 1958).

Liability for Emotional Distress Inflicted on Bystanders. When the defendant directs extreme or outrageous conduct at a third person, he is subject to liability if he intentionally or recklessly causes severe emotional distress:

1) to a member of such person's immediate family who is present at the time, whether or not such distress results in bodily harm; or
2) to any other person who is present at the time, if such distress results in bodily harm.

Restatement (Second) of Torts §46. However, there is no transferred intent; the defendant must intend the emotional harm to the third party, or at least know the third party is present, to be liable to the third party.

B. HARMS TO PROPERTY INTERESTS; TRESPASS TO LAND AND CHATTELS, CONVERSION

1. Trespass to Land

In order for the plaintiff to establish a prima facie case in an action of trespass to land, he must establish that:

1) **he had possession** or the right to possession of the land in question; and
2) that the **defendant interfered with that possessory interest** either intentionally or by some abnormally dangerous activity.

Unlike the action of trespass to person, in trespass to land cases, the matter of consent is a defense rather than part of the plaintiff's case, and hence the burden of proof on the issue of consent is on the defendant.

Possessory Interest. The interest which the plaintiff is protecting in an action of trespass to land is the right to exclusive possession. Hence, he must show that he had possession of the land or the right to possession. Except where the defendant is the real owner of the property or is a person having the right to possession of the property (a lessee, for example), the plaintiff who is in actual possession of the property may prevail in the trespass action, despite the fact that his possession is wrongful. **The New England Box Co. v. C. & R. Construction Company**, 313 Mass. 696, 49 N.E.2d 121 (1943).

Thus, **a person having mere adverse possession of the property may recover in trespass against one not having the right to possession.** **Langdon v. Templeton**, 66 Vt. 173, 28 A. 866 (1893). "Any possession is legal possession against a wrongdoer." **Graham v. Peat**, 1 East 244, 102 Eng. Rep. 95, 96 (1801). It is obvious, therefore, that no claim of title is necessary to recover in a trespass action.

Therefore, with respect to leased property, it is the **lessee** (who has the right to possession), **rather than the lessor** (who has title to the property), who may maintain the trespass action. The lessor, of course, may maintain an action for any permanent harm to the property.

Entry. A trespass may be committed not only by the defendant's entry upon the plaintiff's land, but also by his casting objects upon the plaintiff's land. **Herrin v. Sutherland**, 74 Mont. 587, 241 P. 328 (1925).

Intent. Except where the defendant is engaged in an ultrahazardous activity, **an unintended intrusion upon the plaintiff's land will not constitute a trespass.** Thus, in **Randall v. Shelton**, 293 S.W.2d 559 (Ky. 1956), the plaintiff was injured in her front yard when hit by a stone thrown from the highway by the defendant's passing truck. The Court, citing §166 of the Restatement of Torts, held the defendant not liable.

With respect to the intent necessary for an action of trespass to land, while the defendant's entry must be intentional, **the plaintiff does not have to show that the defendant knew that he was committing a trespass.** A good faith mistake will not excuse the defendant. **Restatement (Second) of Torts**, §164.

Thus, he is liable even where he honestly and reasonably believes that he is on his own property, or that he has the consent of the plaintiff to be on the plaintiff's property, or that he is privileged to be on the plaintiff's property. The intent in a trespass action refers only to the intent to enter upon the land of the plaintiff, and **not to the knowledge** that it is the plaintiff's land. The defendant is liable for the harm caused by his trespass, even though he could not reasonably have foreseen such consequences.

> Example: In Cleveland Park Club v. Perry, 265 A.2d 485 (D.C. 1960), the Court held that a child could be held liable on a trespass theory for damages resulting from placing a tennis ball in a pool drain pipe, so long as he was capable of forming the necessary intent to perform the physical act that released the harmful force; it was not necessary to prove that the child knew or was capable of knowing the possible injurious consequences of such act.

Ultrahazardous Activities. In some jurisdictions, a trespass may result where the defendant, by engaging in some ultrahazardous or abnormally dangerous activity, intrudes upon the plaintiff's property, even where such intrusion is unintentional. **Young v. Darter**, 363 P.2d 829 (Okla. 1961) (crop dusting); **Rochester Gas and Electric Corp. v. Dunlop**, 148 Misc. 849, 266 N.Y.S. 469 (1933) (defendant's airplane crashed into plaintiff's electric transmission line tower). The Restatement would permit recovery in such cases only if actual harm results from the unintentional trespass. Restatement (Second) of Torts, §165.

Nuisance Distinguished. The line separating the action of trespass from the action of nuisance has in recent years become blurred. See Nuisance, *infra*. The distinction between the two actions has traditionally been important because, unlike nuisance, the action of trespass did not involve a balancing of the harm to the plaintiff against the social desirability or necessity of the defendant's conduct.

In **Martin v. Reynolds Metals Co.**, 221 Or. 86, 342 P.2d 790 (1959), the court rejected any distinction between trespass and nuisance based upon the size of the object intruding upon the plaintiff's property, and held that chemical particles, invisible to the naked eye, intruding upon the plaintiff's property were sufficient to constitute a trespass. The Court stated that if the character of the instrumentality which makes the intrusion must be considered, the emphasis should be placed upon the object's energy or force rather than its size.

In another case, **Railroad Commission of Texas v. Manziel**, 361 S.W.2d 560 (Tex. 1962), the Court refused to find a trespass where the defendant pumped salt water into its oil wells, which water crossed under the surface into the plaintiff's wells. The Court emphasized the importance of such secondary recovery operations to avoid the waste of valuable oil.

Low-Flying Aircraft. There is a difference of opinion as to whether low-flying aircraft should be viewed as a trespass or a nuisance. **Smith v. New England Aircraft Company**, 270 Mass. 511, 170 N.E. 385 (1930) (trespass); **Atkinson v. Bernard**, Inc., 223 Or. 624, 355 P.2d 229 (1960) (nuisance). The trend is to treat the situation as a nuisance action.

Damages. Damages in trespass to land may be recovered for mere interference with possession, even though no actual harm is done to the land. **Dougherty v. Stepp**, 18 N.C. 371 (1835). The reason for this rule is that the trespass action is often used either to try the issue of ownership of the land, or the right to possession of the land. Unless the plaintiff could maintain the action without proof of actual harm to the land, the defendant's wrongful conduct might ripen into a prescriptive right.

Obviously, damages may also be recovered for **any harm actually done** to the property as a result of the trespass. See **Guille v. Swan**, 19 Johns. 381, 10 Am. Dec. 234 (N.Y. 1822), where a balloonist who landed in the plaintiff's garden was held liable for the damage done by the crowd which rushed in to view the balloon's landing. A trespass to land subjects the trespasser to liability for any harm to the person or property of the possessor of the land, or the members of the possessor's family, resulting from the trespass. A showing of negligence is not required. Restatement (Second) of Torts, §162.

Privilege of Emergency. A person may be privileged under **emergency circumstances** to enter upon or use the property of another **to protect his own person or property**. Ploof v. Putnam, 81 Vt. 471, 71 A. 188 (1908) (protection of person); Vincent v. Lake Erie Transportation Co., 109 Minn. 456, 124 N.W. 221 (1910) (valuable property). An entry under such circumstances will not constitute a trespass (Ploof v. Putnam, supra), although the person using the property is required to pay the owner or possessor for any damage done to the property. Vincent v. Lake Erie Transportation Co., supra.

© 1995-2018 Celebration Bar Review, LLC   **Multistate Bar Review Book 2**

Where the person using or even destroying the owner's property is acting to protect the public generally rather than his own personal interests, the privilege is complete and he is not required to compensate the owner for any loss, provided he has acted in a reasonable manner. Surocco v. Geary, 3 Cal. 69, 58 Am. Dec. 385 (1853).

Privilege of Police Power and Eminent Domain. Closely allied to the notion of a private person's acting from public necessity is the state's exercise of its police power. This power should be distinguished from the state's power of eminent domain. A person's right to the use and enjoyment of his property is subject to the state's right of eminent domain and the lawful exercise of its police power.

Essentially, the difference between the right of eminent domain and the exercise of the police power is that eminent domain involves the taking of property for the public benefit, whereas the exercise of the police power involves the destruction or limitation on the use of property which under the circumstances represents a danger to the public safety, public health, or public welfare. Thus, the destruction of all the liquor in a town which is being advanced upon by a hostile and licentious army is an exercise of the police power, and not the exercise of eminent domain. Harrison v. Wisdom, 7 Heisk 99 (Tenn. 1872). Likewise is the destruction of petroleum in a city which is about to be captured by an enemy army. United States v. Caltex, 344 U.S. 149 (1952).

When eminent domain is exercised, the owner of the land is entitled to the reasonable value of the property taken. Where, however, the state exercises its police power, the landowner is not entitled to compensation. Harrison v. Wisdom, supra. Whether a particular situation involves eminent domain or the exercise of the police power will depend upon the facts of the particular case.

> For example, the providing of recreational areas for the community is a burden which must be borne by the community and not the individual; hence, a zoning ordinance for this purpose would not fall within the valid exercise of the police power. Aronson v. Town of Sharon, 346 Mass. 598, 195 N.E.2d 341 (1964).

2. Trespass to Chattels and Conversion

Both the actions for trespass to chattels and for conversion involve **an interference with the plaintiff's possessory interest in personal property**. Where the defendant's conduct does not amount to a substantial interference (exercise of dominion) with the plaintiff's possessory interest in the property, but rather consists of intermeddling with, or use of or damage to the personal property, the owner or possessor has an action for trespass to the chattel.

Unlike a trespass to land**, the plaintiff must show actual damage or actual interference with the plaintiff's possessory rights**. The measure of damages is the **actual amount** suffered by reason of the impairment of the property or the loss of its use. Zaslow v. Kroenert, 29 Cal.2d 541, 176 P.2d 1 (1946). Where, however, the defendant's conduct constitutes such a substantial interference with the plaintiff's possessory interest as to amount to an act of dominion over the property, the plaintiff may recover the fair market value of the property in an action for conversion. Id.

If the defendant has exercised dominion over the plaintiff's property, a conversion has been committed even though the defendant acted in good faith and under a reasonable mistake.

Galvin v. Bacon, 11 Me. 28 (1833). While normally a demand and refusal are not necessary in order to show a conversion, if the defendant originally obtained possession rightfully (e.g., a bailee), demand and refusal would be necessary in order to show an exercise of dominion over the property by the defendant. Where the plaintiff wishes to recover the property itself rather than its fair market value, he may bring an action in replevin rather than one in conversion.

Generally, any type of personal property capable of private ownership can be the subject of an action in trespass and conversion. However, most courts require that there be some tangible property involved for there to be a trespass or conversion. Thus, computer software is a proper subject, as are personal writings, books, or pictures if they are of value to their owner. Those jurisdictions that allow recovery for trespass to or conversion of the ideas or thoughts in written documents require that such nontangible property constitute literary or scientific work, or similar product of personal labor or genius.

C. DEFENSES TO CLAIMS FOR PHYSICAL HARMS

1. Consent

Consent is discussed under each of the intentional torts which are harms to the person above.

The actual consent of the plaintiff, express or implied, is a defense to an action of trespass to land. Unlike actions of trespass to person, the defendant has the burden of proof on the issue of consent. If actual consent is lacking, the plaintiff can recover unless plaintiff's conduct misled the defendant into thinking consent had been given. Restatement (Second) of Torts, §164.

A defendant will be liable in trespass even though his original entry upon the land was pursuant to the plaintiff's consent, if he remains on the land **after the consent has been revoked**.

Under the ancient doctrine of trespass ab initio, if the defendant enters upon the plaintiff's property under a license conferred by law (e.g., a public eating place), and he thereafter abuses the license by some act of misfeasance, he will be held as a **trespasser from the beginning**. The doctrine of trespass ab initio has been **rejected in most modern cases**. The Restatement (Second) of Torts, §214 has rejected it. Under the Restatement view, one who properly enters land pursuant to a privilege and thereafter commits a tortious act is subject to liability only for the tortious act, and does not become liable for his original lawful entry, nor for his lawful acts on the land prior to the tortious conduct.

2. Privileges And Immunities: Protection Of Self And Others; Protection Of Property Interests; Parental Discipline; Protection Of Public Interests; Necessity; Incomplete Privilege

Basically, the affirmative defenses available to the actions of intentional torts to the person are **privilege and immunity**.

A privilege is a justification for the defendant's conduct which actually negates its tortious quality; where a privilege existed, no tort occurred. **An immunity**, on the other hand, **goes not to the nature of the conduct, but only to whether or not the defendant may be sued for such conduct**. Thus, for example, a spouse is not ipso facto privileged to commit a battery on his or her marriage partner. Such a harmful or offensive touching is a tort. Yet, some states, for public policy reasons, provide immunity from suit between spouses for such conduct.

Privilege. The burden of proof on the issue of privilege lies upon the defendant. He must prove not only the circumstances giving rise to a privilege, but also that his exercise of the privilege was reasonable under the circumstances.

Privilege of Self Defense. A person who is threatened with bodily harm may meet his aggressor's force with **force sufficient to repel the attack**. A person's right to use force in self defense is not limited to situations where he is threatened with death or serious bodily injury. Boston v. Muncy, 204 Okla. 603, 233 P.2d 300, 25 A.L.R. 1208 (1951). However, unless the defendant was attacked with force apparently sufficient to cause death or serious bodily harm, he may not use in self defense force calculated to cause death or serious bodily harm. Restatement (Second) of Torts §65.

The force used to repel the attack must be **reasonable under the circumstances**. Reasonable force is that force which appears reasonably necessary, in view of all the circumstances of the case, to prevent the impending injury. Fraguglia v. Sala, 17 Cal. App.2d 738, 62 P.2d 783 (1936).

Where the defendant, in self defense, uses some force which is reasonable and some force which is excessive, he is liable only for the excessive force. He is not liable ab initio. Id. The reasonableness of the force used by the defendant in self defense is not determined solely by the nature of the injury which results. That the blow or blows in self defense resulted in more serious injury than might have been sufficient to forestall the attack is not the test of excessive force.

One must **know** that what he does will be excessive - an intent to inflict unnecessary injury must be established. Dupre v. Maryland Management Corp., 283 App. Div. 701, 127 N.Y.S.2d 615 (1954).

Where the defendant has a reasonable belief that self defense is necessary to repel an attack upon him, most jurisdictions hold that the **privilege of self defense exists even though the defendant was in fact mistaken** and the plaintiff was not about to attack the defendant. Restatement (Second) of Torts §63, comment h.

Use of Deadly Force - Obligation to Retreat. A person who has a reasonable belief that he is **being attacked with deadly force has a right to use deadly force in self defense**. However, where a person's means of self defense would involve the use of force likely to cause death or serious bodily harm, the law generally requires that he **first attempt to take any reasonable exit of escape**. [The privilege to use deadly force does not normally exist "if the actor correctly or reasonably believes that he can with complete safety avoid the necessity of so defending himself by ... retreating ..." Restatement (Second) of Torts §65.] "When it comes to a question whether one man shall flee or another shall live, the law decides that the former shall flee rather than that the latter shall die." Commonwealth v. Drum, 58 Pa. 9 (1868).

A generally accepted exception to this rule is that **a person is not required to flee from his own home**. State v. Preece, 116 W.Va. 176, 179 S.E. 524 (1935). This exception extends to the curtilage of the home, which ordinarily means at least the yard around the dwelling house as well as the area occupied by the outbuildings. State v. Frizzelle, 243 N.C. 49, 89 S.E.2d 725 (1955). Some courts have extended the concept of "home" to include an automobile or the defendant's place of business.

Injury to a Third Party. Suppose that, in the reasonable exercise of self defense, the defendant accidentally injures a third party. Absent negligence, the privilege of self defense protects the defendant from liability; in other words, the doctrine of **transferred privilege applies**. Morris v. Platt, 32 Conn. 75 (1864); Restatement (Second) of Torts §75. The rule is different where the defendant deliberately causes injury to the third party in order to protect himself.

Defense of a Third Person. **A person is privileged to use reasonable force in defense of a third person**. Unlike the earlier view, the law today does not generally require, as a condition of the privilege, that the person being defended be a member of the actor's household or one whom he is under a legal or social duty to protect. See Restatement (Second) of Torts §76.

Where the actor makes a mistake as to the need for defending a third person, jurisdictions are split on the issue of his liability. The majority view is that **the actor takes the risk that the person he is defending would not be privileged to defend himself in like manner**. See People v. Young, 11 N.Y.2d 274, 183 N.E.2d 319 (1962).

The minority view is that the standard of liability for an actor who mistakenly goes to the defense of a third person should be the same as when he makes a mistake in believing that self defense is necessary. Thus, a reasonable mistake would preclude liability. The Restatement adopts the minority view. Restatement (Second) of Torts §76.

Note that the rule in criminal cases is the same as this minority rule in torts -- a person who defends another is not criminally liable if the person reasonably believed that the other person had a right of self defense, even if that belief was mistaken. Thus, a person who reasonably but mistakenly defends a third person is not criminally liable in any jurisdiction, but is civilly liable in a jurisdiction that has adopted the majority rule in tort cases.

Defense of Property. It is generally recognized that **reasonable force** may, under some circumstances, be used to protect property or to recover property wrongfully taken. However, there is **no privilege to use any force calculated to cause death or serious bodily injury to repel a threat to land or chattels**, unless there is also a threat to the defendant's personal safety such as to justify the use of deadly force in self defense. Katko v. Briney, 183 N.W.2d 657 (Iowa 1971). Furthermore, since the direct application of deadly force is prohibited, so too is the indirect use of such force as, for example, in setting a spring gun. Id.; State v. Childers, 133 Ohio St. 508, 14 N.E.2d 767 (1938). Also, if the trespass was privileged, there is no right to defense of property, even if it reasonably appeared that there was.

Recapture of Chattels. **Reasonable force may be used to recapture a chattel, provided that the original taking was wrongful** (e.g., by fraud or force), and provided that there is fresh pursuit. Hodgeden v. Hubbard, 18 Vt. 504 (1846). Where, however, the original taking was rightful (e.g., a bailment or conditional sale), but the chattel is retained wrongfully, force may not be used to recapture the chattel. Lamb v. Woodry, 154 Or. 30, 58 P.2d 1257 (1936).

Demand Requirement. Even when force is permitted in the defense or recapture of property, the generally accepted view is that **a request for the return of the property must precede any resort to force**, unless such a request would be useless or dangerous, or would make action by the privileged person futile under the circumstances.

Merchant's Privilege. The most common situation involving the use of force to recapture property wrongfully taken is the detention by merchants of persons whom they suspect of shoplifting.

Multistate Bar Review Book 2

The law recognizes a privilege on the part of a merchant to detain a person when the merchant **has reasonable grounds to believe** that the person is stealing or is attempting to steal his property. The detention, however, must be:

1) for a reasonable period of time; and
2) must be conducted in a reasonable manner.

The purpose of the privilege is to recover the goods and thus if, after the goods are recovered, the defendant continues to detain the plaintiff to obtain a signed confession, an action for false imprisonment will lie. Teel v. May Department Stores Co., 348 Mo. 696, 155 S.W.2d 74 (1941). In many states today the merchant's privilege is covered statutorily.

Threat of Excessive Force. Suppose that the defendant, by some overt gesture, threatens force in defense of his property, but the threatened force would be unreasonable if carried out. Is the defendant liable for assault? There is little authority on point. The Restatement (Second) of Torts §81(2) takes the position that the **actor is privileged in defense of his land or chattels to do an act which is intended to cause apprehension of bodily harm**, even though the threatened force would be excessive if carried out, provided that the act is intended and reasonably believed by the actor to be likely to do no more than to create such apprehension.

Arrest Without a Warrant. Many state statutes provide for warrantless arrests. In the absence of a statute covering the situation, **a private person may arrest without a warrant**:

1) a person who in fact committed a felony;
2) a person attempting to commit a felony in the private person's presence;
3) if a felony has been committed in fact, the person reasonably believed to be the felon; or
4) a person committing a misdemeanor which is a breach of the peace in the presence of the arresting person.

A peace officer possesses the power to make an arrest in each of the situations where a private person is privileged to arrest. In addition, a peace officer may arrest a person he reasonably believes to have committed a felony even if no felony was committed in fact.

It is a **complete defense** to an action for false imprisonment or false arrest **that the party did indeed commit the crime for which he was arrested, regardless of the reasonableness or unreasonableness of the arrest**. Martynn v. Dancy, 333 F. Supp. 1236, 1241 (1971). A private person who is called upon by a peace officer to assist in the making of an arrest is privileged to do so, provided that the peace officer was privileged to make the arrest, or that the private person did not have reason to believe that the peace officer was not so privileged.

Miscellaneous Privileges. There are a few other situations in which a privilege may exist in defense to an action for intentional trespass to person.

While there are very few cases on this point, a privilege may exist to use force to protect the **safety of others**. In the case of Drabek v. Sabley, 31 Wis.2d 184, 142 N.W.2d 798 (1966), the Wisconsin Supreme Court recognized a privilege in the defendant to use some force to prevent boys from throwing snowballs at passing automobiles, although the Court in that case held that the privilege did not extend to placing one of the boys in the defendant's automobile and driving him to the police station.

Multistate Bar Review Book 2

A parent may use **reasonable force upon her child for its proper control, training, or education**. Restatement (Second) of Torts §147. The privilege extends also to those who have been given by law or who have voluntarily assumed the function of controlling, training, or educating the child, except insofar as the parent has restricted the privilege. Id. Thus, most jurisdictions recognize a **privilege in a schoolteacher to use reasonable force to discipline a child** for misconduct. Suits v. Glover, 260 Ala. 449, 71 So.2d 49, 43 A.L.R.2d 465 (1954).

The privilege to discipline a child in such a way, where it exists, is for the benefit of the child and for the purpose of securing his proper education and training. Thus, to sustain the privilege, the evidence must show that the punishment administered was reasonable, and such a showing requires consideration of the nature of the punishment itself, the nature of the pupil's misconduct which gave rise to the punishment, the age and physical condition of the pupil, and the teacher's motive in inflicting the punishment. Tinkham v. Kole, 252 Iowa 1303, 110 N.W.2d 258 (1961). In some jurisdictions, statutes limit or bar the use of corporal punishment by teachers.

Immunity. As mentioned previously, unlike the defense of privilege which, if successful, means that the defendant has not committed a tort, the **defense of immunity is available despite the defendant's tortious conduct**. The defense of immunity is based upon public policy considerations. However, each of the immunities discussed below is less broad today than at common law.

Interspousal Immunity. The original basis for immunity between husband and wife was the preservation of marital harmony. With the advent of the widespread use of liability insurance, the substituted basis was the avoidance of schemes between spouses to defraud insurance companies. If a husband accidentally injures his wife with his automobile, it is obvious that he would want his wife to be successful in her action against him, and thus collect from his liability insurer.

A majority of states have abolished interspousal immunity in at least some situations, on the ground that the mere fact that the husband-wife relationship may provide greater opportunity for fraud or collusion does not warrant the barring of all claims; that the courts must depend upon the judicial process to separate the meritorious claims from the fraudulent ones. See e.g., Freehe v. Freehe, 81 Wash.2d 183, 500 P.2d 771 (1972). This is the position of the Restatement, which recommends abolition of interspousal immunity generally in tort actions. See Restatement (Second) of Torts §895F.

Types of Torts in Which Immunity Abrogated. A number of courts have abolished interspousal immunity only with respect to injuries arising out of the negligent operation of a motor vehicle. See e.g., Richard v. Richard, 131 Vt. 98, 300 A.2d 637 (1973). There is general agreement that no immunity exists between spouses for torts involving property interests, and some states have abolished it with respect to intentional torts. See Aspitz v. Dames, 205 Or. 242, 287 P.2d 585 (1955).

Termination of Husband-Wife Relationship. While there is some disagreement on the matter, actions have been allowed after divorce or annulment for torts occurring prior to (Gaston v. Pittman, 224 So.2d 326 (Fla. 1969)), or during (Sanchez v. Olivarez, 94 N.J. Super. 61, 226 A.2d 752 (1967)), the marriage. Death of a spouse is usually held to eliminate the immunity defense as to prior torts. Mozier v. Carney, 376 Mich. 532, 138 N.W.2d 343 (1965).

Recovery from Spouse's Employer. Even where a spouse may be barred from recovery against the other spouse on the basis of interspousal immunity, recovery may still be had, where appropriate, against the spouse's employer under the doctrine of respondeat superior. In other words, the spouse's immunity does not protect his employer. **Pittsley v. David**, 98 Mass. 552, 11 N.E.2d 461 (1937).

Parent and Child Immunity. Like interspousal immunity, the doctrine of parent-child immunity is increasingly being repudiated. See **Goller v. White**, 20 Wis.2d 402, 122 N.W.2d 93 (1963). **More than half the jurisdictions have abolished it in some fashion**. The Restatement recommends its abolition. **Restatement (Second) of Torts** §895G(1). Some states have eliminated this immunity only with respect to injuries arising out of the negligent operation of a motor vehicle. **Sorenson v. Sorenson**, 369 Mass. 350, 339 N.E.2d 907 (1975).

It is generally held that parent-child immunity does not apply when the claim is brought after the child is legally emancipated, even though the tort occurred before emancipation. **Logan v. Reaves**, 209 Tenn. 31, 354 S.W.2d 789 (1962). Also, the death of the parent or child eliminates the defense. **Brennecke v. Kilpatrick**, 336 S.W.2d 68 (Mo. 1960). Immunity is not present if the child was injured while employed in his parent's business. **Trevarton v. Trevarton**, 151 Colo. 418, 378 P.2d 640 (1963). Further, it has no application in actions between siblings, **Merrell v. Haney**, 207 Tenn. 532, 341 S.W.2d 574 (1960); nor does it apply when the defendant is a stepparent or other person standing in loco parentis. **Xaphes v. Mossey**, 224 F. Supp. 578 (D. Vt. 1963).

In states abolishing the doctrine of parent-child immunity, the problem has arisen regarding the liability of a parent to a young child for negligent supervision. This theory has usually been raised by another defendant (e.g., the operator of a motor vehicle who negligently struck the child), in order to claim contribution from the parent who negligently supervised the child, thus allowing the child to go out into the street. Some courts have taken the position, therefore, that the abolition of immunity applies only where the parent's breach related to a duty owed apart from the family relationship (e.g., driving an automobile). It would thus not be abolished in the case of a breach of duty to supervise. See **Holodook v. Spencer**, 36 N.Y.2d 35, 324 N.E.2d 338 (1974).

Charitable Immunity. The doctrine of charitable immunity was based upon the theory that money donated for charitable purposes should not be diverted to the payment of judgments. With the widespread use of liability insurance, this reasoning is no longer valid and the doctrine has been abolished in most jurisdictions. **Pierce v. Yakima Valley Memorial Hospital Association**, 43 Wash.2d 162, 260 P.2d 765 (1953). The Restatement rejects the doctrine of charitable immunity. See **Restatement (Second) of Torts** §895E. Some states by statute simply limit the amount of damages for which a charity will be held liable.

Governmental Immunity. Varying degrees of governmental immunity exist at the federal, state, and municipal levels of government.

Federal Government. The **federal government may not be sued in tort except to the extent that it has consented to suit by the enactment of the Federal Tort Claims Act**, Title 28, U.S.C.A. Under the Act, the federal government will be liable where "the United States, if a private person, would be liable to the claimant in accordance with the law of the place where the act or omission occurred." (§1346).

The United States government may be liable under this provision, even though the activity giving rise to liability is uniquely governmental. **Indian Towing Company v. United States**, 350 U.S. 61 (1955). The reference in §1346 to "private person" does not mean that the United States government will be liable only if engaged in a type of activity which is normally engaged in by private persons. It relates rather to the theory of liability. The United States government will not be liable under the Act on a theory of liability which would not, under the law of the particular state, be available against a private person. The Act does not create new theories of liability; it merely removes, in some instances, the protection of governmental immunity.

The Federal Tort Claims Act specifically states that **the United States shall not be liable for assault, battery, false imprisonment, false arrest, malicious prosecution, abuse of process, libel, slander, misrepresentation, deceit, or interference with contract rights**. (§1680(h)). Furthermore, the government is not liable under the Act for the performance or nonperformance of a discretionary function or duty on the part of one of its agencies or employees. (§2680(a)). The distinction is basically between functions at the planning level as opposed to functions at the operational level. Liability under the Act exists only as to functions at the operational level. Dalehite v. United States, 346 U.S. 15 (1953).

State Government. It is firmly established that the **doctrine of sovereign immunity applies to the states**. Thus the states may be sued for the torts committed by their employees and agencies **only to the extent that they have, by statute, consented to such suits**. All states, in varying degrees, have consented, usually in limited form by statute. These statutes generally restrict the particular claims for which suit may be brought; some use the Federal Tort Claims Act (see supra), as a guide.

The Restatement (§895B) takes the position that while a state is not liable to suit for its torts without its consent, such consent need not come in the form of legislation. State immunity may be abrogated or restricted judicially. Legislation is clearly the preferable form. Even where consent is given, the Restatement takes the position that it should be limited consent, that is, that a state and its governmental agencies should be immune from liability for actions and omissions constituting:
   a) the exercise of a judicial or legislative function;
   b) the exercise of an administrative function involving a basic policy decision.

Municipal Government. Municipal corporations never enjoyed the complete immunity from tort liability which was formerly enjoyed by the federal and state governments. This is because a municipality performs functions of both a **governmental nature** (e.g., operating a police force), and of a **proprietary nature** (e.g., trash collection).

Traditionally, **municipalities have been held liable for torts committed by their employees in performing proprietary functions, but have not been held liable where the tort arose out of the performance of a governmental function**. A proprietary function is one which might just as well be performed by a private corporation. There is, however, a strong recent trend toward the abolition of municipal immunity on the basis that the loss to a person suffered from the tortious conduct of a municipal employee, even though engaged in governmental activity, should be shifted to the numerous municipal residents who enjoy the benefits of the activity, rather than being required to remain with the victim.

The Restatement (Second) of Torts §895C, takes the position that the municipality should be liable for its torts, except for acts or omissions constituting the exercise of a legislative or judicial function, or for acts or omissions constituting the exercise of an administrative function involving the making of a basic policy decision. Repudiation of municipal immunity does not establish liability for an act or omission which is otherwise privileged or is not tortious. Thus, for example, the privilege of a police officer to make an arrest upon the reasonable grounds that the arrested person had committed a felony likewise protects the municipality.

Public Officers. The immunity of a government, whether federal, state, or municipal, does not necessarily also extend to the government employee who committed the tort. There are, however, separate rules for immunity of public officers. Thus, judges and high-level legislative and executive officers enjoy absolute or qualified immunity from tort liability for their official acts, even where their conduct is intentional. The rationale for such immunity for official acts is to encourage such high-level officials in the fearless pursuit of their duties. Gregoire v. Biddle, 177 F.2d 579 (2d Cir. 1949). Lower echelon executive and legislative officials are protected only from liability flowing from the performance of quasi-judicial, legislative, or discretionary responsibilities.

Necessity. An act which would otherwise be tortious **cannot be the basis for liability if it is justified by necessity (i.e., if it is necessary to avoid a greater harm)**. For example, necessity is a defense to a trespass if the trespass was necessary for the defendant to avoid bodily injury or death. Necessity is not an available defense if the defendant has merely acted to shift the same harm to another person; there must be an objective benefit from the defendant's conduct.

II. NEGLIGENCE

A. THE DUTY QUESTION: INCLUDING FAILURE TO ACT; UNFORESEEABLE PLAINTIFFS; AND OBLIGATIONS TO CONTROL THE CONDUCT OF THIRD PARTIES.

The initial step for the plaintiff in a negligence case is to **establish the duty** which the defendant owed to him. Duty may be divided into two categories:

1) Duty to act.
2) Duty not to act in a negligent or reckless manner.

Duty to Act: No Duty to Act Generally. With few exceptions, **the law does not impose upon individuals the duty to render aid to a person who is ill or in peril; moral obligations in this respect are not transformed into legal obligations**. Yania v. Bigan, 397 Pa. 316, 155 A.2d 343 (1959) (defendant not liable for ignoring the pleas of a drowning man); Hurley v. Eddingfield, 156 Ind. 416, 59 N.E. 1058 (1901) (physician not liable for refusing to answer the call of a dying person).

Creation of Duty: Special Relationships. One exception to the no-duty rule is where some special relationship exists between the plaintiff and the defendant. Such special relationships have been found in the following cases:

1) an employer is liable for the failure to render assistance to a stricken employee. Szabo v. Pennsylvania Railroad, 132 N.J.L. 331, 40 A.2d 562 (1945). See Restatement of Agency, §512.
2) a common carrier has such a duty to its passenger;
3) an innkeeper has such a duty to her guest;
4) a business invitor may be held liable for the failure to render assistance to a business invitee. Dupue v. Flatau, 100 Minn. 299, 111 N.W. 1 (1907)
5) a duty is owed by a school to its pupil, Pirkle v. Oakdale Union Grammar School District, 40 Cal.2d 207, 253 P.2d 1 (1953);

6) a jailor to his prisoner, **Thomas v. Williams**, 105 Ga. App. 321, 124 S.E.2d 409 (1962); and

7) a social invitor to his guest, **Tubbs v. Argus**, 140 Ind. App. 695, 225 N.E.2d 841 (1967).

Defendant Created Peril or Caused Harm to Plaintiff. Furthermore, a person who causes another's injury, even though innocently, is under a duty to render aid to the victim. **Whitesides v. Southern Railway**, 128 N.C. 229, 38 S.E. 878 (1901). In **Rains v. Heldenfels Bros.**, 443 S.W.2d 280 (Tex. Civ. App. 1969), the plaintiff was barred, due to his contributory negligence, from recovering for his original injury, but he still recovered from the defendant for failure to render aid after the original injury.

Also, where the plaintiff is being injured by an instrumentality which is in the defendant's control, the defendant has a positive duty to take steps to **prevent further injury**. **L.S. Ayres Co. v. Hicks**, 220 Ind. 86, 40 N.E.2d 334 (1942) (boy caught fingers in escalator; defendant negligently delayed stopping the escalator). Modern decisions hold that the occupier of land has a duty to use reasonable care to aid an imperiled trespasser on the land. **Pridgen v. Boston Housing Authority**, 364 Mass. 696, 308 N.E.2d 467 (1974).

If the defendant puts into public distribution a product which he subsequently discovers is defective, he has a **duty to notify** all potential purchasers or users. **Ward v. Morehead City Sea Food Co.**, 171 N.C. 33, 87 S.E. 958 (1916).

The defendant may have a **duty to act as the result of a well-established custom or pattern** of action upon which the plaintiff or public has relied. **Wilmington General Hospital v. Manlove**, 174 A.2d 135 (Del. 1961) (emergency patient had relied upon a well-established custom of the defendant, a private hospital, of rendering emergency treatment); **Erie Railroad v. Stewart**, 40 F.2d 855 (6th Cir. 1930) (public had relied upon presence of watchman at defendant's railroad crossing).

Good Samaritan Rule: Generally - Volunteer Owes Duty of Reasonable Care. If a person having no duty to render aid or assistance undertakes to render aid or assistance, he is, under the common law, required to exercise reasonable care. **Zelenko v. Gimbel Bros.**, 158 Misc. 904, 287 N.Y.S. 134 (1935). The rule imposing liability upon the person who, although having no duty to render assistance, does so negligently, is sometimes referred to as the "Good Samaritan Rule."

Thus, while a truck driver may have no duty to signal to an automobile behind him that it may safely pass, he will be liable if he negligently does so. **Haralson v. Jones Truck Lines**, 223 Ark. 813, 270 S.W.2d 892 (1954). The fact that a physician accepts a charity patient does not excuse him from the exercise of ordinary care. **LeJuene Road Hospital, Inc. v. Watson**, 171 So.2d 202 (Fla. App. 1965).

Medical Assistance at Accident Scene. Many states have enacted statutes making the "Good Samaritan Rule" inapplicable to doctors and nurses who render medical assistance at the scene of an accident. **Such statutes usually absolve doctors and nurses from liability for their ordinary negligence in rendering such emergency treatment, although not requiring such persons to render aid**.

Duty Not to Act Unreasonably: Objective Standard. Absent some particular relationship between the parties that the law may recognize as creating a greater or lesser duty, **if a person owes a**

duty to others, the duty is that of exercising reasonable care. This requires that a person's conduct, in light of all the circumstances, does not create unreasonable risks to others.

What is reasonable depends upon a great variety of factors. Basically, a comparison is made between the burden of avoiding the occurrence of harm with the probability that harm will occur and the gravity of that type of harm if it does occur. See **United States v. Carroll Towing Co.**, 159 F.2d 169 (2d Cir. 1947).

Except in the case of minors, **the standard of reasonable conduct is an objective one**. The defendant will not be excused from liability simply because he did the best that he could considering his knowledge, experience, and intelligence. **Vaughan v. Menlove**, 3 Bing. 468 (N.C. 1837).

Emergency Situations. An actor confronted with a sudden emergency will not be required to act as if he had had adequate time to weigh alternatives and decide on the most reasonable course of action. While an objective standard of reasonableness should still be applied in such cases, the standard is one of a **reasonable person under all the circumstances and the emergency will be considered as one of the circumstances**.

Thus, a decision which would not appear prudent upon due deliberation might not be unreasonable if made when emotions were high, there was little time to act, and adequate information was not available. Some courts have distinguished the emergency situation from "instinctive conduct" such as slamming on the brakes when a truck pulls in front of the defendant's car and the defendant has only a "split second" to react, virtually without thought. Instinctive conduct cannot be unreasonable because there was no time to decide on the proper course of action.

Greater Knowledge than Ordinary Reasonable Man. While the adult-defendant's mental shortcomings are not considered in determining whether he has acted in a reasonable manner, if the defendant has greater knowledge or experience in a certain area than that possessed by the ordinary reasonable man, his conduct must be judged in the light of that superior knowledge or experience. **Public Service of New Hampshire v. Elliott**, 123 F.2d 2 (1st Cir. 1941).

Physicians. For years, the standard of care for physicians was whether their conduct measured up to the standard of care and skill ordinarily possessed by others in the profession, practicing in the same community as the defendant. **Small v. Howard**, 128 Mass. 131 (1880). The **"same community"** standard was changed in many jurisdictions to a **"same or similar community"** standard. **Wiggins v. Piver**, 276 N.C. 134, 171 S.E.2d 393 (1970). Some jurisdictions have looked to a statewide standard. **Fitzmaurice v. Flynn**, 167 Conn. 609, 356 A.2d 887 (1975); **Ives v. Redford**, 219 Va. 838, 252 S.E.2d 315 (1979).

Some jurisdictions have completely abandoned a community standard, and have applied a general or nationwide standard, at least in reference to routine medical procedures. See **Pederson v. Dumouchel**, 72 Wash.2d 73, 431 P.2d 973 (1967). In such jurisdictions, the proper standard is whether the physician, if a general practitioner, has exercised the degree of care and skill of the **average qualified practitioner**, taking into account the advances in the profession. In the application of this standard, it is permissible to consider the medical resources available to the physician as one circumstance in determining the skill and care required. Under this standard, some allowance is thus made for the type of community in which the physician carries on his practice. **Brune v. Belinkoff**, 354 Mass. 102, 235 N.E.2d 793 (1968).

A physician presenting herself as a specialist should be held to the **standard of care and skill of the average member of the profession practicing the specialty, taking into account the advances in the profession**. As in the case of the general practitioner, it is permissible to consider the medical resources available to her. Id. The principal benefit arising from the abolition of the community standard is that the plaintiff's expert witness need not be qualified to testify to the standard of any particular community.

Informed Consent. In "informed consent" cases (cases where plaintiff claims that the doctor obtained his or her consent to certain medical treatment by withholding material information concerning the risks involved in such treatment and the other available medical procedures), traditionally plaintiff was required to provide expert testimony that the defendant-doctor's conduct violated the customary or reasonable disclosure standards of medical practitioners under similar circumstances. See Bly v. Rhoads, 216 Va. 645, 222 S.E.2d 783 (1976); Crain v. Allison, 443 A.2d 558 (D.C. App. 1982).

Several jurisdictions, however, have held that, while expert testimony is usually needed as to the degree of the risk involved and the alternative medical procedures, plaintiff is not required to prove by expert testimony that the defendant's nondisclosure was unreasonable by medical standards. Once plaintiff produces evidence that the doctor obtained his or her consent by failing to disclose a material risk and alternative medical procedures, and that injury resulted, the jury may then determine the reasonableness of the doctor's conduct without the help of expert testimony. See Zeleznik v. Jewish Chronic Disease Hospital, 47 App. Div.2d 199, 366 N.Y.S.2d 163 (1975). Some cases have taken the view that the duty of disclosure is measured by the patient's need for information material to her decision whether to accept or reject the proposed treatment. McKinney v. Nash, 120 Cal. App.3d, 174 Cal. Rptr. 642 (1981).

For a discussion on the duties owed by owners of property to invitees, licensees and trespassers, see the discussion under "Claims Against Owners and Occupiers of Land," infra.

B.   THE STANDARD OF CARE

1.   The Reasonably Prudent Person: Including Children, Physically And Mentally Impaired Individuals, Professional People, And Other Special Classes

Generally, the negligence issue is usually put to the jury as:

"Would a 'reasonable person' of ordinary prudence, in the position of the defendant, have conducted himself as the defendant did?"

This is essentially an **objective standard.** It does not ask whether the defendant intended to behave carefully or thought he was behaving carefully. However, this hypothetical "reasonable person" does bear some of the characteristics of the actual defendant, at least to the extent of some of his physical attributes.

Physical characteristics. The test for negligence is whether the defendant behaved as a reasonable person would "under the circumstances" that confronted the defendant. "The circumstances" obviously include the external facts of the case, such as the traffic conditions, speed limits, etc., which confront a motorist.

Most courts have extended "the circumstances" to include the physical characteristics of the defendant himself. That is, they have held that the test is whether a reasonable person with the physical attributes of the defendant would have behaved as the defendant did.

Thus, if the defendant has a **physical disability**, the standard for negligence is what a reasonable person with that physical disability would have done. See Rest. 2d, §283C.

Sudden disability. A key factor will often be whether the disability has struck for the first time immediately preceding the accident. A defendant who reasonably believes himself to be in good health, and who suddenly suffers, for the first time ever, a heart attack or epileptic seizure while driving, would almost certainly not be held to have negligently caused the ensuing accident. But one who knows that he is subject to such attacks or seizures might well be negligent in driving at all. See Rest. 2d, §283C, Comment c.

Blindness. Many disability cases have involved blindness. Typically, it is the plaintiff who is blind, who has been injured, and against whom the defense of contributory negligence is asserted. This defense involves roughly the same definition of negligence, except that this definition is applied to the plaintiff's conduct. In such a case, the issue is: **How would a reasonable blind person behave?** Sometimes, the reasonable blind person will have to be more careful than a reasonable sighted person, sometimes less.

Strict Liability Rejected. If the definition of negligence did not take into account the actor's physical disabilities, something akin to strict liability would be imposed for accidents stemming from such disabilities. For instance, if a driver were held liable for conduct which would otherwise be negligent (e.g., going through a stoplight or off the road), and no account were taken of the fact that he had just suffered an unforeseen heart attack or epileptic seizure, this would not be a true negligence standard at all, but rather, something like the absolute liability for defective products imposed upon manufacturers and sellers.

Mental attributes. The ordinary reasonable person is not, however, deemed to have the particular mental characteristics of the defendant. For instance, the defendant is not absolved of negligence because he is more stupid, hot-tempered, careless or of poorer judgment than the ordinary reasonable person.

> Example: D builds a hay rick (a device for drying hay) near the edge of his property. P is afraid that the stack will ignite, burning his nearby cottages. He repeatedly warns D, but D says he will "chance it." The hay spontaneously catches fire, and the resulting conflagration destroys P's cottages. Held, D is not entitled to a jury instruction that he is not negligent if he acted in good faith and according to his best judgment, and that he should not be penalized for not being of the highest intelligence. Such a standard would be "as variable as the length of the foot of each individual," and would be impossible to administer. Instead, an objective standard, the prudence of an ordinary person, must be applied. Vaughan v. Menlove, 132 Eng. Rep. 490 (1837).

Imbecility. However, **a mental state so low that it must be considered imbecilic or moronic, and which prevents the actor from even understanding that danger exists, will usually be held**

to render negligence impossible. The issue has usually arisen in the case of mentally defective plaintiffs against whom contributory negligence is asserted. (The Second Restatement, however, does not adopt the majority rule that mental deficiency may relieve a person of negligence. Rest. 2d, §283B.)

However, a child's mental deficiency may be taken into account. Rest. 2d, §283A. The Restatement also indicates that mental deficiency will not relieve the plaintiff from contributory negligence, unless the plaintiff is a child (generally, with a chronological age of less than 16 - §283A) or is completely insane.

Insanity. Paradoxically, the courts have been more inclined to impose a "reasonable person" objective standard upon insane persons than upon mentally deficient ones. However, recently courts have begun to hold that insane persons, whether plaintiff or defendant, are not negligent if their insane state prevented them from understanding or avoiding the danger.

As an example, assume that D, driving her car, suddenly becomes convinced that God is taking hold of the steering wheel. As the car nears a truck, D steps on the gas "in order to become airborne because she knew she could fly because Superman does it." She collides with the truck, driven by P, who sues D's insurance company. The verdict is for P, and D appeals. Held, the general rule that insanity is no defense to negligence is too broad. This rule is motivated by several policy considerations:

1) Where loss must be home by one of two innocent persons, the one who caused the loss should bear it;
2) Persons interested in the insane defendant's estate (if she has one) should be induced to restrain and control her; and
3) An insanity defense may lead to false claims of insanity to avoid liability.

However, where the insanity strikes suddenly and without forewarning, so that the defendant has no chance of avoiding the danger, the rule that insanity is no defense is unjust.

In the present case there was some evidence that D had had similar delusions previously, and the jury could have concluded that she should have been forewarned of the danger that delusions would strike her while driving. Therefore, the verdict for P will not be overturned. **Breunig v. American Family Insurance Co.**, 173 N.W.2d 619 (Wis. 1970).

Intoxication. A defendant who is intoxicated at the time of an accident is not permitted to claim that his intoxication stripped him of his ability to comprehend and avoid the danger; he is held to the standard of conduct of a reasonable sober person. See Rest. 2d, §283C, Comment d.

Children. Another exception to the general objective "reasonable person" standard is that children are not held to the level of care which would be exercised by a reasonable adult. A **child must merely conform to the conduct of a "reasonable person of like age, intelligence, and experience under like circumstances."** Rest. 2d, §283A. Note that this is a somewhat **subjective standard**, in that if a child is less intelligent that most children of his age, he is held simply to the degree of care which a similarly unintelligent contemporary would exercise. This should be distinguished from the standard for adults, which makes no allowance for the fact that the individual is less intelligent than the average person.

Fixed Chronological Test Discarded. Many older cases applied an irrebuttable presumption that a child under the age of seven could not be negligent, a rebuttable presumption that one between seven and fourteen was not negligent, and a rebuttable one that a child between fourteen and twenty-one was capable of negligence. However, the arbitrary divisions stem more from the Bible than from any sound judicial reasoning, and they are no longer used by most modern courts. See e.g., Williamson v. Garland, 402 S.W.2d 80 (Ky. 1966).

This special standard is applicable only to children, not to all minors. The Second Restatement, § 283A, Comment a, notes that the test is generally for children of "tender years," and furthermore states that it has "seldom been applied to anyone over the age of sixteen."

Adult Activity. Another exception to the special rules for children is that where a child engages in a potentially dangerous activity that is normally pursued only by adults, he will be held to the standard of care that a reasonable adult doing that activity would exercise. See Rest. 2d, §283A, Comment c. This principle has been applied in cases where a "child" was driving a car, operating a motorboat, and playing golf.

Dangerous But Not Adult. The courts are split as to the standard of care which should be applied where the activity is potentially dangerous, but not one that is usually engaged in by adults rather than children. The Restatement would apply the child rather than adult standard of care, since the adult standard will be applied to children only if the activity is both potentially dangerous and one that is normally engaged in by adults. Rest. 2d, §283A.

But some courts have held that the adult standard of care should be triggered whenever the activity is significantly hazardous, even if it is one which is frequently engaged in by children. See, e.g., Robinson v. Lindsay, 598 P.2d 392 (Wash. 1978), holding that snowmobiling is an "inherently dangerous" activity for which the adult standard should apply, even though children often engage in it. The Robinson court reasoned that this rule "discourages immature individuals from engaging in inherently dangerous activities," while still leaving them free to enjoy "traditional childhood activities without being held to an adult standard of care."

Knowledge. Assuming that the general "reasonable person" standard is the one which applies to a case at hand, there a number of basic issues about how a reasonable person generally behaves. One of these troublesome areas has to do with knowledge that a reasonable person would possess.

1) **Ordinary Experience.** Items of knowledge that virtually every adult in the community possesses will be imputed to the "reasonable adult" and thus to the defendant. This is true whether the defendant herself actually knows the fact in question or not.

2) **Stranger to Community.** Facts generally known to all adults in a particular community will be imputed to a stranger who enters the community without having had the experience of knowledge in question. Thus a city dweller who visits a farm, and who has never learned that a bull can be dangerous, will nonetheless be held to the standard of behavior that would be exercised by one who did have such knowledge, since that knowledge is common to dwellers in rural areas.

3) **Duty to Investigate.** Even where a certain fact is not known to members of the community at large, or to the defendant herself, she may be under a duty to end her ignorance. A driver who senses that something is wrong with his steering wheel, for instance, would have a duty to find out what the problem is before an accident is caused.

4) **Memory.** Just as the reasonable person knows certain facts, she also has a certain level of memory. Thus, a motorist who has passed a particular intersection many times will be charged with remembering that it is dangerous in a certain way, whereas one who never or seldom had passed that intersection before would not have the same burden. See Rest. 2d, §289, Illustr. 4.

5) **Distractions.** Similarly, the reasonable person pays attention to what she is doing, and is not distracted, unless there is a legitimate reason for such distraction. Thus, a driver who turns to look at his passenger and slams into another car would be held to have failed to behave like a reasonably prudent person. See Rest. 2d, §289, Comment k.

6) **Frailties Remain.** The "reasonable person" is not, however, completely without imperfections. Her care for her own safety and that of others is merely reasonable, not flawless.

Custom. In litigating the defendant's negligence, one thing that either side may point to is custom, that is, the way a certain activity is habitually carried out in a trade or a community. The plaintiff may try to show that the defendant did not follow the safety-motivated custom that others in the same business follow, or the defendant may try to show that he exercised due care by using the same procedures as everyone else in the trade.

Not Conclusive. The vast majority of courts allow evidence as to custom for the purpose of showing the presence or absence of reasonable care, but do not treat this evidence as conclusive. Thus, the fact that everyone else in the defendant's industry does a certain thing the same way the defendant did it does not mean that that way was not unduly dangerous, if there are other factors so indicating.

> **Example:** Two tugboats owned by D are towing cargo owned by P. Most tugboats have not yet installed radio receiving sets, although some have; D's two tugs do not yet have these sets. They are therefore unable to receive messages that a strong storm is overtaking them, and are sunk. Held, the fact that most tugs have not installed sets does not conclusively establish that D was non-negligent in not having installed them. For custom is not dispositive on the issue of negligence – "a whole calling may have unduly lagged in the adoption of new and available devices. . . . Courts must in the end say what is required; there are precautions so imperative that even their universal disregard will not excuse their omission." Here some tug owners had already installed the sets, so D's case is even weaker, and was liable. The TJ Hooper, 60 F.2d 737 (2d Cir. 1932).

Even though custom is **not conclusive** on the issue of negligence, it is nonetheless evidence on this question, and if there is no evidence in rebuttal, the fact that the defendant did or did not follow custom may be sufficient for him to prevail.

Advances in Technology. The technological "state of the art" at a particular moment is, similarly, relevant to what constitutes negligence. For instance, the defendant's failure to take action to prevent a certain known risk might be either negligent or non-negligent, depending upon whether technology exists that could reduce that risk. Consequently, conduct that would be non-negligent in earlier times may have become negligent today due to technological advances.

Emergency. The general rule is that the defendant must follow the standard of care that a reasonable person would exercise "considering all of the circumstances." One of the circumstances of a particular case may be that the defendant was confronted with an emergency, and was forced to act with little time for reflection. If this is so, **the defendant will not be held to the same standard of care as one who has ample time for thinking about what to do; instead he must merely behave as would a reasonable person confronted with the same emergency.** See Rest. 2d, §296.

Emergency Caused By Defendant. But if the emergency was caused by the defendant's negligence, the fact that the emergency leads the defendant into an accident will not absolve him of liability. In such a situation, it is the initial negligence leading to the emergency, not the subsequent response to the emergency, that makes the defendant negligent.

Even if the emergency is not of the defendant's own making, he must still live up to the standard of care of a reasonable person confronted with such an emergency. That is, if he behaves unreasonably, even conceding the fact that he had little time for reflection, he will nonetheless be negligent. Thus a person driving on an undivided highway who sees an accident ahead of him, and who swerves left into oncoming traffic instead of right onto a shoulder, might well be held liable notwithstanding the fact that he had little time for reflection.

Activity Requiring Special Training. There are certain activities which by their nature require an unusual capacity to react well in an emergency. In a case involving such an activity, the defendant will therefore be held to this higher standard of preparedness. A bus driver, for instance, should by her training be better prepared than the average driver to anticipate various traffic emergencies, and she will be held to this higher standard. See Rest. 2d, §296, Comment c. In fact, even the average motorist will probably be held to bear the burden of being capable of anticipating certain kinds of common emergencies (e.g., a child rushing out into the street after a ball), and will be charged with reacting more quickly in such a situation than if that kind of emergency arose less frequently.

Anticipating Conduct of Others. Just as the reasonable person must possess certain knowledge, so she must possess a certain ability to anticipate the conduct of others. The defendant may be required to anticipate the possibility of negligence on the part of others. Generally, this will be so only if the likelihood of injury is great, or the magnitude of the injury is very substantial.

> Example: An automobile driver is normally entitled to assume that other drivers will drive non-negligently. But if she has reason to know that the car ahead of her is being driven by a drunk driver, or if the road conditions are such that a short stop by the driver ahead is very likely to cause the defendant to run over a pedestrian, the defendant will be required to guard extra carefully against these consequences.

Furthermore, the defendant is charged with anticipating careless or dangerous conduct on the part of children, since they are commonly known to be incapable of exercising the degree of care of the average adult. Thus one who drives down a street crowded with children playing is not entitled to assume that the children will stay out of the car's path and must take extra precautions to guard against their carelessness.

Duty Owed by Automobile Operator to a Guest. In some states, the duty owed by the operator of a motor vehicle to a social guest is something less than ordinary care, usually the avoidance of gross negligence or reckless conduct. This lesser duty of care is imposed by so-called **"guest statutes."** See Murray v. Land, 252 Iowa 260, 106 N.W.2d 643 (1960), interpreting the Iowa guest statute as meaning that under some circumstances, the owner of the automobile could be a guest passenger in his own automobile.

Some states, by common law, make a distinction between active conduct of the operator toward the guest (holding the operator liable for ordinary negligence), and a defective condition in the automobile (holding no duty on the operator to inspect). **Most states now hold that the operator of a motor vehicle owes the same duty of care to a social guest as he owes to anyone else, namely, ordinary care.** Cohen v. Kaminetsky, 36 N.J. 276, 176 A.2d 483 (1961).

2.   Rules Of Conduct Derived From Statutes And Custom

Violation of a Criminal Statute or Ordinance: Negligence Per Se. Often the plaintiff in a negligence action asserts that a statute or ordinance which imposes criminal liability should be used by the court in a civil action to establish the standard of conduct for the reasonable man. The vast majority of jurisdictions agree with this contention, holding that **the unexcused violation of a criminal statute is itself negligence, that is, negligence per se**. Martin v. Herzog, 228 N.Y. 164, 126 N.E. 814 (1920).

The negligence per se doctrine means that for purposes of determining whether a party's conduct was negligent, **the criminal statute fixes the standard**; that is, rather than a common law reasonable person standard, the statutory standard (even though in a criminal statute) controls. Osborne v. McMasters, 40 Minn. 103, 41 N.W. 543 (1889).

A small minority of jurisdictions adopt the rule that the violation of a criminal statute is **only evidence of negligence**; that is, in determining whether defendant violated the standard of reasonable conduct, the jury is entitled to consider as evidence the fact that defendant's conduct violated a criminal statute. The jury, however, is not bound by the standard established by the criminal statute.

Excuse. Even in negligence per se jurisdictions, the courts generally consider whether defendant's conduct, although technically in violation of the criminal law, was nevertheless excused. Thus, where plaintiff was able to demonstrate that, due to traffic conditions, it was safer for plaintiff to walk on the wrong side of the road in violation of a statute, such conduct was held not to constitute contributory negligence. Tedla v. Ellman, 280 N.Y. 124, 19 N.E.2d 987 (1939). Many courts impose a more rigorous standard for violations of safety equipment statutes, McConnell v. Herron, 240 Or. 486, 402 P.2d 726 (1965) (faulty brakes), than for violations of operational statutes. Pozsgai v. Porter, 249 Or. 84, 435 P.2d 818 (1967) (vehicle on wrong side of road).

Violation of Ordinance. While there is a slight difference of opinion on the matter, most states treat the violation of ordinances in the same manner as statutes.

Relationship Between Harm that Occurred and Harm that the Statute Seeks to Avoid. There is general agreement among the states, whether negligence per se or evidence of negligence jurisdictions, that the criminal violation, to be relevant, **must be shown to have contributed to the harm**. Thus, in Brown v. Shyne, 242 N.Y. 176, 151 N.E. 197 (1926), it was held that plaintiff had failed to prove that defendant was liable for medical malpractice simply on a showing that defendant, in violation of a statute, had no license to practice medicine. Proof had to be forthcoming that

Multistate Bar Review Book 2

defendant, in treating plaintiff, did not exercise the care and skill which would have been exercised by qualified practitioners within the state, and that such lack of skill and care caused the injury.

Also, the statutory violation will not be considered **unless plaintiff was a member of the class that the criminal statute was designed to protect and the harm was the type that the statute was designed to prevent**. Thus, suppose defendant, in violation of a criminal statute, parks his automobile next to a fire hydrant, leaving a passenger in the vehicle. Shortly thereafter, the passenger is injured when another vehicle strikes defendant's parked automobile. The mere fact that the passenger would not have been injured had defendant parked the automobile elsewhere rather than in violation of the statute does not make defendant liable for the passenger's injury. The purpose of the statute was not to protect against this hazard.

Direct Evidence of Negligence. Obviously, the plaintiff may establish the defendant's breach of duty by the introduction of direct evidence of negligence even apart from violations of criminal statutes. The major problems in this area are:

a) the need in some cases for expert testimony;
b) the sufficiency of the evidence to avoid a directed verdict; and
c) the relevancy or materiality of the evidence on the issue of negligence.

Compliance with Professional Standards or Custom in the Trade. When a plaintiff charges that the defendant was negligent in rendering services in the practice of a profession or trade, the plaintiff must normally prove that the **defendant's conduct fell below the standard of skill and knowledge** which is commonly possessed by members in good standing of that trade or skill. Restatement (Second) of Torts §299A. Where the matter involved is of such a nature that the jury cannot, on the basis of its common knowledge and experience, determine whether the standard has been violated, expert testimony will be required in order for the plaintiff to avoid a directed verdict.

There are aspects of a trade or a profession with which even laymen are sufficiently familiar to be able to determine from their own knowledge and experience whether the defendant has been negligent. Thus, in Lipman v. Lustig, 342 Mass. 182, 190 N.E.2d 675 (1961), the court held that expert testimony was not required in a negligence action against a dentist who had dropped an instrument in the plaintiff's mouth, requiring abdominal surgery to have it removed.

However, an expert may testify that although the defendant acted consistently with the standard of care currently applied in the community, the defendant was negligent because the community standard was set too low. With respect to some trades or callings, evidence that the defendant's conduct was consistent with the custom in the trade or calling is merely evidence of due care; it does not establish due care. A whole calling may have unduly lagged in the adoption of new and available devices.

> Example: In The T.J. Hooper, 60 F.2d 737 (2d Cir. 1932), the court held the defendant liable for failing to have a receiving set in its tugboat, thereby preventing it from receiving the weather forecast. Merely because most tugboat owners did not equip their boats with receiving sets did not make the defendant's conduct reasonable. The court stated that there are precautions which are so imperative that even their universal disregard will not excuse their omission.

Multistate Bar Review Book 2

In medical malpractice cases, though, doctors are generally held only to the standard established by **reasonably prudent peers, acting in the same or similar circumstances**. See Harris v. Robert C. Groth, M.D., Inc., P.S, 99 Wash.2d 438, 663 P.2d 113 (1983). Thus, expert evidence that the prevailing professional standards are negligent is not generally allowed.

C. PROBLEMS RELATING TO PROOF OF FAULT, INCLUDING RES IPSA LOQUITUR

The doctrine of res ipsa loquitur permits the finder of fact to find negligence on the part of the defendant even though the plaintiff has produced no direct evidence of the defendant's negligence; such negligence may be inferred from circumstantial evidence. The doctrine of res ipsa loquitur is a common sense appraisal of the probative value of circumstantial evidence. George Foltis, Inc. v. City of New York, 287 N.Y. 108, 38 N.E.2d 455 (1941).

The plaintiff must ultimately establish under res ipsa loquitur that it is **more likely than not that the harm to the plaintiff resulted from the defendant's negligence rather than from some other cause**. The plaintiff attempts to do this by excluding as the cause of the harm possibilities other than the defendant's negligence. The plaintiff is not, however, required to exclude every possibility other than the defendant's negligence as the cause of the harm. Rocona v. Guy F. Atkinson Co., 173 F.2d 661 (9th Cir. 1949). The primary consideration should be whether, in the particular case, the circumstances are such as to sustain an inference that the injury was the result of the defendant's negligence.

Restatement View. The Restatement (Second) of Torts §328 D sets forth the doctrine of res ipsa loquitur as follows:

(1) It may be **inferred** that harm suffered by the plaintiff is caused by negligence of the defendant when:
   a) the event is of a kind which ordinarily **does not occur in the absence of negligence**;
   b) other responsible causes, including the conduct of the plaintiff and third persons, **are sufficiently eliminated** by the evidence; and
   c) the indicated negligence is **within the scope of the defendant's duty to the plaintiff**.

Application and Examples. In Evangelio v. Metropolitan Bottling Co., 339 Mass. 177, 158 N.E.2d 349 (1959), the court allowed a case to go to the jury under res ipsa loquitur where a carbonated beverage bottle exploded in the plaintiff's hand. While there were several possible explanations for the incident (e.g., a defective bottle, mishandling of the bottle by the retailer, etc.), the court held that the doctrine was available against the defendant bottling company on the inference of over-carbonation of the beverage.

In a later case, Hadley v. Hillcrest Dairy Inc., 341 Mass. 624, 171 N.E.2d 293 (1961), the court refused to allow a case to go to the jury under res ipsa loquitur against a bottler of milk, where a bottle of milk shattered in the plaintiff's hand causing injury. As in the Evangelio case, the defendant bottler did not manufacture the bottle. The inference of over-carbonation which permitted the case to go to the jury in the Evangelio case was not present in the Hadley case, and thus there was no sufficient inference of negligence on the part of the defendant to allow the case to be sent to the jury.

Failure to Rebut Evidence of *Res Ipsa Loquitur*. A res ipsa case will get the plaintiff to the jury. Most jurisdictions hold that a plaintiff is **not entitled to a directed verdict** merely because he has presented a res ipsa case which the defendant has failed to rebut. Res ipsa loquitur means that the facts warrant the inference of negligence, not that they compel such an inference. George Foltis, Inc. v. City of New York, supra. The doctrine does not create a presumption of negligence or shift the burden of proof to the defendant, but rather **permits the factfinder to infer negligence from the evidence presented**.

Use of Doctrine in Medical Malpractice Cases. Most states today permit res ipsa loquitur to be used in a medical malpractice case; in most instances, however, expert testimony is still required. Expert testimony is not required when a layman is capable of inferring negligence from the happening of an event, based upon his common knowledge and experience. These situations have included the following:

1) an object (e.g., sponge or clamp) left in the patient's body at the time of surgery (Martin v. Perth Amboy General Hospital, 104 N.J. Super. 335, 250 A.2d 40 (1969);

2) injury to a healthy part of the body in the treatment area or to a part of the body remote from the treatment area;

3) removal of the wrong part of the body;

4) tooth dropped down patient's throat during extraction;

5) patient burned by such devices as hot water bottles, X-rays, heat lamps, vaporizers, etc.; and

6) infection from unsterilized instruments.

Where, however, the jury is incapable of inferring negligence from common knowledge and experience, expert testimony is required. The expert testimony would take the form of a statement that when this particular unfortunate result occurs during the particular medical treatment or surgery, it is more likely due to the negligence of the defendant-physician than to some other cause. Brannon v. Wood, 251 Or. 349, 444 P.2d 558 (1968).

Sometimes a close question exists on whether the matter is one from which the jury may infer negligence based upon common knowledge and experience. In Pipers v. Rosenow, 39 A.D. 240, 333 N.Y.S.2d 480 (1972), the Court held that expert testimony was required to prove negligence where the plaintiff suffered injury to his radial nerve following the use of a needle by defendant to withdraw blood from the plaintiff's arm, even though the use of such a needle is not in most instances followed by serious harm.

Shift of Burden to Defendants to Prove Lack of Culpability. The doctrine of res ipsa loquitur has been used in a few states against a group of doctors and nurses where the plaintiff, while unconscious during surgery, was injured in an area of the body remote from the surgery in some unexplained manner, apparently by one of the doctors or nurses. The doctors and nurses who had been in contact with the plaintiff during his period of unconsciousness were held jointly and severally liable. Ybarra v. Spangard, 25 Cal.2d 486, 154 P.2d 687, 162 A.L.R. 1258 (1944).

In Anderson v. Somberg, 67 N.J. 291, 338 A.2d 1 (1974), the Ybarra doctrine was expanded. In Anderson, a surgical instrument broke during an operation on the plaintiff and lodged in his spinal column. The plaintiff sued the manufacturer and distributor of the instrument as well as the surgeon and the hospital. It was unknown whether the instrument was defective when it left the manufacturer or became defective while in possession of the hospital or was negligently misused by the surgeon.

Multistate Bar Review Book 2

The court, citing Ybarra, held that the burden was on the defendants to establish their lack of culpability and that a verdict had to be given in favor of the plaintiff against at least one of the defendants.

D.   PROBLEMS RELATING TO CAUSATION

1.   But For And Substantial Causes

Most cases dealing with causation relate to **proximate cause**, namely, whether the defendant's negligent act was sufficiently connected with the plaintiff's harm to be considered the legal cause of it. Before reaching matters relating to proximate cause, it must first be determined that the defendant's conduct was actually connected with the plaintiff's harm. If the plaintiff is unable to prove that his harm actually resulted from the defendant's negligence, the plaintiff is not entitled to recover.

Probability. In Barnes v. Bovenmyer, 255 Iowa 220, 122 N.W.2d 312 (1962), the court held that even though the defendant doctor may have been negligent in his delay in removing a piece of steel from the plaintiff's eyeball, the plaintiff could not recover in the absence of expert testimony that such negligent delay caused the plaintiff's loss of his eye. Expert testimony of causal connection between an act of negligence and a particular injury to the plaintiff must indicate a probability of such a causal connection. Thus, the testimony of a doctor that the decedent's leukemia might possibly have resulted from his exposure to benzene was held insufficient to sustain recovery from a Workers' Compensation insurer for the death of the plaintiff's husband. Matter of Miller v. National Cabinet Co., 8 N.Y.2d 277, 168 N.E.2d 811 (1960).

"But For" Causation. Except as discussed below, **the defendant's conduct cannot be considered the cause of the plaintiff's harm if such harm would have occurred even had the defendant not so acted.** Cole v. Shell Petroleum Corp., 149 Kan. 25, 86 P.2d 740 (1939). This rule is often referred to as the **"but for" test** or the **"sine qua non" rule**.

The question is not, however, whether a like harm or similar harm would have occurred without the defendant's negligent act, but whether the same harm would have occurred. Thus, in Dillon v. Twin States Gas & Electric Co., 85 N.H. 449, 163 A. 111 (1932), the plaintiff's intestate fell from a bridge and was electrocuted by coming in contact with the defendant's uninsulated live wires which were dangerously close to the bridge. Regardless of the defendant's negligence, the deceased would undoubtedly have been killed or gravely injured when he struck the surface below. The court held that the trial judge correctly refused to direct a verdict for the defendant. If the defendant's negligence caused the decedent's death by electrocution, what might have happened when the decedent struck the surface was relevant on the issue of damages, but not on the issue of liability.

Substantial Factor Test. The "substantial factor" rule is used in a special class of cases where, under the "but for" test, the defendant would escape liability because other causes have contributed to the result and each cause would have been sufficient to produce the result. In such cases, **the defendant's conduct is a cause of the event if it was a material element and substantial factor in bringing about the event.** Anderson v. Minneapolis, St. Paul & Sault St. Marie Railway Co., 146 Minn. 430, 179 N.W. 45 (1920).

2.   Harms Traceable To Multiple Causes

Where the plaintiff is injured from the negligent act of co-defendants who **shared a common duty** toward the plaintiff or **acted in concert** with each other, the "but for" test can usually be readily applied to make the **defendants jointly and severally liable** for the full amount of the plaintiff's damages. See Johnson v. Chapman, 43 W.Va. 639, 28 S.E. 744 (1897).

Occasionally, however, the plaintiff's harm may result from two independent acts or events, either alone being insufficient to cause the plaintiff's harm. Thus, for example, the plaintiff's cottage may burn down from a fire which was a combination of two separate fires. In such situation, the "but for" test or the "sine qua non" rule will not fit the situation. The courts have taken the position that where the defendant's negligent act **unites with another event**, the defendant's negligence will be considered the **cause of at least part of the harm**. If the other human agent is another negligent defendant, the defendants will be held jointly and severally liable.

Also, where two defendants have **acted negligently, although independently**, but due to the circumstances it is impossible to determine which defendant caused the plaintiff's injury (as where two defendants fire shotguns in the general direction of the plaintiff but only one hit the plaintiff), the **courts have treated the defendants as joint tortfeasors, even though in actuality only one of the defendants has caused the plaintiff's injury**. See Oliver v. Miles, 144 Miss. 852, 110 So. 666 (1962); Summers v. Tice, 33 Cal.2d 80, 199 P.2d 1 (1948).

3.   Questions Of Apportionment Of Responsibility Among Multiple Tortfeasors, Including Joint And Several Liability

Joint Tortfeasors. If two or more defendants, by their **concurrent negligent acts**, bring about harm to the plaintiff, and it is **not possible to separate portions of the harm** as being the result of each act, the **defendants may be held jointly liable**. Johnson v. Chapman, 43 W.Va. 639, 28 S.E. 744 (1897). The word "concurrent" does not mean "simultaneous." Thus, joint liability may be possible even though the separate acts occurred weeks or even months apart. Further, joint liability does not require that the defendants have acted in concert (contrast with joint enterprise as a theory of imputed negligence).

The effect of joint liability is that **each defendant is liable for the entire amount of the damages to the plaintiff**. Obviously, the plaintiff can collect only the amount of the judgment; he is not entitled to a double recovery.

A question may arise as to the application of **comparative negligence** where joint tortfeasors are involved. The majority of jurisdictions hold that the defendants are jointly and severally liable for plaintiff's damages (reduced by plaintiff's negligence), **despite the different percentages** of negligence attributed to each defendant.

Thus, if plaintiff suffered damages of $50,000 and the jury found that plaintiff's negligence was 20%, defendant A's negligence was 30%, and defendant B's negligence was 50%, then plaintiff could obtain a $40,000 judgment against defendant A and defendant B (joint and several liability). If defendant A pays the entire judgment, his remedy would be for contribution against defendant B. A very few comparative negligence jurisdictions do not hold the defendants jointly liable in such cases. Instead, they hold each defendant severally liable only for the percent of the total damages attributable to each defendant's fault, e.g., Bartlett v. N.M. Welding Supply Co., 646 P.2d 579 (N.M. 1982).

Multistate Bar Review Book 2

Suppose plaintiff, in a jurisdiction that bars recovery where plaintiff is more negligent than defendant, is found to be 30% negligent, and defendant A is 20% negligent, while defendant B is 50% negligent. May plaintiff obtain a judgment against defendant A? The jurisdictions which have responded to this issue are split. Some say that as long as plaintiff is not more negligent than both defendants combined, plaintiff may recover from either defendant. Other jurisdictions will dismiss the action against the defendant who is less negligent than the plaintiff. Any Multistate question raising these issues would have to tell you the approach taken in the particular jurisdiction.

Contribution. A plaintiff is not required to join two or more defendants in an action, since liability is also several. If, however, the plaintiff sues fewer than all of the potential joint tortfeasors, those defendants who are sued may implead the remaining tortfeasors as third party defendants for contribution. Knell v. Feltman, 174 F.2d 662 (D.C. 1949).

A plaintiff may normally make a settlement with one of several joint tortfeasors. Such a settlement, however, will in no way prejudice the rights of the remaining tortfeasors, since any judgment obtained against them will be proportionately reduced, usually on a pro rata basis. Theobald v. Kenney's Suburban House, Inc., 48 N.J. 203, 225 A.2d 10 (1966).

If one joint tortfeasor pays more than his pro rata share of the judgment, he has the right of contribution over against the other joint tortfeasor for the excess. In most jurisdictions, the pro rata basis is determined by the number of joint tortfeasors involved and not upon their relative degrees of fault. Wisconsin, New York and some other comparative negligence jurisdictions, however, determine the amount of contribution on the basis of the relative percentages of causal negligence of the joint defendants. Bielski v. Schulze, 16 Wis.2d 1, 114 N.W.2d 105 (1962).

Whichever approach is adopted does not, in most jurisdictions, have any effect upon the amount of plaintiff's recovery, because contribution is a matter affecting only defendants. The jurisdictions which have adopted a contribution rule based upon degrees of fault have done so because they viewed such an approach as consistent with their comparative negligence rule. Packard v. Whitten, 274 A.2d 169 (Me. 1971).

In summary, suppose the jury finds that plaintiff's damages are $100,000, plaintiff was not negligent, defendant A was 30% negligent, and defendant B was 70% negligent. Suppose further that plaintiff sued only defendant A, but defendant A impleaded defendant B for contribution. Plaintiff would, in most states, obtain a $100,000 judgment against defendant A, and defendant A would obtain a $50,000 judgment against defendant B (pro rata contribution). Some states, however, while still holding defendant A liable for $100,000 to plaintiff, would nevertheless permit defendant A to obtain a $70,000 judgment for contribution against defendant B (contribution based upon percentages of negligence).

Indemnification. Contribution should be distinguished from indemnification. Contribution involves the sharing of the financial burden among joint wrongdoers. Indemnification involves **recovery by one who was found liable but was not an active wrongdoer against the actual wrongdoer or against the one primarily responsible for the harm**. Thus, a retailer who incurs a judgment for breach of warranty as the result of injury sustained by the purchaser of a defective product may obtain indemnification from the manufacturer of the defective product.

The most common situation involving the action for indemnification is where the party seeking indemnification has incurred a judgment based upon derivative or vicarious liability (see below).

Thus, for example, a master who has incurred a judgment as the result of a tort committed by his servant, under the doctrine of respondeat superior, may obtain indemnification from the servant for the entire amount of the judgment incurred. The plaintiff in an action for indemnification seeks the entire amount of the judgment incurred by him; the plaintiff in an action for contribution seeks a part of the amount of the judgment incurred by him.

E.   LIMITATIONS ON LIABILITY AND SPECIAL RULES OF LIABILITY

1.   Problems Relating To "Remote" Or "Unforeseeable" Causes, "Legal" Or "Proximate" Cause, And "Superseding" Causes

Assuming that actual causation exists between the defendant's conduct and the plaintiff's harm, **no recovery will be allowed unless the defendant's act was the "proximate" (or "legal") cause of the harm to the plaintiff**. Proximate cause is an indefinite term of art, often subject to policy considerations.

For example, courts are less likely to be concerned with proximate cause in an intentional tort (as opposed to negligence) case. If a defendant intends harm, and by some action causes such harm, courts will often hold that defendant liable, no matter how distant or unlikely the harm is from the defendant's act.

Quite broadly, the area of proximate cause may be divided into two categories:

1) persons within the risk; and
2) harm within the risk.

Persons Within the Risk: Foreseeability of Risk of Harm to Plaintiff - Palsgraf v. Long Island Railroad. The concept of proximate cause with respect to persons is actually a question of **whether the defendant owed a duty to the plaintiff**. The two views relating to persons within the risk are set out in the majority and dissenting opinions of the case of Palsgraf v. Long Island Railroad, 248 N.Y. 339, 162 N.E. 99 (1928).

The problem is this: Suppose the defendant's conduct is negligent as to X (in the sense of imposing an unreasonable risk of harm upon him), but not negligent as to P (i.e., not imposing an unreasonable risk of harm upon P). If P is nonetheless injured through some fluke of circumstances, may she in effect "tack on" to the negligence against X, and establish the defendant's liability for her injuries?

Facts of Palsgraf. In Palsgraf, a man running to board the defendant's train seemed about to fall; one of the defendant's employees, attempting to push him onto the train from behind, dislodged a package from the passenger's arms. The package, unbeknownst to anyone (except perhaps the passenger) contained fireworks, which exploded when they fell. The shock of the explosion made some scales at the other end of the platform fall down, hitting the plaintiff.

Issue. It was clear from the facts of the case that, although the defendant's employee may have been negligent toward the package-carrying passenger (by pushing him), his conduct did not involve any foreseeable risk of harm to the **plaintiff,** who was standing far away. The issue was whether,

Multistate Bar Review Book 2

given the fact that the defendant had been negligent toward someone, this negligence was enough to give rise to liability to the plaintiff, injured by fluke.

Holding. The court, in a decision by Judge Cardozo, held that the defendant was **not liable.** "The conduct of the defendant's guard, if a wrong in its relation to the holder of the package, was not a wrong in its relation to the plaintiff, standing far away. Relative to her it was not negligence at all. Nothing in this situation gave notice that the fallen package had in it the potency of peril to persons thus removed. The plaintiff sues in her own right for a wrong personal to her, and not as the vicarious beneficiary of a breach of duty to another." Furthermore, generally speaking, [A] wrong is defined in terms of the natural or probable, at least when unintentional."

Since the defendant's conduct did not involve an unreasonable risk of harm to the plaintiff, and the damage to her was not foreseeable, the fact that the conduct was unjustifiably risky to someone else is irrelevant. "Proof of negligence in the air, so to speak, will not do. "

"Duty" formulation. The majority opinion phrased its rule in terms of "duty", more than "foreseeability". The question, the court said, was whether the defendants had a duty of care to the plaintiff which was violated by their acts. But this formulation simply poses the same question as to the scope of liability; if the rule is that a defendant will be liable only to a plaintiff as to whom his conduct imposed a foreseeable risk, it will also be the case that the defendant violated no duty to a plaintiff as to whom there was no forseeable risk. Phrasing the question in terms of duty does, however, have the advantage of not making the question sound like one of factual causation when it is really one of policy.

The majority opinion, written by Cardozo, C.J., in essence takes the position that for a defendant to be liable in a negligence action, his conduct must have created an **unreasonable risk of harm to the plaintiff**; it is insufficient to show that the defendant's conduct created an unreasonable risk of harm to a **third party which resulted in actual harm to the plaintiff**. "The plaintiff sues in her own right for a wrong personal to her, and not as the vicarious beneficiary of a breach of duty to another."

The **dissenting opinion**, written by Andrews, J., took the position that the plaintiff who is injured by the defendant's unreasonable act should **not** be barred from recovery **simply because the act did not, at the time of its commission, create a foreseeable risk of harm to the plaintiff.** He indicated that an unreasonable or negligent act is a wrong "not only to those who happen to be within the radius of danger, but to all who might have been there - a wrong to the public at large. Given such a negligent act, the defendant is liable to all persons proximately harmed by the act. By proximate we mean that there is a cutoff, but the cutoff is not based upon foreseeable consequences. It is based rather upon public policy; by a rough sense of justice, the law arbitrarily declines to trace a series of events beyond a certain point. It is not logic. It is practical politics."

The Andrews view would allow the jury to decide whether, from a post-event perspective, there had been a continuous and uninterrupted sequence of events harming the plaintiff. While the law in this area is not fully settled, **the majority of jurisdictions probably follow the Cardozo view requiring foreseeability of harm to the plaintiff.**

Rescue Doctrine. In Wagner v. International Railway, 232 N.Y. 176, 133 N.E. 437 (1921), the court held that a **defendant who negligently places a victim in a perilous position owes a duty to the person coming to the aid of the victim**. Thus, if the rescuer is injured in effectuating the rescue, the defendant will be liable to him as long as the rescuer exercised reasonable care in attempting the rescue.

However, most courts take into consideration the fact that the rescuer is acting under emergency circumstances. The defense of assumption of the risk is not available to the defendant. This rule is sometimes referred to as the "danger invites rescue doctrine." The doctrine applies also to the situation where the defendant negligently places himself in a perilous position, and the rescuer is injured in attempting to prevent injury to the defendant. Carney v. Buyea, 271 App. Div. 338, 65 N.Y.S.2d 902 (1946). (Defendant started her automobile and then got out and stepped in front of the automobile to remove an object in front of it. The automobile started to move. The plaintiff, a bystander, was injured when he attempted to push the defendant out of the path of the moving automobile.)

Harm Within the Risk. Once we have established that the plaintiff was a **foreseeable victim** of the defendant's conduct, the question becomes whether the defendant should be held responsible for the particular type or manner of harm to the plaintiff which resulted. While there are various theories of proximate cause of the harm, basically, jurisdictions adopt one of two general theories.

Some courts hold that the defendant is liable only for the harm that was a foreseeable consequence of his unreasonable act. Liability under this theory is confined to that resulting harm which **a reasonable man would have foreseen as a probable consequence of his act**. See Overseas Tankship (U.K.), Ltd. v. Mort's Dock and Engineering Co. [The "Wagon Mound Case"], 1 All E.R. 404 (1961), overruling Re Polemis and Furness, Withy and Co., Ltd., 3 K.B. 560 (1921). A common variant of the foreseeability test is that the defendant is liable for harm resulting from his unreasonable conduct which was foreseeable, despite the fact that the precise form in which the harm resulted could not have been foreseen. Hill v. Windsor, 118 Mass. 251 (1875).

The second general view of proximate cause is the one expressed in Dellwo v. Pearson, 259 Minn. 452, 107 N.W.2d 859 (1961). If the defendant has committed a negligent act (determined by whether his conduct created an unreasonable risk of harm), he may be liable for **any harm which follows in unbroken sequence, without an intervening efficient cause**, from the negligent act. The test is whether, in hindsight, given the events that actually occurred, it is fair and just to extend liability for all harm actually caused by the defendant's acts.

This latter view has been adopted by the **Restatement (Second) of Torts** in Restatement §435, as follows:

Foreseeability of Harm or Manner of Its Occurrence

(1) If the actor's conduct is a substantial factor in bringing about harm to another, the fact that the actor neither foresaw nor should have foreseen the extent of the harm or the manner in which it occurred does not prevent him from being liable.

(2) The actor's conduct may be held not to be a legal cause of harm to another where, after the event and looking back from the harm to the actor's negligent conduct, it appears to the court highly extraordinary that it should have brought about the harm.

Negligent Intervening Acts. The most common problem in the area of proximate cause (regardless of which general view of proximate cause is adopted), is whether the intervening negligence of a third party, which combines with the negligence of the defendant to cause the plaintiff's injury, will legally break the proximate causal connection between the defendant's negligence and the plaintiff's injury. In a "foreseeability test" jurisdiction, the defendant will be held liable for all of the consequences brought about by the combination of his negligent act and that of a third party, **if the defendant should have foreseen that his negligence would be followed by the negligence of the third party**, thereby causing additional injury to the plaintiff.

For example, in **Vataloro v. Thomas**, 262 Mass. 383, 160 N.E. 269 (1928), the court held that defendant could be held liable for the harm resulting from the negligent treatment by a physician of the injuries to the plaintiff, injuries which had originally been caused by the defendant.

On the other hand, see **McLaughlin v. Mine Safety Appliance Co.**, 11 N.Y.2d 62, 181 N.E.2d 430 (1962), where the court held that the defendant, a manufacturer of heat blocks, could not reasonably foresee that a fireman, specifically instructed by the defendant as to the proper precautions to be exercised in using the heat blocks, would totally disregard such instructions.

While ordinary intervening negligence may be foreseeable, **gross negligence will not be deemed foreseeable** unless the defendant had reason to believe, based on past experience, that the gross negligence of others would follow his acts.

Intentional Intervening Acts. While negligent intervening acts are, generally speaking, more foreseeable than intentional intervening acts, the mere fact that an intervening act is intentional, or even criminal, does not ipso facto mean that it was unforeseeable. **Brower v. New York Central & Hudson River Railroad**, 91 N.J.L. 190, 103 A. 166 (1918) (robbery); **Hines, Director General of Railroads v. Garrett**, 131 Va. 125, 108 S.E. 690 (1921) (rape); **Liberty National Life Ins. Co. v. Weldon**, 267 Ala. 171, 100 So.2d 696 (1958) (murder).

Efficient Cause. In a jurisdiction following the proximate cause theory set out in **Dellwo v. Pearson, supra** (proximate cause is determined by hindsight), the **defendant is not liable only if the second actor's conduct has become the efficient cause of the plaintiff's injury**. The efficient cause test generally will operate more strictly against the defendant than the foreseeability test.

Injury to Person or Property of Another. While a person may be liable in negligence for injury to the plaintiff's person or physical property, it is generally held that, except for wrongful death actions, **proximate cause does not extend to economic harm suffered by the plaintiff as a result of injury to another individual's person or property**.

Thus, an employer may not normally recover in negligence for injury to an employee. Chelsea Moving & Trucking Co. v. Ross Towboat Co., 280 Mass. 282, 182 N.E. 477 (1932). Nor may a person recover in negligence for lost wages against a defendant who negligently burned down the plaintiff's place of employment. Stevenson v. East Ohio Gas Co., 47 Ohio Law Abs. 586, 73 N.E.2d 200 (1946).

Nor may an insurance company recover in negligence the amount which it had paid out on a life insurance policy against the defendant who had negligently caused the death of the insured. Connecticut Mutual Life Ins. Co. v. New York, New Haven & Hartford Railroad, 25 Conn. 265 (1856). In all these situations, however, if the plaintiff could establish that the defendant acted with the intent to injure the plaintiff, recovery may be had on a theory of intentional interference with contractual or advantageous relations.

2. Claims Against Owners And Occupiers Of Land

Defect in Premises. With respect to premises, the mere existence of a slight defect (e.g., a slight ridge in a carpet) does not establish negligence, since **the appropriate standard is generally reasonable care** and not perfection. The issue is whether the defendant's conduct has created an unreasonable risk of harm.

Many factors are involved in that determination, including expense. See Beatty v. Central Iowa Railway, 58 Iowa 242, 12 N.W. 332 (1882). With respect to even ordinary defects, the **defendant is not an insurer**. He is given a reasonable opportunity to discover defects and make repairs.

With respect to foreign substances on a floor or step, it is incumbent upon the plaintiff to prove either that the defendant or his employees had actual knowledge of the presence of the foreign substance and failed to remove it, or that they had a reasonable time to discover the presence of the foreign substance and remove it, and failed to do so. Often the only evidence available to the plaintiff on the issue of the period of time that the substance was on the floor or step is the appearance of the substance (e.g., discoloration, hardness, presence of dirt on the substance, etc.). Sustaining the burden of proof in this situation is often difficult.

Duty of Owner or Possessor of Property to a Business Invitee. One who invites a business visitor to enter his premises owes to such visitor the duty of exercising reasonable care to keep the premises in a **reasonably safe condition** for the visitor's use. Thus, the invitor is under an affirmative duty to protect the invitee not only against defects known to the invitor, but also against those which the invitor could discover by the exercise of ordinary care. See Rest. 2d of Torts §343. Thus, the invitor has a duty of inspection as well as a duty to repair or warn of known defects.

A person accompanying a business invitee upon the defendant's premises will also be classified as a business invitee, even though that person has no intention of dealing with the defendant. Farrier v. Levin, 176 Cal. App.2d 791, 1 Cal. Rptr. 742 (1959). Thus, a child accompanying an adult in the defendant's store is owed a duty of ordinary care. Hostick v. Hall, 386 P.2d 758 (Okla. 1963).

There is a split regarding whether persons coming into business establishments for purposes which do not directly benefit the owner should be classified as business invitees or licensees. In Argus v. Michler, 349 S.W.2d 389 (Mo. App. 1961), the court held that a person coming into a gasoline station solely for the purpose of using the telephone was not a business invitee, since the owner derived no profit from the telephone's use.

Many courts have taken a contrary position, holding that potential profit may accrue to such business owners by encouraging or allowing people to come into the establishment for such purposes (e.g., goodwill) and thus the duty of ordinary care is owed. See Renfro Drug Co. v. Lewis, 149 Tex. 507, 235 S.W.2d 609, 23 A.L.R.2d 1114 (1951) (short-cut passageway through the defendant's store - ordinary care required). The Restatement advocates the latter approach. Restatement (Second) of Torts §332, comment f.

Liability for Obvious Conditions. Where the defective or dangerous condition is obvious to the business invitee, recovery will not ordinarily be allowed for resultant injury. This result is based upon a theory either that the plaintiff-invitee assumed the risk or that the obviousness of the condition was the equivalent of a warning by the defendant-invitor, and thus no duty was breached. See Paubel v. Hitz, 339 Mo. 274, 96 S.W.2d 369 (1936). For a contrary result, however, see Pribble v. Safeway Stores Inc., 249 Or. 184, 437 P.2d 745 (1968), holding that the owner of a store may be liable despite the customer's knowledge of the slippery floor.

Areas to Which Duty Extends. The duty of ordinary care owed to a business invitee does not extend to areas of the defendant's premises with respect to which the invitee has not been invited. Paris v. Howard D. Johnson Co., 340 Mass. 739, 166 N.E.2d 735 (1960) (customer entering restaurant through service door rather than regular door for customers was owed only the duty of refraining from willful and wanton conduct). If a customer is invited or encouraged to enter an unusual part of the premises, as for example, the storeroom, he will remain a business invitee. Bullock v. Safeway Stores, 236 F.2d 29 (8th Cir. 1956) (back room).

Duty to Prevent Injury to Invitee by Third Parties. In some cases, the duty of a business invitor extends to using reasonable care to prevent injury to the business invitee by third persons, whether the acts of the third person are accidental, negligent, or intentional.

Policemen and Firemen. Most states treat policemen and firemen as licensees rather than business invitees. See Mulcrone v. Wagner, 212 Minn. 478, 4 N.W.2d 97 (1942). This rule is based upon the idea that policemen and firemen are likely to enter the premises at unforeseeable times and in unforeseeable ways.

Some states have held that they are invitees when they enter under the same circumstances as other members of the public and to a part of the premises that is normally open to the public. Meiers v. Fred Koch Brewery, 229 N.Y. 10, 127 N.E. 491 (1920). Several cases have held that firemen and policemen are to be treated in all respects as business invitees, and that the unusual aspects of the time and location of their entry upon the premises merely go to the issue of foreseeability. Dini v. Naiditch, 20 Ill.2d 406, 170 N.E.2d 881 (1960).

Duty of Owner or Possessor of Property to a Social Guest or Licensee. Unlike the duty owed to the business invitee to maintain the premises in a reasonably safe condition, generally the duty owed to a social guest or licensee is to **make reasonably safe those conditions on the premises which are known by the owner or occupier to be defective, or to give a warning** to the guest or licensee of the condition. The owner or occupier is not under a duty to such persons to inspect the premises for unknown perils. Rushton v. Winters, 331 Pa. 78, 200 A. 60 (1938).

Most states hold that with respect to active conduct, the duty to a licensee or social guest is ordinary care. Restatement (Second) of Torts §341. To create liability, the active negligence must be more than the prior creation of the defective condition. Kaslo v. Hahn, 36 Wis.2d 87, 153 N.W.2d 33 (1967).

Duty of Owner or Possessor of Property to a Trespasser. The owner or possessor of property is generally held to be under **no duty** to a trespasser to exercise reasonable care to put his land in safe condition. Restatement (Second) of Torts §333. Some states have abolished the concept of categories, holding that the owner or occupier of premises has a duty to maintain the premises in a reasonably safe condition for all persons coming upon the premises. See Rowland v. Christian, 69 Cal.2d 108, 70 Cal. Rptr. 97, 443 P.2d 561 (1968); Barker v. Parnossa, Inc., 39 N.Y.2d 926, 352 N.E.2d 880 (1976).

Some states impose a duty of ordinary care to all lawful visitors on the property. Poulin v. Colby College, 402 A.2d 846 (Me. 1979). These states do not distinguish between categories of licensees and invitees, but do hold that a lesser duty is owed to a trespasser. Jurisdictions differ in whether the lesser duty is to avoid gross negligence or to avoid willful and wanton conduct.

There are, in either event, certain exceptions to this general rule discussed below:

Infant Trespassers and The Attractive Nuisance Doctrine. Practically all jurisdictions today have established a special rule for infant trespassers (often called the attractive nuisance doctrine); in most instances, the states have adopted the rule set out in the Restatement (Second) of Torts §339. This section provides that a possessor of land is subject to liability for physical harm to children trespassing thereon caused by an artificial condition upon the land if:

1) the possessor **knows or has reason to know that children are likely to trespass** in the location of the danger; and
2) the possessor knows or has reason to know that the **condition will involve an unreasonable risk of death or serious bodily harm** to such children; and
3) the children **because of their youth** do not discover the condition or realize the risk involved; and
4) the utility to the possessor of maintaining the condition and the burden of eliminating the danger are slight as compared with the risk to children involved; and
5) the possessor **fails to exercise reasonable care** to eliminate the danger or otherwise to protect the children.

Despite the label "attractive nuisance," it is not necessary that the child realized its danger. While only a few jurisdictions have established an arbitrary age limit, most cases applying the attractive nuisance doctrine have involved children under twelve. Courts have refused to apply the attractive nuisance doctrine to natural conditions; see e.g., Loney v. McPhillips, 521 P.2d 340 (Or. 1974) (wind-swept ocean cave dangerous at high tide).

Deceptive Appearances. A landowner may be liable for breach of ordinary care to one not permitted on the land where the plaintiff was misled by deceptive appearances to believe the property was public property. Where premises adjoining a public way are so connected with the public way as to indicate a public use, the property owner must use reasonable care to see that there is no danger to

Multistate Bar Review Book 2

those who are misled into using it. Southern v. Cowan Stone Co., 188 Tenn. 576, 221 S.W.2d 809 (1949).

Frequent Trespassers. Where the defendant knows that members of the public are in the habit of trespassing upon his land with great frequency, he is under a duty of reasonable care to take steps to prevent injury to them from known dangers or to warn the public of such dangers. See Clark v. Longview Public Service Co., 143 Wash. 319, 255 P. 380 (1927); Restatement (Second) of Torts §334.

Discovered Trespassers. A great majority of the courts hold that once the presence of a trespasser is discovered, even simply as a member of a large crowd, there is then the duty to use ordinary care to avoid injury to him, just as in the case of any other person. Herrick v. Wixom, 121 Mich. 384, 80 N.W. 117, aff'd, 81 N.W. 333 (1899) (boy who crawled under a circus tent and became a member of a large crowd was owed the same duty of care as was owed to persons who paid to get into the circus, namely, ordinary care).

3. Claims For Mental Distress Not Arising From Physical Harm; Other Intangible Injuries

If Defendant causes an actual **physical impact** to the plaintiff, Defendant is liable not only for the physical consequences of that act but also for all of the **emotional** or mental **suffering** which flows naturally from it. Such mental-suffering damages are called "parasitic" because they attach to the physical injury. But where there has been no physical impact or direct physical injury to Plaintiff, courts limit Plaintiff's right to recover for mental suffering.

Where there is not only no impact, but **no physical symptoms** of the emotional distress at all, the majority of states **deny recovery.**

> Example: Defendant narrowly misses running over Plaintiff. No one is hurt. P has no physical symptoms, but is distraught for weeks. Few if any courts will allow P to recover for her emotional distress.

Exceptions. Some courts recognize an exception to this rule in special circumstances, such as the negligence by telegraph companies in wording messages, and by funeral homes in handling corpses.

The general rule means that if P, by virtue of his exposure to a certain substance, suffers an increased likelihood of a particular disease, P may generally not recover for the purely emotional harm of being at risk.

Remember that the general rule applies only to **negligent** conduct. If the defendant's conduct is intentional or willful, the plaintiff may recover for purely emotional harm with no physical symptoms, by use of the tort of intentional infliction of emotional distress, *supra.*

Physical Injury Without Impact. Nearly all courts allow recovery where the negligent act:

1) physically endangers the plaintiff;
2) does not result in physical impact on the plaintiff; and
3) causes the plaintiff to suffer emotional distress that has **physical consequences.**

> Example: Defendant narrowly avoids running over plaintiff and plaintiff is thereby so frightened that she suffers a miscarriage, plaintiff may recover.

Fear for Others' Safety. If Plaintiff suffers purely emotional distress (without physical consequences), and Plaintiff's distress is due solely to fear or grief about the danger or harm to third persons, courts are split. If Plaintiff was in the **"zone of danger"** (i.e., physically endangered but not struck), nearly all courts allow her to recover for emotional distress due to another person's plight.

> Example: Defendant narrowly avoids running over Plaintiff, and in fact runs over Plaintiff's child. Most courts will allow Plaintiff to recover for her emotional distress at seeing her child injured.

Abandonment of zone requirement. A number of states - probably still a minority have abandoned the "zone of danger" requirement. In these courts, so long as Plaintiff **observes** the danger or injury to X, and X is a **close relative** of Plaintiff, Plaintiff may recover. (Example: Plaintiff is on the sidewalk when Defendant runs over Plaintiff's son. In a court which has abandoned the "zone of danger" requirement, Plaintiff will be able to recover for his emotional distress at seeing his son injured, even though Plaintiff himself was never in physical danger.)

4.   Claims For Pure Economic Loss

Problems of pure economic loss arise where a defendant (D) behaves negligently towards X, in a way that causes X personal injury or property damage. D's conduct also injures Plaintiff (P), but P's only loss is **economic,** not personal injury or property damage. May P recover in tort from D for those economic damages?

If D behaves negligently towards P, and causes P both personal injury and economic loss, all courts agree (and have always agreed) that P, in addition to recovering for his personal injury, may **"tack on" his intangible economic harm as an additional element of damages.**

> Example: P owns a retail store, which he personally operates. P is injured by the negligence of D, a careless driver who hits P while P is walking. P can of course recover damages for his physical harm (e.g., his medical bills plus pain and suffering). Once P shows that he has suffered physical harm, he will be permitted to "tack on," as an additional element of damages, his loss of profits from being unable to operate the store. In other words, P's suffering of physical harm qualifies him to recover for the full range of damages which he has suffered, including intangible economic ones.

Property Damage. Similarly, if P suffers property damage (even if he does not suffer personal injury), this property damage will qualify him to tack on intangible economic loss as well. Thus suppose, on the facts of the above example, that P's car was struck by D's car, and that as a result: (1) P's car was damaged; (2) P himself was not physically injured; and (3) P lost two days of profits at the store because he could not commute to the store. Once P showed that he suffered direct property damage from P's negligence, all courts would allow him to recover his loss-of-business damages, even though those are purely intangible economic losses.

© 1995-2018 Celebration Bar Review, LLC   **Multistate Bar Review Book 2**

156

Traditional Rule Disallows Pure Economic Losses to Third Party. Now, let's return to the three-party situation, in which D's negligence causes physical injury or property damage to X, but only economic loss to P. The traditional rule in this situation is that P may not recover anything for his economic losses, since he has not suffered any personal injury or property damage. This is true even though D is clearly a tortfeasor (vis-à-vis X), and even though D's negligence has quite clearly, and foreseeably, brought about the injuries to P.

> Example: Defendant (a ship, the Donau Maru) spills fuel oil into Boston Harbor. The spill damages a dock owned by X. P (owner of a different ship, the Tamara) is thus prevented from docking at a nearby berth. P's ship has to discharge her cargo at another pier, thereby incurring significant extra labor and docking costs. P sues D to recover these economic losses. The court rules for the defendant, stating:. "Controlling case law denies that a plaintiff can recover damages for negligently caused financial harm, even when foreseeable, except in special circumstances. There is present here neither the most common such special circumstance physical injury to the plaintiffs or to their property – nor any other special feature that would permit recovery. . . . " Barber Lines AIS v. M/V Donau Maru, 764 F.2d 50 (Ist Cir. 1985).

The reason for this restrictive rule is the fear of open-ended liability. Allowing liability for economic loss unaccompanied by physical injury or property damage would result in "liability in an indeterminant amount for an indeterminant time to an indeterminant class." **Ultramares Corp. v. Touch**, 174 N.E. 441 (N.Y. 1931) (an accountant's liability case). For instance, "the typical downtown auto accident, that harms a few persons physically and physically damages the property of several others, may well cause financial harm (e.g., through delay) to a vast number of potential plaintiffs." **Barber Lines, supra.**

Foreseeability is really not a very good tool for handling cases like these. It is foreseeable that if the utility cuts off power to a plant, every worker at the plant is likely to lose wages. This is an identifiable class of people, and we don't have to worry much about fraudulent or hard-to-verify claims.

So rather than rely on proximate cause/foreseeability as a way to keep claims from getting out of hand, the common law has traditionally used a blanket prohibition - no recovery for economic loss unaccompanied by physical injury or property damage together with a few exceptions for special kinds of situations where we don't have to worry about unduly widespread liability (e.g., negligent misstatements about financial matters, such as by accountants, when these cause financial harm to a third party who could be expected to rely on them, such as a bank or supplier.)

Modern Approach. Since the early 1980s the traditional rule denying recovery has been significantly weakened. Even though most recent decisions have probably **abandoned the blanket no-liability rule**, there has not emerged a single predominant method for determining which claims should and should not be allowed. The foreseeability of the injury, and the number of plaintiffs that would be permitted to sue if recovery were allowed, are clearly two important factors. The moral blameworthiness of the defendant also seems to be significant. Courts that have retreated from this position have adopted various approaches including the following:

> A defendant owes a duty of care to take reasonable measures to avoid the risk of causing economic damages, aside from physical injury, to particular plaintiffs or plaintiffs comprising an identifiable class **[who] defendant knows or has reason to know are likely to suffer such damages from its conduct**. An "identifiable class," however, is not simply a "foreseeable class." "An identifiable class of plaintiffs must be particularly foreseeable in terms of the type of persons or entities comprising the class, the certainty or predictability of their presence, the approximate numbers of those in the class, as well as the type of economic expectations disrupted." People Express Airlines, Inc. v. Consolidated Rail Corp., 495 A.2d 107 (N.J. 1985). (In this case a railroad, negligently performed the "coupling" of one rail car with another, allowing ethylene oxide to escape and to ignite. Municipal authorities, responding to the fire, evacuate an area within a one-mile radius surrounding the fire. The plaintiff, an airline whose airport operations are within the evacuated zone, is forced to close for 12 hours and loses business. P sues D for these lost-business damages.)

Another approach can be illustrated as follows:

> **Where a special relationship exists between the parties, a plaintiff may recover for loss of expected economic advantage through the negligent performance of a contract although the parties were not in contractual privity** ...... Among the factors that the court should consider in determining whether the requisite "special relationship" exists between the parties, are (1) the extent to which the transaction was intended to affect the plaintiff, (2) the foreseeability of harm to the plaintiff, and (3) the moral blame attached to the defendant's conduct. Applying these criteria to these facts, a duty was owed by D to P. JAire Corp. v. Gregory, 598 P.2d 60 (Cal. 1979). (In this case, P, the operator of a restaurant, rents its premises from X, a county government. X enters into a contract with D, a general contractor, whereby D is to make improvements to the premises, including renovation of the heating and air-conditioning systems. D performs the work negligently and with undue slowness. P is unable to operate the restaurant for some time, and suffers lost profits from lost business. P sues D for negligence.)

F.   LIABILITY FOR ACTS OF OTHERS

A defendant may be liable under some circumstances for a tort committed by another person. Such **vicarious liability** is generally based upon a relationship existing between the defendant and the person committing the tort, **wherein the negligence of the actor is imputed to the defendant**. The most common situation involving vicarious liability is the liability of a master for the torts of his servant under the doctrine of respondeat superior.

There is under the common law no vicarious liability of a parent for the torts of the child based solely upon that relationship; nor is there any vicarious liability imposed upon one spouse for the torts of the other spouse based solely upon the marital relationship.

1.   Employees And Other Agents

Master and Servant Relationship. A master is vicariously liable for the torts of his servant who is acting within the scope of his employment. Thus, the issue of vicarious liability of a master generally involves three questions:

    1)   was the actor a servant or an independent contractor;
    2)   did the act constitute a tort to the plaintiff; and
    3)   did the actor commit the tort while acting within the scope of his employment?

Right of Control. The test of the existence of a master and servant relationship is whether, with respect to the physical conduct of the employee and the performance of his service, he is subject to the **employer's control or right of control**. Throop v. F.E. Young & Co., 94 Ariz. 146, 382 P.2d 560 (1963). It is not necessary that there be any actual control by the alleged master; the **right to control** is sufficient. However, the right to control must not merely relate to the end result sought; it must also relate to the **manner and means of bringing about that end result**. Khoury v. Edison Illuminating Company, 265 Mass. 236, 164 N.E. 77 (1928).

An independent contractor is a person who contracts with another to do something for him, but who is not controlled by the other nor subject to the other's right to control with respect to his physical conduct in the performance of the undertaking. Restatement (Second) of Agency, § 2.

Agents. An agent is a person retained by another (called a principal) **to deal with third parties contractually on behalf of the principal**. An agent may be either a servant or an independent contractor. An agent who is not subject to control as to the manner in which he performs the acts that constitute the execution of his agency is not a servant, and thus the principal is not liable for incidental acts of negligence in the performance of the agent's duties. Throop v. F.E. Young & Co., supra.

Factors that Indicate a Right of Control. On the issue of control, there are certain factors which should be considered:

1) the extent of control which, by the agreement, the master may exercise over the details of the work;
2) whether or not the person employed is engaged in a distinct occupation or business;
3) the kind of occupation, with reference to whether, in the locality, the work is usually done under the direction of the employer or by a specialist without supervision;
4) the skill required in the particular occupation;
5) whether the employer or the workman supplies the instrumentalities, tools, and the place of work for the person doing the work;
6) the length of time for which the person is employed;
7) the method of payment, whether by the time or by the job;
8) whether or not the work is a part of the regular business of the employer; and
9) whether or not the parties believe they are creating the relation of master and servant. Restatement (Second) of Agency, § 220.

Control of General Activities. A master-servant relationship may be found despite the fact that the negligent employee at the time of the accident was using his own automobile and could choose his own route and speed. If there is a right to control the employee's general activities, he is a servant, even though the master may not have the right to control the details of the operation of the car when the servant is carrying out an errand for his master. Konick v. Berke, Moore & Co., 355 Mass. 463, 245 N.E.2d 750 (1969).

Borrowed Servants. In order to establish a master-servant relationship, it is not necessary to prove that the servant was being paid by the master. Thus, under the borrowed servant rule, the defendant may be responsible for the servant's tort where the servant was doing the work of the defendant under the defendant's control, **even though the servant was being paid by a third party**. Nepstad v. Lambert, 235 Minn. 1, 50 N.W.2d 614 (1951). In fact, it is possible that two masters may be liable for the tort of the borrowed servant, the one immediately using the services of the borrowed servant, and the one paying the servant for those services.

Scope of Employment. The master is liable for the torts of the servant committed while acting within the scope of his employment. Scope of employment refers to "those acts which are so closely connected with what the servant was employed to do, and so fairly and reasonably incidental to it, that they may be regarded as **methods,** even though quite improper ones, of **carrying out the objectives of the employment**." See Prosser & Keeton on Torts, 502 (5th ed. 1984).

Often, questions which involve the issue of whether a tort was committed within the scope of the servant's employment revolve around a servant in transit. The general rule, applicable to almost all situations, is that an employee traveling to or from work is not within the scope of the employment. However, an employee whose work involves traveling for the company is within the scope of the employment while in transit after starting work. The following rules will help to clarify the factual issues.

Advancing Employer's Business. If the servant's tortious conduct relates to the advancing of his master's business, the master is liable even though such conduct may be of a willful or malicious nature. Houston Transit Co. v. Felder, 146 Tex. 428, 208 S.W.2d 880 (1948). The master cannot escape liability by showing that he did not condone the servant's act, or even that he had ordered the servant not to act in that manner. Grant v. Singer Manufacturing Co., 190 Mass. 489, 77 N.E. 480 (1906).

Frolic and Detour. A master will not be held liable for the negligence of his servant where the servant, at the time of the accident, had **substantially deviated from his authorized route**. In such situations it is said that the servant was on a "frolic" of his own, and not within the scope of his employment. Where, however, the "detour" is slight, the courts generally have taken the position that the master must take the risk that an accident may occur while the servant is on a detour which is to be reasonably foreseen. Such slight deviations have been referred to as being within the permissible "zone" of deviation, in the sense that they should be reasonably expected by the master. Kohlman v. Hyland, 54 N.D. 710, 210 N.W. 643 (1926).

Sub-employees. Where there is neither express nor implied authority given a servant to employ another to perform or to assist him in the performance of his work, or subsequent ratification by his employer of such employment, the relation of master and servant does not exist between the employer and one so employed by his servant; and the employer, under the doctrine of respondeat superior, is not liable for the negligent acts of one so employed by his servant. See Potter v. Golden Rule Grocery Co., 169 Tenn. 240, 84 S.W.2d 364 (1935). A master may be liable, however, if his servant entrusts another with an instrumentality where the servant should realize that there is an undue risk that such person will harm others by its management.

> Example: A master may be liable for the negligence of the servant in permitting a thirteen-year-old boy to drive a truck. It is the negligence of the servant in allowing the thirteen-year-old boy to drive the truck, rather than the negligence of the thirteen-year-old operator, that is imputed to the master. Id.

Liability for Negligent Hiring. Most courts have recognized negligent hiring or retention of an employee as an independent, non-agency basis of liability for the employer. Thus, even where liability cannot be based on respondeat superior because the employee acted outside the scope of his employment, the **employer may be liable for his own negligence in hiring a dangerous employee and placing him in a position to commit harm.** Thus, in Ponticas v. K.M.S. Investments, 331 N.W.2d 907 (Minn. 1983), an employer was found liable for hiring as an apartment manager a man with a criminal record who later raped a resident of the apartment complex.

Joint Enterprise. Just as partners are liable for the torts of each other while acting for the partnership business, **vicarious liability exists among members of a joint enterprise for torts committed in carrying out the purposes of the enterprise.** A joint enterprise is like a partnership, except that it is for a limited period of time and for a limited purpose.

While there are a minority of cases applying vicarious liability on a joint enterprise theory where the purpose of the association was purely social **most states limit the application of the doctrine to situations where the association is for a business or commercial purpose**. See Edlebeck v. Hooten, 20 Wis.2d 83, 121 N.W.2d 240 (1963).

A theory of joint enterprise or concert of action may be used to impose collective liability on a group of defendants where commission of a tort can be proven but it cannot be established which individual defendant caused the plaintiffs injury (e.g., which company's drug had been ingested by each of the plaintiffs' mothers during pregnancy). Payton v. Abbott Labs, 512 F. Supp. 1031 (D. Mass. 1981). Although there is disagreement as to whether an implied agreement must be shown or whether mere parallel activity is sufficient, an express agreement among the manufacturers to market a drug without adequate testing need not be shown. Bichler v. Lilly & Co., 55 N.Y.2d 571, 436 N.E.2d 182 (1982).

Other theories of liability have been utilized by some courts. **"Enterprise liability,"** which is joint and several, may be available as a theory where the plaintiffs are unable to identify the manufacturers specifically at fault but the defendants comprise virtually the entire manufacturing industry for that product, and the product was manufactured to meet industry-wide safety standards set by their own trade association. "Market share liability" limits the individual defendant's liability to that percentage of the plaintiffs injuries corresponding to its percentage share of the market at the time of the injury. See Martin v. Abbott Labs, 102 Wash.2d 581, 689 P.2d 368 (1984); Sindell v. Abbott Labs, 26 Cal.3d 588, 607 P.2d 924 (1980).

Automobiles: Nonliability of Owner for Driver's Negligence. Generally, in the absence of a statute to the contrary, the owner of a motor vehicle is not liable for the negligence of a person who borrows the automobile for his own purposes, on the basis that the negligence of a bailee is not imputed to the bailor. If the bailee is using the automobile on an errand for the bailor, then vicarious liability may attach on a respondeat superior theory.

Some states have enacted statutes (often referred to as consent statutes), whereby the owner of a motor vehicle is held liable for the negligence of a bailee up to a certain amount, on the basis that the owner is in a position to obtain liability insurance to protect himself. Such statutes have been held to replace the family purpose doctrine (see infra). Jacobsen v. Dailey, 228 Minn. 201, 36 N.W.2d 711 (1949). They impute negligence only one way - that is, for the purpose of imposing liability on the owner to a third person. They have been interpreted as not imputing negligence to the owner for the purpose of contributory negligence.

Where, for example, the owner sues another person to recover for damages to the owner's vehicle, the bailee's negligence is not attributed to the owner. See McMartin v. Saemisch, 254 Iowa 45, 116 N.W.2d 491 (1962).

Negligent Entrustment of Automobile. If the owner of an automobile entrusts the vehicle to an unfit person, he may be held liable for resulting injury if he knew of the operator's unfitness or was in possession of knowledge from which he should have known. Liability here, however, is not based upon a theory of imputed negligence. It is based upon the owner's actual negligence in entrusting the vehicle to an unfit person. The most obvious situation involving such liability is where the owner of the vehicle allows it to be operated by a person known to the owner to be intoxicated.

Owner's Presence in Automobile. Where an owner is present in an automobile, jurisdictions differ on whether the operator's negligence is imputed to the owner. If, prior to the accident, the operator was driving in a negligent or reckless manner, most states would agree that the owner is liable. As owner of the vehicle, he had the duty not to allow it to be driven in a negligent or reckless manner. See **Wheeler v. Darmochwat**, 280 Mass. 553, 183 N.E. 55 (1932). Liability in such a case is not, however, vicarious. The defendant-owner is being held liable for actual negligence in allowing his vehicle to be driven in a negligent or reckless manner. Most states hold that mere presence alone is insufficient to fasten liability upon the owner. See **Sackett v. Haeckel**, 249 Minn. 290, 81 N.W.2d 833 (1957); **Darman v. Zilch**, 56 R.I. 413, 186 A. 21 (1936). Where there has been no such pattern of conduct, a few states still hold that the mere presence of the owner in the vehicle is sufficient to fasten liability upon him for the negligence of the operator. See **Sutton v. Inland Construction Co.**, 144 Neb. 721, 14 N.W.2d 387 (1944).

Family Purpose Doctrine. Under the family purpose doctrine, the owner of the vehicle is liable for the negligent operation of the vehicle by members of his family, relative to any family purpose. A family purpose will include all normal family activities, including the mere driving for pleasure on the part of one of the family members. **Harinon v. Haas**, 61 N.D. 772, 241 N.W. 70 (1932).

Liability of Parents for Conduct of Their Children. Under the common law, parents are **not vicariously liable for the torts of their children**. **Ellis v. DAngelo**, 116 Cal. App.2d 310, 253 P.2d 675 (1953). However, a parent may be held liable for injury caused by a child where the parent has allowed the child to use a dangerous instrumentality which caused injury to the plaintiff, or where the parent has failed to take corrective measures to restrain a child from committing certain harmful conduct where the parent knew or should have known of the child's propensity for such conduct. **Cardwell v. Zaher**, 344 Mass. 590, 183 N.E.2d 706 (1962). This is not, however, vicarious liability. Liability in these cases is based upon the actual negligence of the parents.

2.   Independent Contractors And Nondelegable Duties

The general rule is that **an employer is not liable for the torts of an independent contractor**. This is based on the idea that the employer has **no right to control the activities of the independent contractor**. There are, however, a few exceptions to this general rule. Case law and statutes have recognized certain situations where an employer is said to have a **nondelegable duty**, and will thus be held liable for the negligence of even an independent contractor in carrying out that duty.

Following are some examples of nondelegable duties:

1) The duty of a municipality to keep the streets in a reasonable state of repair cannot normally be delegated to an independent contractor. **City of Baltimore v. Leonard**, 129 Md. 621, 99 A. 891 (1917).
2) Likewise, the duty of a landlord to maintain common passageways cannot be so delegated. **Brown v. George Pepperdine Foundation**, 23 Cal.2d 256, 143 P.2d 929 (1943).
3) The duty of a business invitor to business invitees to keep the premises in a reasonably safe condition cannot be delegated. **Besner v. Central Trust Company of New York**, 230 N.Y. 357, 130 N.E. 577 (1921).
4) Also, an employer cannot remove from himself the potential liability to others in carrying out inherently dangerous activities by employing an independent contractor to carry out such activities. **Id**.

G. DEFENSES

1. Contributory Fault: Including Common Law Contributory Negligence And Last Clear Chance, And The Various Forms Of Comparative Negligence

The two substantive defenses to a negligence action are contributory negligence and assumption of the risk. In a minority of jurisdictions today, both defenses, if sustained, are complete defenses.

a. Contributory Negligence

The essence of the defense of contributory negligence is that **a plaintiff who is negligent (in the sense of not taking reasonable care to protect his own safety), and whose negligence contributes proximately to his injuries, is totally barred from recovery.** The defense is a complete one - it shifts the loss totally from the defendant to the plaintiff, even if the plaintiff's departure from reasonable care was much less marked than that of the defendant. Rest. 2d, §467.

The most common rationale supporting the contributory negligence defense is that where the plaintiff's negligence has contributed to his injuries, it has become the proximate cause of those injuries, and the defendant's conduct is no longer a proximate cause. However, this theory is not at all in accord with the general rules of proximate cause we examined previously, insofar as those general rules often allow for several distinct proximate causes of a single result.

Burden of Pleading and Proof. In all states which employ contributory negligence, the defendant must specifically plead contributory negligence as a defense. Furthermore, she must bear the burden of proof on it; thus if there is no evidence at all (or evenly weighted evidence on both sides) as to the existence of contributory negligence, the defense does not apply.

Standard of Care. The plaintiff is held to essentially the same standard of care as the defendant, i.e., the care of a **"reasonable person under like circumstances."** Rest. 2d, §464. However, the care a reasonable person will exercise to protect his own safety may in some circumstances be less than he will use to protect others. For instance, the Restatement suggests that a motorist driving with a passenger, if he allows himself to be distracted by a call from a friend on the sidewalk, may be negligent as to his passenger, but not contributorily negligent with respect to his own safety.

Child Plaintiffs. Where the plaintiff is a child, the standard of care to which he is held is that of a **reasonable child with similar age, intelligence and experience**. This is, in essence, the same "subjective" standard as is applied where the child is a defendant.

Insane or Mentally Deficient Plaintiffs. Where the defendant is an insane or mentally deficient adult, courts are split as to whether he should be held to the standard of care of the ordinary reasonable adult. Where such a person is a plaintiff, courts have generally been somewhat more willing to judge him by a subjective standard (i.e. one taking into account his shortcomings); they have probably done so out of a general sense that where he has hurt only himself, he should be judged less harshly.

Jury Issue. In any event, the issue of what constitutes reasonable care on the part of the plaintiff is left to the jury in all but a very few cases.

Proximate Cause. The contributory negligence defense only applies where the **plaintiff's negligence contributes proximately to his injuries**. In general, the rules for determining actual and proximate causation are the same as those discussed previously in the context of defendants' conduct. Thus the plaintiff's negligence must, for one thing, be a **"cause in fact"** of his harm. This means that it must be either a "but for" cause of that harm, or a "substantial factor" in it. For instance, if the defendant starts a fire that burns down the plaintiff's house, the fact that the plaintiff has thrown a match into the flame will not constitute contributory negligence, since the match is not a "substantial factor."

Same Result, Different Risk. There is, however, one important respect in which proximate cause is construed more narrowly in the case of contributory negligence than in the case of defendant's negligence. Where the plaintiff's act is negligent as to his own safety because it threatens a particular harm in a particular manner, and the harm occurs in some other manner, the plaintiff's conduct is usually held not to be the proximate cause of the harm. See Rest. 2d, §468.

> Example: D Co. loads and unloads its trucks in a public alley. D warns P that because of this activity, the alley is dangerous, and that he should keep out. P goes into the alley anyway, and is hit by a railroad car that gets loose from a siding negligently maintained by D. P's negligence is not the proximate cause of his own injuries, because, although the risk that made his conduct negligent was the risk of being run down, this harm came to pass in a different way from the threatened one (i.e., railroad car rather than truck). See Rest. 2d, §468, Illustr. 1.

Avoidable Consequences. The defense of contributory negligence must be distinguished from that of avoidable consequences. The latter is generally held to apply only to conduct by the plaintiff after the accident which unreasonably fails to mitigate his damages. Contributory negligence, on the other hand, applies to the plaintiff's conduct prior to the accident. Hence, although both the doctrines of contributory negligence and avoidable consequences rest on the policy of requiring the plaintiff to exercise proper care to protect himself, the rule of avoidable consequences is usually held to come into play only after a legal wrong has occurred but while some damages can still be averted.

Seat Belt Defense. Perhaps the most interesting context in which the apportionment issue has arisen is that of the "seat belt defense." In this defense, the defendant argues that the plaintiff's injuries from a car accident could have been reduced or entirely avoided had the plaintiff worn a seat belt. An increasing number of states - though probably not yet a majority - reduce the plaintiff's damages in some way to reflect the fact that the plaintiff's injuries would have been less if he had worn a seat belt

Excessive Speed. A similar apportionment issue is presented by accidents in which the plaintiff's car is traveling at an excessive speed. If the speed has not increased the risk of the accident, but does increase the damage which results to the plaintiff from it, what is the consequence? Again, as with seat belts, some courts have tried to apportion the damage, and others have not.

Conscious Exposure to Danger. One way in which the plaintiff may fail to use due care for his own safety is if he consciously puts himself in a position of unreasonable danger (as opposed to merely unwittingly and "casually" doing so.) For instance, one who agrees to be a passenger in a car driven by a person he knows to be drunk may be contributorily negligent. Such conscious exposure to risk also usually gives rise to the defense of "assumption of risk," discussed infra.

Claims Against Which Defense of Contributory Negligence is not Usable. The contributory negligence defense, based as it is upon general negligence principles, may be used as a bar only to a claim that is itself based on negligence. Thus, it may not be used in the following circumstances:

1) **Intentional torts.** The defense may not be used where the plaintiff's claim is for an intentional tort.

2) **Willful and wanton tort.** Similarly, if the defendant's conduct is found to have been willful and wanton" or "reckless," the contributory negligence defense will not be allowed. (But if the defendant's negligence is merely "gross" (i.e., differing in degree from that of the plaintiff, but not in kind), contributory negligence will be allowed. Obviously it may sometimes be hard to distinguish between negligence that is merely "gross", and that which is "willful." But the idea is that the latter applies to conduct by the defendant which disregards a conscious risk.)

3) **Strict liability.** See infra.

4) **Negligence per se.** Contributory negligence can generally be asserted as a defense even to the defendant's "negligence per se". i.e., his negligence based on a statutory violation. (Exceptions where responsibility placed on defendant: But there are some statutes which are enacted solely for the purpose of protecting a class of which the plaintiff is a member, and which show an intent to place all responsibility for violations upon the defendant. Where the plaintiff shows a violation of such a statute, contributory negligence may not be asserted as a defense.)

> Examples: One kind of "special protection" statutes are child labor laws; an employer who hires a child under the legal age may not assert contributory negligence if child is injured. A statute prohibiting the sale of guns to minors might also fall in this category, as do many statutes whose purpose is to protect employees against occupational hazards.

Last Clear Chance. Most states mitigated the harshness of the doctrine of contributory negligence as a complete bar to recovery by the so-called "last clear chance" rule. If the plaintiff is successful in establishing that **the defendant had the last clear chance to avoid injury to the plaintiff, the plaintiff will have a full recovery despite his own contributory negligence**.

While there is some difference of opinion as to what the plaintiff may establish to invoke successfully the last clear chance doctrine, most jurisdictions agree that the plaintiff must show:

1) that the defendant is aware of the plaintiff's presence;

2) that he is also aware of the plaintiff's ignorance of his peril or of his inability to save himself; and

3) that the defendant may then in due care act to avoid injury.

Clark v. Boston & Maine Railroad, 87 N.H. 434, 182 A. 175 (1935).

Some jurisdictions have viewed "last clear chance" as merely an application of the requirement that for the plaintiff's negligence to operate as contributory negligence, it must be a proximate cause of the plaintiff's injury. See Wall v. King, 280 Mass. 577, 182 N.E. 855 (1932).

Multistate Bar Review Book 2

In several jurisdictions which enacted comparative negligence statutes, the courts have held that the last clear chance rule was no longer an appropriate doctrine. See Cushman v. Perkins, 245 A.2d 846 (Me. 1968). This is based upon the idea that the last clear chance doctrine was designed to mitigate the harshness of the doctrine of contributory negligence as a complete defense, and since comparative negligence does away with this harshness, the last clear chance doctrine is no longer appropriate.

Imputed Negligence. Except in cases of vicarious liability (discussed supra), the general rule is that **the negligence of one party cannot be attributed to another.** Thus, the contributory negligence of a driver cannot be raised by a negligent third party to bar an action by a passenger in the driver's car. Likewise, the negligent supervision of parents will not act to bar a suit by their child to recover for harm resulting from the negligence of a third party, and the negligence of the plaintiff's spouse will not defeat the plaintiff's cause of action against a third party. The one exception to this rule is that the negligence of the deceased will bar (or reduce) a wrongful death recovery by the decedent's estate.

b.   Comparative Negligence

The great majority of jurisdictions have adopted some form of comparative negligence. The effect of comparative negligence is to abolish the doctrine that plaintiff's contributory negligence operates as an absolute bar to recovery; instead, **plaintiff is allowed to recover his or her damages reduced by the percentage of negligence attributable to plaintiff.**

> Thus, for example, if the jury finds that plaintiff suffered $50,000 in damages, but that plaintiff's own negligence contributed to his injury to the extent of 20%, the jury should award the plaintiff $40,000, calculated as follows: $50,000 minus 20% of $50,000.

While there are variations of comparative negligence, **two basic approaches exist.**

Modified Comparative Negligence. The modified approach is that the plaintiff who is guilty of contributory negligence may obtain the reduced recovery, demonstrated above, **provided plaintiff's negligence is not equal to or greater than defendant's.** A total bar exists where plaintiff's negligence is equal to or exceeds defendant's. Some jurisdictions allow the partial recovery provided plaintiff's negligence is not greater than defendant's, so that where plaintiff's and defendant's negligence are equal, plaintiff may recover half of his damages.

Pure Comparative Negligence. The second basic pattern is the so-called "pure" comparative negligence. Here, **plaintiff may obtain the reduced recovery even where plaintiff's negligence exceeds defendant's.**

> Thus, under the pure form, if plaintiff's damages were $50,000 and the jury found plaintiff 60% negligent, plaintiff would recover $20,000, calculated as follows: $50,000 minus 60% of $50,000.

Most states which have adopted comparative negligence have done so by statute; a few states (e.g., Florida, California, Illinois, and New Mexico) have done so by judicial decision. A Multistate question on comparative negligence would have to give you the type of statute applicable. If the question indicates that the applicable doctrine was judicial, you should assume then that it is the pure form of comparative negligence, since that is the only type which has been (or probably could be) judicially adopted.

2. Assumption Of Risk

A plaintiff is said to have **assumed the risk** of certain harm if she has **voluntarily consented** to take her chances that harm will occur. Where such an assumption is shown, the plaintiff is, at common law, completely barred from recovery. If P explicitly agrees with D, in advance of any harm, that P will not hold D liable for certain harm, P is said to have "expressly" assumed the risk of that harm.

> Example: P wants to go bungee jumping at D's amusement park. P signs a release given to him by D in which P agrees to "assume all risk of injury" that may result from the bungee jumping. If P is injured, he will not be able to sue D, because he has expressly assumed the risk.

Public Policy Against Assumption. But even P's express assumption of the risk will not bar P from recovery if there is a public policy against the assumption of the risk involved. For instance, if D's position as a unique provider of a certain service gives him greater bargaining power than P, and D uses this power to force P into a waiver of liability, the court is likely to find that public policy prohibits use of the assumption of risk doctrine. (Example: D is a public utility or common carrier, whom P must patronize because of D's monopoly. Even if P expressly assumes the risk, this will probably not bar recovery.) Public policy usually prohibits a waiver of liability for D's willful and wanton or "gross" negligence, and for D's intentionally tortious conduct.

Health Care. Courts almost never allow P to expressly assume the risk of harm with respect to **medical services**. Therefore, even if P signs a contract with D, her doctor, saying, "I agree not to sue you for malpractice if anything goes wrong with my operation," no court will enforce this.

Implied Assumption of Risk. Even if P never makes an actual agreement with D whereby P assumes the risk, P may be held to have assumed certain risks by her conduct. Here, the assumption of risk is said to be "implied." There are **two requirements** to find an implied assumption of the risk. It must be shown that:

1) The plaintiff **knew of the risk** in question; and
2) The plaintiff **voluntarily consented** to bear that risk herself.

> Example: D owns a baseball team. D posts big signs at the gates warning of the danger of foul balls. P has attended many games, and in each game buys a seat right behind home plate, a place where she and all other fans know many foul balls are hit. If P is hit by a foul ball, she will not be able to recover against D even if D negligently failed to screen the home plate area. This is because P knew of the risk in question, and voluntarily consented to bear that risk.

Requirements Strictly Construed. The requirement that the plaintiff be shown to have known about the risk is strictly construed. For instance, the risk must be one which was **actually known** to P, not merely one which "ought to have been" known to her. The requirement that P consented voluntarily is also strictly construed.

The defense of assumption of the risk has become disfavored, and has been abolished in certain situations by some courts or by statute. In *Siragusa v. Swedish Hospital*, 60 Wash.2d 310, 373 P.2d 767 (1962), the court held that the defense of assumption of the risk was not available to any employer who failed to provide reasonably safe working conditions for his employee. The court indicated, however, that if the employee's voluntary exposure to the risk is unreasonable under the circumstances, he will be barred from recovery because of his contributory negligence. The same rule is also applied in product liability cases - assumption of the risk is a defense only if the assumption of the risk was unreasonable (i.e., negligent). Many comparative negligence jurisdictions have also abolished assumption of risk as a separate full defense, and merge the conduct which formerly constituted assumption of risk into comparative negligence. *Blackburn v. Dorta*, 348 So.2d 287 (Fla. 1977).

III. STRICT LIABILITY: CLAIMS ARISING FROM ABNORMALLY DANGEROUS ACTIVITIES; THE RULE OF RYLANDS V. FLETCHER AND OTHER COMMON LAW STRICT LIABILITY CLAIMS; DEFENSES

The common law recognized two types of no-fault or strict liability: **harm resulting from escape of materials kept on the land and harm resulting from the keeping of animals.** In an 1866 English decision, *Rylands v. Fletcher*, L.R. 3 H.L. 330, Justice Blackburn stated that "the person who for his own purposes brings on his lands and collects and keeps there anything likely to do mischief if it escapes, must keep it in at his peril, and if he does not do so, is prima facie answerable for all the damage which is the natural consequence of its escape."

The rule was modified by the House of Lords, which confined the doctrine to non-natural uses of the land, i.e., an activity that is not ordinary or appropriate for its locality. L.R. 3 H.L. 330 (1868). The concept of "non-natural uses" is reflected in the language of the *Restatement (Second) of Torts*, which would impose strict liability for "abnormally dangerous activities," those not ordinary or appropriate for the particular community involved.

Restatement Provisions On Abnormally Dangerous Activities. Many jurisdictions have adopted the rule of the *Restatement (Second) of Torts* in this area. Section 519 provides that one who carries on an "abnormally dangerous" activity is subject to liability for harm to the person, land or chattels of another resulting from the activity, even if he has exercised the utmost care to prevent the harm.

The rule of strict liability is limited to the kind of harm for which the activity was determined to be abnormally dangerous; the risk must be of physical harm to persons or tangible property. Determining whether an activity is abnormally dangerous involves consideration of the following factors listed in Section 520:

1) existence of a high degree risk of some harm to the person, land or chattels of others;
2) likelihood that the harm that results from it will be great;
3) inability to eliminate the risk by the exercise of reasonable care;
4) extent to which the activity is not a matter of common usage;
5) inappropriateness of the activity to the place where it is carried on; and
6) extent to which its value to the community is outweighed by its dangerous attributes.

Concurrence of Risk of Harm and Unusual Nature of Activity. Although the Second Restatement advocates a balancing of all the above factors, the harm threatened generally must be major; if the potential harm is great enough, the activity may be abnormally dangerous even if the likelihood of its occurrence is small, e.g., a nuclear explosion. Restatement (Second) §520, comment g.

When safety cannot be guaranteed despite the exercise of all due care, the activity may be considered abnormally dangerous.

Common Usage. On the other hand, even those activities or instrumentalities which cannot be made safe by the utmost precaution and care may be carried on or used without incurring absolute liability if the activity or instrumentality is one which is commonly carried on or used. See Hudson v. Peavy Oil Co., 279 Or. 3, 566 P.2d 175 (1977) (storage of gasoline in underground tanks at gasoline station in commercial area not an uncommon usage). Blasting and the manufacture, storage, or transportation of high explosives are carried on by a relatively small class of persons and therefore are not matters of common usage.

The operation of automobiles is a matter of common usage, whereas the operation of a large tank truck is not. Restatement (Second) §520, comment i. The locality in which the activity is being conducted should be considered with respect to whether the activity is one of common usage. Some states apply the doctrine of Rylands v. Fletcher in the name of liability for nuisance. The utility of the activity must be sufficient to outweigh the risk, or it may be negligent to carry on the activity at all.

Function of Court and Jury. "What facts are necessary to make an activity ultrahazardous under the rule stated in this Section is a matter for the judgment of the court." Restatement (Second) of Torts, §520, comment l. In this, a strict liability question differs from questions of negligence, which are ordinarily within the province of the jury. The jury in a strict liability case, such as Silkwood v. Kerr-McGee Corp., 485 F. Supp. 566, aff'd in part, rev'd in part, 667 F.2d 908 (10th Cir. 1981), rev'd on other grounds, 104 S. Ct. 615 (1984), will not be asked whether a material such as plutonium is ultrahazardous but may be asked whether the defendants were responsible for the material's escape and whether the plaintiff in fact was injured as a result of that escape.

Animals Trespassing Off The Possessor's Property. As regards liability of the possessor of a trespassing animal, the common law draws a distinction between livestock or wild animals on the one hand, and domestic pets on the other. **The possessor of livestock** (cattle, hogs, sheep, etc.) or of a kept wild animal **is strictly liable for damage done by the animal's trespass.** See Restatement (Second) of Torts, §504. The possessor in effect is deemed to have trespassed.

Damage done by trespassing dogs, cats, or other domestic pets is **compensable only on proof that the possessor had knowledge of the animal's mischievous propensity.** Some states, however, have statutes imposing strict liability on the possessor for damage caused by a trespassing dog.

Other Types of Harm by Animals. Apart from the trespassing animal situation, the possessor of an animal is liable for harm caused by the animal as follows:

1) **Wild Animals.** A wild animal is defined as an animal which is not by custom devoted to the service of mankind at the time and in the place in which it is kept. Restatement

(Second) of Torts, §506. In addition to the rule on trespass described supra, a possessor of a wild animal is **strictly liable** for harm to another's person or property caused by the wild animal, provided the harm results from a dangerous propensity that is characteristic of wild animals of that particular class, or of which the possessor knows or has reason to know. Restatement (Second) of Torts, §507.

2) **Domestic Animals.** A domestic animal is defined as an animal that is by custom devoted to the service of mankind at the time and in the place in which it is kept. Restatement (Second) of Torts, §506. This generally covers livestock and domesticated pets. **Liability for harm done by such animals is generally in negligence.** However, a possessor of a domestic animal that he knows or has reason to know has dangerous propensities abnormal to its class is subject to liability for harm done by the animal, even though the possessor exercised the utmost care to prevent it from doing the harm, provided that the harm results from the abnormally dangerous propensity of which the possessor knows or has reason to know. Restatement (Second) of Torts, §509. Cases not coming within the above rules require proof of negligence, although some states have statutes imposing strict liability for harm done by dogs.

3) **Injury to Trespassers.** The above rules of liability are modified when the injured person is a trespasser on the possessor's land. In that instance, **strict liability does not apply** (Restatement, §511), but the **rules of negligence pertaining to other artificial conditions or activities on the land do apply.** Restatement (Second) of Torts, § 512. Thus, the possessor of land or chattels is privileged to employ a watchdog or other animal to protect his property, but only to the same extent that he is privileged to use a mechanical device for the same purpose. Also, since the purpose of privilege is to protect the property rather than to cause injury to trespassers, usually the possessor is required to post warnings. Restatement (Second) of Torts, §516.

IV. PRODUCTS LIABILITY: CLAIMS AGAINST MANUFACTURERS AND OTHERS BASED ON DEFECTS IN MANUFACTURE, DESIGN, AND WARNING; AND DEFENSES

When a person or property is injured by an unsafe product, a cause of action may be premised on any or all of three broad theories - negligence, strict liability, and/or misrepresentation or breach of warranty.

A. LIABILITY FOR NEGLIGENCE

Sellers of products, like anyone else, can be held liable for injuries caused by their failure to exercise due care.

Types of Negligence. A breach of this duty can be found in any one of the following circumstances.

1) **Negligence with Regard to a Particular Unit.** A defendant can be liable under a negligence products liability theory when his failure to exercise due care causes a product to differ from its intended design and this difference causes the product to be more dangerous than others of its type. This type of negligence may result from **carelessness in manufacturing** (as

when a product is improperly assembled) or from a **mishandling of the product** (as when it is dropped or improperly exposed to the elements).

2) **Negligence in Design.** Negligence may be found even if a product meets the specifications of its designer if the design unreasonably fails to protect potential plaintiffs from harm. This so-called "negligence in design" requires a careful consideration of whether the defendant could have reasonably foreseen the danger, the extent to which the technology in existence at the time of its manufacture could minimize the risks, and the degree to which the consumer could be reasonably expected to appreciate and protect himself from harm.

3) **Negligence in Instructions or Warnings.** A product might be suitable for its intended purpose when used properly, but unreasonably dangerous if it is handled differently. In such a case, a defendant can be liable in negligence if he fails to provide adequate instructions or warnings with regard to foreseeable uses to which the product may be put.

Individuals Who May Be Liable (and the Duty to Inspect). Any seller who is physically responsible for the product's dangerous condition can be liable under a negligence theory. In addition, sellers further down the chain of distribution can be liable if a reasonable inspection would have revealed a product's dangers and they unreasonably failed to protect possible plaintiffs from such dangers.

The question whether a wholesaler or retailer should inspect goods at all, and the kind of inspection that is appropriate, is determined by ordinary concepts of **reasonableness and foreseeability**. Factors which would weigh in the balance include:

1) the potential dangerousness of the product;
2) any safety history with regard to the product or predecessors in possession;
3) the presence of any physical evidence of danger (as when the product arrived in a damaged container); and
4) the practical ability of the defendant to inspect the product (including costs).

Individuals Protected. Any person who was **foreseeably endangered** by the defendant's negligence (and who is, in fact, injured thereby) can bring a negligence action. **Privity of contract is not required**. MacPherson v. Buick Motor Co., 217 N.Y. 382, 11 N.E. 1050 (1916).

Defenses. The usual defenses to a negligence action (i.e., contributory/comparative negligence and assumption of risk) are available in products liability actions based on negligence.

B.   STRICT PRODUCTS LIABILITY

In jurisdictions which follow the Second Restatement of Torts , **a manufacturer or supplier of a product which is defective and unreasonably dangerous can be held strictly liable in tort when the product causes injury to the user or his property.** This theory is found in §402A of the Restatement of Torts (Second) and is often referred to as strict products liability.

The rationale behind this theory is that it encourages manufacturers and sellers to make products as safe as possible in an area in which it is particularly difficult to prove negligence. In addition, strict liability is justified by the belief that it is unfair to make the injured plaintiff bear the costs of his injury when the supplier, even if he cannot prevent the loss, is able to spread the risks among all consumers by increasing the price of its goods to cover the potential injuries.

Elements of Strict Products Liability Action. Strict liability requires that the product have been **marketed in a defective condition that is unreasonably dangerous**. The defect may be a manufacturing defect, a design defect, or a failure to warn. Furthermore, the plaintiff must prove **causation** between the defendant's conduct and the harm suffered by the plaintiff.

Defective Product: Manufacturing and Design Defects. A manufacturing defect results in a product which does not conform to the manufacturer's specifications; the flaw occurred in the manufacturing process, making the product more dangerous than it was intended to be. The plaintiff need not prove negligence in creating or failing to discover the defect.

Defective design cases differ from manufacturing defect cases in that the final product is exactly what the manufacturer intended. Imposing strict liability for so-called defective design creates greater problems than in other defective product cases. All of defendant's products made to that design are the same. Whether the particular design is unreasonably dangerous involves a weighing of such facts as the fortuitousness of the injury which occurred, whether the design change would destroy or substantially impair the utility of the article, and whether the cost of the design change necessary to alleviate the danger would price the article out of the market.

However, normally such balancing of factors relates to negligence cases, not strict liability ones. Also, it has been held in cases involving defective design that it is no defense that the design defect was obvious. "The law, we think, ought to discourage misdesign rather than encouraging it in its obvious form." Palmer v. Massey-Ferguson, Inc., 3 Wash. App. 508 (1970).

The problems of so-called defective design are compounded when the issue is the crashworthiness of an automobile. These are cases where plaintiff is not claiming that defective design caused the automobile to crash; rather, plaintiff is claiming that some or all of his injuries from the crash could have been avoided had the automobile been properly designed. These are often referred to as second collision cases. A typical second collision case is where an automobile involved in an accident flips over, and the operator is injured when the roof collapses and comes into contact with his head. Plaintiff claims that a different design of the roof would have prevented its collapse. Initially, most cases denied recovery here even on a negligence theory. The rationale for this approach was that the intended purpose of a car does not include its participation in collisions. Evans v. General Motors Corp., 359 F.2d 822 (7th Cir. 1966). The prevailing view allows recovery on a defective design theory. Larson v. General Motors Corp., 391 F.2d 495 (8th Cir. 1968).

Here the rationale is that the intended use of the automobile necessarily entails the risk of injury-producing accidents. A few jurisdictions have imposed strict liability in this area (see e.g., Turner v. General Motors Corp., 514 S.W.2d 497 (Tex. 1974)). However, since a balancing test is used in either case, whether the theory adopted is negligence or strict liability makes little difference. Such factors as cost, utility, and even style or aesthetic appeal must be considered.

Further, consumer expectation is a factor. While it is foreseeable that an automobile may leave the road and go into a lake, the average consumer does not expect his car to float, and the manufacturer has no duty to equip the automobile with pontoons. However, the average consumer may well expect the roof of his automobile not to collapse in a roll-over accident. Id.

Failure to Warn. Strict liability may be applied even if a product does not otherwise contain a defect, if the product is unreasonably dangerous and the manufacturer fails to give proper warning of the danger or proper directions as to its use. See Davis v. Wyeth Laboratories, Inc., 399 F.2d

121 (9th Cir. 1968) (polio vaccine - even though risk of contracting the disease from the vaccine was less than one in a million).

The defendant is required only to warn of dangers which were or reasonably should have been known to him at the time of delivering the product. The supplier may defend against a strict liability action with the fact that the "state of the art" was not such that he should have known of the danger. See Christofferson v. Kaiser Foundation Hospitals, 15 Cal. App.3d 75, 92 Cal. Rptr. 825 (1971). However, the duty to warn may be present even where the use of defendant's product was abnormal if the abnormal use is a foreseeable one.

> For example, in Spruill v. Boyle-Midway, Inc., 308 F.2d 79 (4th Cir. 1962), a fourteen-month-old child died as the result of ingesting furniture polish manufactured and bottled by defendant. The court held that defendant could be held liable for its failure to warn adequately the parents of the child of the dangerous toxic nature of the polish.

Unreasonably Dangerous: Foreseeable Uses. For an action in strict liability, the product must not only be "defective," but the defect must render the product **unreasonably dangerous for its intended use or for any unintended but foreseeable use**. A product causing harm through an unforeseeable use is not actionable. Colosimo v. May Department Store Co., 466 F.2d 1234 (2d Cir. 1972). If the defendant can establish an unforeseeable misuse of the product by the plaintiff, then there has been no breach of duty to the plaintiff. Swain v. Boeing Airplane Co., 337 F.2d 940 (2d Cir. 1964).

Unavoidably Unsafe Products. The Restatement (Second) of Torts §402A, comment k, recognizes that there are certain products which are presently unavoidably unsafe but whose need justifies their marketing. Comment k states: "There are some products which, in the present state of human knowledge, are quite incapable of being made safe for their intended and ordinary use."

> Example: The vaccine for the Pasteur treatment of rabies not uncommonly leads to very serious and damaging consequences when it is injected. Since the disease itself invariably leads to a dreadful death, both the marketing and the use of the vaccine are fully justified notwithstanding the unavoidably high degree of risk which they involve. Such a product, properly prepared, and accompanied by proper directions and warnings, is not defective, nor is it unreasonably dangerous.

In Hines v. St. Joseph's Hospital, 86 N.M. 763, 527 P.2d 1075 (1974), the Court held that blood containing hepatitis virus came within the category of an unavoidably unsafe product. The Court pointed out that, at the time of the plaintiff's transfusion, no test could adequately detect the hepatitis virus in the blood and no process could destroy it without damaging the blood. See also Brody v. Overlook Hospital, 127 N.J. Super. 331, 317 A.2d 392, aff'd 6 N.J. 448, 332 A.2d 5

If the drug is a prescription drug, most courts hold that the drug company may rely upon the warning that it provides to physicians as to any risks involved in the use of the drug. However, in Davis v. Wyeth Laboratories, Inc., 399 F.2d 121 (9th Cir. 1968), the Court held that the manufacturer of live polio vaccine could be held strictly liable for its failure to communicate directly to users of the vaccine the risk of contracting polio, no matter how slight, involved in its use. The vaccine was denominated a prescription drug, but it was not dispensed as such. It was dispensed to all comers at mass clinics without an individualized balancing by a physician of the risks involved.

Reasonableness of Design. Various tests have been developed to determine whether the design of a product is unreasonably dangerous. The Restatement (Second) of Torts, §402A adopts the **consumer-contemplation test,** under which courts look at the dangerousness of the product from the point of view of the ordinary, prudent purchaser or other foreseeable user with respect to the contemplated uses of the product. Most courts apply the consumer contemplation test except in design defect cases, where many courts prefer the balancing of risks and utility.

The **risk-utility** test, which is adopted by the Restatement (Third) of Torts weighs the danger of the design against its benefits. The court will consider the feasibility of safer alternative designs. Some courts require the plaintiff only to prove that the design of the product proximately caused the injury. The burden then shifts to the defendant to show that the utility of the design outweighs its inherent danger. Barker v. Lull Engineering Co., 20 Cal.3d 413, 573 P.2d 443 (1978).

Causation. The defendant's liability may be cut off if the product defect was not created by the defendant but by a substantial subsequent change in the product caused by a third party. The plaintiff must plead and prove that the product reached the user or consumer without a substantial intervening change. **An unforeseeable modification or alteration constitutes a superseding cause of the injury.**

Furthermore, the defendant will not be liable if the **plaintiff's misuse of the product,** rather than the condition of the product itself, is responsible for the plaintiff s injuries. Strict liability applies in some cases even though the defective product was being misused at the time of the injury, provided that the misuse was foreseeable. Ford Motor Co. v. Matthews, 291 So.2d 169 (Miss. 1974); Moran v. Faberge, Inc., 273 Md. 538, 332 A.2d 11 (1975).

Just as in the area of negligence, where negligence and causation may be proved by circumstantial evidence, in the area of strict liability, whether the plaintiff's injury resulted from the defendant's defective product **or** some other cause may likewise be proved by circumstantial evidence. The evidence, however, must be sufficient to warrant the inference that a defective condition existed which caused the plaintiffs injury. Elmore v. American Motors Corp., supra.

Individuals Who May Be Liable. Manufacturers, Suppliers and Lessors of Defective Products. Strict liability is imposed upon a manufacturer or supplier (whether wholesaler or retailer) of any product which is in a defective condition, unreasonably dangerous to the user or consumer or to his property, for physical harm caused thereby to such persons or property, provided:

1) the manufacturer or supplier is engaged in the business of selling such a product; and
2) the product is expected to and does reach the user or consumer without substantial change in the condition in which it is sold. Restatement (Second) of Torts §402A.

There must be a "sale" of a "product" by the manufacturer for strict products liability to apply. Case law has found products liability inapplicable to the transmission of electricity, either on the ground that electricity is a service, not a product, or that there has been no sale before the electricity enters the consumer's home and is metered.

It is not necessary that the supplier be engaged solely in the business of selling such product, or that it be a principal part of his business. Thus, strict liability would apply to the owner of a motion picture theater who sells popcorn or ice cream. Id., comment f. It would not apply, however, to an occasional seller, as for example the owner of an automobile who sells it to a used car dealer, even though he is fully aware that the dealer plans to resell it.

Strict liability applies also to lessors of defective products. Price v. Shell Oil Co., 2 Cal.3d 245, 466 P.2d 722 (1970). Further, as with negligence cases, manufacturers are strictly liable for defective component parts which are manufactured or supplied by others, but which are assembled into the defendant's product. Goldberg v. Kollsman Instrument Corp., 12 N.Y. 432, 191 N.E.2d 81 (1963).

Since the theory of recovery is strict liability, it is irrelevant that the defect in the component part was not discoverable by a reasonable inspection on the part of the manufacturer of the final product. The manufacturer of the final product, if adjudged liable to the injured party, is normally entitled to indemnification from the manufacturer of the defective component part.

Manufacturer's Liability for Assembly by Dealer. Normally a manufacturer is strictly liable only if the product was defective when it left the hands of the manufacturer. However, if the manufacturer ships a product which is not totally assembled, and relies upon the dealer to complete the assembly, the manufacturer is still strictly liable even though the defect in the final product is solely the result of improper assembly by the dealer. Vandermark v. Ford Motor Co., 61 Cal.2d 256, 391 P.2d 168 (1964). The rationale for this result is that the manufacturer cannot escape liability because he entrusts final assembly to an authorized dealer, rather than to some employee of the manufacturer. See Sabloff v. Yamaha Motor Co., Ltd., 133 N.J. Super. 279, 273 A.2d 606, affd 59 N.J. 365, 283 A.2d 321 (1971).

Liability of Component Part Manufacturers. The Restatement (Second) of Torts §402A takes no position on whether the manufacturer of a defective component part may be held strictly liable when it causes the final product to be defective, but a majority of courts hold that the **ultimate user cannot sue the component part manufacturer**, at least when the manufacturer of the completed product is solvent and subject to liability. Goldberg v. Kollsman Instrument Corp., supra.

Nonliability for Providing Services. Strict liability does not apply to the performance of services; negligence must be proved. In Hoffman v. Simplot Aviation, Inc., 97 Idaho 32, 539 P.2d 584 (1975), the Court refused to extend strict liability to the repair of an airplane.

Sometimes, however, a transaction is a hybrid having incidents of both a sale and a service. Where the plaintiff is harmed by a defective product being applied upon the plaintiff as part of the service, and where the defendant in the regular course of its business sells or applies the product, strict liability may apply. In Newmark v. Gimbel's Inc. 54 N.J. 585, 258 A.2d 697 (1969), the Court held that implied warranty principles applied to the application of a permanent wave solution upon the plaintiff by the defendant beauty parlor, which caused acute dermatitis.

Multistate Bar Review Book 2

Individuals Protected. Users, Consumers and Bystanders. Clearly, **users or consumers** of a defective product are protected by the strict liability rule. Plaintiff need not be a purchaser of the product in order to qualify as a user or consumer. A passenger in an automobile, airplane, or other vehicle is a user.

The clear weight of authority also permits **bystanders** and other persons to recover on a strict liability basis following the leading case of Piercefield v. Remington Arms Co., 375 Mich. 85, 133 N.W.2d 129 (1965). The Restatement (Second) §395 **recommends extension of liability to all foreseeable plaintiffs**. Thus, a bystander may recover as the result of being struck by a defective automobile. Elmore v. American Motors Corp., 70 Cal.2d 578, 451 P.2d 84 (1969). The same applies to persons in another automobile struck by the defective automobile. Caruth v. Mariani, 11 Ariz. App. 188, 463 P.2d 83 (1970).

Rescue Doctrine. It is generally held that the rescue doctrine applies in strict liability cases. Thus, where a defective product threatens or causes injury to an individual, the manufacturer or seller of the product **may be strictly liable for injury sustained by a person attempting to rescue the imperiled individual**.

Defenses. Contributory negligence of the plaintiff is not a defense to strict liability when such negligence "consists merely in a failure to discover the defect in the product, or to guard against the possibility of its existence. On the other hand, the form of contributory negligence which consists in voluntarily and **unreasonably** proceeding to encounter a **known** danger, and commonly passes under the name of assumption of risk, is a defense. If the user or consumer discovers the defect and is aware of the danger, and nevertheless **proceeds unreasonably** to make use of the product and is injured by it, he is barred from recovery." Restatement (Second) of Torts §402A, comment n.

Assumption of Risk Must Be Unreasonable. The above defense is basically an unreasonable assumption of risk. It requires that plaintiff was **actually aware of the defect** (a subjective test), and not merely that as a reasonable person he should have been aware. Williams v. Brown Manufacturing Co., 45 Ill.2d 418, 261 N.E.2d 305 (1970). The jury, however, is not compelled by the subjective nature of this test to accept a user's testimony that he was unaware of the danger, if, in light of all the evidence, he could not have been unaware of the hazard.

The factors of the user's age, experience, knowledge, and understanding, as well as the obviousness of the defect and the danger it poses, will all be relevant to the jury's determination of the issue. Id. The **use** of the product by the plaintiff with knowledge of the defect must be **unreasonable.**

> For example, in Devaney v. Sarno, 125 N.J. Super. 414, 311 A.2d 208 (1973), defendant sold plaintiff an automobile that had an inoperable seatbelt. Plaintiff informed defendant of the defect, and defendant ordered a new seatbelt from the factory. While the order was pending, plaintiff was involved in an accident and sued defendant for aggravation of his injuries due to the inoperable seatbelt. Defendant successfully moved for summary judgment, on the basis that plaintiff knew of the defect and unreasonably continued to use the product. The appellate court reversed, holding that it was a jury question whether plaintiffs use of the vehicle was, under the circumstances, unreasonable.

Multistate Bar Review Book 2

Diminution of Recovery Under Comparative Fault Principles for Contributory Negligence. In jurisdictions that have adopted comparative negligence, a plaintiff who is found guilty of contributory negligence will have his damages reduced by the extent to which (percentage-wise) the plaintiff's own negligence contributed to his injury, despite the fact that the plaintiff is suing on a strict liability theory and despite the fact that plaintiff's contributory negligence did not involve an assumption of risk and therefore was not a defense to strict tort liability prior to the adoption of comparative negligence. Daly v. General Motors Corp., 144 Cal. Rptr. 380, 575 P.2d 1162 (1978); Thibault v. Sears Roebuck Co., 395 A.2d 843 (N.H. 1978). Because comparative negligence does not constitute a complete bar to the plaintiff's recovery, courts may be more willing to take into consideration the plaintiff's conduct than where contributory negligence or assumption of the risk is a complete bar.

C.   LIABILITY FOR MISREPRESENTATION AND BREACH OF WARRANTY

Several potential products liability theories are based upon express or implied assertions concerning the nature and quality of a seller's goods.

Misrepresentation Under Restatement §402B. Under §402B of the Restatement of Torts (Second), a commercial seller's **public misrepresentation of material fact concerning the character or quality of a product** is actionable if the plaintiff is injured thereby. While, as a technical matter, the plaintiff must actually have relied upon the seller's assertions, many cases have ignored this rule on the theory that a seller ought to be held to his self-proclaimed standards. The defenses under this theory are the same as those applicable to strict products liability actions.

Implied Warranty in Torts. At one time, many cases talked in terms of an **implied warranty in tort.** While actions brought under this theory were generally covered by tort principles, contract concepts of warranty crept into the area and caused considerable confusion. Today, most states have totally abandoned this theory in favor of strict products liability.

Furthermore, those states which still speak in terms of implied warranty in tort generally agree with the approach of §402A of the Restatement. See, e.g., Swartz v. General Motors Corp., 375 Mass. 620, 378 N.E.2d 61 (1978). Indeed, in most cases, the two theories reach the same results upon a consideration of the same evidence. Thus, while the vocabulary may differ slightly, the actual analysis of a modern "implied warranty in tort" action is essentially identical to the analysis of strict products liability as discussed above.

Warranties Under the Uniform Commercial Code. Since warranties under the Uniform Commercial Code are discussed in the **Contracts and Sales** materials, only a brief outline of these actions is presented here.

Express Warranty Under U.C.C. §2-313. Section 2-313 of the Uniform Commercial Code imposes liability for injuries resulting from a **breach of express warranty.** Insofar as its applicability to Torts questions is concerned, an express warranty claim is essentially the same as an action under §402B except that:

1) liability can be imposed on **any seller** (not just on commercial suppliers);
2) the warranty need not be made to the public at large;

3) specific reliance on the warranty is not required so long as it was "part of the basis of the bargain;" and

4) the plaintiff must fall within the class of people protected by the relevant state's version of §2-318.

Finally, U.C.C. §2-607(3)(a) generally provides that an aggrieved buyer loses his rights under the Code unless he notifies the seller of any breach "within a reasonable time;" many courts, however, have abandoned this requirement in the case of personal injury (at least when the defendant cannot show that the failure to give prompt notice was prejudicial).

Implied Warranty of Merchantability Under U.C.C. §2-314. Under U.C.C. §2-314, every **commercial seller** warrants that the goods he sells are of "fair average quality within the description" and "fit for the ordinary purposes for which such goods are used" unless this implied warranty of merchantability is clearly disclaimed or modified. The privity, notice, and defense issues with regard to this action are the same as those relating to express warranty as discussed above.

Implied Warranty of Fitness for a Particular Purpose Under U.C.C. §2-315. When a seller has reason to know of the buyer's particular purpose for certain goods and that the buyer is relying on the seller's skill or judgment to select a product appropriate for such needs, the seller impliedly warrants that the goods are fit for that use. This **implied warranty of fitness for a particular purpose** applies whether or not made by a commercial distributor. The other issues are essentially the same as those applying to the other U.C.C. theories.

V. OTHER TORTS

A. CLAIMS BASED ON NUISANCE, AND DEFENSES

While trespass has been traditionally defined as an interference with the plaintiff's possessory interest in his land, the concept of nuisance generally involves an **interference by the defendant with the plaintiff's use and enjoyment of his property.** Historically, the more common types of interferences which would be classified as nuisances are noise, odors, vibrations, light, and similar intangibles.

The practical distinction between an action for nuisance and one for trespass is that in a nuisance action, the court will usually weigh and balance all the factors involved and, unless the defendant's conduct is actionable under some other theory, will grant relief only where the defendant's conduct is unreasonable under all of the circumstances. Trespass, on the other hand, does not involve such a balancing.

Elements of a Cause of Action for Nuisance. The plaintiff may sustain his nuisance action upon a showing that:

1) the defendant's conduct with respect to the use of neighboring land substantially interferes with the use and enjoyment of the plaintiffs property; and
2) that such interference is unreasonable.

Reasonableness. Whether the defendant's conduct is reasonable or unreasonable involves **weighing the gravity of the harm** done to the plaintiff against **the utility of the defendant's activity**, together with **the suitability of the location** of the defendant's activity. See Patterson v. Peabody

Multistate Bar Review Book 2

Coal Co., 3 Ill. App.2d 311, 122 N.E.2d 48 (1954). Thus, a determination of whether the defendant's conduct is reasonable or unreasonable will primarily depend upon a balancing of three factors:

1) the locality and character of the surroundings;
2) the nature, extent, and frequency of the harm; and
3) the utility and social value of the activity involved.

Locality and Character of the Surroundings. In determining whether the defendant's interference is so unreasonable as to constitute a nuisance, **the character of the locality is of great importance**. A noise which is permissible in an industrial area may constitute a nuisance in a residential area. While the zoning of a particular area is important on the appropriateness of the activity, it is not controlling. Tortorella v. H. Traiser & Co., Inc., 284 Mass. 497, 188 N.E. 254 (1933).

Priority of occupation does not give the defendant the absolute right to conduct his activity. In Guarina v. Bogart, 407 Pa. 307, 180 A.2d 557 (1962), homeowners in a rural area sought an injunction restraining the operation of a drive-in motion picture theater. The court held that the operation of the theater, equipped with loudspeakers which were hung from trees, constituted a nuisance; and the fact that adjoining property owners knew of the operation of the theater before they acquired the property and improved it was not determinative when defendants could, for a reasonable cost, equip the theater with individual automobile speakers.

Nature, Extent, and Frequency of the Interference. The degree of the interference, its frequency, and the time that it occurs, will be important considerations on the question of the existence of a nuisance. It must be an interference which affects in an unreasonable manner persons of normally sensitive characteristics. Injury to a particular person in a peculiar position or of specially sensitive characteristics will not render the interference actionable. See Rogers v. Elliot, 146 Mass. 349, 15 N.E. 768 (1888) (court refused to enjoin the ringing of a church bell on Sunday).

The time of day that an activity takes place is important. Noise taking place for long periods in the early morning may be actionable, whereas the same noise taking place during normal working hours may not be actionable. Tortorella v. H. Traiser & Co., supra.

Utility and Social Value of the Activity. The utility and social value of the defendant's activity will have some bearing on the issue of reasonableness. City of Harrisonville v. W.S. Dickey Clay Mfg. Co., 289 U.S. 334 (1933). Many courts today take the position that the question of the utility and social value of the defendant's activity is important only where an injunction is sought. When, however, the action is for damages only, no balancing of the social utility against the gravity of the injury should take place. Jost v. Dairyland Power Cooperative, 45 Wis.2d 164, 172 N.W.2d 647 (1970).

Relief. Since the action for nuisance is equitable in nature, the court has a great deal of flexibility in determining the relief which should be granted. The court may order a **complete abatement of the nuisance**, with or without damages for past harm, or it may order the defendant to take certain steps to **reduce the interference**, with or without damages. If, because of social utility, the court is not inclined to enjoin the defendant's activity, it will treat the defendant's activity as a permanent nuisance and award the plaintiff **damages for the diminution of the value of his property**. Boomer v. Atlantic Cement Co., 26 N.Y.2d 219, 257 N.E.2d 870 (1970).

Sometimes the court will take this latter approach because of the great economic hardship which would result to the defendant if the activity were enjoined, as contrasted with the slight economic loss to the plaintiff as the result of the activity. Finally, the court may decline to find a permanent nuisance and instead award damages for the past nuisance, while authorizing plaintiffs return to court periodically if the nuisance continues, for the award of additional damages. See Restatement (Second) of Torts, §930.

Public Nuisance. A public nuisance is one which **affects an interest common to the general public, rather than solely to one or several persons**. Examples of public nuisances are the pollution of a stream or the blocking of a public highway. Public nuisances are usually detailed in criminal statutes enforceable only by the state.

The general rule has been that **a private individual has no cause of action for a public nuisance** unless he can establish that his harm or damage is different in kind rather than merely in degree from that suffered by the public generally. See Smedberg v. Moxie Dam Co., 148 Me. 302, 92 A.2d 606 (1952). The purpose of this rule is to avoid a multiplicity of suits. It has, however, occasionally been ignored where the plaintiff's harm, although not different in kind from that suffered by the public generally, was significantly greater in degree.

Contributory Negligence. It is generally held today that whether contributory negligence is a defense in a nuisance action for personal injury depends upon the conduct underlying the nuisance. If the defendant intentionally created the nuisance (i.e., for the purpose of invading another's interest or knowing that such invasion is resulting or is substantially certain to result), contributory negligence is not a defense to the action. If, however, the underlying conduct is simply negligence, contributory negligence will operate as a defense. See Deane v. Johnson, 104 So.2d 3 (Fla. 1958).

Defense of Compliance with Statute or Administrative Regulation. Usually evidence of compliance with a statute or ordinance as a defense is relevant and admissible but not binding on the fact-finder. Sometimes compliance with a statute or regulatory scheme constitutes a defense to an action for public nuisance. For example, consideration may appropriately be given to the fact that defendant adjusted downward the pollution level of his manufacturing plant to reduce the pollution level to the maximum permitted by applicable statutes and regulations. Restatement (Second) of Torts, §821B, comment f.

B. CLAIMS BASED ON DEFAMATION AND INVASION OF PRIVACY; DEFENSES AND CONSTITUTIONAL LIMITATIONS

1. Defamation

Defamation is the **wrongful and unprivileged invasion of the interest in reputation of a person**. Defamation may be either libel or slander.

Libel and Slander Distinguished. Libel is defamation in which the defamatory statement is made **in writing**. Slander is defamation in which the defamatory statement is made **orally**.

The difference between libel and slander is important only when determining the type of damages that must be pleaded and proven. In general, **libel does not require proof of special damages**. A writing is libel per se if the defamatory meaning is apparent on its face. In contrast, **slander actions**

Multistate Bar Review Book 2

do require proof of special damages with four exceptions described below. In effect, it is easier to recover for libel than for slander because of this difference in the damages requirement.

The reason for this distinction is the belief that the written word has more permanence and is more likely to do serious harm. Spence v. Funk, 396 A.2d 967 (Del. 1978). The advent of television with the likelihood of great harm from oral defamation has led some jurisdictions to treat televised defamation as libel. See Annot., Defamation by Television and Radio, 50 A.L.R.3d 1311.

Who May Be Plaintiff in Defamation Action. Any living person may be a plaintiff in a defamation action. The common law rule is that the death of the plaintiff is also the death of any libel action the plaintiff may have had at the time of his death. E.g., Gruschus v. Curtis Publishing Co., 342 F.2d 775 (10th Cir. 1965). Some states provide by statute for the survival of defamation actions.

Corporations and other business entities may also sue for libel. Restatement (Second) of Torts §561. In addition, if the corporation's product has been disparaged, the corporation may sue for the related tort of product disparagement. Bose Corp. v. Consumers Union of United States, Inc., 466 U.S. 485 (1984).

Elements of Defamation Action. In all defamation actions, the plaintiff has the burden of proving the following elements, each of which is described in more detail in sections which follow:

1) the defendant **published a communication**;
2) the communication was expressed as a communication of **fact**;
3) the communication was **concerning the plaintiff**;
4) the communication was **false**;
5) the communication was **defamatory**;
6) the person receiving the communication **understood it to be defamatory and to apply to the plaintiff**;
7) the defendant was guilty of **fault**; and
8) the communication **proximately caused harm** to the plaintiff.

Publication. For a communication to be defamatory, it must be "published." Publication occurs when the defamatory matter is **communicated by the defendant to a third person other than the plaintiff** intentionally or by a negligent act. Restatement (Second) of Torts §577(i). Thus, a letter sent only to the plaintiff by the defendant is not normally a publication. If, however, the defendant should have reasonably expected a third person to read the letter, there is a publication even though the letter is addressed only to the plaintiff. First State Bank of Corpus Christi v. Ake, 606 S.W.2d 696 (Tex. Civ. App. 1980); e.g., Western Union Telegraph Co. v. Lesesne, -198 F.2nd 164 (4th Cir. 1952) (telegram addressed to husband; wife opened it. Held: Publication occurred because it could reasonably be expected that a telegram, with its implication of emergency, might be opened and read by a spouse in absence of other spouse).

Communication to One Person Sufficient. It is not necessary that the defamatory matter be communicated to a large or even a substantial group of persons. It is enough, to meet the publication requirement, that it is communicated to a single individual other than the one defamed. Restatement (Second) of Torts §577, comment b. **Dictation** of a letter by the defendant to a secretary, without more, does not constitute a publication according to some cases. E.g., Mims v. Metropolitan Life Insurance Co., 200 F.2d 800 (5th Cir. 1952). The Restatement takes the position that this is a sufficient publication to support a defamation action, however. Restatement (Second) of Torts §577, comment h.

Republication. A person who **repeats or otherwise republishes defamatory matter is subject to the same liability** as if that person had originally published it. Cianci v. New Times Publishing Co., 639 F.2d 54 (2d Cir. 1980); Restatement (Second) of Torts §578. A defendant may be liable for republication of defamatory matter if he negligently allows defamatory matter to remain for an unreasonable time on property over which he has control. See Restatement (Second) of Torts §577.

Statement of Fact. In order to be actionable defamation, the statement must be one of "fact." This means that **hyperbole and satire** which could not reasonably be construed as statements of fact are **not actionable**. However, opinions are actionable if they merely state a personal belief on a matter of fact which can be proven true or false. For example, the statement "I think that Sue is a liar" is as actionable as "Sue is a liar." A speaker cannot immunize a statement by couching it in the terms of an opinion. Milkovich v. Lorain Journal Co., 497 U.S. 1 (1990).

Of and Concerning the Plaintiff. The defamation must be "of and concerning the plaintiff," i.e., the person to whom it was published reasonably must have understood it to refer to the plaintiff. Restatement (Second) of Torts §564. Sometimes a statement that seems to refer to one person, actually is "of and concerning" a different person, and the other person can sue for defamation.

> For example, if A states to B that C is an illegitimate child, A has made a defamatory statement "of and concerning" the mother of C. Id. at comment e.

A statement directed to a group or class of persons can be "of or concerning" a particular person only if the group or class is small enough for the statement reasonably to be understood as referring to the plaintiff, who is a member of the group, or the circumstances give rise to the conclusion that there is a reference to a particular member of the group. Loeb v. Globe Newspaper Co., 489 F. Supp. 481 (D. Mass. 1980).

> For example, the statement that the saleswomen at a large department store were prostitutes did not support a defamation action by one of the 382 saleswomen at the store because "[the] group was too large to infer defamation of a member thereof." Neiman-Marcus v. Lait, 13 F.R.D. 311 (S.D.N.Y. 1952).

Falsity. The plaintiff must establish, as part of his cause of action, that the statement is false. See Gertz v. Robert Welch, Inc., 418 U.S. 323 (1974); Philadelphia Newspapers, Inc. v. Hepps, 475 U.S. 767 (1986). However, if the defendant can show that the statement is true, the plaintiff's case is defeated. Truth is an "absolute defense."

Proof of slight inaccuracies will not be sufficient to demonstrate falsity. Plaintiff must prove that the published statement was substantially false. See Anderson v. Stanco Sports Library, Inc., 542 F.2d 638 (1976) (finding that publication was substantially true precludes recovery).

"Defamatory" Defined. A communication is defamatory if it tends to **harm the reputation of the plaintiff so as to lower the plaintiff in the estimation of the community, or to deter third persons from associating with the plaintiff.** Restatement (Second) of Torts §559. It is not enough that some people think less of the plaintiff. The statement must discredit the plaintiff in the minds of a considerable and respectable segment in the community.

The court makes a threshold decision whether a statement may be defamatory. Where the language is unambiguous, the question whether the statement is defamatory is for the court. McCort v. Morris, 58 A.D.2d 700, 396 N.Y.S.2d 107 (1977). If the publication is susceptible of both defamatory and harmless meanings, it presents a question for the jury and cannot be ruled nondefamatory as a matter of law. Smith v. Suburban Restaurants, Inc., 374 Mass. 528, 373 N.E.2d 215 (1978).

Occasionally, a written communication is not defamatory when considered in isolation but becomes defamatory when combined with information that is in the possession of some of the persons to whom the communication is published. Such defamation is called **libel per quod**. The significance of this type of libel is that the defendant will not be liable unless the plaintiff can establish that the plaintiff suffered "special damages" as a result of the libel per quod. (See discussion of damages, infra.)

The communication to a third person must be in such a way that the third person understood the words in a defamatory sense. Bergman v. Oshman's Sporting Goods, Inc., 594 S.W.2d 814 (Tex. Civ. App. 1980).

> If A falsely accuses B of murder in the presence of several persons, none of whom understand the language used by A to make the charge, there can be no recovery because, although the communication was defamatory and was published, no person to whom it was published understood the defamatory nature of the communication. Restatement (Second) of Torts §577, comment d.

Fault. The United States Supreme Court has ruled that there **cannot be a cause of action for defamation in the absence of proof of fault of some sort**. Gertz v. Robert Welch, Inc., 418 U.S. 323 (1974).

Multistate Bar Review Book 2

The standard of familiarity is quite liberal. A person who has exchanged correspondence with the purported author over a period of time is qualified, even though he has not seen the author write his signature. One who has seen signatures in a business office where the genuine signature is present on many documents is likewise qualified.

The familiarity need not be recent. In one case, a witness was allowed to identify a signature, even though it was twenty years since he saw a genuine signature. In re Diggins Estate, 68 Vt. 198, 34 A. 196 (1896).

Authentication by Comparison with a Genuine Signature. An admittedly genuine specimen or one which can be authenticated as a specimen of the purported author can be admitted to authenticate a document. **A comparison of the features of the disputed document and the specimen can be made by a handwriting expert, but not by a lay witness**. Even if a handwriting expert is not present, the jury can find the disputed document genuine by making a comparison between the genuine and disputed documents themselves. Many courts require that the judge make a determination that the specimen is in fact genuine before it can be admitted. The Federal Rules of Evidence require only that it be authenticated, Rule 901(b)(3).

Authentication by Circumstantial Evidence. In addition to direct testimony, distinctive characteristics of the document may serve to authenticate it. See Fed. R. Ev. 901(b)(4). For example, information in the document may be shown to have been available only to the author, or the author may have a peculiar way of expressing himself.

Custody. Writings also may be authenticated by proof of their custody. If a writing purports to be an official or public document and is shown to have come from the custody of the official upon whom the law places an obligation to keep the document, this constitutes sufficient authentication. This rule applies to court records, deeds, tax returns, and other documents in official custody. See Fed. R. Ev. 901(b)(7).

Reply Doctrine. To authenticate a letter or other document under the reply doctrine, it must be shown that a communication was sent to the purported author of that letter or document, and that the person who sent the first communication received a document shortly thereafter, which either referred to the prior communication or contained information which could only be known by its recipient. The regularity of the mails and the presumption that the addressee received the first letter provide the circumstantial basis necessary for authentication.

Ancient Documents. Federal Rule 901(b)(8) provides that if a document or data compilation is **over twenty (20) years old, in such condition as to create no suspicion of its authenticity**, and was kept in a place where it would likely be if it was authentic, then it is **admissible without further authentication**. The rule is not restricted to deeds. A deed authenticated under the ancient document rule is admissible, even though the grantee under that deed did not go into possession under it.

Authentication by Process or System. Federal Rule 901(b)(9) has added a new type of circumstantial authentication. If the process or system which produces the document is shown generally to have produced an accurate result, then the particular document will be authenticated. Printouts from computers and X-rays are the most common examples.

Where Authenticity Is at Issue. The methods described above relate solely to the condition precedent to admissibility, authentication. When the central issues in the case are the genuineness of documents, the common procedure is to call **handwriting experts** to testify by comparing admittedly genuine signatures with the questioned ones and then give their opinion on authenticity. However, this is not a field where expert testimony is necessary to make out a prima facie case. If the plaintiff authenticates a document without expert testimony, the defendant is not entitled to a directed verdict merely because he produces an expert who says it is a forgery.

Authentication of Voices. When the relevancy of a voice communication depends upon the identification of the author of the voice, evidence of that authorship must be produced. Oral testimony by a person familiar with that voice, even if the familiarity is obtained by mechanical or electronic means, and even if acquired subsequent to the time of the communication in issue, is sufficient authentication.

Identification of voices is not a subject of expert testimony except in the field of voiceprints. Therefore, a non-expert witness can compare a voice to be identified with an undisputed sample of the individual's voice. A layman cannot perform a similar function in handwriting identification.

Authentication of Telephone Calls. The problem of authenticating voices most commonly arises in the authentication of telephone calls. If the witness recognizes the voice of the caller, sufficient authentication has been accomplished. If the witness cannot recognize the caller's voice, the conversation is authenticated circumstantially if the witness dialed the number of the person, asked for him, and the voice identified itself as that person.

Likewise, if the witness dials the number of a business and talks to someone at the other end of the phone about business usually transacted over the phone, there is a presumption that the person at the other end of the phone was authorized to transact business for that company. A telephone call will be inadmissible because it is not authenticated if the purported author calls the witness who is not familiar with his voice and identifies himself. See Fed. R. Ev. 901(b)(5), (6).

Self-Authentication - Fed. R. Ev. 902. Certain types of documents, because of their official nature, are of undisputed authenticity and need not be authenticated by extensive proof. A document bearing the seal of the United States or any political subdivision or agency thereof or a public document not under seal but attested to by another officer needs no further authentication. A foreign official document ordinarily must be finally certified by a United States official before it is properly authenticated. Certified copies of public records, or summaries thereof, and official publications need no further authentication.

The Federal Rules of Evidence add four new categories to the self-authentication of documents where the risk of forgery is slight. **Newspapers and periodicals** do not have to be authenticated, but their admissibility may be barred by hearsay and other problems. **Commercial and mercantile labels are self-authenticating under the Federal Rules, because companies ordinarily spend great sums inducing reliance and protecting brand names**. Cases such as Keegan v. Green Giant Co., 150 Me. 283, 110 A.2d 599 (1954), where a can of Green Giant Peas was held not to be self-authenticating, no longer are generally accepted. Notarized documents and commercial paper are also self-authenticating under the Federal Rules.

Authentication of Documents with Attesting Witnesses. Many states require that any document such as a will which requires attesting witnesses before it is valid must be authenticated by those attesting witnesses. They must be shown to be unavailable before it can be authenticated in any other way. The Federal Rules of Evidence only require such authentication when state law governs the transaction and so requires it. Fed. R. Ev. 903.

Even where authentication by attesting witnesses is required, the testimony of the attesting witnesses is not conclusive, and its genuineness may be disputed by other witnesses. Likewise, if the attesting witnesses testify that the document is not genuine, other witnesses may prove its authenticity. Subscribing witnesses are also not needed if the opponent admits the genuineness of the document, where it is "collateral" to the lawsuit, or where ancient documents are involved.

C.   CHARACTER AND RELATED CONCEPTS

1.   Admissibility Of Character

Character presents two completely different evidence problems.

Character in Issue. Occasionally, the question of a person's character trait is an issue to be determined in the lawsuit. For example, the plaintiff's character is in issue when determining damages in a defamation case. Meiners v. Moriarity, 563 F.2d 343 (7th Cir. 1977). Character may also be in issue in a criminal case when the defendant raises an entrapment defense and the prosecution offers evidence that the defendant was predisposed to commit the offense. See, United States v. Burkley, 591 F.2d 903 (D.C. Cir. 1978), cert. den., 440 U.S. 966 (1979). There is no relevancy problem under these circumstances. **Character, when at issue, can ordinarily be proved by specific instances of conduct**. Fed. R. Ev. 405(b).

Character Not Directly in Issue. Character evidence might be offered to prove circumstantially that the person acted on a specific occasion in conformity with a certain character trait. Because the rules concerning admissibility of character evidence when used circumstantially are crystallized, they are frequently asked on the Multistate Examination. To answer questions concerning them, it is important to commit the basic rules to memory.

a) **Prosecution may not introduce bad character.** The prosecution may not introduce character evidence to show that the criminal defendant was the kind of person likely to commit a crime. Fed. R. Ev. 404(b).

b) **Defendant can introduce good character and Prosecution may rebut.** The criminal defendant has the right to introduce evidence of his good character to prove that it was unlikely that he committed the alleged act. **Once he does so, he opens the door and the prosecution may then prove bad character.** Fed. R. Ev. 404(a)(1). Furthermore, under a 2000 amendment, if the defendant offers evidence of a trait of character of the alleged victim, the prosecution may offer evidence of the same trait of character of the accused. This amendment permits a more balanced presentation of character evidence when an accused chooses to attack the character of the victim.

c) **No character evidence in civil cases.** In civil cases, character evidence may not be introduced by either side unless character itself is in issue. While some commentators have advocated allowing proof of "accident proneness" in negligence cases, this has not been accepted. Fed. R. Ev. 404(a).

d) **Defendant may introduce victim's character and Prosecution may rebut.** In a criminal case where the defendant has raised the issue of self defense, he may introduce evidence of the victim's reputation for turbulence and violence. The introduction of such evidence of the victim's character gives the prosecution the opportunity to introduce evidence of the good character of the victim. Fed. R. Ev. 404(a).

e) **Prosecution can show peacefulness of homicide victim if self defense is in issue.** If the defendant in a homicide case introduces evidence showing that the victim was the first aggressor, the prosecution may rebut that evidence by showing the character trait of peacefulness of the victim. Fed. R. Ev. 404(a)(2). In this instance, the prosecution may introduce character evidence even though the defendant introduced evidence other than character evidence to show the victim was the aggressor.

f) **Character of witness for truthfulness may be impeached.** The character of a witness may be impeached by proof of character with respect to truth and veracity.

2. Methods Of Proving Character

Federal Rule 405(a) provides that in all cases where character evidence is admissible, it **may be proven by testimony as to reputation and by testimony in the form of opinion.** When character is directly in issue, it may be proven by specific instances of conduct. Fed. R. Ev. 405(b).

Proof of Reputation. When character is proven by reputation, a **foundation must be laid by showing that the character witness is familiar with that reputation**. He must know and have contact with persons with whom the individual lives and works. Once that foundation is laid, he may testify as to his generalized conclusion of what such others think about that individual's character trait. This statement of the opinion of others is admissible despite the fact that it is hearsay. Fed. R. Ev. 803(21).

Opinion. When a witness testifies to his own opinion of the character of an individual, a foundation must be laid by showing that the witness had familiarity with the individual sufficient to form the opinion.

Cross-examination of Character Witness by Inquiry into Contrary Conduct. When a witness testifies to character, he may be cross-examined by inquiry into his or her knowledge of contrary conduct by the person in question. Fed. R. Ev. 405(a).

3. Habit And Routine Practice

Habit. When a practice becomes a habit, it is done **as a regular response to a given situation without much independent thought on each occasion**. Habit is narrower in scope than character. Character is a generalized description of traits such as dishonesty, morality, aggressiveness and sobriety, whereas habit is a regularized reaction to a specific situation. When speaking of character we might say a man is prudent, but we speak of a habit when we speak of a motorist always applying his brakes when he sees a red light.

The trial judge must decide if habit has actually been proven. Where the activity is likely to be performed with varying regularity, proof of a number of specific instances of conduct will not prove habit. The court may require a comparison of the number of instances in which the alleged conduct occurred with the number of instances in which such conduct did not take place. Wilson v. Volkswagen of America, Inc., 561 F.2d 494 (4th Cir. 1977), cert. den., 434 U.S. 1020 (1978). Religious practices and drunkenness are examples of character and not habit, and therefore do not come within the proscription of Rule 406.

Because it is so regularized, proof of a habit is extremely probative on the issue of whether a particular individual acted in a certain way when met with the specific fact situation. Therefore, it is permissible to show habit in order to prove that an individual reacted in accordance with that habit on a particular occasion. Fed. R. Ev. 406. The habit can probably be proven by the opinion of a person who has made sufficient specific observations to conclude that an individual does in fact possess a particular habit, and can also be proven by enough specific instances so that the trier of fact can draw the inference that the habit exists. Such evidence is not conclusive and may be rebutted by showing specific instances of deviation from the habit.

Routine Practice or Custom. In the business world, the analogy to a habit is a routine practice or custom. **Proof of a routine practice or custom is admissible to raise the inference that it was followed on a particular occasion**. For example, if a business organization must show the mailing of a letter, it can prove the custom of delivery of the original to the mail room and the placing of a carbon copy in the appropriate file. Proof of the routine business mailing practice, together with the carbon copy in the file will permit an inference that the letter was mailed. Again, the judge has discretion to exclude such evidence if he does not find that the routine was regularly followed.

Corroboration of Habit or Routine Practice Not Necessary. Evidence of habit or routine business practice need not be corroborated to be admissible. Fed. R. Ev. 406. Thus, habit concerning safety practices is admissible whether or not there were eyewitnesses to the particular accident at issue.

Character and Habits of Animals. The character and habits of animals are admissible on the theory that animal conduct is more regular than human conduct, and therefore an animal's conduct at one time is probative of its conduct at the time in issue. In this category are habits such as that of a horse to start up of its own accord, and the vicious propensity of certain animals. Thus, in an action for personal injuries arising out of a dog bite, it would be permissible to ask anyone who has knowledge of the dog's history if the dog has bitten anyone in the past.

4.   Other Crimes, Acts, Transactions, And Events

Admissible on Issue Other than Character. Proof that a criminal defendant has committed other crimes, whether or not he has been convicted of them, is admissible **if offered for some reason other than to show the character of the defendant**. Such evidence is admissible to prove **motive, opportunity, intent, preparation, plan, knowledge, identity, or absence of mistake or accident**, if, upon request from the defendant, the prosecution gives reasonable notice of the general nature of any such evidence of prior crimes it intends to use. Fed. R. Ev. 404(b).

Many courts have read the balancing test of Rule 403 into Rule 404(b), requiring that such **evidence be excluded if clearly more prejudicial than probative**. See, United States v. Fosher, 568 F.2d 207 (1st Cir. 1978). Other courts follow a more "inclusionary" approach. See, United States v. Long, 574 F.2d 761 (3rd Cir.) cert. den. 439 U.S. 985 (1978). If not admissible for one of these specific purposes, the prosecution should not be allowed to "sneak in" references to other crimes, such as by suggesting that the defendant is a member of the underworld, United States v. Shelton, 628 F.2d 54 (D.C. Cir. 1980), or by having the defendant's probation officer testify on other issues. United States v. Pavon, 561 F.2d 799 (9th Cir. 1977).

Examples of the **specific exceptions** to the general rule that prior crimes committed by the accused are inadmissible are:

a) **If the accused takes the witness stand, evidence of prior convictions** (to the extent permitted by Federal Rule 609 discussed above) is **admissible to impeach his credibility**.

b) If the accused raises the **defense of entrapment**, his propensity to commit the crime without assistance from the police is in issue. **Evidence of his committing the same offense on previous occasions is therefore admissible**.

c) When the **identity** of the person who committed the crime is a principal issue, the fact that **the accused committed similar crimes by some peculiar method can be shown**.

d) When the defendant admits the act which constitutes the crime, but **denies having the required mental state** (as for example when a person accused of receiving stolen goods denies knowing the goods were stolen), **evidence that he perpetrated the same act previously is admissible to show the required mental state**. When malice is an element of a crime, such as murder, proof of a previous assault reasonably near in time is admissible on that issue. The same is true where he claims he perpetrated the act through accident or mistake. For example, when a defendant charged with the murder of his child claims that the death was accidental, the court can admit evidence of injuries suffered by the child on other occasions. United States v. Harris, 661 F.2d 138 (10th Cir. 1981).

e) **One crime may furnish the motive for another**. For example, if W was an eyewitness to a robbery and identified D, the fact would be admissible if D were later charged with the murder of W, and the fact that he committed the crime which furnished the motive is admissible.

Conviction of Prior Crime Not Generally Required. Except in the first example, where a conviction was required to impeach a witness, all that is required when evidence of other crimes is not being offered to show character is substantial evidence that the defendant was the person who committed the other crime. Proof of the other crime beyond a reasonable doubt is not required. This can be proven by witnesses as well as by documentary evidence.

However, the judge, to avoid confusion and side issues, can, in his discretion, limit the proof of other crimes. Several federal circuits have held that an acquittal of the prior crime estops the government from using evidence of the charge as "other crimes" evidence in subsequent cases. See, United States v. Day, 591 F.2d 861 (D.C. Cir. 1979). However, evidence of a prior acquittal has been admitted in other circuits where relevant to issues such as motive and knowledge as specified in Rule 404(b). See, United States v. Rocha, 553 F.2d 615 (9th Cir. 1977).

Similar Happenings and Transactions. Evidence of happenings similar to those in issue in the lawsuit are relevant in the broadest sense because they have some probative worth. Many times, however, their probative worth is outweighed because they will confuse the issues and consume excessive time. Many questions of the admissibility of similar transactions will be determined by the trial judge in his discretion. However, the standards in some areas are quite specific.

The mere fact that a plaintiff is a chronic litigant is not admissible. However, if any of the other lawsuits claim compensation for the same injuries or damages claimed in the present lawsuit, the fact that other lawsuits were begun would be admissible to show a claim which is possibly inconsistent with the present lawsuit, or that the plaintiff has already been compensated for the injuries he is now claiming. If the other lawsuits were for claims very similar but not identical to the present lawsuit, the relevancy is stronger but they are still not admissible, unless it could be proven that the similar claims were fraudulent.

If property is **fungible**, such as stock of the same class in the same corporation or bushels of wheat, **evidence of sales of similar property is the best evidence of value and is regularly admitted**. Fed. R. Ev. 803(17).

> For example, if the value of 100 shares of Xerox stock on a certain day were in issue, quotes of the sales prices of that stock on the stock exchange for that day would in most circumstances be conclusive on the issue of value. The stock quotation could be proven from the newspaper reports of exchange transactions as an exception to the hearsay rule.

If the asset is **not fungible**, as in the case of land taken by eminent domain, sales of similar parcels are admissible if the sale was between a willing buyer and a willing seller, each free from coercion, and took place near in time to the time for valuation. To be similar enough to be admissible, the comparable land must be reasonably close in proximity, similar in size, topography, permitted use, and physical improvement. There are bound to be differences between any two parcels of land, but the judge has the discretion to admit a sale into evidence if there is enough similarity to be a fair indication of the value of the subject parcel, or if differences in value can be readily computed because of the differences in characteristics.

A purchase price of the subject parcel at some time prior to the valuation date is admissible if it is not too remote in time, and if the property has not changed significantly since the purchase. Offers to purchase other parcels are not admissible. However, some states will permit the state to introduce the price at which the owner offered to sell the subject parcel as an admission of its value by the owner.

Fraud. Where the plaintiff is attempting to prove fraud or misrepresentation in a civil case, **evidence of similar fraudulent acts is admissible to show intent to defraud and to show knowledge that the representations were false**. If the making of the fraudulent misrepresentation is denied, proof that similar representations were made to others is admissible to show that they were made in the instant case, if it can be proven that they were part of a grand scheme or design.

Contract Dealings. Evidence of a **course of dealings between the parties to a contract are admissible in a dispute over the meaning of the words in the contract**. Uniform Commercial Code, §1-205. Previous contracts negotiated by an agent are admissible on the issue of the agent's authority. Other contracts between the two litigating parties are also admissible on the theory of custom and usage on the issue of the substantive language of the contract, when the precise terms of the contract are oral and are in dispute. However, similar contracts made between one of the litigants and third parties are not admissible.

Accidents and Defective Goods. **Evidence of similar accidents, particularly automobile accidents, is not admissible**. However, if the defendant is being sued as an owner or occupier of land, similar prior accidents at the same spot are admissible on the issue of knowledge of a dangerous condition. Here substantial similarity between the two accidents is not required, as long as the first accident would have brought a dangerous condition to the landowner's attention before the second one occurred. Evidence of similar injuries is admissible to prove causation if the cause and the injuries are almost identical.

Generally, **evidence of lack of similar accidents is admissible** in the landowner or defective product situation where, if the plaintiff's allegations are to be believed, other people would have had to be injured also. See Roth v. Black & Decker, Inc., 737 F.2d 779 (8th Cir. 1984) (evidence of similar accidents admissible in products liability case).

> For example, if A is suing a restaurant claiming food poisoning, proof that others who ate the same food there the same day also got sick is highly probative on the issue of causation. Likewise, evidence that no one else who ate the same food got sick is admissible because it is probative to show the absence of causation.

Evidence of Company Rules or Custom in an Industry. Proof of a company safety rule and its violation by an employee is admissible as evidence of negligence. Proof of an industry-wide standard or custom is admissible on the issue of the appropriate standard of care, but is not conclusive on that issue.

D.   EXPERT TESTIMONY AND SCIENTIFIC EVIDENCE

1.   Qualifications Of Witnesses

There are two preliminary matters to be considered before a witness can give an opinion as an expert.

First, the witness must be qualified as an expert. Evidence must be presented of the knowledge, skill, education, training, or experience possessed by the witness, and his familiarity with the particular problem on which he is to give an opinion. Fed. R. Ev. 702.

> For example, a real estate appraiser must be qualified by showing his education in the field of appraisal technique, his experience in buying and selling real estate, and his appraisal experience. If that background is sufficient to qualify him as an expert appraiser, he must then explain his familiarity with the property to be appraised before he can give an opinion on value.

It is unlikely that you will be given a multiple choice question in which you must determine if a particular expert is qualified, because qualification involves subjective value judgments made in the discretion of the trial judge. However, beware of the question where a witness is asked a question calling for expert testimony and there is no indication that he has been qualified. Under those circumstances, the question is inadmissible because a proper foundation for the testimony has not been laid.

2.   Bases Of Testimony

General Test. Expert testimony is permitted when (1) the testimony is based upon sufficient facts or data, (2) the testimony is the product of reliable principles and methods, and (3) the witness has applied the principles and methods reliably to the facts of the case. Fed. R. Ev. 702.

Reliability. Expert testimony is permitted when the procedures or methodology involved in reaching conclusions have received **"general acceptance in the particular field to which it belongs."** See, for example, United States v. Stifel, 433 F.2d 431 (6th Cir. 1970), where the neutron activation analysis technique for identification of materials was found to be a proper subject matter for expert opinion.

Expert testimony is **not permitted** where the state of knowledge in the field is such that the methodology in which the person is qualified has **not received general acceptance**. For example, polygraph tests offered to prove the truthfulness of a witness are not generally admissible, despite the presence of a trained polygraph operator. See United States v. Morrow, 731 F.2d 223 (4th Cir. 1984); United States v. Feldman, 711 F.2d 758 (7th Cir. 1983).

Assistance of the Trier of Fact. Another **prerequisite** to the admissibility of expert testimony is that the **scientific, technical, or other specialized knowledge** of the witness **will assist the trier of fact to understand the evidence or determine a fact in issue.** Fed. R. Ev. 702.

Expert Opinion Permitted. Expert opinions are permitted (and in some instances are necessary to avoid a directed verdict), in cases involving:

    a)   valuation;

    b)   physical or mental condition of an individual;

    c)   ballistics;

    d)   fingerprints;

    e)   handwriting; and

    f)   other issues where some scientific, business, literary, or other skill not possessed by the ordinary layman is required to reach an intelligent conclusion concerning the facts necessary to decide the case.

Many cases have involved opinions by professional accident investigators or police officers on such matters as the speed and location of the vehicle at the time of impact. Although a jury is permitted to draw inferences on those matters unaided by expert opinion, a trial judge's discretionary decision to allow expert testimony on the cause of the accident will be upheld if the expert had a sufficient factual basis from which to draw his conclusion. Gladhill v. General Motors Corp., 743 F.2d 1049 (4th Cir. 1984).

Expert Opinion Not Permitted. Expert opinions are not permitted where the trial judge in his discretion finds that the subject matter of the proposed expert opinion is one **where the jury is capable of drawing inferences from the facts, and that an expert opinion would not aid them.** For example, testimony of an architect concerning safety of a restroom, Skelton v. Sinclair Refining Co., 375 P.2d 948 (Okla. 1962), and testimony of an engineer that certain shoes were slippery, Bennet v. International Shoe Co., 275 Cal. App.2d 797, 80 Cal. Rptr. 318 (1969), were excluded on the ground that the jury did not need expert opinions in these areas.

Factual Basis of Expert Opinion. In addition to possessing the necessary background and experience to be qualified, **an expert witness must have sufficient knowledge of the immediate subject matter before his opinion is admissible.** This information can be obtained by the expert's personal observation. For example, the doctor who treated a patient can give a medical opinion of the patient's condition, using his own faculties to get the necessary information in the case. A real estate expert can gather some of the facts necessary to value a building by making a personal inspection of the premises.

Many times expert testimony will be necessary and the expert will not have access to first-hand knowledge about the subject matter of his opinion. **An expert is permitted to give an opinion even though he has not personally observed the facts necessary to form an opinion.** For example, a psychiatrist may be asked to testify in a will contest even though he never saw the testator, or an engineer may be asked to testify to the cause of a building collapse even though he never saw the debris.

Evidence Reasonably Relied Upon by Experts in Field. Federal Rule 703 permits an expert to obtain such information by listening to the evidence presented at the hearing or by gathering it before the hearing. If of a type reasonably relied upon by experts in a particular field in forming opinions or inferences on the subject, the facts or data need not be admissible in evidence in order for the opinion or inference to be admitted. See Zenith Radio Corp. v. Matsushita Elec. Indus. Co., 723 F.2d 238 (3d Cir. 1983). In fact, facts or data that are otherwise inadmissible do not become admissible merely because they were used to form an expert opinion or inference. The **inadmissible information may not be disclosed to the jury by the proponent of the opinion unless the court determines that its probative value in assisting the jury to evaluate the expert's opinion substantially outweighs its prejudicial effects.** Fed. R. Ev. 703.

This means that an expert can rely upon such hearsay information as nurses' opinions of other doctors' reports, statements by a patient's friends or relatives about his past condition, and various types of public opinion polls. The expert may be asked to rely on such information by means of a hypothetical question, but a hypothetical question is not required. See United States v. Mann, 712 F.2d 941 (4th Cir. 1983). However, a statement by a bystander at an accident concerning the point of collision could not be used by an expert in the cause of accidents, because such statements are not commonly relied upon by such experts.

Limitations on the Use of Another Expert's Opinion. Likewise, while an expert can rely on another expert's opinion on a subsidiary matter, he cannot testify to another expert's opinion on the very issue upon which he is testifying. For example, a medical examiner could rely upon a pathologist's classification of a blood type, but could not testify that another medical examiner thought that the cause of death was suffocation.

Use of Secondary Sources by an Expert on the Stand. An expert witness is also permitted to take into account hearsay information acquired during his training and education. In addition, he can rely upon facts and theories told to him while practicing his profession. For example, a real estate expert can rely upon institutional information concerning the sale price of a similar parcel of property.

However, if the expert has received from secondary sources evidence of the specific facts upon which he is basing his opinion, he may use that evidence only in forming his opinion. He may not relate those facts to the jury for them to use independently in deciding the case. For example, if a real estate expert was told about the physical condition of a building on the date it was taken by eminent domain, he may base his opinion on these facts, but he cannot himself testify to these facts while on the stand. The court has the power to appoint its own experts and to disclose their court-appointed status if they testify. Fed. R. Ev. 706.

3.   Ultimate Issue Rule

Once a witness is qualified as an expert in a field where expert opinion may properly be admitted, he is still subject to limitations in giving his testimony.

Generally, an expert opinion or inference is not objectionable merely because it embraces the ultimate issue to be decided by the trier of fact. Fed. R. Ev. 704(a).

Limitations. When the question is not phrased in terms of a factual opinion, but rather in terms of inadequately explained legal criteria, the question will be excluded. For example, the question, "Did T have the capacity to make a will?" will be excluded. On the other hand, a question such as "Did T have sufficient mental capacity to know the nature and extent of his property and the natural objects of his bounty, and to formulate a rational scheme of distribution?" would be allowed. The former question is inadmissible because neither the judge nor the jury knows what standard the expert is applying to determine capacity.

Likewise, **conclusory statements applying legal concepts** such as "D was negligent" or "P was permanently disabled" **are not permitted**.

In a criminal case, no expert may state an opinion or inference as to whether the defendant had the mental state constituting an element of the crime charged or of his defense. Fed. R. Ev. 704(b). Thus, the insanity defense is a matter for the trier of fact alone, without the aid of expert opinion, although an expert may testify to underlying facts or data on the issue.

4.   Reliability Of Scientific Evidence

An expert may testify to and, if other evidentiary rules allow, produce experimental or scientific evidence if the evidence will assist the trier of fact in determining a fact in issue. The probative value of most experiments depends upon their similarity or identity to conditions in issue. Therefore, the most common test to determine if evidence of an experiment performed outside of the courtroom is admissible is whether the conditions under which the experiment was conducted were identical or substantially similar to the conditions in issue in a lawsuit.

If the experiment relates to the composition or analysis of some relevant piece of evidence, no problem of similarity is presented when the relevant evidence itself is analyzed. If a defendant wishes to prove that a specific event could have occurred in his absence or in the absence of the thing for which he is responsible, then similarity or identity is not required.

Tests are not rendered inadmissible if the opposing party does not participate in conducting them, or if the court does not supervise them.

There are **two categories** of scientific procedures, each of which involves a different procedure for admissibility of the evidence concerning the test.

1. Scientific Procedure Not Seriously in Dispute. Many scientific testing procedures are so generally accepted as valid that **no testimony is required concerning the validity of the process itself. The court will take judicial notice of that fact**. Examples are fingerprint tests for identification, blood tests in paternity cases, ballistics tests, and radar tests to determine automobile speed. In addition, legislation in most states has sanctioned the validity of blood and breathalyzer tests for alcohol to determine drunkenness.

However, even when the validity of the testing procedure has been established, expert testimony is still required to show that the particular test was conducted in accordance with established test procedures, and that the specimens or subjects tested were relevant to the particular lawsuit. Finally, the test itself must be relevant to the determination of a material issue.

The expert must also interpret the test results. Sometimes this procedure can be easily accomplished. For example, a police officer who can testify that he has received adequate training in the operation of a breathalyzer machine can testify that he administered a test to the defendant, and that the machine registered a particular reading. Statutory provisions then determine the effect of that reading on the issue of the defendant's drunkenness. Note, however, that it is a violation of the Confrontation Clause for the prosecution in a criminal trial to prove a fact using laboratory analysis or a report without a witness who signed the report's certfiication or personally performed or observed the test. Melendez-Diaz v. Massachusetts, 557 U.S. 305 (2009); Bullcoming v. New Mexico, 564 U.S. ____ (2011).

2. Scientific Procedure Not Universally Established. Even if the scientific procedure has not become generally accepted, **it is possible to introduce evidence of test results, provided that expert evidence is produced at the trial concerning the validity of the test procedure involved, and that the trial judge finds sufficient evidence of its reliability**. The judge must perform a "gatekeeping" function, finding that the testimony or evidence is not only relevant to the issue at hand, but also rests on a reliable scientific foundation. Reliability of a scientific technique is determined by many factors, including whether the technique can be or has been **tested**, whether it has been subjected to **peer review and/or publication**, its known or potential **rate of error**, and the existence and observation of **standards controlling the application** of the technique. Daubert v. Merrell Dow Pharmaceuticals, Inc., 509 U.S. 579 (1993). Neutron activation analysis to determine the identity of goods, and voiceprints to determine identity by voice comparison are examples of techniques which require expert evidence concerning the technique itself before testimony concerning the test will be accepted. Of course, expert testimony would also be required concerning the way the test was conducted and the way the results should be interpreted.

In Kumho Tire Co., Ltd. v. Carmichael, 526 U.S. 137 (1999), the Court held that the Daubert "gatekeeping" obligation applies not only to "scientific" testimony but to all expert testimony. The Court found that Rule 702 does not distinguish between "scientific" knowledge and "technical" or "other specialized" knowledge in this regard. The Rule was subsequently amended to incorporate this standard.

Multistate Bar Review Book 2

Weight of Scientific Tests. The weight given by the fact finder to scientific tests will vary with the type of test, the way in which it was conducted, and its relevancy to the issue in the case. Except in the case of blood tests to absolve a particular male of paternity, a verdict will rarely be granted in favor of the proponents of the test on the basis of test results alone. In paternity cases, if there is no dispute concerning the procedure under which the tests were conducted, or concerning the particular elements found in the blood samples, the tests are conclusive if they show that the individual named as the father could not be the parent. Because of the danger of overreliance or admittedly inconclusive results, the tests are ordinarily inadmissible if they show a possibility of paternity. However, recent legislation in some jurisdictions would make such evidence admissible in the judge's discretion when the tests exclude such a large segment of the population that they are highly probative on the paternity issue.

E. REAL, DEMONSTRATIVE, AND EXPERIMENTAL EVIDENCE

Demonstrative evidence is a generic classification given to evidence which a trier of fact can perceive without substantial reliance on the testimony of witnesses. It is functionally divided into **real evidence,** i.e., those physical objects which played a part in the issues being litigated, and **illustrative (or demonstrative) evidence** such as maps, diagrams, charts, and photos, whose relevancy depends on its ability to explain and describe the facts of a case.

There is little question of the relevancy of items of real proof which are directly in issue in a lawsuit, such as the weapon which inflicted the violence, or the actual part of the body which was injured.

Real proof can also be circumstantial. In People v. Adamson, 27 Cal.2d 478, 165 P.2d 3 (1946), evidence of parts of women's stockings found in the defendant's room were admitted into evidence in a murder case wherein other parts of women's stockings were also found near the victim, on the ground that possession of such an item by the defendant, even if it did not match the ones found in the victim's room, were relevant as circumstantial evidence on the issue of identity. A comparison of the features of the putative father and a child in a paternity suit is usually permitted as circumstantial evidence of paternity.

Counterweights to Relevancy. In considering the admissibility of real proof, its **probative value must be weighed against the possibility it will mislead, confuse, or prejudice the jury**. The possibility of prejudice is especially acute with real evidence, particularly with parts of the human body. Therefore, even though certain parts of the anatomy may be relevant, the trial judge in his discretion can exclude exhibition of them if he finds that such exhibition will unduly inflame the jury, and that a testimonial description will serve the same function. See, People v. Cavanaugh, 44 Cal.2d 252, 270-271, 282 P.2d 53, 64 (1955).

Requirement of Authentication. Real evidence must be authenticated before it is admissible. If the object is distinctive, such as a gun with a serial number, the only authentication required is for a witness who is familiar with the object's relationship to the issues in the case to testify to that relationship. For example, a police officer can testify that the gun offered in evidence is the same one he saw at the scene of the crime.

Chain of Custody Authentication. When the object is **not distinctive** and can be easily confused with other objects, such as a bullet or a laboratory slide, or some type of fungible material such as a white powder, the requirements for proper authentication are substantially more rigid. The party offering the object into evidence must produce evidence of a chain of custody from the time the particular object becomes relevant until its introduction in court. This can best be accomplished by the testimony of each custodian accounting for the object during his period of custody. It can also be accomplished by distinctively marking an object at the time it becomes relevant, and then identifying those markings at the time of the trial.

Evidence that Physical Evidence Is in the Same Condition at Trial as at the Time of Occurrence. Testimony is also required that the physical object is either in the same condition at the time of trial as it was at the time it became relevant, or that any difference can be easily explained and will not mislead the trier of fact.

> For example, a damaged shipment of cocoa beans might have changed further between the time of the contract breach and the time of trial, due to natural deterioration or poor storage. In that case, the trial judge could exclude it.

Demeanor and Views. In addition to hearing evidence and viewing objects introduced into evidence, the court can take the demeanor of witnesses appearing before it and any information obtained on a properly authorized view into consideration in making its decision. For example, a jury can disbelieve a witness because of his demeanor while testifying, or because the testimony of a witness contradicts physical facts observed on a view.

A jury may also take into consideration the demeanor of parties off the witness stand who are present in the courtroom. Thus, a jury could find limited damages for a plaintiff who claimed he was partially yet permanently crippled, but who walked in an able manner in the courtroom. However, **an unauthorized view of a scene by a single juror is not permitted and is grounds for a mistrial**.

Tape Recordings, Photographs, and Motion Pictures of the Relevant Event. There are increasing instances in which the record of a relevant event in either sound or picture or both has been preserved by mechanical means. **Evidence produced by such recording devices is highly relevant and admissible when properly authenticated**. Authentication is accomplished by the testimony of either the person running the recording equipment, or a person present at the scene, that the mechanical equipment has in fact accurately portrayed the relevant event. If a tape recording of sound is offered into evidence, it is also necessary to show that the tape is the original, or to account for nonproduction of the original and to offer some evidence that the tape has not been altered or erased.

Tape recordings, even if properly authenticated, may nevertheless be inadmissible if the recording was made in violation of the defendant's Fourth Amendment rights. See, Katz v. United States, 389 U.S. 347 (1967). Although courts have not yet reached such a conclusion, it is possible that where the relevant event has been carefully recorded by mechanical equipment, a court cannot let stand a verdict inconsistent with what is shown on the reproduction. See, People v. Eisenberg, 22 N.Y.2d 99, 238 N.E.2d 719 (1968).

Pictures, Maps, and Models Which Illustrate the Relevant Event. Graphic illustrations of a relevant event, whether by way of photograph, diagram, or model, are **admissible when accompanied by testimony relating them to the relevant event or place**. To be admissible, maps, models, and diagrams should conform at least to one party's theory of the facts in all essential details. Photographs taken after the event may depict conditions which have changed in the interim. They would still be admissible if a witness can point out any changes, and then testify that except for them the photograph is an accurate representation of a relevant scene. X-ray photographs are admissible if they are authenticated by a doctor or other expert who can demonstrate their relevancy. The testimony of the photographer who took a particular picture is not necessary to introduce the photograph.

Demonstrations. The **trial judge in his discretion can permit a demonstration to be conducted by a witness in front of the jury**. Limitations on physical activity caused by an accident are the most common kind of demonstration. However, wherever the physical properties of some substance or machine are in issue, the judge can permit a demonstration if it will not greatly inconvenience the jury or consume excessive time.

Test Procedure Inadmissible Unless Parties Stipulate that Results Will Be Admissible. Scientific tests to determine the credibility of witnesses have not been well received by the courts. Although the polygraph and chemical and hypnotic devices have been used in many applications to assist in determining if an individual is telling the truth, courts have not admitted such evidence even when buttressed by expert testimony. The reasons for judicial reluctance to admit such evidence are:

a) doubts about the scientific reliability of the tests;
b) the difficulty of interpreting the raw test data; and
c) the danger that the jury would place undue reliance on the accuracy of the tests if they were admitted.

However, if all counsel agree to their admissibility, courts will usually admit them.

III. PRIVILEGES AND OTHER POLICY EXCLUSIONS

A. SPOUSAL IMMUNITY AND MARITAL COMMUNICATIONS

There are two distinct privileges which may apply when a witness is asked to testify against his or her spouse (or former spouse). The first is the right in criminal cases to prevent the spouse from testifying, and the second is the right to prevent the disclosure of marital communications.

When a Spouse Is a Criminal Defendant. The right of a criminal defendant to keep his spouse off the witness stand altogether has its roots in the common law incompetency of husband or wife to testify in any case in which they were interested parties. This disqualification was transformed into a privilege of one spouse to keep the other from testifying at all in a criminal case, and was based upon the rationale that such a rule would foster marital harmony.

The United States Supreme Court in Trammel v. California, 445 U.S. 40 (1980), held that the **right to refuse to testify is in the witness spouse. The spouse who is the criminal defendant does not have the right to keep her spouse off the stand**.

There must be a marriage relationship at the time of the trial for the rule to be operative. The United States Supreme Court in Obergefell et. al. v. Hodges et. al. 576 U. S. ____ (2015) held that the Fourteenth Amendment guarantees same-sex couples the fundamental right to marry in all states. A divorced witness spouse cannot claim the privilege. Most courts allow the rule to bar testimony concerning events occurring before the marriage. The privilege also renders inadmissible extra-judicial statements of the witness spouse, which would otherwise be admissible under an exception to the hearsay rule.

One further rule of disqualification in most states prohibits a spouse from testifying concerning lack of access of her mate at the time of conception, if the purpose of such testimony is to bastardize the child.

The Right to Prevent a Spouse from Testifying About Confidential Communications. The right to prevent a spouse from testifying about confidential communications, commonly called the **marital privilege, applies to civil as well as criminal cases**.

What Is a Communication? While all courts would agree that an **oral or written message** from one spouse to the other are communications, and would probably agree that acts or bodily motions which are intended by one spouse to send information to the other are communications, there is **sharp disagreement about information which a spouse obtains merely from observing acts of the other spouse, actions which are not intended by him to communicate**, as for example when wife observes husband in possession of stolen goods. A small minority of courts would go so far as to classify general information about health or mental condition learned through observation during the marriage as "communication."

Multistate Bar Review Book 2

Confidential. To be protected by the privilege, the communication must be confidential. The manner in which the communication is made is the key to confidentiality. Communications **made in private**, that is, with no third parties present, are ordinarily confidential, and are clearly so if they are about a subject the parties would desire to keep secret because its publication to third parties would be embarrassing.

On the other hand, **the presence of third parties ordinarily destroys the confidential nature of the communication, and with it the privilege**. The exception is when the third parties present are the children of the spouses. If they are too young to understand the conversations, the confidentiality is not destroyed. If the children can understand, then it is destroyed. Even if spoken in private, words said during heated arguments, expletives, and sometimes conversations about business affairs may not be confidential.

The holder of the privilege is ordinarily the spouse who originates the communication, and not the spouse receiving it. However, if there is a dialogue with each communication building upon the previous one, both spouses are the holders as to the entire communication.

Marriage Necessary at the Time of the Communication. The critical time when the marital relationship must exist for the privilege to apply is at the time of the communication. Private communications made before marriage are not privileged, even though the parties are married at the time of trial. Likewise, a former spouse or the executor of the estate of a dead spouse cannot testify to those private communications made during the marriage. Once made during marriage, the private communications are protected by the privilege unless waived by the holder.

Waiver. Since the private communication rule is one of privilege, it can only be claimed by the holder or someone authorized to claim it for him. It may not be claimed by any party to the lawsuit merely because he would be adversely affected by the testimony. Like other privileges, it can be waived by making public the information contained in the private communication, by failing to claim the privilege when a spouse is asked about the private communication, or by introducing part of the communication into evidence.

Exceptions. The privilege does not apply to suits between spouses, including divorce and support hearings, to actions of tort for damage to the marital relationship, such as alienation of affections, or to criminal actions against one spouse where the confidential communication of the other spouse might, by showing consent, reduce the offense.

Eavesdroppers. A problem may arise where a supposed confidential communication is overheard by one not known to be present. The person overhearing the conversation may be an eavesdropper, or he may have overheard the conversation completely by accident. The question is whether either spouse can prevent such a person from testifying as to what he heard. **The majority rule (and the rule to be applied on the MBE) is that an eavesdropper will not be permitted to testify to privileged communications if either spouse exercises the privilege**.

Examples of Inapplicability. Any of the following situations in a fact pattern will make the marital privilege inapplicable:

1) The offered evidence is not a communication because it does not involve an attempt to send any kind of message.
2) The parties were not married at the time of the communication.
3) The conversation took place in front of someone old enough to understand it, and therefore was not confidential.
4) The person objecting to the marital communication is not one of the spouses.
5) The action involves one spouse suing the other.
6) The party claiming the privilege has already testified about the conversation so that there is a waiver.

B.   ATTORNEY-CLIENT AND WORK PRODUCT

The attorney-client privilege was codified in 503 of the Uniform Rules of Evidence Act. Although not enacted as part of the Federal Rules of Evidence, this section has become an authoritative source on the nature and extent of the attorney-client privilege.

Rule 503 sets forth the attorney-client privilege by first defining the persons among whom confidential communications are protected and then prescribing the circumstances under which communications among them are privileged. It then deals with the mechanics of claiming the privilege and the exceptions to its operation.

An understanding of the scope of the attorney-client privilege starts with the definitions of the participants.

Client. For purposes of the rule, a client is a person, public officer, corporation, or other entity which has consulted a lawyer in his professional capacity. The client need not pay a fee nor actually retain the lawyer, but will be considered a client if the consultation was made with the prospect of hiring the lawyer.

Representative of a Client. A representative of a client is a person who:

1) has authority on behalf of the client to hire a lawyer and obtain professional legal services; or
2) has authority to act on behalf of the client on the advice rendered by a lawyer; or
3) is an employee of the client and communicates with an attorney for the employer while in the performance of his duties under the direction of the employer. Upjohn Co. v. United States, 449 U.S. 383 (1981).

Lawyer. The definition of a lawyer includes not only persons actually authorized to practice law in any state or county, but also persons reasonably believed to be so authorized.

Representatives of a Lawyer. This term includes all persons used by a lawyer in the rendition of professional legal services. Its breadth is such that not only do secretaries, law students, paralegals and employees of the lawyer's office come within this term, but professionals such as accountants and doctors whom the lawyer uses in the preparation of litigation are also included. It does not include **witnesses.**

Confidential. The term confidential is defined in terms of intent. If the communication was not intended to be disclosed to third persons other than those to whom disclosure is normally made in furtherance of those services, or those reasonably necessary for the transmission of the communication, then it is confidential. At times such a person could be the spouse, parent, confidant or business associate of the client. If the communication goes astray or is overheard by an eavesdropper, the communication is still confidential because it was not intended to be disclosed.

Operation of the Rule. The client, as the holder of the privilege, has a right:

1) to refuse to disclose, and
2) to prevent any other person from disclosing,
3) confidential
4) communications
5) made for the purpose of facilitating the rendition of professional legal services to the client
6) if the communication is between the persons discussed below.

Each of these elements requires discussion.

Refusal to Disclose. The client has a personal right not to disclose matters himself.

Attorney's Duty to Prevent Disclosure. The attorney is under an ethical duty not to disclose privileged communications to anyone, and **must claim the privilege unless the client waives it**. The attorney also has an ethical duty to supervise those in his employ so that they do not disclose confidential communications, and claim the privilege if they are compelled to disclose confidential communications by judicial process.

If eavesdroppers or persons to whom disclosure has been made in an unauthorized manner attempt to disclose confidential communications, the holder of the privilege has a right to prevent that disclosure, by objecting to the question if it is asked in a judicial proceeding, whether or not he is a party.

Confidential. Confidential has been defined above in terms of intent.

Communication. Communications clearly include words spoken and written intending to convey a message. Acts, such as the exhibition of a physical characteristic or a gesture to call the attorney's attention to some physical object, are also considered communications.

However, if a lawyer while working on his client's case **obtains information from witnesses and third parties, those communications are not within the attorney-client privilege, but are protected from pretrial discovery by the opponent**. If the client is called to testify, he may only refuse to testify about the communications made to his lawyer, and not the facts or actions which are the subject matter of those communications. Written documents are communications within the privilege only when they were written specifically to or from the lawyer, to or from the client.

Pre-existing written documents such as contracts, leases, or inter-company memos do not become privileged merely because they are handed over to the lawyer. The fact of employment, the identity (name, address, and occupation) of the client, the scope of employment, and the identity of the lawyer, are not within the privilege.

Facilitation of Legal Services. The communications must be for the purpose of obtaining legal advice or legal services. Consultation of a lawyer in the role of business advisor, friend, or confidant is not within the privilege. Even if the lawyer is consulted in his professional capacity, statements made to the attorney that are not related to the legal advice or legal services sought (e.g., the fee arrangement of the parties) would not be protected by the privilege. See In re Grand Jury Investigation, 723 F.2d 447 (6th Cir. 1983), cert. denied, 467 U.S. 1246 (1984).

This aspect of the rule is of crucial importance when dealing with communications between parties other than the lawyer and the client. Such communications are not privileged unless they are made for the purpose of obtaining legal advice for the client.

Parties Protected. Both sides of confidential communications between the following persons are protected provided that they are made for the purpose of rendering legal services.

Between a client and	his lawyer [503(b)(1)] or his lawyer's representatives [503(b)(1)].
Between a client and	representatives of the client [503(b)(4)].
By a client	to a lawyer or his representative representing another party in a pending action concerning a matter of common interest in that action [503(b)(3)].
Between a lawyer and	his client [503(b)(1)], his client's representatives [503(b)(1)], or his own representatives [503(b)(2)].
By a lawyer to	a lawyer representing another party in a matter of common interest in that action [503(b)(3)].
Among lawyers	and their representatives representing the same client [503(b)(5)].
Between representatives of a client	and the lawyer [503(b)(1)], the lawyer's representative [503(b)(1)], other representatives of the client [503(b)(4)], and the client [503(b)(4)].

By a representative of a client	to a lawyer or his representative representing another party in a pending action concerning a matter of common interest in that action [503(b)(4)].
Between a representative of a lawyer and	the client [503(b)(1)], the client's representative [503(b)(1)], the lawyer [503(b)(2)], and another representative of the lawyer [503(b)(5)].
By a representative of a client	to a lawyer or his representative representing the client in a pending action concerning a matter of common interest in that action [503(b)(4)].

Notice that the rule operates to confer the privilege on communications between the various protected parties. The lawyer's statements to the client are privileged because in the give and take of conversation each party adopts the other's language.

This formulation in Rule 503(b) gives wide scope to the attorney-client privilege. However, it ordinarily does not apply to protect the identity of the client or the fee arrangement made.

Rule 503(c) - Who May Claim the Privilege. The privilege **belongs to the client** and no one else. However, if the client is not competent to claim it, it may be claimed by a guardian or conservator if the client is alive, and his personal representative if he is deceased. If the client is a corporation, it can be claimed by successors to the corporate entity. A trustee in bankruptcy was held to have the power to waive the bankrupt corporation's attorney-client privilege with respect to prebankruptcy communications in C.F.T.C. v. Weintraub, 471 U.S. 343 (1985).

The attorney, or his representative, to whom the statement was made is presumed to have authority to claim it on behalf of his client even if the lawyer's services have been terminated. A lawyer has an ethical duty to claim the privilege unless the client has waived it and authorized disclosure.

Rule 503(d) - Exceptions. Even though all other conditions for the existence of the privilege exist, it does not exist under the following conditions:

Rule 503(d)(1) - Furtherance of Crime or Fraud. If the purpose of the communication to the lawyer is to plan or perpetrate a **future** crime or fraudulent act, then the privilege will not arise. Discussions of past frauds or crimes held for the purpose of defending an individual are within the privilege. Examples of conversations which might come within this exception would be conversations held in preparation for litigation, where the attorney condones or encourages perjury, or in the criminal situation, where the lawyer gives advice on how to cover up the crime. The party seeking to introduce the evidence must make a showing of crime or fraud before the judge may admit the evidence of the conversation.

Rule 503(d)(2) - Claimants Through the Same Deceased Client. Death ordinarily does not terminate the attorney-client privilege. It may be claimed after the death of the client by his executor. However, in a will contest, the testimony of the attorney who drew the will about his conversation with the deceased is not privileged, because all claimants are trying to inherit through the same deceased client, and there is no person who has the right to claim the privilege.

Moreover, since the attorney is often in the best position to know the testator's wishes, there is an overriding public policy reason for this vital evidence to be brought before the trier of fact. The inapplicability of the privilege in this instance has also been justified on the ground that the testator did not intend his instructions concerning his will to remain confidential after his death. The privilege is applicable, however, in suits against an estate for breach of contract to make a will or for services rendered.

Rule 503(d)(3) - Breach of Duty by the Lawyer or Client. If a client sues the lawyer for malpractice or for breach of contract, the lawyer may defend himself by revealing previously privileged communications. Likewise, he may use privileged conversations to prove his case if he is suing a client for a fee or other breach of duty. The extent of the disclosure, however, is limited to communications necessary to establish his (the attorney's) claim or defense. See American Bar Association Model Code of Professional Responsibility, DR 4-101(C)(4).

Rule 503(d)(4) - Documents Attested by the Lawyer. In this instance the lawyer is acting more as a witness than as a lawyer and the client is presumed to have waived any privilege.

Rule 503(d)(5) - Joint Clients. If two clients consult a single lawyer on a common legal problem, statements made among all three are confidential and protected by the privilege, except where the two clients are later engaged in litigation against each other. In that case, the communications are not considered confidential, and the attorney is not bound to remain silent. Likewise, if a client and his agent make statements in confidence to an attorney, they would not be privileged in a later suit between the client and agent.

Work Product. The documents or other items prepared by an attorney (or his or her agent) in preparation for trial are privileged, unless the other party has substantial need for the material and is unable to obtain the substantial equivalent of the materials by other means. Even then, the attorney's (or the agent's) mental impressions, conclusions, opinions and theories are absolutely privileged. See Fed. Rule of Civ. Proc. 26(b)(3).

C.   PHYSICIAN/PSYCHOTHERAPIST-PATIENT

Although it did not exist at common law, a statutory privilege has been created in most states for **confidential communications** between a physician and patient, **where the communications were made to the physician for the purpose of treatment or diagnosis related to treatment**.

The Relationship. The physician-patient privilege only applies when the patient has consulted the physician **for treatment or diagnosis for the purpose of treatment**. It does not apply to examinations made in preparation for litigation, for examinations by court-appointed physicians, or for life insurance examinations. Consultation for illegal purposes, such as obtaining illegal narcotics, does not come within the privilege. Since an autopsy cannot possibly be for purposes of treatment, the facts discovered in such an examination are not privileged. Likewise, information obtained for the preparation of a death certificate is not privileged.

Scope of the Privilege. Unlike the attorney-client privilege and the marital privilege, the physician-patient privilege **protects information** obtained during consultation in addition to communications. Observations made by the physician of the patient's physical or mental condition are protected by the privilege. However, the fact of the consultation, the time and place of the consultation, or the fee charged is not protected.

Confidentiality. Information and communications obtained by the doctor when he is alone with the patient are clearly confidential unless intended to be disclosed to third parties. Those persons necessary to the doctor's performance of his duties, such as nurses, lab technicians, and secretaries, do not destroy the privilege and are entitled to refuse to testify where the privilege is applicable. The presence of an advisor, parent, or counselor of the patient likewise would not destroy confidentiality.

In many jurisdictions there is a **psychotherapist-patient privilege**. Because of the nature of psychotherapy, communications made in group sessions, or made in conjunction with family members and a psychotherapist are privileged, despite the presence of these third parties. This privilege has recently been codified in Rule 503 of the Uniform Rules of Evidence Act, but it has not been enacted by the Federal Rules.

> A Supreme Court decision held that conversations between a patient and her psychotherapist as well as the notes taken during their counseling sessions are protected from compelled disclosure under Rule 501. Jaffee v. Redmond, 518 S.Ct. 1 1996.

The **social worker- patient privilege** is also recognized in many states and codified in the Uniform Rules. It, however, has been narrowed throughout recent years protecting only communications relating to the treatment of a mental or emotional condition including alcohol and drug addiction. The social worker – patient privilege is substantially incorporated in the physician and psychotherapist privilege of Rule 503.

Holder. The patient is the holder of the privilege. However, if the patient is not present, the **physician must claim it on his behalf**. If the privilege is applicable, the patient can refuse to disclose (and can prevent the physician or anyone who obtained information as the agent of the physician from disclosing), any communication made to the physician or information obtained as a result of the consultation.

In the case of the patient-psychotherapist privilege, the patient as holder has the right to prevent all persons who participated in the therapy from disclosing information obtained in the course of the patient's treatment. The privilege survives the patient and may be claimed by the executor, but does not apply in a will contest.

Waiver. The patient can waive the privilege by **contract** (when he takes an examination for life insurance), or he can waive it **voluntarily**. He impliedly waives it when he testifies to events relating to his consultations with the physician, or puts the physician on the stand to ask him about the patient's physical or mental condition. Failing to object when his physician is called by the adversary is likewise a waiver. A suit against the physician for malpractice is a waiver of the privilege.

Some courts have gone so far as to find a waiver whenever the patient voluntarily puts his physical or mental condition in issue in a lawsuit. Statutes in various states make the privilege completely inapplicable in certain proceedings, such as criminal cases, malpractice actions, or commitment proceedings.

Relationship to Hearsay Exception. There is a substantial overlap of material covered by the physician-patient privilege and the hearsay exception for statements made for the purpose of diagnosis or treatment. If the patient wants to admit statements which fall into the hearsay exception, there is no problem, since the privilege can be waived.

In order to be admissible over the objection of the patient, though, statements to a doctor must be both not hearsay and not privileged (i.e., they must fall within the hearsay exception and outside the privilege). The most common example is a statement made to a physician consulted only for the purposes of testifying or a court-appointed physician. Also, statements made for the purpose of diagnosis or treatment to one other than a doctor (an ambulance driver or the like) would fall within the hearsay exception but would not be privileged, and so would be admissible over the patient's objection.

D. SELF-INCRIMINATION

The Fifth Amendment to the United States Constitution provides in part that "No person . . . shall be compelled in any criminal case to be a witness against himself." Through the due process clause of the Fourteenth Amendment, this provision and the Federal constitutional standards with respect to its application must be applied by the states. **Malloy v. Hogan**, 378 U.S. 1, 8-9 (1964).

There are two separate branches of this privilege - First, the privilege of a witness not to answer questions which might tend to incriminate him; and second, the right of the accused in a criminal trial not to take the stand and testify at all.

1. Witness Privilege

Type of Proceeding. The privilege of a witness not to answer questions which might tend to incriminate him **extends to all kinds of proceedings where compulsory process to summons and interrogate witnesses is available**. A witness may claim this privilege at civil and criminal trials, administrative hearings, legislative investigations, pretrial discovery proceedings, and grand jury proceedings.

Holder of the Privilege. The privilege against self-incrimination is **limited to natural persons who claim that the answer or the documentary evidence sought would tend to incriminate them**. A person may not claim the privilege on the ground that the answer would tend to incriminate a third person. The privilege against self-incrimination does not permit an individual to prevent a witness from testifying about an incriminating statement made in the past, unless the individual's Miranda rights were violated.

Likewise, privileged records which an individual places in the hands of a third party such as a tax accountant are **not privileged in the hands of that third party**. **Couch v. United States**, 409 U.S. 322 (1973). The privilege is **not available to corporations**, **George Campbell Painting Corp. v. Reid**, 392 U.S. 286 (1968), or to any unincorporated organization such as a three member law partnership, **Bellis v. United States**, 417 U.S. 85 (1974). Property of a corporation in the hands of its agents or officials cannot be withheld by an agent on the ground that it will tend to incriminate the agent. **Wilson v. United States**, 211 U.S. 361 (1911).

Type of Answer Which Is Privileged. The privilege only protects against incrimination; that is, legal criminal liability. The privilege is not available if the answer to the question would possibly subject the holder to no more than embarrassment, social disgrace, loss of status, loss of private employment, or civil liability, unless the liability, such as a forfeiture proceeding, although civil in form, is criminal in nature. **Boyd v. United States**, 116 U.S. 616 (1886).

Crimes Barred by the Statute of Limitations. If the questioning is only related to a crime for which the guilt of the witness has been finally adjudicated, or which is clearly beyond the statute of limitations and therefore there is no longer any chance of conviction, the **privilege cannot be claimed on account of those crimes**. However, if testimony concerning such a crime could lead to conviction of a crime for which the witness has not been tried, or a crime which is not barred by the statute of limitations, the privilege can be claimed. **Malloy v. Hogan**, 378 U.S. 1, 13 (1964).

Criminal Liability in Another Jurisdiction. Even though a witness is being asked about facts which do not lead to criminal liability in the forum jurisdiction, he may claim the privilege if the forum is a Federal one and testimony could lead to conviction of a crime in any state; or, conversely, if the forum is a state one and the testimony could lead to Federal conviction. **Murphy v. Waterfront Commission**, 378 U.S. 52, 77-78 (1969). By implication, that case would permit claim of the privilege if the testimony in a state proceeding could lead to conviction of a crime in a sister state or foreign country.

Determining When Answer Will Be Incriminating. The trial judge must rule on the claim of privilege without knowing what the answer will be. The answer need not admit criminal liability in order to be privileged. The answer need only furnish a link in the chain of circumstantial evidence necessary for a conviction. **Blau v. United States**, 340 U.S. 159 (1950).

In addition, the answer itself need not be admissible evidence in a criminal trial if it would provide a lead to evidence which might be so used. Even though the judge ultimately decides if the claim of privilege is justified, his right to require the witness to answer is limited. To sustain the privilege under the standard required by **Hoffman v. United States**, 341 U.S. 479, 486, 487 (1951), "it need only be evident from the implications of the question in the setting in which it is asked, that a responsive answer to the question or an explanation of why it cannot be answered might be dangerous because injurious disclosures could result."

The Supreme Court reversed a contempt conviction in Hoffman because it was not completely clear whether the answer could not possibly tend to incriminate. The witness, however, cannot refuse to appear at a proceeding and still get the benefit of the privilege. He must be sworn and claim the privilege in response to questions asked.

Immunity. If the government desires a witness to testify despite a justified claim of privilege, it can obtain his testimony by properly giving the witness immunity. For the witness to claim immunity successfully in a later prosecution, he must first be questioned, then claim the privilege, and finally be given immunity by an authority empowered to do so.

Transactional Immunity vs. Testimonial Immunity. The scope of protection which an immunity statute must give before evidence can be compelled has been defined by the Supreme Court in two cases: Zicarelli v. New Jersey, 406 U.S. 472 (1972) (dealing with a state witness immunity statute), and Kastigar v. United States, 406 U.S. 441 (1972) (dealing with the Federal witness immunity statute). In both cases, the Court decided that the United States Constitution does not require a witness immunity statute to encompass "transactional immunity" that is, immunity from prosecution for any crime which was referred to in the testimony. **The statute need only afford "testimonial immunity" which merely prevents the prosecution from using the actual testimony of the witness and any evidence derived therefrom in any future trial**. The Court found the protection conferred by the statutes (immunity from use and derivative use) to be co-extensive with the privilege against self-incrimination, and so sufficient to compel testimony without jeopardizing the privilege against self-incrimination. While "transactional immunity" confers broader protection than the Fifth Amendment privilege, the Supreme Court found it was not constitutionally required.

A deponent's testimony at a civil deposition, with questions repeating verbatim or closely tracking his prior immunized grand jury testimony, is not immunized testimony within the meaning of the use immunity statute. Without an additional assurance of immunity, the deponent may assert his Fifth Amendment privilege. Pillsbury Co. v. Conboy, 459 U.S. 248 (1983).

Immunity in Other Jurisdictions. A state immunity statute can give effective immunity from a Federal prosecution, and a Federal immunity statute can give effective protection against a state prosecution. Murphy v. Waterfront Commission, 378 U.S. 52 (1964).

Use of Immunized Testimony in Perjury Prosecutions. Both truthful and false immunized testimony may be used against a witness in a subsequent perjury prosecution where the testimony is relevant to prove that the false statements were made with knowledge of their falsity. United States v. Apfelbaum, 445 U.S. 115 (1980).

Waiver by the Witness. If a witness voluntarily testifies and makes significant incriminating disclosures, he can be required to testify further if the additional disclosures will **not additionally incriminate,** but will rather only add details concerning the earlier testimony. Rogers v. United States, 340 U.S. 367 (1951). Ellis v. United States, 416 F.2d 791, 805 (1969), held that a nondefendant witness who has waived his privilege in front of the grand jury cannot later claim it at a trial resulting from a grand jury indictment.

A contractual agreement to waive the privilege, which is usually incident to an employment contract, is not specifically enforceable. A witness may break his contract and claim the privilege. Steven v. Marks, 383 U.S. 234 (1966). A state cannot as a condition of public employment require that a contractor waive his privilege. Lefkowitz v. Turley, 414 U.S. 70 (1973).

Privilege to Prevent Production of Documents. There are two distinct procedures whereby the state might attempt to obtain documentary evidence.

If the state, pursuant to a valid search warrant, seizes the private, incriminating papers of an individual, the privilege against self-incrimination has not been violated. While the Fourth Amendment protects the defendant's privacy rights, the Fifth Amendment only protects the defendant from testimonial compulsion. As long as he is not required to tell the police where the records are, or to vouch for their authenticity, the privilege against self-incrimination will not bar their admission. Andresen v. Maryland, 427 U.S. 463 (1976).

On the other hand, if the police summons a witness and require him to bring with him the documents which the state requires, he can successfully refuse to produce them by claiming the protection of the privilege against self-incrimination, Curcio v. United States, 354 U.S. 118, 125 (1952), on the theory that bringing the records in response to a summons would in effect be testimony that the records are the ones which were summonsed.

There is an **exception** to the right to claim the privilege against self-incrimination if the government can bring the records it seeks within the required records exception. To qualify for this exception, the purpose for which the record is kept must be essentially regulatory; the records must be the kind which are customarily kept; and the records must have "a public aspect which render them analogous to public documents." Grosso v. United States, 390 U.S. 62, 67, 68 (1968). Under this test, price records kept under a price regulation statute were not privileged, but the privilege was a defense to a prosecution for failing to file under the Subversive Activities Control Act, Federal wagering statutes, and a Federal firearms act.

Right of a Witness to Be Warned of his Privilege Against Self-Incrimination. Statements made by a party as a result of interrogation while in police custody are inadmissible, unless the **party has been advised that his constitutional privilege against self-incrimination gives him the right to remain silent**, and unless he **freely waives that right**. Miranda v. Arizona, 384 U.S. 436 (1966). However, a witness in a civil or criminal trial or grand jury hearing is not entitled to such a warning, and can incriminate himself by not claiming the privilege. Such testimony can then be used against him later. A person compelled to appear before his probation officer to answer questions similarly must assert the privilege despite the lack of a warning. Minnesota v. Murphy, 466 U.S. 945 (1984).

2.   Privilege of the Accused

In addition to the rights of a witness described above, the accused in a criminal case has the **right not to testify at his criminal trial**. He **may testify at a preliminary hearing** concerning the admissibility of evidence **without waiving his privilege** not to take the stand at his trial. The evidence given at the preliminary hearing is not admissible at trial, nor may it be commented on. Simmons v. United States, 390 U.S. 377 (1968).

Multistate Bar Review Book 2

When the Rights Attach. A person does not achieve the status of an accused **until formal legal process has been commenced against him**. Thus, while he may invoke the privilege as a witness at a grand jury investigation, administrative hearing, or legislative inquiry, he may not refuse to testify altogether. However, once formal criminal proceedings are begun, he can refuse to answer any question and thus is not subject to pretrial discovery unless he requests pretrial discovery from the prosecution. In that case, the right of the accused to pretrial discovery can be made subject to his giving similar rights to the prosecution. Fed. R. Crim. R. 16.

The Scope of the Privilege. The privilege against self-incrimination is a **testimonial privilege**. Thus, while the accused cannot be compelled to take the witness stand to testify, **he can be required, without violating his rights, to try on clothing before a jury to see if it fits him**, Holt v. United States, 218 U.S. 245 (1910); to provide a **sample of his blood** for the purpose of determining alcohol content, Schmerber v. California, 384 U.S. 757 (1966); to provide fingerprints; to participate in a lineup; to give a sample of handwriting for comparison purposes, United States v. Mara, 410 U.S. 19 (1973); and to give a sample of his voice for analysis and comparison. United States v. Dionisio, 410 U.S. 1 (1973).

The privilege only protects an accused from being compelled to testify against himself, or otherwise to provide the state with evidence of a testimonial or communicative nature. Schmerber v. California, 384 U.S. 757, 761 (1966). Four members of the five member majority in California v. Byers, 402 U.S. 424 (1971), held that a statute requiring a driver involved in an automobile accident to stop and identify himself was not of a testimonial or communicative nature, and therefore did not violate his privilege against self-incrimination. The admission into evidence of a defendant's refusal to submit to a blood-alcohol test does not violate the privilege. South Dakota v. Neville, 459 U.S. 533 (1983).

Comment Upon Failure of Accused to Testify. The prosecution in a criminal case **may not comment upon the failure of the accused to take the witness stand**, and the judge must instruct the jury to draw no inference from it. Griffin v. California, 380 U.S. 609 (1965). A state criminal defendant's right, upon proper request, to receive such jury instruction is protected by the Fifth and Fourteenth Amendments. Carter v. Kentucky, 450 U.S. 288 (1981). However, unexplained possession of stolen goods permits the jury to infer that the accused stole them. Comment by the prosecution on this unexplained possession and on similar inferences does not constitute comment upon the failure of the accused to take the stand.

Waiver of the Privilege by the Accused. By voluntarily taking the witness stand in his own defense, the accused **waives the privilege and may be cross-examined** at least on those matters concerning which he testified on direct examination. Because he has the right to stay off the stand altogether, if the accused testifies, he is more likely to create a waiver than in the case of an ordinary witness. Brown v. United States, 356 U.S. 148 (1958).

In addition to cross-examination on the matters testified to on direct examination, he is also subject to impeachment in a manner similar to any witness. The rule in some jurisdictions that a witness called on direct examination may be cross-examined on any matter relevant to the case probably does not apply to an accused, because Federal standards which restrict the scope of cross-examination govern the standards for claim of the privilege against self-incrimination. **Malloy v. Hogan**, 378 U.S. 1 (1964).

Therefore, since in a Federal court an accused could not be asked on cross-examination about matters unrelated to his direct testimony or his impeachment, the same rule should apply in states where there is wide-open cross-examination. The accused has the right to take the stand at any time during his defense. A statute requiring him to take the stand, if at all, at the conclusion of the prosecution's case is unconstitutional. **Brooks v. Tennessee**, 406 U.S. 605 (1972).

Pretrial Psychiatric Tests for the Accused Valid. When the issue of the ability of the accused to stand trial is raised, the court has the power, without violating the accused's privilege against self-incrimination, to require him to submit to psychiatric examination. Most courts, however, would limit information obtained at such an examination to the competency of the accused to stand trial, while others would permit the evidence to be used on the sanity issue generally. To permit evidence communicated during the psychiatric examination to be used to prove the substantive facts of the crime charged, or to allow such evidence to be used at a presentence hearing without informing the defendant, prior to the examination, of her Miranda rights would violate the privilege against self-incrimination. **Estelle v. Smith**, 451 U.S. 454 (1981).

E.   OTHER PRIVILEGES

Priest-Penitent Privilege. Most states provide by statute, and a few by decision, that a person has a privilege to refuse to disclose, and to prevent another from disclosing, a **confidential communication by the person to a clergyman in his capacity as a spiritual advisor**. A clergyman is a priest, minister, rabbi, or similar functionary of a religious organization, or someone reasonably believed to be one. The requirement of confidentiality is similar to that of the attorney-client privilege. Some state statutes require that the communication be made as part of a prescribed church rite, but the more generally accepted view confers the privilege on any information confidentially communicated for the purpose of seeking spiritual advice. **A "Religious Privilege" is codified in the Uniform Rules of Evidence Act. Rule 505, but is not enacted in the Federal Rules of Evidence.**

Required Reports. If a person or entity must make a report to a governmental agency as required by law, and the statute requiring the report also confers the privilege to refuse to disclose its contents, then the person making the report is not obliged to disclose its contents, and the government official to whom it is made is forbidden to disclose it. Federal tax returns are not so privileged. Some state returns enjoy greater protection under state statutes. The privilege does not exist in prosecutions for fraud or perjury in connection with the returns themselves.

Political Vote. Unless he has cast his vote illegally, a voter has a privilege to refuse to disclose the tenor of his vote at a political election conducted by secret ballot.

Trade Secrets. There is no absolute privilege protecting trade secrets. Federal Open Market Comm. v. Merrill, 443 U.S. 340 (1979). A person has a qualified privilege to refuse to disclose a trade secret owned by him when that refusal would not tend to conceal fraud or otherwise work an injustice. Even if disclosure is required, the judge must take protective measures to limit the persons to whom disclosure is made.

The Accountant-Client Privilege. A substantial minority of states have created by statute a privilege for clients of accountants similar to that enjoyed by clients of lawyers. There is **no accountant-client communications privilege under federal law**, however. United States v. El Paso Co., 682 F.2d 530 (5th Cir. 1982), cert. den., 104 S. Ct. 1927. Nor can a client's records in the possession of an accountant be protected from discovery by the Internal Revenue Service under the "work product" doctrine. United States v. Arthur Young & Co., 466 U.S. 936 (1984). The Supreme Court stated that a certified public accountant serving as an independent auditor assumes a public responsibility different from the relationship of loyalty and confidence between lawyer and client.

Newsperson Privilege. A number of states by statute have given a newsperson a qualified privilege to refuse to disclose sources of information. However, the Supreme Court has refused to give that privilege constitutional status under the First Amendment. In Branzburg v. Hayes, 408 U.S. 665 (1972), the court upheld the right of the grand jury to subpoena a newsperson and ask him about sources of information in his news story when that information is relevant to the crime it is investigating.

Governmental Privileges: State Secrets. The government has a privilege to refuse to disclose secret information relating to national defense or international relations. All that is required to claim this privilege is for the head of the government agency involved to demonstrate a reasonable likelihood that the evidence will disclose a secret of state. The judge has the limited function of determining that the government's claim is reasonable. The government may request that the hearing be held in camera.

Governmental Privileges: Official Information. Official information not involving state secrets is not privileged except for intragovernmental opinions or recommendations, investigatory files for law enforcement purposes, and information not available to the public under freedom of information acts. Investigatory files compiled for law enforcement purposes are available after the witness who is the subject of those files has testified in a particular case. Grand jury minutes are available upon the showing of a particularized need. Pittsburgh Plate Glass Co. v. United States, 384 U.S. 855 (1966). The privilege for information in a government file may be claimed by an attorney for the government. The trial judge has full power to make a determination whether the government's claim of privilege is justified, but can require that inspection of the documents be done in secret.

Governmental Privileges: Identity of Informers. The government has **a privilege to refuse to disclose the identity of a person who has furnished information relating to a possible law violation. Only identity is privileged**. Communications are privileged only to the extent that disclosure would protect the informer's identity. If the identity of the informer has already been disclosed to those who would have cause to resent the communication, or if he appears as a government witness, then the purpose of the privilege is gone and it may no longer be claimed. Roviaro v. United States, 353 U.S. 53 (1957).

If it appears that the informer may be able to give testimony necessary to a fair determination of the issues of a case, the government can show in camera whether the informer can supply that testimony. If the judge finds that the informer is in a position to give necessary testimony, then the government must either produce the witness or suffer a determination of the case adverse to the government. Roviaro v. United States, supra. The identity and reliability of an informer may be decisive evidence on the validity of a search warrant and the admissibility of evidence found pursuant thereto. Therefore, the judge may require that the identity of the informer be disclosed, but at the government's request this will be done in camera. See McCrory v. Illinois, 368 U.S. 800 (1967).

Executive Privilege. The case of United States v. Nixon, 418 U.S. 683 (1974), recognized a **constitutional privilege in the President of the United States to refuse to disclose military, defense, or foreign policy secrets to anyone in any proceeding**, because such a privilege is necessary to the discharge of his constitutional functions. Moreover, to require the disclosure of any presidential conversation, there must be a strong showing of the need for disclosure, which in this case was met by the need for the evidence in a pending criminal proceeding, and a demonstration that the specific evidence sought was relevant in that proceeding. Finally, even where that evidence is required, the disclosure must be made in camera and the judge must permit only the most limited disclosure.

Effect of the Exercise of the Privilege by the Government. If the government is not a party to a case where it successfully invokes a governmental privilege, then the case will proceed with the evidence unavailable. If the government is a party and its opponent is deprived of material evidence, the judge may make any further orders which the interests of justice require, including striking the testimony of a witness, declaring a mistrial, finding against the government on the relevant issue, or dismissing the action.

F. INSURANCE COVERAGE

General Rule of Inadmissibility. Federal Rule 411 provides that evidence that the defendant is or is not covered by liability insurance is **not admissible to prove that the defendant acted negligently or otherwise wrongfully**. Such evidence is only marginally relevant to these issues, but can be highly prejudicial.

Exceptions. The fact that the defendant is insured may be admissible on a number of other grounds, such as **agency** and the **control or ownership** of the vehicle or instrument involved. It may also be relevant on the credibility or bias of a witness. For example, a physician who examined the plaintiff can be required to testify that he was employed by the defendant's liability carrier. Charter v. Chleborad, 551 F.2d 246 (8th Cir.), cert. den., 434 U.S. 856 (1977). Finally, the fact of insurance may also be brought to the jury's attention in an unresponsive answer by the witness. In this case, the answer will be stricken but will ordinarily not automatically require a mistrial.

G.   REMEDIAL MEASURES

General Rule of Inadmissibility. Federal Rule 407 provides that **evidence of measures taken after an event which would have made that event less likely to occur if taken previously is not admissible to prove negligence, culpable conduct, a defect in a product or its design, or a need for a product warning in connection with the event**. Although such evidence could be relevant on the issue of negligence to indicate the appropriate standard of care in the particular situation, it is not admissible on that issue because of the public policy to encourage repairs or other safety measures. This rule would exclude evidence of subsequent activities such as repairs made after an accident, installation of safety devices, changes in rules or regulations, changes in construction or manufacturing processes, or discharge of an employee who caused the injury.

Previously, it had been held in some states that this rule was inapplicable in strict liability actions because the issue is the product's defect rather than the manufacturer's conduct. Ault v. Int'l Harvester Co., 13 Cal.3d 113, 528 P.2d 1148 (1974). Federal courts were divided on the question of whether Rule 407 applied in strict products liability cases as well as negligence cases. See Grenada Steel Indus., Inc. v. Alabama Oxygen Co., 695 F.2d 883 (5th Cir. 1983) (Rule 407 applicable in products liability cases); Roth v. Black & Decker, Inc., 737 F.2d 779 (8th Cir. 1984) (Rule 407 not applicable in strict liability cases). But, in 1997, Rule 407 was amended to provide that evidence of subsequent remedial measures might not be used to prove a defect in a product or a defect in design. Thus, today, Rule 407, uniformly applies to strict liability cases. Also, the adequacy of the manufacturer's warnings falls within Rule 407, and evidence of a subsequently revised warning will not be admissible. DeLuryea v. Winthrop Laboratories, 697 F.2d 222 (8th Cir. 1983).

Exceptions. Subsequent safety measures **are admissible when offered to prove some relevant issue other than negligence**. The most common example is proof that the defendant made repairs offered to show that the defendant is in **control of the premises** upon which the accident occurred.

> For example, in Powers v. J.B. Michael & Co., 329 F.2d 674 (6th Cir. 1964), evidence of the subsequent placing of warning signs on a stretch of road was admitted to show the contractor's control over that road, even though the theory of negligence was the failure to install such signs at the time of the accident.

Such evidence is also admissible to show **feasibility of precautionary measures**. In Boeing Airplane Co. v. Brown, 291 F.2d 310 (9th Cir. 1961), evidence of alterations to the design of a plane of the type involved in a crash was admissible to show that such changes were feasible.

If the view of the accident scene as shown to the jury differs from that at the time of the accident because of subsequent safety measures, this fact can be called to the jury's attention. Evidence of subsequent safety measures used to show control and the other uses of such evidence can be prevented if the control or other issue is not seriously in dispute, and is therefore admitted by the defendant.

H. COMPROMISE, PAYMENT OF MEDICAL EXPENSES, AND PLEA NEGOTIATIONS

General Rule of Inadmissibility. Federal Rule 408 provides that evidence of a settlement, or of an offer to settle or compromise a claim which is disputed as to either validity or amount, or to receive such a settlement or offer of settlement, is not admissible to prove either the validity or invalidity of that claim or its amount. This universal principle is based upon the public policy to encourage settlement negotiations and thereby avoid litigation.

Exceptions. The following are four situations in which this rule will not apply:

1. When There Is No Dispute. There must be a claim or dispute, or at least a threatened claim or dispute, before the rule will be applicable. A statement made at the scene of an auto accident such as, "I guess I owe you a fender" before any claim is made or threatened is not excluded.

2. When Offered for Purposes Other than to Show Liability. If the offer in compromise is accepted and the contract thus formed is not performed, then in a suit to enforce the settlement contract, the offer is admissible because it is the central fact of such a suit, and no public policy encourages nonperformance of settlement agreements. See, United States v. Stirling, 571 F.2d 708 (2d Cir.), cert. den., 439 U.S. 824 (1978). The offer is likewise admissible to show that the settlement negotiations operated as a waiver by the defendant of time limitations imposed upon the plaintiff to give notices or file pleadings. If the settlement offer is relevant to impeach the credibility of any witness, it would be admissible. A consent decree between the defendant and its federal regulators has been held admissible in a subsequent case on the issue of the defendant's knowledge and intent to defraud. See, Wegerer v. First Commodity Corp., 744 F.2d 719 (10th Cir. 1984).

3. When Liability and Amount Are Not in Dispute. If the claim is admitted as to both liability and amount, the rule banning evidence of offers of settlement is inapplicable to negotiations to pay a lesser amount, or to pay over a period of time.

4. Obstructing a Criminal Investigation or Prosecution. The act of a criminal defendant in settling or attempting to settle civil claims with criminal prosecution witnesses is not protected by the policy of encouraging settlements. Evidence of such activity by a criminal defendant is admissible against him as circumstantial evidence of his guilt. Fed. R. Ev. 408.

     Conduct or Statements Made During Compromise Negotiations. Evidence of conduct or statements **made during compromise negotiations is inadmissible**, even though in the form of an unequivocal admission, and even though counsel failed to stipulate that the negotiations were without prejudice. The principal factual issue to be determined concerning such statements is the dimensions of settlement negotiations. Any statements made during a conversation in which an offer in compromise is made, whether occurring before or after the actual compromise offer, would be protected under the rule.

     However, Federal Rule 408 does not permit a party to keep documents or statements out of evidence deliberately by bringing them forward at a compromise negotiation. If they are otherwise discoverable, they are admissible.

> For example, if the defendant had a statement from an eyewitness that said that he went through a red light, the defendant could not keep that statement out of evidence by showing it to the other side during the course of settlement negotiations.

     Payment of Medical Expenses. Federal Rule 409 provides that evidence of furnishing, or offering or promising to pay medical, hospital, or similar expenses occasioned by an injury is **not admissible to prove liability for the injury**. Statements made which are not a part of the paying or offer to pay are not excluded in the same way in which statements made in the course of compromise negotiations are excluded under Rule 408.

     Settlement with Third Parties. Where two persons are injured by the same act of the defendant, he will frequently settle or attempt to settle one claim before the trial of the other. The **fact of the offer of settlement with the third party is ordinarily inadmissible** for the policy reasons discussed previously.

     However, if the third party is called as a witness by the defendant and testifies in support of his defense, the fact of the settlement may be shown to impeach the witness's credibility by raising the inference that the payment biased his testimony in the defendant's favor, and by showing that his claim and settlement are inconsistent with his testimony that the defendant is not at fault.

Criminal Cases. Plea bargaining, i.e., an offer to plead guilty or to plead nolo contendere in exchange for a lighter sentence in the criminal law is analogous to a settlement negotiation in civil cases. Therefore, an **offer to plead guilty or nolo contendere is not admissible against a criminal defendant in any criminal or civil action or proceeding against the person making the offer**. Fed. R. Ev. 410. Statements made in connection with such an offer are similarly excluded. There must be a showing that the government agents involved had authority to plea bargain and in fact offered a "deal." Rachlin v. United States, 723 F.2d 1373 (8th Cir. 1983).

Likewise, a plea of guilty which is later withdrawn is inadmissible because it would frustrate the policy which permitted withdrawal in the first place. However, Federal Rule 410 provides that statements made in court on the record and in the presence of counsel are admissible in a subsequent perjury prosecution.

I.   PAST SEXUAL CONDUCT

Federal Rule 412(a) renders **inadmissible reputation and opinion evidence concerning a victim of rape's other sexual behavior**. Evidence of specific incidents of that other sexual behavior is admissible if constitutionally required to be admitted, or to prove sexual activity with a third person for the purpose of showing that the third person and not the defendant engaged in the criminal conduct.

Evidence of other sexual conduct with the accused is admissible on the issue of consent. A defendant must ordinarily give advance notice prior to trial of his desire to introduce evidence of other sexual conduct, and the judge must conduct a hearing in chambers to determine if its probative value outweighs its prejudicial effect before it may be admitted at trial.

The Rule (as amended) applies to all proceedings (criminal and civil) in which alleged sexual misconduct is an issue (rather than just the criminal proceedings specified in the old Rule). The Rule continues to prohibit, in general, all evidence of other sexual behavior and now also generally prohibits any evidence of the alleged victim's "Sexual predisposition."

The prior exceptions to these general prohibitions continue to be the same in criminal cases -- evidence is admissible if it is:

1)   constitutionally required;
2)   offered to prove that someone other than the defendant was the perpetrator; or
3)   offered to prove consent.

In a civil case, the Rule now provides that evidence of sexual behavior or predisposition is admissible **only if its probative value substantially outweighs the danger of harm to any alleged victim and unfair prejudice to any party**. Evidence of the alleged victim's reputation is admissible only if that reputation is put in controversy by the alleged victim.

As with the prior Rule, any party who wants to use such evidence must generally give advance notice of the intent to do so, and the judge must conduct an in camera hearing to decide whether the evidence should be admitted.

IV. WRITINGS, RECORDINGS, AND PHOTOGRAPHS

Definitions

Writings and Recordings. "Writings" and "recordings" consist of letters, words, or numbers, or their equivalent, set down by handwriting, typewriting, printing, photostating, photographing, magnetic impulse, mechanical or electronic recording, or other form of data compilation.

Photographs. "Photographs" include still photographs, X-ray films, video tapes, and motion pictures.

Original. An "original" of a writing or recording is the writing or recording itself or any counterpart intended to have the same effect by a person executing or issuing it. An "original" of a photograph includes the negative or any print therefrom. If data are stored in a computer or similar device, any printout or other output readable by sight, shown to reflect the data accurately, is an "original."

Duplicate. A "duplicate" is a counterpart produced by the same impression as the original, or from the same matrix, or by means of photography, including enlargements and miniatures, or by mechanical or electronic re-recording, or by chemical reproduction, or by other equivalent techniques which accurately reproduces the original.

A. REQUIREMENT OF ORIGINAL

Federal Rule 1002 defines the best evidence rule as follows:

> To prove the content of a writing, recording, or photograph, the original writing, recording, or photograph is required except as provided in the rules or by act of Congress.

Applicability: Proof of Contents. The best evidence rule applies only where the **contents of a document, recording, or photograph must be proven**. It does not apply to proof of the existence of documents. It most frequently applies to contracts, wills, deeds, and other instruments of operative legal effect where the policy of the rule in providing the trier of fact with the exact language used is most important.

Inapplicable to Records of Events When Record Not Used to Prove Event. The rule does not apply to require the introduction of contemporaneously made records of events where the event and not the record is in issue. Here the fact to be proven has an existence independent of the writing.

> For example, it is not necessary to produce the stenographic transcript to introduce the testimony of a witness at a previous hearing, because the testimony itself and not the record is in issue. A witness who heard the testimony may testify. Persons who have personal knowledge of births, marriages, and deaths may testify about them without producing appropriate certificates. A doctor who performed an autopsy can testify about its results without introducing the autopsy report. A purchaser may testify that he paid for goods without producing a receipt.

Applied When Record Used to Prove Event. If a witness does not have personal knowledge of an event and relies upon the document for his information, then he is introducing the contents of the document and the best evidence rule would apply.

> For example, a party who desired to introduce the findings of an autopsy by showing what was contained in the autopsy report would be required to comply with the best evidence rule. Likewise, if a party did not have a witness who was present and remembered testimony given at a former trial, he would have to comply with the best evidence rule if he sought to introduce that testimony through a transcript.

Not Applicable to Physical Objects. The best evidence rule does not apply to physical objects, even if they have inscriptions on them, unless the exact wording is crucial and the object can be easily transported to court.

Applies to More than Writings. The best evidence rule applies to much more than conventional writings. Under the Federal Rules of Evidence, it applies to "writings and recordings consisting of letters, words, or numbers, or their equivalent, set down by handwriting, typewriting, printing, photostating, photographing, magnetic impulse, mechanical or electronic recording, or other form of data compilation." Fed. R. Ev. 1001(1). Photographs (which include still photographs, X-ray films, videotapes, and motion pictures) are also included. Rule 1001(2). However, as in the case of writings, the best evidence rule would apply to those other forms of recorded data when the contents of that data must be proven.

What Is an Original. For purposes of the rule, the original document is the one which affects the rights of the parties under the substantive law controlling in the lawsuit.

> For example, if D sends P a letter defaming P, and also sends a copy to P's friend, the copy is the original document for purposes of libel, because publication to a third party is a substantive law requirement of torts. If the parties sign a carbon copy of a contract instead of the ribbon copy, the carbon is the original document.

Original in Multiple Counterparts. If a contract is signed in two counterparts, both are originals even though one is a carbon copy and the other is the ribbon copy. Where there is more than one original, the nonproduction of all must be accounted for before secondary evidence is admissible.

"Duplicates." The Federal Rules of Evidence have introduced a new concept called a "duplicate." A "duplicate" is a counterpart produced by the same impression as the original, or from the same matrix, or by means of photography, including enlargements and miniatures, or by mechanical or electronic re-recording, or by chemical reproduction, or by other equivalent technique which accurately reproduces the original. Fed. R. Ev. 1001(4).

A "duplicate" is admissible to the same extent as an original, except where there is a genuine question of the authenticity of the original, or where it would be unfair to admit the duplicate in place of the original (Rule 1003). A paper which is hand copied from an original or duplicate does not have the status of a duplicate.

Admissibility of Other Evidence of Contents. The best evidence rule is a rule of preference. As long as it has been shown that there was in fact a genuine original, then secondary evidence of its contents is permissible under the following circumstances:

Original in Hands of Party Opponent. If the original is in the hands of the party opponent and a notice to produce it has been given the opponent, then secondary evidence can be admitted if the party opponent refuses to produce the original. Fed. R. Ev. 1004(3).

Original Unobtainable. If the original is in the possession of a third party who is not amenable to summons, then secondary evidence is admissible. However, an original is considered obtainable if it can be obtained by a subpoena duces tecum incident to an out-of-state deposition. Fed. R. Ev. 1004(2).

Original Lost or Destroyed. If the original has been lost or destroyed and a diligent search has been made to find it, secondary evidence is admissible in the discretion of the trial judge, who must be satisfied that the search has been diligent. If the party himself has destroyed the original, he will not ordinarily be able to introduce a copy, unless he can convince the judge that there was good reason for its destruction other than the fact that it contained evidence unfavorable to him.

Public Documents. A court will ordinarily not require the original of a public record such as a court document. To require removal might prove inconvenient for a member of the public who might wish to consult them, and might expose the documents to damage or loss. For this reason, a properly authenticated copy is sufficient. Certification is the usual means of authenticating such a public record. Fed. R. Ev. 1005.

Collateral Matters. Where the contents of a document need to be proven, but the issue is not one of the important matters in litigation, and there is little controversy about the existence of the original, the writing will be deemed collateral and secondary evidence allowed. For example, if the issue is possession of certain premises, the original lease under which possession is claimed would ordinarily not be necessary under the best evidence rule. Likewise, it is not necessary to produce a transfer to show status as a passenger.

Degrees of Secondary Evidence. The Federal Rules of Evidence do not recognize degrees of secondary evidence, except for the requirement of a certified copy of an official document. Fed. R. Ev. 1005. Therefore, any form of secondary evidence, including oral testimony, is admissible once production of the original has been excused.

Admissibility of Admissions by Party Opponent of Contents of Writings. The case of Slatterie v. Pooley, 51 Eng. Rep. 579 (Exch. 1840), permitted the contents of a writing to be **proven by the oral admissions of the party against whom it was offered**. That rule has been generally followed in the United States. The Federal Rules of Evidence would restrict its operation to those cases where the party admits the contents of the writing in his testimony, a deposition, or by another writing. In each of these cases, the precise nature of the admission is before the court. Fed. R. Ev. 1007. Of course, if secondary evidence is admissible under one of the theories previously discussed, it is not necessary to rely on the admission of a party opponent in order to introduce secondary evidence of the contents of a writing.

Function of Judge and Jury. Ordinarily, questions relating to the admissibility of evidence under the best evidence rule, such as whether the contents of a document are to be proved, whether the document is collateral, or what is sufficient excuse for nonproduction of the original, are **preliminary questions of fact which are resolved by the trial judge**, not the jury. In some instances, the issue controlling the admissibility of evidence and the ultimate issue in the case coincide.

> For example, if P desires to introduce secondary evidence of a crucial document on the ground that the original was destroyed, and the defendant says the document never existed, a judge's determination that the document never existed and that secondary evidence is inadmissible would deprive the jury of the principal issue in the case. Therefore, the judge will allow the jury to decide that issue under appropriate instructions.

The same rule allows the jury to decide the issue of whether the document produced is in fact the original, and whether the evidence of the contents when introduced by secondary evidence accurately reflects the contents of the original document. See Fed. R. Ev. 1008.

B.   SUMMARIES

The contents of voluminous writings, recordings, or photographs which cannot conveniently be examined in court **may be presented in the form of a chart, summary, or calculation**.   The originals, or duplicates, shall be made available for examination or copying, or both, by other parties at a reasonable time and place.   The judge may order that they be produced in court.   Fed. R. Ev. 1006.

V.   HEARSAY AND CIRCUMSTANCES OF ITS ADMISSIBILITY

In the evidence portion of the Multistate Examination, the correct answers to many questions will depend upon your ability to distinguish hearsay from nonhearsay, and then decide whether the evidence, even if hearsay, is admissible under an exception to the hearsay rule.   A common pattern of choices is:

(A)   admissible because it is not hearsay;

(B)   inadmissible because it is hearsay and comes within no exception to the hearsay rule;

(C)   admissible because, even though hearsay, it comes within the present mental state exception to the hearsay rule;

(D)   admissible because, even though hearsay, it comes within the excited utterance exception to the hearsay rule.

To answer such a question, it is necessary first to determine whether the evidence offered is hearsay and, if it is, whether it comes within any recognized exception to the hearsay rule.

One of the overriding principles of the law of evidence is that the trier of fact ought to have **first-hand knowledge** available to it in making its decision.   Rule 602, which requires that, with very few exceptions, a witness may testify only from first-hand knowledge, is an example of this principle.   The hearsay rule complements the first-hand knowledge rule by prohibiting a person from testifying about the knowledge of another person.

An out-of-court statement is less likely to help the trier of fact obtain the truth because the out-of-court declarant's statement may become garbled in its transmission to the court; the out-of-court declarant may be lying and his veracity cannot effectively be impeached; his perception of the subject matter of the statement may have been faulty; and his memory could be inaccurate.   All of these dangers can be mitigated if the declarant is present in the courtroom and subject to cross-examination.

The reason for the hearsay rule is that it:

1) forces parties to bring their witnesses into court, thereby preserving the right of the other party to cross-examine;
2) preserves testimony under oath;
3) allows the trier of fact to observe the demeanor of the witness; and
4) permits more accurate testimony of the events which are the subject of the litigation.

The Federal Rules of Evidence approach the hearsay rule by defining hearsay in Rule 801; promulgating the general rule that hearsay is inadmissible in Rule 802; and defining the exceptions where unavailability of the declarant is [Rule 804] and is not [Rule 803] required.

Exceptions to the hearsay rule are usually based upon a **special need** to receive the out-of-court statement, and some **reason why it is particularly reliable**.

Cases Where Unavailability Required. The Federal Rules of Evidence divide hearsay exceptions into two categories, those where it must be shown that the **declarant is unavailable** (Rule 804), and those where **unavailability is immaterial** (Rule 803).

The hearsay exceptions where unavailability is required are:

1) the prior recorded testimony exception (Rule 804(b)(1));
2) the statement under belief of impending death (Rule 804(b)(2));
3) the statement against interest (Rule 804(b)(3));
4) the statement of personal family history (Rule 804(b)(4));
5) and the broad catch-all exception (Rule 804(b)(5)).

None of the other hearsay exceptions require that the witness be unavailable.

Definition of Unavailability. Federal Rule 804(a) defines unavailability more broadly than the common law. It provides that a witness is unavailable if **one** of the following conditions is met:

1) He is exempted from testifying about a subject because he has successfully claimed a privilege. The judge must rule that he has actually claimed the privilege.
2) He defies a court order and refuses to testify about a subject.
3) He testifies that he has no memory of the subject matter. In this case, the witness must be produced and is subject to cross-examination.
4) He is absent because of death, or then existing physical or mental illness or infirmity.
5) He cannot be required to attend by process or other reasonable means.

A party who procures the unavailability of a witness is estopped from asserting his unavailability.

A. DEFINITION OF HEARSAY

1. What Is Hearsay

There is a close relationship between the exclusionary features of the hearsay rule and the rule on qualification of witnesses, which requires them to testify personally only to facts of which they have personal knowledge.

> For example: if W, on the stand, testifies that the defendant was on the wrong side of the road at the time of the accident, and it later turns out that he did not see D's car but learned this fact from talking to witnesses, his testimony will be stricken, not because it is hearsay, but because he did not have personal knowledge of the facts to which he testified.

The two rules work toward the same goals - that is, to provide the trier of fact with the freshest evidence possible upon which to decide the case, and to provide counsel an opportunity to subject this evidence to cross-examination.

The scope of the hearsay rule is determined by the definitions of its essential terms. Rule 801 contains those definitions.

Statement. The scope of the hearsay rule depends upon the definition of the word statement. The Federal Rules of Evidence define a statement as:

1) an oral or written assertion; or
2) nonverbal conduct of a person, if it is intended by him as an assertion. Fed. R. Ev. 801(a).

Nonverbal conduct is within the definition of a statement only when it is intended by the out-of-court declarant as an assertion.

> For example, if the victim of a crime pointed to a participant in a line-up in response to a question about the identity of his assailant, then even though neither written nor spoken words have been used, his conduct is hearsay.

Sign language is another example of conduct which is hearsay.

Even **silence could be hearsay** under the Federal Rules if the out-of-court declarant intended that silence as an assertion. For example, if he remained silent in response to a statement such as, "If you did not see X sign this document then you must speak up now," then the fact of his silence would be hearsay if it could be shown that the declarant remained silent because he intended to communicate the fact that he did see X sign the document.

However, by restricting the definition of hearsay to nonverbal conduct intended by the declarant to be assertive, evidence of conduct which is offered circumstantially to show the opinion of the person pursuing that conduct is no longer hearsay.

Conduct Offered Circumstantially to Show Opinion of Out-of-Court Declarant Is Not Hearsay. The following are examples of conduct which would have been considered hearsay under some earlier cases, but which would not be considered hearsay under the present definition of statement.

1) To prove that X is insane, testimony is offered that X's doctor committed him to a mental institution. This evidence is being offered to show the doctor's opinion that X was insane. However, since the doctor's action was intended merely to facilitate treatment rather than express his belief regarding X's sanity, evidence offered regarding the commitment is not hearsay even though there is no chance to question the doctor on what he observed unless he is called by the party objecting. Its admissibility would be governed by the probative quality of the inference drawn from the doctor's conduct, and not by the hearsay rule.

2) To prove that a ship was seaworthy at the time of sailing, testimony is offered that the captain made a thorough inspection of the ship and sailed with his family. Again, the purpose of this evidence is to show that the captain must have thought the ship seaworthy or he would not have sailed with his family. There was no intention on the captain's part to make this assertion and, therefore, it is not a statement for purposes of the hearsay rule.

3) To prove that a sleeping car on a train was not cold, testimony is offered that none of the passengers complained about a cold car to the porter as they left in the morning. The silence of the passengers is offered as evidence of their opinion that the car was not cold. However, this silence was not intended to be an assertion, and hence is not hearsay.

4) To prove that an establishment is an illegal gaming parlor, evidence is offered by a policeman that he answered incoming calls and heard the person calling direct that bets be placed. The person calling is engaged in the act of placing a bet. That act is offered as circumstantial evidence that the caller thought the place was a betting parlor. Again, the caller did not intend to assert an opinion about the character of the place. Therefore, under the Federal Rule's definition, this evidence is not hearsay.

Declarant. The term declarant is defined as the **person who makes a statement**. The purpose of this definition is to distinguish the declarant from the witness on the stand who is testifying about the declarant's statement. Rule 801(b)

Hearsay. The most important definition in Article VIII is that of hearsay. It is defined as **"a statement, other than one made by the declarant while testifying at the trial or hearing, offered in evidence to prove the truth of the matter asserted."** Rule 801(c)

In deciding if evidence is hearsay, the first thing you must do is to determine the purpose for which it is offered. If you must believe that the out-of-court statement is true before it is relevant to any issue in the lawsuit, then you are relying on the credibility of the out-of-court declarant, and the reasons for the hearsay rule become important.

> Example of Hearsay: If W, the witness, is on the stand and testifies that he heard X say, "D is a bank robber," this evidence is hearsay if the case happens to be a criminal trial of D for bank robbery, and X is a witness to the crime. The statement is hearsay because it is being offered to prove that D is in fact a bank robber, that is, it is being offered for the truth of the statement made. Under these circumstances, D's attorney should have the right to cross-examine the eyewitness, X, in order to test his credibility, inquire about any possible bias, test his memory and ability to perceive, and accomplish anything else which is proper in cross-examination. X's testimony should be taken under oath, and the jury should have the opportunity to observe X as he describes D as the bank robber. X should not be shielded by W, who can only testify as to what he heard X say.

> Example of Nonhearsay: If the case is a slander action where D is suing X for saying that he is a bank robber, W's testimony that he heard X say "D is a bank robber" is not hearsay, because it is the fact that the statement was made rather than the truth of it which is important in a slander suit. W is the percipient witness, and can be cross-examined on this point since he was the one who actually heard the statement. He can be asked whether his hearing is good, whether he is sure it was X that he heard make the statement, and other questions that he can answer from first-hand knowledge.

Hearsay Includes Written as Well as Oral Statements. Assertive written statements as well as assertive oral statements are hearsay, since by their very nature they cannot be made by a witness while testifying at a trial. Common examples of written hearsay are accident reports and statements reporting on the chemical composition of real evidence. Most written business records and official records are likewise hearsay. The only written documents which are not hearsay are those which are not offered for the truth of matters contained therein. The fact that the written out-of-court statement is given under oath or in the form of an affidavit does not prevent it from being hearsay.

Nonassertive Out-of-Court Statements. The hearsay rule does not apply when it does not make any difference whether the out-of-court statement is believed in order for that statement to be relevant. There are three kinds of out-of-court statements whose relevancy does not depend upon the truth of the matters contained in them. The credibility of the out-of-court declarant is, therefore, unimportant, and they are not hearsay.

1) Those statements which have an **operative legal effect**;
2) Those which constitute **verbal acts;** and
3) Those where the fact that the **statement was made is used circumstantially to prove some matter in issue**.

Each of these will be discussed below.

Legally Operative Effect. Both oral and written statements can have legal significance irrespective of the truth of any words contained in them. Where the words themselves bring about legal consequences regarding an issue in the lawsuit, those words are not hearsay.

The following examples illustrate this principle:

> Example: Writings Which Constitute a Contract. A is suing B on a written contract. Since the objective interpretation of the words of the document will govern the rights of the parties, it is an operative legal document and not hearsay. The fact that one party did not intend to be bound by the promises contained therein is not relevant to the issues in the case.

> Example: Words Which Form a Contract. In a lawsuit where P is suing D for damages resulting from D's breach of a contract to sell P a bushel of apples, P must prove the contract. If P testifies that he said to D, "I will buy one bushel of apples for four dollars," and that D said in return, "O.K.," the words in quotes actually form a contract, and thus are not hearsay for the same reason as in the previous example.

> Example: Words of Defamation. In a defamation action, the publication of the words, "X is a thief," is the actual libel or slander and constitutes the tort. Therefore, since the speaking or writing of the words creates the legal liability, the words are operative facts and not hearsay.

> Example: Words of Deceit. In a deceit action, the statement, "The car has only been driven 10,000 miles," is the basis of the action if in fact the car had been driven 50,000 miles, and the buyer could prove that the seller spoke these words to the buyer knowing they were false, and that the buyer relied on them. Here the words constitute the basis of Seller's deceit liability and, therefore, are not hearsay. In this case, the statement is not being offered for its truth, but rather because it is false.

> Example: Words Which Give Notice. If a contract requires that a notice be given before liability accrues, then the words which constitute the notice have a legal effect and give rise to legal liability in the same manner that the physical delivery of goods gives rise to an obligation to pay for them.

Verbal Acts or Partial Verbal Acts. In many instances, the physical actions of a person are ambiguous. The words which accompany those actions form an integral part of their legal significance and, therefore, are not offered for their truth. Wigmore attaches the following conditions before words can be considered a verbal act:

1) the conduct involved must be material to some issue in the case and must be ambiguous; and
2) the words must aid in giving legal significance to the conduct and must accompany the conduct. 6 Wigmore, Evidence, §1772.

The following examples illustrate this principle:

> Example 1. If the issue in a case where the plaintiff is claiming title to land by adverse possession is the open and notorious occupancy of the land, the statement, "I own Blackacre because X gave me a deed," made by him to a group of people, is not hearsay because it is not being offered to show that X gave him a deed or that he owned Blackacre, but that he possessed it in an open and notorious manner – an element which he must prove to establish adverse possession.

> Example 2. If the issue is whether a transfer of money from the plaintiff to X was a loan or a gift, a statement accompanying the transfer, such as, "I hope you enjoy this birthday present," is not hearsay because it is the embodiment of the donative intent which is left ambiguous by the simple act of transfer, and thus has operative legal effect even if Plaintiff secretly intended not to make a gift. On the other hand, if one week after the transfer Plaintiff said to W, "I gave X some money last week," the statement would be hearsay because it is offered for its truth and relies upon Plaintiff's credibility.

> Example 3. Assume A and B have a dispute concerning the ownership of commingled assets which are in a storage area and both of them go to that area. If A says to B, "I'll take the ones to the North of the road, and you take the ones to the South," then (assuming B assents) that statement will effect a physical division of the assets and, therefore, it is not hearsay.

> Example 4. If decedent, upon giving his son some money, said, "Consider this as part of your inheritance," it would characterize the gift as an advance in the later division of his estate, and thus would not be hearsay.

When Offered Circumstantially To Show the Effect upon the Hearer. Legal rights frequently turn upon the state of mind of the actor at the time he acted. Inferences can be drawn concerning his state of mind by showing what information was communicated to him prior to the time where his state of mind was relevant. This evidence is not offered to show the truth of the statements, but only for their **effect upon the actor's state of mind**.

The following examples illustrate this principle:

> Example 1. In a lawsuit, P is attempting to establish the priority of his mortgage over D's mortgage. Even though P's mortgage was given earlier, D was first to record. To prevail in the relevant jurisdiction, P must show that D knew of P's mortgage at the time D recorded. If P offers evidence of witness W, who testifies that he heard the mortgagor tell D before he executed D's mortgage, "I gave P a mortgage on this property last week," it is not hearsay because it is only being offered to show D's knowledge of the prior mortgage.
>
> Whether the statement is true, that is, whether the mortgagor in fact gave P a mortgage the previous week, is irrelevant to the issue of notice. The only reason the statement is offered is for the fact that it was said and that the witness, W, has first-hand knowledge of this fact. However, if W were not available, but X, a friend of W's, were to testify that W told him of the conversation between D and the mortgagor, then there would be a hearsay problem because W's conversation with X would have to be offered for the truth of the matters which W related to X, namely that W heard the mortgagor make the statement to D.

> Example 2. In a lawsuit, P is attempting to prove D negligent by showing that D knew that the brakes of his car, which had been in an accident with P's car, were bad at the time he let X drive it. If he could prove by independent evidence that the brakes were in fact bad, then the statement, "Your brakes are bad," made to D before the accident by a mechanic, is not hearsay. On the other hand, this statement would be either hearsay or irrelevant if it were made after the accident, because it could not then have any bearing on D's knowledge at the relevant time.

Example 3. If the defendant in a criminal action claims self-defense, threats made by the victim, which are communicated to the defendant are not hearsay, since the very making of the threat could cause a reasonable person to believe that he would be attacked if he encountered the victim.

Example 4. In an accident case, a claim may be made that the defendant did not produce as witnesses in the proceeding all of his employees who observed the accident. In such instance, statements made by Defendant to his employees regarding the identity of such witnesses are admissible, not to establish who in fact the witnesses were, but rather to show that the defendant, on the basis of the information received, acted in good faith in not calling any more witnesses.

Example 5. If a claim is made that the defendant cancelled a franchise because the dealer refused to finance sales through Defendant's finance facility, letters sent to the defendant complaining about Dealer's service are admissible, not to show that the dealer's service was in fact poor, but rather to show that the defendant had a good faith reason for believing that Dealer's service was poor and for thus canceling the franchise. When offered for that purpose, the complaints are not hearsay. Emich Motors Corp. v. General Motors Corp., 181 F.2d 70 (7th Cir. 1950).

Statements Offered to Show the Feelings or State of Mind of the Declarant. The substantive law frequently attaches legal significance to an individual's state of mind. Statements made by that individual can be used circumstantially to draw inferences about his state of mind and are not hearsay when offered for that purpose unless they directly describe the state of mind in question.

The following examples illustrate this principle:

Example 1. If the issue is X's sanity, and evidence was offered that X said, "I am insane," it would be hearsay because it is offered to prove the truth of the matter asserted by X – that he is insane. On the other hand, if X had said, "I am Superman," it would not be hearsay, but rather would be circumstantial evidence of that state of mind.

> Example 2. If the issue is the knowledge possessed by the out-of-court declarant at a particular time, any statement made by him before that time may be used to show that he had that knowledge. If X's knowledge of a defective floor on June 15 were in issue, X's statement to Y on June 14 that, "Z told me the floor is defective," would not be hearsay, because whether or not Z actually made the statement to X, X's repetition of it implies that he had knowledge of its defective condition.

> Example 3. If the issue in a will contest were the undue influence of M, the sole legatee, then T's statement, "I care more for M than anyone else," would be strong circumstantial evidence that any influence by M was not undue and, therefore, the statement is not hearsay.

> Example 4. If the issue is compensatory damages in a death action, an element of which is loss of love and affection, a statement in the decedent's will, "I disinherit P because he has been mean to me," is circumstantial evidence of the decedent's feeling toward P and, therefore, is not hearsay.

Any verbal statement made by the declarant is circumstantial evidence that he is alive and conscious.

To Show Lack of Credibility. Sometimes an out-of-court statement of a declarant is offered and is then proven to be false in order to raise the inference that similar in-court statements of the same declarant probably are also false.

> For example, assume that the key issue in a case is, "Did D make a particular telephone call?" W identifies the voice on the phone as D's. Evidence could be admitted that on a previous occasion W announced, "D is calling," and that, in fact, the caller was someone else. W's statement, "D is calling," is offered as a statement of W's belief (which is in fact erroneous) in order to show circumstantially that W was wrong on the occasion in issue.

Statements Which Are Not Hearsay. The Federal Rules of Evidence, under Rule 801(d), define certain statements which would otherwise be hearsay as not hearsay, so that the exceptions to the hearsay rule are not applicable. There are two categories of such statements:

1) Statements made by persons while witnesses at a trial prior to the time they became witnesses in the present proceeding; and
2) Admissions by a party opponent.

2.   Prior Statements By Witness

General Principle: Out-of-Court Statements by Witnesses on the Stand Are Hearsay.
Because the often-stated purpose of the hearsay rule is to preserve the right of cross-examination, it is often thought that any out-of-court statement which was made by a person who is now a witness should not be hearsay because the witness is available to be cross-examined on the statement. While this reasoning would seem logical, history and precedent apply the same tests to hearsay, whether or not the person who made the out-of-court statement is present and available for cross-examination.

Thus, if W, a witness to an automobile accident, tells a friend about the accident, W cannot come into court and testify that he told his friend that car X was at fault, because that statement to his friend is hearsay. He can, however, testify to what he remembers about the accident itself from his memory. Here the rule making the out-of-court statement hearsay does no harm, because the witness is able to testify on the stand to facts which were asserted in the out-of-court statement.

Prior Inconsistent Statements Are Not Hearsay When Offered to Impeach Credibility. The rule making out-of-court statements of witnesses hearsay is most important when the witness's story on the stand is contrary to his out-of-court statement. At the least, **the out-of-court statement is then admissible to impeach the witness's credibility**. It is not hearsay for this purpose, since it is being offered only to raise the inference that the testimony given on the stand is not credible. The out-of-court statement is not being offered for its truth but only for the fact that it is inconsistent with the testimony on the stand.

Note, though, that extrinsic evidence of a prior inconsistent statement is not admissible unless:

1) the witness is afforded the opportunity to deny or explain it; and
2) the opposing party is given the opportunity to question the witness on the statement. Rule 613(b).

Prior Inconsistent Statement Admissible Substantively if Given Under Oath. Federal Rule 801(d)(1) allows out-of-court statements of witnesses to be used substantively in two limited instances. That rule has deleted from the definition of hearsay a prior statement of a witness if it is inconsistent with his testimony at trial and was given under oath at a prior trial, hearing, or other proceeding or in a deposition. All statements made by a witness at trial or to a grand jury, and statements made at a deposition, are admissible substantively under Fed. R. Ev. 801(d)(1)(A).

Prior Consistent Statement Admissible to Rebut Charge of Recent Fabrication, Improper Influence, or Motive. Likewise, out-of-court statements of a witness which are consistent with his testimony are admissible substantively if they are offered to rebut an express or implied charge against the witness of recent fabrication, improper influence, or motive. Such prior consistent statements are only admissible in rebuttal to rehabilitate a witness whose credibility has been attacked in such a way that the very making of the prior consistent statement will bolster his credibility. Fed. R. Ev. 801(d)(1)(B).

Prior Eyewitness Identification Permitted. Federal Rule 801(d)(1)(c) exempts from the definition of hearsay evidence a prior identification made by an eyewitness who is testifying at the trial.

Self-Serving Statements Are Hearsay. The rule which classifies out-of-court statements of witnesses as hearsay also applies to out-of-court statements made by a party who is a witness if offered on behalf of that party. They are ordinarily hearsay and are not admissions, because the party is offering his own statements, not his opponent's statements. Such statements are also ruled inadmissible because they are "self-serving." This is just another way of saying that they are hearsay and come under no exception.

Witness May Not Introduce Joint Opinion of Himself and Out-of-Court Declarant. Except for the right of an expert witness under Rule 703 to rely on the type of information reasonably relied upon by experts, a witness on the witness stand is ordinarily bound by the rule that he testify only from first-hand knowledge. He may not testify about a conclusion he reached jointly with other persons who are not witnesses, because he is in effect putting into evidence conclusions which are partly those of the out-of-court declarants. Unless within an exception, such joint conclusions are inadmissible as hearsay when only one of the persons reaching the conclusion is a witness.

3.   Statements Attributable To Party-Opponent

While most earlier formulations of evidence considered admissions to be hearsay, the Federal Rules of Evidence (Rule 801(d)(2)) excludes them from the definition of hearsay on the theory that their admissibility in evidence is the result of the adversary system rather than satisfaction of the conditions of the hearsay rule. **Therefore, on the Multistate Examination, the admissions specified under 801(d) are not hearsay**.

Must Be Introduced by Opposing Party. An out-of-court statement by one party to a lawsuit may be introduced by the opposing party as an admission. A party cannot introduce his own out-of-court statement under this rule. Since an admission is only a statement by a party opponent, it is most important to ascertain the precise parties to the lawsuit before determining if a statement is an admission.

Admissible Even if Declarant Available or if Declarant Lacked Personal Knowledge. All of the exceptions to the hearsay rule discussed below have some guarantee of trustworthiness of the out-of-court statement. This is not true with an admission. It is admissible even if the declarant is available, even if it was in the interest of the party when it was made, even if it is in the form of opinion, and even if the declarant did not have personal knowledge of the facts which are the basis of the statement.

Five Types of Admissions. The Federal Rules of Evidence divide admissions into five categories:

a) The Party's Own Statement. The statement of a party himself is admissible against him if he is a principal. It is also admissible against him if he is merely an agent speaking for someone else. Fed. R. Ev. 801(d)(2)(A).

While not hearsay because they are not statements under the definition of the Federal Rule, admissions can be made by a party by conduct as well as verbally. Examples of admissible conduct are flight from the scene of a crime; destruction of relevant records; conveying away property after an accident; failure of a party to take the stand in his own behalf in a civil case (in a criminal case the defendant has a constitutional right not to take the stand, and this refusal may not be commented on by the prosecution), or refusal of a party to submit to a medical examination after an accident. These actions must ordinarily be proven by evidence at trial. However, if the activity is obvious in the course of trial, such as the refusal of the defendant to take the stand, counsel in a civil case may comment in final argument.

b) A Statement of Which He Has Manifested His Adoption or Belief in its Truth. If a statement is made to a party under circumstances where he hears and understands it, and where an ordinary person would deny the statement if it were not true, and the party remains silent, then an inference arises that the party has adopted the statement made to him, and both the statement and the fact of his silence are admissible as admissions. If instead of remaining silent he makes an equivocal statement, both the statement made to the party and the reply are admissible. Most face-to-face statements call for contradictions if false. However, if the same statement has been denied previously, or there is other good reason for the party to remain silent, the trial judge may hold as a preliminary question of fact that the party did not adopt the statement and exclude it. Fed. R. Ev. 801(d)(2)(B).

The rule on adoptive admissions is **not applicable to a defendant accused of a crime, because he has a right to remain silent**, Miranda v. Arizona, 384 U.S. 436 (1966), and no inference can be drawn from that silence. Doyle v. Ohio, 426 U.S. 610 (1976).

The failure to respond to a letter about the litigation is not an admission. Letters and telegrams sent in the general course of business by one party to the other are also inadmissible, unless they come within a hearsay exception or are not hearsay in the first place.

An adoptive admission is not limited to the case where the party knows precisely the statement he is adopting. If a party were approached and said, "X is a reliable person and knows what he is talking about," a statement made by X would be admissible as an adoptive admission even though the party did not know what X was going to say.

Whenever you have a hearsay problem, pay particular attention to the persons present at the time any offered statement is made. If the party opponent was present, then you should consider whether or not he was under a duty to contradict a statement. If he was and failed to do so, the statement will be admissible as an admission by silence.

c) Statements by a Person Authorized by Him to Make a Statement Concerning the Subject. If an agent has authority to make a statement on behalf of a principal, then that statement has the status of an admission. The Federal Rules also classify a statement made by an agent to his principal as an admission against the principal. A lawyer ordinarily has the authority to speak for his client on matters for which he has been retained. If he files a pleading in a case admitting some fact which is not an evidentiary admission but a conclusive admission, the matter admitted is no longer contestable in the lawsuit. See Fed. R. Ev. 801(d)(2)(C).

A partner has authority to make statements binding his co-partners on matters of partnership business. Most close questions in this area deal with the extent of the authority of the agent, which must be shown by independent proof.

d) A Statement by an Agent or Servant Concerning a Matter Within the Scope of his Agency or Employment Made During the Existence of the Relationship. In the past, courts have applied a strict agency test to statements made by employees. If the employee was not authorized to speak for the principal, then his statement concerning the way in which he performed his job (usually operating a motor vehicle), was not admissible as a vicarious admission against the principal. The Federal Rules of Evidence would admit such statements as vicarious admissions, provided they covered matters concerning the employee's employment, and were made while the employment relationship still existed. Fed. R. Ev. 801(d)(2)(D).

e) A Statement Made by a Conspirator During the Course of and in Furtherance of the Conspiracy. For the statement of one conspirator to be admissible against the other conspirators, the conspiracy itself must be proven independently. To determine if the statement is in furtherance of the conspiracy, it is necessary to determine its scope. Once the objectives of the conspiracy have been obtained or it has failed, the conspiracy is ended and statements of one conspirator are no longer admissible against the others. **Krulewitch v. United States**, 336 U.S. 440 (1949). Thus, an out-of-court statement made by one conspirator after he has been arrested implicating the other conspirators is not admissible against them. See also Fed. R. Ev. 801(d)(2)(E).

Inadmissible Hearsay. The discussion of hearsay has focused on those out-of-court statements which are not hearsay. In actual practice, it is much more likely that a statement of a nonparty not presently testifying is being offered because the proponent of the evidence wants the trier of fact to believe what the out-of-court declarant said or wrote. In that case, the statement is hearsay, even if it is in writing and under oath, and made contemporaneously with the happening of the event. Any statement which is hearsay must come within one of the exceptions discussed below, or the hearsay rule will bar its admissibility.

4.   Multiple Hearsay

Sometimes an out-of-court statement which contains a second out-of-court statement is offered for the truth of the matter contained in the second statement. Unless an exception is found to **justify each layer** of hearsay, the statement is inadmissible.

> For example, suppose that X heard D say "I was driving on the wrong side of the road." The plaintiff can call X and he can testify concerning D's statement, because it comes within the admissions exception to the hearsay rule. However, if X were not called as a witness but Y was called instead, Y could not testify to what X told him about D's statement unless X's statement to Y also came within an exception to the hearsay rule. For example, if X recorded D's statement in a business record, and Y were the keeper of those records, then Y could put the record into evidence, even though X was not on the stand. In this instance, X's out-of-court statement (the record of his conversation with D) would be admissible under the business records exception, and the statement of D (contained in the record) would be admissible because it was an admission.

Where there is a hearsay statement, you must find an exception for each layer before the statement can be admitted. The only exception to this rule is where an admission is based upon information of which the party to the lawsuit had no personal knowledge and obtained from hearsay sources. Here, because a party relied upon hearsay enough to repeat it, the admission is admissible. Fed. R. Ev. 805.

B.   PRESENT SENSE IMPRESSIONS AND EXCITED UTTERANCES

Present Sense Impressions. Federal Rule 803(1) permits testimony regarding statements made by persons who are **observing some event at the exact time they are making the statement, whether or not the declarant is unavailable**. Unlike the excited utterance exception, the event in this case need not be startling. Houston Oxygen Co. v. Davis, 139 Tex. 1, 161 S.W.2d 474 (1942).

This exception applies to " . . . a statement describing or explaining an event or condition made while the declarant was perceiving the event or condition, or immediately thereafter." The guarantees of reliability of the present sense impression are that there is no memory problem, and that the person to whom the statement is made is usually in a position to check the accuracy of the sense impression.

To be admissible as a **present sense impression**, the statement **must be a description of the event**, whereas an **excited utterance need only relate to the exciting event**. A statement such as "the enchilada has been on the floor for two hours" could be admissible as a present sense impression but not as an excited utterance. .

Excited Utterances. Federal Rule 803(2) exempts from the hearsay rule (whether or not the out-of-court declarant is unavailable), a statement relating to a **startling event or condition made while the declarant was under the stress of excitement caused by the event or condition**. The critical factor in the admissibility of such statements is the **time lapse** between the event and the statement. The trial judge may admit such a statement in his discretion, even though not made contemporaneously, if made before the exciting event has lost its sway and before there has been time to contrive and misrepresent.

This exception applies to statements of all persons present at the so-called exciting event. Thus, it is not limited to the victim of the event, but also applies to a bystander. There is a requirement, however, that the out-of-court declarant be shown to have personal knowledge of the facts about which he speaks.

C. STATEMENTS OF MENTAL, EMOTIONAL, OR PHYSICAL CONDITION

Statements of Present Physical or Mental Condition. Federal Rule 803(3) permits introduction of statements made by the declarant, **whether or not he is unavailable, of a statement of his existing state of mind, emotion, sensation, or physical condition**. The statement may be made to any person.

Circumstantial Use of Proof of Mental State. Where proof of mental state is made under this rule, the existence of that mental state may be used as circumstantial evidence that the mental state continued into the future, and that the declarant at some time in the future acted in accordance with that mental state.

> For example, if the issue was whether a will was executed, statements by decedent in a bank that he intended to make a will while visiting the bank are admissible to show that he did in fact make the will.

In *Mutual Life Insurance v. Hillmon*, 45 U.S. 285 (1891), the issue was whether the declarant made a trip with one X. A letter written the day before the scheduled trip, expressing an intention to make it, was admitted for the purpose of showing his present mental intent, from which the inference could be drawn that his future actions were in accordance with that intent. However, such evidence is admissible only to prove the declarant's conduct, not the future conduct of a person other than the declarant.

Declarations of Mental State Not Admissible to Show Past Conduct. Declarations of mental state are not admissible to show past conduct. *Shepard v. United States*, 290 U.S. 96 (1933). Thus, the statement "X has stabbed me" is not admissible to show the present mental state of the declarant for the purpose of showing that X's actions were in accordance with that statement.

The **rule specifically excludes a statement of memory or belief to prove a fact remembered or believed.** The one exception to this exclusion of mental state to prove past conduct is the execution, revocation, identification, or terms of the declarant's will. Thus, a statement by the declarant, "I signed my will last night and left all my property to X," would be admissible under this exception to the hearsay rule.

D.   STATEMENTS FOR PURPOSES OF MEDICAL DIAGNOSIS AND TREATMENT

Federal Rule 803(4) greatly expands the common law rule which held that statements of past physical conditions were admissible when made to a physician for purposes of diagnosis **and** treatment, by changing the conjunctive word to or.

Need Not Be Made to a Physician. Under the federal rule, the statement need not be made to a physician, but can be made to an ambulance driver, nurse, or anyone, so long as the purpose of making the statement is diagnosis or treatment.

Under the federal rule, the statement is not limited to present or past physical condition, but also includes the general source of the cause or external source of the pain. Thus, a statement to a nurse, "I was hit by a car," would be admissible, but a statement, "The car went through a red light," would not.

Admissible Even if Doctor Examines for Purpose of Testifying. Under common law rules, statements of past physical condition made to a doctor conducting an examination for the purpose of testifying were not admissible because they were not for the purpose of treatment. While the common law rule required that the statements be made for the purpose of diagnosis and treatment, the federal rule only requires diagnosis or treatment. The testifying physician is performing diagnosis, and, therefore, statements of past physical condition made to him are admissible for substantive purposes under the federal rule.

Relationship to Physician-Patient Privilege. Even if a statement to a physician falls within a hearsay exception, the statement may be inadmissible if it is privileged and the patient claims the privilege, as discussed infra at "Physician-Patient Communications" in the Privileges section.

E. PAST RECOLLECTION RECORDED

Federal Rule 803(5) excepts past recollection recorded from the hearsay rule.

Witness Must Be Available. The witness who once had personal knowledge of the contents of the record must take the witness stand. This exception to the hearsay rule is unique in that the **statement is not admissible unless the person who made the out-of-court statement has been a witness in the case**. The witness need only take the stand to establish the foundation for the admission of the evidence (that he made the record when his memory was fresh and he no longer has any memory of the event).

The Witness Must Have Insufficient Recollection. The judge must find that at the time of testifying, the witness had insufficient recollection to testify fully and accurately about the contents of the record. The record must be shown to the witness, who will testify that it does not refresh his memory.

The Record Must Satisfy the Admissibility Requirements of a Writing. Since the contents of the record and not the testimony of the witness is the evidence, the record must be authenticated, and it must satisfy the best evidence requirements of Federal Rules 1001 to 1008.

Record Must Have Been Made When Memory Was Fresh. The record must have been made or adopted by the witness when the matter was fresh in his memory, and it must reflect the knowledge accurately. The most common case is where the witness makes the record himself and testifies that he made it soon after the matter occurred. However, the record can be adopted by him after it is made by another, as long as he has knowledge. If two or more persons cooperated in the making of the record, then each would be required to testify about their part in its preparation under this exception.

> For example, if A made observations which he conveyed to B, who recorded them, A would have to testify that he accurately repeated what he saw to B, and B would have to testify that he accurately recorded what A said.

The Record Itself Is Not Admissible by its Proponent. Because a jury might give undue weight to a record if it were admitted as an exhibit, the proponent of its admissibility is only permitted to read it into evidence and to the jury. However, the adverse party can require the record itself to be admitted. He will most often require admission of the record when he feels that its form and physical features will impeach the credibility of the evidence it contains.

Comparison with Business Records Exception. There can be a substantial overlap between the business records exception discussed below and past recollection recorded. The principal distinctions are that there is **no requirement of a regularly conducted business activity for past recollection recorded**.

However, the business records exception does not require the presence of the witness, or the exhaustion of memory required by the past recollection recorded exception. It is possible that a document could qualify for admissibility under both exceptions.

Comparison with Present Memory Refreshed. Where past recollection recorded applies, the contents of the document is the evidence. The witness cannot be effectively cross-examined because he has no present memory. However, for the contents of the document to be admissible, the prerequisites to admissibility discussed above must be satisfied. If memory is refreshed so that a witness is testifying on the stand from present memory, the contents of the document used to refresh memory is not the evidence, and no hearsay problem is presented. Here the witness can be effectively cross-examined, and under Rule 612 the writing used to refresh memory can, at the option of the adverse party, be admitted to impeach credibility or for substantive purposes.

Requirement of a Permanent Record. While the Federal rule requires a record, it can be a record, memorandum, report, or data compilation in any form.

Subject Matter of Record. In addition to records of acts, events, and conditions, the Federal rule permits, if other conditions are satisfied, records of opinions and diagnoses.

F.   BUSINESS RECORDS

Federal Rule 803(6) excepts business records (memoranda, reports, records or data compilations in any form, regarding acts, events, conditions, opinions or diagnoses) from the hearsay rule.

Prerequisite: Kept in the Course of a Regularly Conducted Business Activity. The guarantee of trustworthiness for business records is the routine nature and regularity with which they are kept. The word "business" is defined in the rule to include institutions, associations, professions, and occupations, whether or not conducted for profit. Therefore, records of a hospital or police records could qualify as records kept in the course of a regularly conducted business.

Prerequisite: Regular Practice of the Business Activity to Make the Record. The type of record introduced must be kept as a matter of business routine. If it were a record kept on an occasional or haphazard basis by a business, it would not be admissible.

Prerequisite: Made At or Near the Time of the Event. The requirement of freshness of knowledge required by the past recollection recorded exception is also present in the business records exception. The language "at or near" contained in the rule gives the trial judge discretion to admit the record if the regularized routine practice is to wait a reasonable time before the entry is recorded.

Requirement of Personal Knowledge. The entry must have either been made by a person with personal knowledge of the event, or it must have been received by the maker from a person with personal knowledge who transmitted the information in the course of business. Thus, the rule affirms the holding of Johnson v. Lutz, 253 N.Y. 124, 170 N.E. 517 (1930), that the statement of a bystander contained in a police report prepared in the regular conduct of the police business was inadmissible, because the bystander was not making his report to the police officer in the regular course of the bystander's business.

Must Satisfy the Requirements for a Writing. Since the record itself is to be introduced into evidence, it must be authenticated in one of the ways provided in Rule 901 or 902 and it must comply with the requirements of the best evidence rule as prescribed in Rules 1001-1007.

Witness Required. The person making the entry need neither testify nor be shown to be unavailable. The records **may be introduced either through their custodian or other qualified witness**. That witness should be able both to authenticate the records, and to provide testimony concerning the other prerequisites to their admissibility.

Motivation of the Declarant - Lack of Trustworthiness. The United States Supreme Court in Palmer v. Hoffman, 18 U.S. 109 (1943), held inadmissible records made in the usual course of business if they were prepared especially for litigation. The federal rule carries this policy into the rule by providing that a record which otherwise qualifies will be **excluded if lack of trustworthiness is indicated by the source of the information or the method or circumstances of preparation of the record.** Records **prepared specifically for litigation** will be excluded under this provision. The trial judge would have discretion to exclude other records for the same reason.

Absence Of Records. Federal Rule 803(7) permits the introduction of a record admissible under 803(6) to prove the nonoccurrence or nonexistence of a matter if it can be shown that if the event occurred or matter existed, it would have appeared in such a record. The most common example of this rule is the use of a receipt book, which recorded all the receipts of a business to show the absence of an entry to prove nonpayment.

G.   PUBLIC RECORDS AND REPORTS

Federal Rule 803 excepts public records and reports from the hearsay rule.

The same expansive language contained in the business records exception applies to public records. The record must be of a public agency.

Requirements of a Writing. While the document must comply with the admissibility requirements of a writing, Rule 902 provides that public records are self-authenticating if certified by a public official, and Rule 1005 admits certified copies in lieu of originals. No testimony is required to show the authenticity of the record if certified. Furthermore, extrinsic evidence of authenticity is no longer required to admit certified records of regularly conducted activity (if admissible under Rule 803(6)).

The rule admits **three kinds of reports**:

1) The **activities of the agency** itself are admissible. Fed. R. Ev. 803(8)(A).
2) **Matters observed by a public official pursuant to a duty imposed by law** are admissible, as long as there was a duty to report. However, because of the adversary nature of the criminal process, reports of police and other law enforcement personnel concerning matters they observed are not admissible in criminal trials under this section, even if the report is required by law. Fed. R. Ev. 803(8)(B).
3) **Factual findings resulting from an investigation made pursuant to law** are admissible. However, such reports are not admissible against the defendant in a criminal action. Fed. R. Ev. 803(8)(C).

While the rule restricts this latter category to factual findings, the reports indicate that conclusions and opinions contained in the reports would be admissible, subject to the trustworthiness requirement described below.

Exclusion if Untrustworthy. As in the case of the business records exception, an official record will be excluded if circumstances indicate its lack of trustworthiness. **The factors helpful to determine lack of trustworthiness are the timeliness of the investigation, the special skill and experience of the official, whether a hearing was held and the level at which it was held, and the possible motive of the public official to misrepresent.**

Absence of Public Record. Federal Rule 803(10) permits the introduction of evidence in the form of a certificate, or in the form of testimony that a diligent search failed to disclose a record or entry in order to prove the absence of the record, or to prove the nonoccurrence or nonexistence of the matter of which a report was regularly made by the agency.

Records of Vital Statistics. Federal Rule 803(9) exempts from the hearsay rule records in any form of births, marriage, and deaths if the report thereof was made to public office pursuant to law.

Records of Documents Affecting Property. Federal Rule 803(14) exempts from the hearsay rule records of documents recorded in the registry of deeds or other public office to prove the contents of the original document and its execution and delivery.

Judgments. Federal Rule 803(22) exempts from the hearsay rule evidence of a previous conviction of a crime punishable by more than one year in prison to prove any fact necessary to sustain the judgment. Such judgments are always admissible in civil actions, but are admissible in criminal actions only against an accused. A judgment of conviction may, of course, be offered for impeachment purposes against any witness under Rule 609. Pleas of nolo contendere are not admissible under Rule 803(22). Also, the declarant need not be unavailable for this exception to apply.

While a judgment of guilt in a criminal action is admissible in a later civil action to show negligence or other type of liability, the converse is not true. A civil judgment is not admissible in a criminal action because the burden of proof is lighter in the civil case.

H.   LEARNED TREATISES

Federal Rule 803 excepts learned treatises from the operation of the hearsay rule under limited circumstances. The requirements for admissibility are as follows:

Used Only After an Expert Testifies. An expert witness must have testified on the subject matter of the treatise on direct examination. The treatise must either be relied upon by him in direct examination, or called to his attention on cross-examination. See Fed. R. Ev. 803(18).

Treatise Must Be Established as a Reliable Authority. This requirement can be satisfied if the expert admits its reliability, another expert establishes it as a reliable authority, or the court takes judicial notice that it is a reliable authority.

Admissible Substantively, But Not as an Exhibit. Once these conditions are satisfied, a published treatise, periodical, or pamphlet on science or art is admissible not only to impeach the expert, but also for the truth of the statement contained in the treatise. The treatise itself is not admissible as an exhibit. It may only be read to the jury.

I.   FORMER TESTIMONY; DEPOSITIONS

Federal Rule 804(b)(1) admits, as an exception to the hearsay rule (when the declarant is unavailable), testimony given at another hearing of the same or a different proceeding, or in a deposition taken in compliance with law in the course of the same or another proceeding. The reason for this exception is that the witness was under oath at the prior proceeding and, as discussed below, was subject to or available for effective examination or cross-examination.

When Parties Are Identical - Civil and Criminal Cases. The Federal Rule goes on to provide that such former testimony is admissible in both civil and criminal cases when the parties in the former and the present proceeding are the same. Here, the ability to cross-examine at the prior hearing is in the precise party against whom it is offered. If that earlier cross-examination was ineffective or was waived, this is the responsibility of the party against whom it is offered, and he cannot complain at the later hearing.

Actual cross-examination at the former hearing is not required in civil and criminal cases, as long as the opportunity to cross-examine is present. In criminal cases, there must be an identity of parties for the prior recorded testimony exception to apply.

The evidence is also admissible under the Federal Rule when offered against the party who presented the evidence at the earlier hearing. While the opportunity for cross-examination is not available in such an instance, the party calling the witness in the earlier proceeding had the ability to develop the testimony on both direct and redirect examination.

When Parties Are Not Identical - Civil Cases Only. The evidence of testimony at a prior hearing is admissible in civil cases, not only where there is an identity of parties at the prior and later hearings, but also where there is not such an identity, and the predecessor in interest at the prior hearing had an opportunity and similar motive to develop the testimony by direct, cross, or redirect examination at the former hearing.

A person who is in privity would qualify as having an identity of interest, as would a person whose claim against a common defendant is based upon the same act of negligence.

J. STATEMENTS AGAINST INTEREST

Must Be Against Interest when Made - Declarant Must Be Unavailable. The evidence which may be admitted under the declaration against interest exception is considerably narrower than that which is admitted as the admission of a party (discussed above) in that the statement must have been against a limited type of interest at the time it was made; the out-of-court declarant must have first-hand knowledge of the subject matter; and the declarant must be unavailable before it is admissible. However, it is broader than an admission in that it applies to any out-of-court declarant, not just a party.

> For example, if a declarant testifies to a low value of his property for the purpose of obtaining a lower property tax assessment, that statement is not admissible to show that lower value in an eminent domain proceeding, because the statement was in his interest when he made it. If the person making the statement were a party, then his earlier statement would be admissible as an admission, even though it was in his interest when made.

Type of Interest Required. Federal Rule 804(b)(3) admits statements against interest when, at the time of their making, they are **so far contrary to the declarant's pecuniary or proprietary interest that he would not have made the statement unless he believed it to be true**. A statement that a declarant owes a debt is against his pecuniary interest. A statement that she does not own a piece of property is against her proprietary interest.

Civil Liability. The rule also admits statements which would subject a declarant to civil liability or render invalid a claim which he might have. A statement at the scene of the accident admitting fault would be admissible under this section of the rule if the other requirements of the rule were satisfied.

Criminal Liability - Rule of Corroboration. A statement which would tend to expose a declarant to criminal liability is also admissible under the rule. However, such a statement is not admissible if the statement is offered to exculpate the accused, unless corroborating circumstances indicate the trustworthiness of the statement. Where corroborating circumstances exist and the statement is offered to exculpate the accused, it is a violation of due process to exclude the statements. Chambers v. Mississippi, 410 U.S. 284 (1973). The purpose of the corroboration requirement is to allow the trial judge to exclude statements of third parties which are fabricated by the accused.

A statement against penal interest might implicate the accused as well as the declarant and then be offered by the prosecution against the accused, as long as the declarant is unavailable. As long as the statement was not made when in custody, it would be against interest when made and would seem to be admissible under this rule. However, the extent to which the confrontation clause of the Constitution would render such evidence inadmissible has not been determined. See Pointer v. Texas, 380 U.S. 400 (1965).

K.   OTHER EXCEPTIONS TO THE HEARSAY RULE

Dying Declaration: Criminal Cases. At common law, the dying declaration exception applied only to criminal homicide prosecutions. The statement could only be made by the victim of the homicide at a time when he had knowledge of his impending death, and could only relate to the cause and circumstances of that impending death.

Federal Rule 804(b)(2) retains the original common law rule in criminal cases. A dying declaration is not admissible in a criminal prosecution for any other crime than homicide, but would seem admissible in a prosecution for the homicide of someone other than the declarant.

Dying Declaration: Civil Cases. The rule expands the exception to civil cases, but the exception is still limited to statements made while the declarant believed his death was imminent, and is limited to the causes and circumstances of what he believed to be his impending death.

Requirement of Unavailability. While unavailability of the declarant is required for this exception, that unavailability is **not limited to death**. If a statement was made under belief of impending death and the declarant did not die but was unavailable for some other reason, the statement would be admissible.

A dying declaration will be admissible even though it is in the form of opinion. It must, however, either be based upon the first-hand knowledge of the declarant, or come to him in the form of hearsay which is independently admissible.

Exceptions to Prove Family and Ancestral Relationships. In addition to the exception for reports of vital statistics discussed above under the official records exception, the Federal Rules provide for many separate exceptions to the hearsay rule to prove family relationships.

Federal Rule 803(11) exempts from the hearsay rule facts of personal or family history contained in regularly kept records of religious organizations (i.e. statements of birth, marriages, divorces, death, relationship by blood or marriage).

Although they would appear to be admissible under either the business records exception or the records of religious organizations exception, Federal Rule 803(12) excepts from the hearsay rule statements of fact contained in a certificate that a sacrament was performed.

Family Records. Federal Rule 803(13) excepts from the hearsay rule statements of fact concerning personal or family history contained in family bibles, genealogies, charts, engravings, inscriptions on family portraits, and engravings on urns, crypts, or tombstones.

Reputation Concerning Family History. Federal Rule 803(19) excepts from the hearsay rule reputation evidence among members of an individual's family by blood, adoption, or marriage, reputation among his associates, or reputation in the community concerning personal or family history.

Market Quotations. Federal Rule 803(17) excepts from the hearsay rule market quotations, tabulations, lists, directories, or other published compilations generally used and relied upon by the public or by persons in particular occupations.

Statements, Reputations, and Judgments Affecting Property. Federal Rule 803(15) excepts from the hearsay rule a statement in a document creating or affecting an interest in property, if the matter stated was relevant to the purpose of the document. However, if dealings with the property have been inconsistent with the truth of the statement in the document, then it will be inadmissible.

Federal Rule 803(20) excepts from the hearsay rule reputation in the community arising before the controversy as to boundaries or customs affecting lands in the community.

Federal Rule 803(23) excepts from the hearsay rule judgments on the position of boundaries.

Note, the availability or unavailability of the declarant is immaterial in Rule 803 hearsay exceptions.

Statement of Personal or Family History. If the declarant is unavailable, Federal Rule 804(b)(4) excepts from the hearsay rule a statement by the declarant of his own personal or family history, or a statement about another person's family history, if the declarant was related to the other person by blood or marriage or was so intimately associated with the family that he was likely to have accurate information.

The Residual Exception. Federal Rules 803(24) and 804(b)(5) give the courts limited discretion to find exceptions to the hearsay rule not specifically covered in the earlier exceptions. The requirements of these rules are strict. They were not intended to be the instrument of a broad expansion of the hearsay exceptions. In answering multiple choice questions on hearsay exceptions, you should not disregard the answer "inadmissible because it is hearsay" merely because of these rules.

The specific requirements for these exceptions to apply are:

1) The statement is offered as evidence of a material fact. Statements on collateral matters would not come within this rule.
2) The statement must be more probative on the point for which it is offered than any other evidence which the proponent can procure through reasonable efforts.
3) The general purposes of the Federal Rules and the interests of justice must be served by the admission.
4) The proponent must notify the adverse party prior to trial that he intends to introduce a statement under the rule, of the particulars of the statement, and of the name and address of the declarant.

FEDERAL JURISDICTION & CIVIL PROCEDURE

I.   JURISDICTION AND VENUE

A complaint must contain "a short and plain statement of the grounds upon which the court's jurisdiction depends." Fed. R. Civ. P. 8(a). The defense that there is no federal jurisdiction may be raised by motion or by answer. Fed. R. Civ. P. 12(b). If the record fails to disclose a basis for federal jurisdiction, the claim must be dismissed, whether the case is at the trial stage or at the appellate stage. The whole record may be looked to for the purpose of curing a defective averment of jurisdiction, however. Defective allegations of jurisdiction may be amended upon terms in the trial or appellate courts. 28 U.S.C. §1653. Note that the defect of lack of jurisdiction is not waived and the court is required to dismiss the action "whenever it appears by suggestion of the parties or otherwise that the court lacks jurisdiction of the subject matter." Fed. R. Civ. P. 12(h).

A. ORIGINAL JURISDICTION

"In all cases affecting ambassadors, other public ministers and consuls, and those in which a state shall be a party, the Supreme Court shall have original jurisdiction." Article III, Section 2. The constitutional provisions delineating the original jurisdiction of the Supreme Court are self-executing. Thus, Congress can neither add to the original jurisdiction of the Supreme Court, *Marbury v. Madison*, 5 U.S. 137 (1803), nor take away any of that jurisdiction. *Chisholm v. Georgia*, 2 Dall. 419 (1793). However, Congress can make such jurisdiction concurrent with that of the district courts, and may also confer appellate jurisdiction over cases that are otherwise within the original jurisdiction of the Supreme Court (*e.g.*, where it has appellate jurisdiction of a federal question case, but original jurisdiction because a state is a party).

B. APPELLATE JURISDICTION

The Constitution provides that in all other cases within the judicial power of the United States, "the Supreme Court shall have appellate jurisdiction, both as to law and fact, with such exceptions, and under such regulations as the Congress shall make." Article III, Section 2. In *Ex parte McCardle*, 7 Wall. 506 (1868), the Supreme Court held that, under this provision, Congress could deprive the Supreme Court of its appellate jurisdiction to review a denial of habeas corpus, even though the Act limiting the Court's jurisdiction was passed after the Court had taken jurisdiction of the case.

The extent of Congress's power to limit Supreme Court review is still uncertain. However, the congressional power is probably restricted by the Court's responsibility for upholding the supremacy of federal law, and for providing a check on any congressional attempt to exceed its constitutional powers. Furthermore, total denial of Supreme Court review might violate litigants' rights to due process or equal protection.

C. CONCURRENT AND EXCLUSIVE JURISDICTION

Congress has broad powers over the jurisdiction of the lower federal courts. It can provide that a particular court shall hear certain types of cases, and can deny to all other courts the power to hear such cases. It can also deny the courts the power to grant certain remedies. Generally, absent express limitation or implication, federal jurisdiction is concurrent with that of the state courts - *i.e.*, the suit may be brought in either a federal or a state court. However, Congress has made certain areas of jurisdiction exclusive in the federal courts.

Congress has granted the federal courts exclusive jurisdiction in the following actions:

(1)   Bankruptcy proceedings (28 U.S.C. §1334).

(2)   Patent and copyright cases (28 U.S.C. §1338).

(3)   Actions against foreign consuls and vice-consuls (28 U.S.C. §1351).

(4)   Admiralty and maritime cases (28 U.S.C. §1333). However, federal jurisdiction is exclusive only in limitation of liability proceedings and in maritime actions in rem.

(5)   Antitrust cases (15 U.S.C. §§15, 26). Here, exclusive jurisdiction is not expressly granted by statute; rather, the antitrust statutes have been judicially interpreted to allow exclusive jurisdiction. *Freeman v. Bee Machine Co., Inc.*, 319 U.S. 448 (1943).

(6)   Cases under the Securities Exchange Act of 1934 (15 U.S.C. §78a(a)).

(7)   Foreign state. 28 U.S.C. §1441(d) permits a foreign state, or agency thereof, which is sued in a state court, to remove the action to federal court.

(8)   Actions where the United States is involved. This includes cases involving fines, penalties, or forfeitures under the laws of the United States, crimes and tort suits against the United States, and customs decisions review.

The doctrine of sovereign immunity prevents the United States from being sued without its consent. However, in the Federal Torts Claims Act the United States has consented to suits based on the negligence of government employees, if a private person would be liable under the same circumstances. Likewise, suits for tax refunds and for contract claims of $10,000 or less may be brought in federal district court. 28 U.S.C. §1346.

D. FEDERAL SUBJECT MATTER JURISDICTION

The first issue in federal jurisdiction is to determine whether the court has jurisdiction to decide the particular controversy brought before it. This power of adjudication is known as subject matter jurisdiction.

Federal courts have subject matter jurisdiction in: (1) suits between citizens of different states; (2) suits involving a federal question; (3) cases involving ambassadors, admiralty, and maritime jurisdiction; and (4) cases where the United States is a party.

Subject matter jurisdiction may not be conferred by agreement or consent of the litigants. The defense of lack of subject matter jurisdiction may be raised at any point in the trial, and may even be raised for the first time on appeal. However, if the jurisdictional issue was actually litigated and expressly decided, the court's finding of subject matter jurisdiction is res judicata; similarly, if the jurisdictional issue was not contested, the judgment is res judicata unless the suit was "plainly outside the rendering Court's jurisdiction." *Chicot County Drainage District v. Baxter State Bank*, 308 U.S. 371 (1940).

1.   Federal Question
a.   *The Meaning of "Arising Under"*

The Constitution allows federal courts to be given jurisdiction over cases "arising under this Constitution, the laws of the United States, and treaties made, or which shall be made, under their authority." Article III, Section 2. The statutory basis for federal question jurisdiction is 28 U.S.C. §1331, which provides that district courts have original jurisdiction in all civil actions where the matter in controversy "arises under the Constitution, laws, or treaties of the United States."

i.   Federal Right or Immunity Must Be Essential Element

No definitive test of when a case "arises under" federal law has been enunciated. However, a right or immunity created by the Constitution or federal law must be an essential element of the plaintiff's cause of action, and the right or immunity must be such that it will be supported if the Constitution or laws are given one construction or effect, and defeated if they receive another. *Gully v. First Nat'l Bank in Meridian*, 299 U.S. 109 (1936).

Federal "common law" (*i.e.*, judicial interpretation of statutes) can serve as the basis for federal question jurisdiction. *Illinois v. City of Milwaukee*, 406 U.S. 91 (1972). Federal question jurisdiction does not arise merely because a corporation was incorporated by Congress; it exists only if the United States owns more than half of the corporation's capital stock. 28 U.S.C. §1349.

ii.   Federal Right May Be Implied

The right of action may be either express or implied. Thus, federal question jurisdiction existed where plaintiff sued for damages, claiming that his arrest violated his Fourth and Fifth Amendment rights, even though the Constitution does not provide a right to sue for damages. *Bell v. Hood*, 327 U.S. 678 (1946). Likewise, a right of action was implied from the Securities Exchange Act of 1934, even though the Act did not expressly create a remedy for the violation alleged. *J.I. Case v. Borak Co.*, 377 U.S. 426 (1964). However, if the right infringed upon is not protected by the Constitution or a federal statute, the cause of action will not raise a federal question merely because the federal government was somehow involved. *Wheeldin v. Wheeler*, 373 U.S. 647 (1963) (claim for damages based on alleged abuse of federal subpoena power).

b.   *Federal Question Must Appear In Complaint*

The federal question must appear on the face of the well-pleaded complaint. Anticipation of a defense based on federal law is insufficient to constitute a federal question. *Louisville & Nashville R.R. v. Mottley*, 211 U.S. 149 (1908). Likewise, an answer that raises a defense based on federal law is insufficient to grant federal question jurisdiction.

If a complaint states a plausible claim that arises under federal law, federal jurisdiction exists even if the court later determines that the plaintiff, on the merits, has no federal right. In that instance, the complaint is dismissed for failure to state a claim on which relief may be granted, rather than for lack of subject matter jurisdiction. *Bell v. Hood*, 327 U.S. 678 (1946). Dismissal for lack of jurisdiction is proper only if the allegations are immaterial and are made solely for the purpose of creating federal jurisdiction, or if the claim is wholly insubstantial and frivolous.

2.   Federal Diversity Jurisdiction

Article III, Section 2 of the Constitution allows Congress to confer jurisdiction on the federal courts over controversies "between citizens of different states . . . and between a state, or the citizens thereof, and foreign states, citizens or subjects." Congress has implemented this provision in 28 U.S.C. §1332(a), which grants federal district courts original jurisdiction of all civil actions where the matter in controversy exceeds the sum or value of $75,000 (exclusive of interest and costs), and is between (1) citizens of different states; (2) citizens of a state, and foreign states or citizens or subjects thereof; and (3) citizens of different states and in which foreign states or citizens or subjects thereof are additional parties. However, the U.S. Supreme Court has held that diversity jurisdiction does not extend to domestic relations cases seeking the issuance or modification of divorce, alimony, or child custody decrees, but does include jurisdiction over related matters (such as the enforcement of such decrees validly entered by state courts, and tort actions involving family members). *Ankenbrandt v. Richards*, 112 S.Ct. 2206 (1992).

a.   *Requirement of Complete Diversity*

Complete diversity between the parties on each side of the controversy is required, *i.e.*, each plaintiff must be from a state that is different from that of each defendant. *Strawbridge v. Curtiss*, 3 Cranch 267 (1806).

> *For example, if A, a Pennsylvania citizen, and B, a New York citizen, sue X, a Florida citizen, and Y, a Massachusetts citizen, complete diversity exists. However, if A and B sue X, Y, and Z, another New York citizen, diversity jurisdiction is destroyed.*

The one exception to the complete diversity requirement is the Federal Interpleader Act, 28 U.S.C. §1335, which requires only "minimal diversity." The statute permits one who is holding property claimed by two or more persons to deposit the property with the court and let the claimants litigate ownership. If there is diversity between any two of the claimants, the other claimants can all be citizens of the same state.

> *For example, an insurance company brings a statutory interpleader action to determine ownership of insurance benefits; four of the claimants are Virginia citizens, and one is a New York citizen. Minimal diversity is achieved because at least one claimant has state citizenship different from that of the others.*

i.   Time For Determination Of Diversity

Diversity is determined as of the date the action is commenced. Diversity need not have existed when the cause of action arose. Neither a subsequent change in citizenship nor a subsequent change in the parties (*e.g.*, by intervention or substitution) will divest the court of diversity jurisdiction.

The complaint must plead the existence of the diversity jurisdiction. If the plaintiff fails to allege the citizenship grounding diversity jurisdiction, the defendant may bring a Rule 12(b) motion to dismiss, or the court may dismiss on its own motion, unless the plaintiff amends.

ii.   Citizenship of Natural Persons

Citizenship means (1) United States citizenship (or permanent resident alien status), and (2) domicile in a state.

> *Thus, an American citizen who is domiciled in Mexico can neither sue nor be sued in the federal courts under diversity jurisdiction.*

Mere residence in a state is insufficient for diversity purposes. Domicile is defined as the place where a person has his fixed and permanent residence and to which he has the intention of returning whenever he is absent therefrom. Change of domicile may be effected by physical presence in the new domicile with the intent to remain there. If these requirements are met, it is immaterial that the change of domicile was made solely to create diversity jurisdiction.

iii.   Citizenship of Corporations

For purposes of diversity jurisdiction, a corporation is deemed a citizen of (1) any state in which it has been incorporated, and (2) the state in which it has its principal place of business. 28 U.S.C. §1332(c).

The principal place of business is usually the place where the bulk of the corporate activity takes place; however, if no one state is clearly predominant, then the state of the home office will be deemed the principal place of business.

> *For example, if P, a citizen of New York, sues D Corp., which is incorporated in Delaware but has the bulk of its manufacturing facilities in New Jersey, and only a small sales office in New York, diversity will exist. However, if D Corp.'s manufacturing facilities are in four different states and their activities are directed from a corporate headquarters in New York, diversity will not exist.*

Diversity is destroyed if an opposing party is a citizen of any of the states of which the corporation is a citizen.

> *Thus, if B, a citizen of Pennsylvania, and A, a citizen of Delaware, sue S Corp. which has its principal place of business in New York, but is incorporated in Delaware, A's citizenship destroys diversity.*

In any direct action against a liability insurer, to which the insured is not a party, the company is deemed to be a citizen of the same state as the insured, as well as of the state of its incorporation and its principal place of business. 28 U.S.C. §1332(c). This provision prevents cases that are purely in-state disputes from entering federal court under diversity jurisdiction solely because the defendant is an out-of-state insurer.

iv.   Citizenship of Unincorporated Associations

Where a partnership, labor union or other unincorporated association is a party, the citizenship of each member must be considered in determining diversity.

> *For example, P, a citizen of Massachusetts, sues the ABC Partnership, which is located in New York; A and B are New York citizens, but C is a Massachusetts citizen. No diversity exists because of C's citizenship.*

If membership of the association is large enough, a class action can be brought, naming as representatives only those members whose citizenship satisfies the diversity requirement.

v.   Citizenship of Legal Representatives

The legal representative of an estate (*e.g.*, an executor or administrator) is deemed to be a citizen of the decedent's state only; the actual citizenship of the representative is irrelevant.

> *For example, if B, a citizen of State X, dies and C, a citizen of State Y, is appointed executor, diversity jurisdiction exists between C acting as executor of B's estate and any citizen of State Y, but not between C (as executor) and any citizen of State X. Likewise, the legal representative of an infant or incompetent is deemed to be a citizen of the infant or incompetent's state. This rule prevents the appointment of a legal representative solely to create diversity.*

Where an action is brought on behalf of a trust, the citizenship of the trustee (not that of the beneficiary) controls, as long as the trustee has actual powers with regard to the litigated matter. If the trustee is merely a nominal party, the court will look to the citizenship of the aggrieved persons. The citizenship of receivers and subrogees is likewise controlling.

vi.   Citizenship of Substituted Parties

If an original party dies, becomes incompetent or transfers his interest, or if a public officer has been succeeded, a successor party may be substituted under Fed. R. Civ. P. 25. The citizenship of the substituted party is irrelevant; for diversity purposes, the citizenship of the original party is governing.

vii.   Citizenship in Class Actions

In class actions, the court looks only to the citizenship of the named representatives of the class. *Snyder v. Harris*, 394 U.S. 332 (1969). Likewise, diversity can be created in a stockholders' derivative suit by making the plaintiff a stockholder who is not a citizen of any of the states of the corporation's citizenship.

viii.   Devices to Create Or Destroy Diversity

A.   Assignment or Subrogation of Claim

If a claim is assigned to an out-of-state assignee for collection only and the assignment was motivated by desire to obtain diversity jurisdiction, the assignment is collusive under 28 U.S.C. §1359 and diversity does not exist. *Kramer v. Caribbean Mills, Inc.*, 394 U.S. 823 (1969). (§1359 provides that a district court shall not have jurisdiction of a civil action in which any party "by assignment or otherwise, has been improperly or collusively made or joined to invoke jurisdiction.") Likewise, a sham subrogation will not create diversity. However, if substantial consideration was paid, or if the assignor has no further interest in the claim, diversity will be upheld.

B.   Change of Domicile

If a person moves to a new domicile before bringing suit, diversity will be achieved, as long as the change of domicile is bona fide. A corporation cannot create diversity by transferring a claim to an out-of-state subsidiary.

C.   Collusive Joinder to Prevent Removal

Conversely, a plaintiff may sue in state court and try to prevent the defendant from removing to federal court under diversity jurisdiction. She might appoint an administrator from the same state as the defendant, or name another defendant who is from her own state to destroy diversity. Section 1359 does not prohibit a collusive action to defeat jurisdiction, but a federal court will strike down fraudulent joinder. Likewise, plaintiff's reduction of the amount claimed after removal in order to violate the amount-in-controversy requirement will not defeat jurisdiction. *St. Paul Mercury Indemnity Co. v. Red Cab Co.*, 303 U.S. 283 (1938).

ix. Realignment of Parties

The court need not adhere to the plaintiff's alignment of parties. It "will look beyond the pleadings and arrange the parties according to their sides in the dispute." *Dawson v. Columbia Ave. Savings Fund*, 197 U.S. 178 (1905). This may create or destroy diversity.

> *Thus, if the plaintiff in a stockholders' derivative action alleges that the corporation is controlled by antagonistic directors, the court will align the corporation as a defendant, even though the recovery will belong to the corporation so that its ultimate interest coincides with that of the plaintiff.*

b. *Amount in Controversy Requirement*

In diversity jurisdiction, the amount in controversy must exceed the sum or value of $75,000, exclusive of interest and costs. 28 U.S.C. §1332(a). One exception to this is federal statutory interpleader actions, in which the amount in controversy need only be $500. 28 U.S.C. §1335.

The amount-in-controversy requirement in federal question jurisdiction was eliminated in December, 1980, except in suits under the Consumer Product Safety Act §23(a) against defendants other than the United States, its agencies or employees.

The purpose of the $75,000 amount is to reduce congestion in the federal courts by excluding "insubstantial" controversies.

i. The Plaintiff's Complaint Determines Amount in Controversy

The amount in controversy is determined from the plaintiff's viewpoint. The court looks to the prayer in the complaint or the allegations of damage. The amount is measured at the time suit is commenced; thus, a subsequent reduction in the amount sought does not defeat jurisdiction if the original claim was made in good faith. *St. Paul Mercury Indemnity Co. v. Red Cab Co.*, 303 U.S. 283 (1938).

If the plaintiff's allegation of an amount more than $75,000 is made in good faith, a motion to dismiss for lack of jurisdiction will be denied. It must appear to a legal certainty that the claim is really for less than the jurisdictional amount to justify dismissal. *Id.* The plaintiff need not itemize his damages; an allegation that the matter in controversy exceeds $75,000 is sufficient.

If the plaintiff actually recovers less than $75,000, jurisdiction is not thereby retroactively destroyed. *Rosado v. Wyman*, 397 U.S. 397 (1970). However, to discourage the filing of exaggerated claims, the court has discretion to deny costs to, or to impose costs on, the plaintiff, if the plaintiff's recovery (without regard to any set-off or counterclaim) is $75,000 or less. 28 U.S.C. §1332(b).

ii.   Measure of Amount In Controversy

If the plaintiff seeks something other than damages, determination of the amount in controversy is more difficult. Where the plaintiff seeks an injunction, the amount in controversy is the value of the right to be protected or the extent of the injury to be prevented. Suits to protect a civil or constitutional right are generally presumed to involve an inherent value of more than $75,000.

In certain instances, the court may look to the monetary value to the plaintiff or the defendant to determine the amount in controversy.

> *For example, in a suit to quiet title to water rights, it was stipulated that the rights were worth less than the jurisdictional amount to the plaintiff, but worth far more to the defendant. The court held that the test for the amount in controversy was "the pecuniary result to either party which the judgment would directly produce."* Ronzio v. Denver & R. G. W. R. R., *116 F.2d 604 (10th Cir. 1940).*

The stare decisis or collateral estoppel effects of the decision cannot be used to determine the amount in controversy.

> *Thus, in an action on bond coupons, the amount in controversy is only the amount of the coupons, not the value of the bonds, even though the decision will conclusively determine the value of the bonds.* Elgin v. Marshall, *106 U.S. 578 (1882).*

Similarly, in an action to enjoin a regulatory statute that will harm a business, the amount in controversy is the difference between the value of the unregulated business and the value of the regulated business. However, if the statute would prohibit conduct of the business, the value of the entire business would be the measure.

iii.   Interests and Costs

Interest and costs are specifically excluded by §1332 in calculating the amount in controversy. However, attorneys' fees may be included if they are authorized by contract or by state statute, provided the fee is reasonable. Furthermore, interest is not excluded if it is part of the basis of the suit (*e.g.*, an action to collect on bond coupons), rather than interest that has accrued after the cause of action arose (*e.g.*, after the maturity of the coupon).

iv.   Aggregation of Claims

When a single plaintiff sues a single defendant, the plaintiff may join as many claims as he has against an opposing party, regardless of the nature of the claim. Fed. R. Civ. P. 18. The plaintiff may likewise aggregate his claims to achieve the jurisdictional amount.

> *Thus, if A has one claim against B for $50,000, and another unrelated claim against B for $26,000, A may join both claims and sue in federal court, provided there is the requisite diversity.*

The claims of several plaintiffs against a single defendant cannot be aggregated, even though the parties join under the rule relating to the joinder of parties.

> *Thus, if A has a claim against C for $50,000, and B has a claim against C for $26,000, they cannot aggregate their claims and sue in federal court if the claims are separate and distinct. Likewise, if a single plaintiff has claims against several defendants, she can aggregate her claims only if the defendants are jointly liable; if they are separately liable, each of her claims must satisfy the $75,000 requirement.*

However, aggregation is permitted where several plaintiffs have an undivided right, title or interest, *e.g.*, an action on bonds by joint owners, a suit by holders of two notes to enforce a vendor's lien securing both notes, or a suit by joint owners of realty to quiet title.

> *If one plaintiff has a claim for an amount exceeding $75,000, and another plaintiff has a similar claim for $75,000 or less, the second plaintiff cannot join in the original action; she must satisfy the amount individually.*

Snyder v. Harris, 394 U.S. 332 (1969) held that a class action will not meet the amount in controversy requirement (now $75,000) if no individual member has a claim for that amount. *Zahn v. International Paper Co.*, 414 U.S. 291 (1974), extended this rule, holding that even if each of the named class representatives has an individual claim for more than the required amount, they cannot represent a class in which the members have claims for less than that amount. Note that in a shareholders' derivative action, the measure would be the amount by which the corporation would benefit from a recovery, rather than the amount by which individual stockholders would benefit.

v.   Jurisdictional Amount in Counterclaims

The amount of a counterclaim cannot be aggregated with the plaintiff's claim to satisfy the $75,000 requirement.

A counterclaim that arises out of the same transaction or occurrence is compulsory. Fed. R. Civ. P. 13(a). A compulsory counterclaim need not meet the jurisdictional amount requirement, because the federal court has supplemental jurisdiction over it. (See Section IV(D), *infra*.)

A counterclaim that does not arise out of the same transaction or occurrence is permissive. Fed. R. Civ. P. 13(b). A permissive counterclaim must have an independent jurisdictional basis.

If P sues in state court for $75,000 or less, and D counterclaims for more than $75,000, P cannot remove the case to federal court, because removal is allowed only by defendants. 28 U.S.C. §1441; *Shamrock Oil & Gas Corp. v. Sheets*, 313 U.S. 100 (1941).

> *If, in this situation, D asserts a counterclaim that is permissive under state law, he too will be unable to remove, since P's claim does not meet the requirement. Where D asserts a counterclaim that is compulsory under state law, the courts are divided as to whether D can remove, but the majority hold that he cannot.*

c. State Subject Matter Jurisdiction

In state courts, as in federal courts, a court must have jurisdiction over the subject matter of the litigation. Subject matter jurisdiction is the authority to hear and decide a general type of suit; it is granted by the constitution or statutes of the state, and cannot be waived by the parties. The lack of subject matter jurisdiction may be raised at any time by the parties or by the court on its own motion. If a court lacks subject matter jurisdiction, its judgment is void and can be collaterally attacked.

A state court's jurisdiction may be either general or limited, and either exclusive or concurrent. A court of general jurisdiction is authorized to hear and decide all suits, regardless of the nature of the case or the amount involved, unless exclusive jurisdiction has been conferred on another court by constitution or statute. A court of limited jurisdiction has only that jurisdiction expressly granted it by the state constitution or statute (e.g., a probate court may be limited to jurisdiction over probate, adoption and divorce). If a suit may be brought only in one court, that court has exclusive jurisdiction over it; if a suit might be brought in either of two courts, those courts have concurrent jurisdiction over it. Besides courts of original jurisdiction (those in which cases are commenced and tried), there is always at least one state court of appellate jurisdiction which reviews the decisions of the lower courts.

3. Supplemental Jurisdiction

Congress has enacted a statute, 28 U.S.C. §1367, which codifies (and to some degree extends) the prior practice of pendent and ancillary jurisdiction for actions filed on or after December 1, 1990. Pendent jurisdiction allows a federal court to take jurisdiction of a state law claim between the parties if it derives from the same "common nucleus of operative fact" as the federal question properly before the court. *United Mine Workers v. Gibbs*, 383 U.S. 715 (1966). Ancillary jurisdiction allows a federal court in diversity cases to join parties over which it has no independent jurisdiction (*i.e.*, nondiverse parties or parties with claims of $50,000 or less) under essentially the same standard as pendent jurisdiction. Under the new statute, a district court generally will have supplemental jurisdiction over any claims so related to the claim upon which federal jurisdiction is founded that "they form part of the same case or controversy." 28 U.S.C. §1367(a).

> *This statute reinstates the doctrine of pendent party jurisdiction over state law claims in federal question cases as promulgated prior to Finley v. U.S., 109 S.Ct. 2003 (1989). Finley held that federal courts could assert pendent party jurisdiction only where expressly authorized by Congress.*

The district court may refuse to exercise supplemental jurisdiction if:

(1)   the claim raises a novel or complex issue of state law;

(2)   the state law claim substantially predominates over any claim(s) over which the court has original jurisdiction;

(3)   the district court has dismissed all claims over which it had original jurisdiction; or

(4)   exceptional circumstances and compelling reasons exist for the court to decline jurisdiction.

Of course, the court may decide a state law claim without deciding the federal question on which jurisdiction is based. If the federal claim raises a significant constitutional issue, courts generally prefer to dispose of the case by deciding the state law claim, if by doing so, they can avoid the constitutional question. *See Hagans v. Lavine*, 415 U.S. 528 (1974).

Filing the claim in federal court tolls all applicable statutes of limitations (including state statutes) while the claim is pending and for 30 days after dismissal (unless state law provides for a longer tolling period). 28 U.S.C. §1367(d).

Supplemental jurisdiction usually extends to the joinder or intervention of additional parties. 28 U.S.C. §1367(a). However, it does not extend to plaintiffs that would destroy the required diversity in cases based solely on diversity jurisdiction. 28 U.S.C. §1367(b).

a.   *Counterclaims (Rule 13)*

Supplemental jurisdiction extends to compulsory counterclaims, *i.e.*, a counterclaim that must be brought because it arises out of the same transaction or occurrence as the main claim (as defined in Fed. R. Civ. P. 13(a)).

However, permissive counterclaims (any counterclaim that does not arise out of the same transaction or occurrence, Rule 13(b)) require an independent jurisdictional ground. The one exception is that a permissive counterclaim in the nature of a set-off used only to reduce the plaintiff's judgment does not require an independent jurisdictional ground.

b.   Cross Claims (Rule 13(g))

A cross-claim (*i.e.*, a claim against a co-defendant) also probably falls within the court's supplemental jurisdiction.

> For example, P, a citizen of Maine, sues D-1 and D-2, both citizens of Massachusetts; D-1 cross-claims against D-2 for indemnification. The court has supplemental jurisdiction, and diversity between D-1 and D-2 is not required.

However, a few cases have held that if D-1's suit against D-2 is for D-1's own injury (*i.e.*, an issue different from that in the main claim), the court may refuse to exercise jurisdiction.

c.   Impleader (Rule 14)

Through impleader (also known as a third-party action) a defendant can bring in as a third-party defendant someone whom the defendant asserts will be liable to him for all or part of the defendant's liability to plaintiff. A court has supplemental jurisdiction of the third-party action and neither the diversity requirement nor the jurisdictional amount requirement need be met where the defendant (or third-party plaintiff) and the third-party defendant are citizens of the same state.

> For example, P, a citizen of New York, sues D, a citizen of Pennsylvania; D impleads T, a citizen of Pennsylvania, for indemnification. The third-party action is supplemental to the main claim, and the federal court has jurisdiction.

However, if the plaintiff in the main action amends his complaint to sue the third-party defendant, diversity between them is required. *Owen Equipment & Erection Co. v. Kroger*, 437 U.S. 365 (1978).

> For example, P, a citizen of Massachusetts, sues D, a citizen of New York, and D impleads T, a citizen of Massachusetts. Since P could not originally have sued T in federal court (due to lack of diversity), P cannot now use supplemental jurisdiction to evade the diversity requirement.

d.   Intervention (Rule 24)

A person may intervene as of right in an action if she claims an interest relating to the subject property or transaction, and the disposition of the action may impair or impede her ability to protect that interest, unless her interest is adequately represented by existing parties. Fed. R. Civ. P. 24(a).

However, supplemental jurisdiction extends only to a defendant intervenor's claim. A party seeking to intervene as a plaintiff must show independent grounds for jurisdiction.

Permissive intervention may be allowed in the court's discretion when an applicant's claim or defense and the main action have a question of law or fact in common. Fed. R. Civ. P. 24(b). Independent jurisdictional grounds are required where intervention is permissive.

e. *Joinder of Claims (Rule 18)*

Supplemental jurisdiction does not extend to joinder of claims under Rule 18, unless the federal and nonfederal claims are so closely related as to constitute separate grounds in support of a single cause of action.

f. *Joinder of Parties (Rules 19 & 20)*

Supplemental jurisdiction does not apply to an absent "indispensable" party under Rule 19 (*i.e.*, a party needed for just adjudication) or to parties permissively joined under Rule 20. Therefore, the diversity and jurisdictional amount requirements must be met.

g. *Process and Venue Under Supplemental Jurisdiction*

The party to be brought in under supplemental jurisdiction must be served in accordance with Fed. R. Civ. P. 4, which permits service (1) within the state where the federal court is located, and (2) as to third-party defendants or necessary parties under Rule 19, outside the state if the place of service is within 100 miles from the place the action is commenced.

If the federal court has supplemental jurisdiction, the venue statutes with regard to the additional claim or party need not be satisfied.

4. Removal

A civil action brought in a state court may be removed by the defendant to the federal district court if the plaintiff could have brought the action in federal court originally. 28 U.S.C. §1441(a). This statutory right of removal protects the defendant from any local prejudice in a diversity case, and allows the defendant to avail himself of a hearing in federal court when a federal question is at issue.

a. *Prerequisites to Removal*
i. Federal Subject Matter Jurisdiction - Plaintiff's Claim Governs

Since only a civil action that could have been brought in federal court originally is removable, the ground for removal must appear in the plaintiff's claim. 28 U.S.C. §1441(b). *See also Merrell Dow Pharmaceuticals, Inc. v. Thompson*, 478 U.S. 804 (1986). A federal question raised in a defense

Multistate Bar Review Book 2

or counterclaim is not a basis for removal. Thus, a plaintiff can prevent a defendant from removing by simply failing to assert a federal claim, or by joining a nondiverse party. However, after removal, the plaintiff cannot defeat jurisdiction by reducing the amount claimed or by joining a nondiverse party.

ii.   Time of Determining Removability

Generally, the right to remove is determined by the pleadings as of the time of filing the petition for removal. However, there is an exception to this rule: where diversity of citizenship is the basis for federal jurisdiction, the diversity must have existed at the time the original action was filed in state court, and at the time the petition for removal was filed. This restriction prevents the defendant from changing his citizenship after the suit is filed, and then petitioning for removal on the ground of diversity. On the other hand, if a case was not initially removable, but the plaintiff then drops a nondiverse party, the defendant may remove, because that change was not within the defendant's control. Likewise, if diversity of citizenship did not exist at the time of filing of the action, a party's postfiling change of citizenship cannot cure a lack of subject matter jurisdiction that existed at the time of filing. (See *Grupo Dataflux v. Atlas Global Group, L.P.*, ___ U.S.___ (2004) wherein plaintiff filed suit in federal court based on alleged diversity. In fact, diversity of citizenship did not exist at the time of filing and the suit was dismissed. Plaintiff unsuccessfully tried to argue that since diversity of citizenship existed before trial began that dismissal should not take place. The Court stressed the long-standing rule that subject matter jurisdiction in diversity cases depends on the state of facts that exist at the time of filing).

b.   Only the Defendant Can Remove

Only a defendant can remove an action from state to federal court. 28 U.S.C. §1441(b). A plaintiff cannot remove on the basis that a counterclaim could have been brought originally in federal court.

A diversity case is removable "only if none of the parties in interest properly joined and served as defendants is a citizen of the state in which such action is brought." 28 U.S.C. §1441(b).

> For example, P, a resident of Massachusetts, sues D, a resident of New York, in a New York state court; D cannot remove to federal court if the only basis for federal jurisdiction is diversity. However, if P had sued D in a Massachusetts state court, D could have removed.

A suit involving a federal question is removable even by a resident defendant.

All defendants who have been properly joined and served must join in the petition for removal.

c. *State Court Jurisdiction No Longer A Prerequisite*

Under former practice, a federal court could exercise jurisdiction over a case removed from state court only if the state court had proper subject matter jurisdiction. Therefore, if the action was one within the exclusive jurisdiction of the federal courts (*e.g.*, an antitrust suit), the case could not be removed; the case would have to be dismissed in the state court so that it could be refiled in federal court. This cumbersome process is no longer necessary because of the passage of 28 U.S.C. §1441(e), which expressly permits the federal court to take jurisdiction of the removed claim, even though the state court did not have proper subject matter jurisdiction.

d. *Waiver of Right To Remove*

The defendant may waive his right to remove. However, the courts are reluctant to find a waiver; even where defendants have appeared, answered, and taken depositions in the state court action, federal courts have held that defendants did not thereby waive their right to remove.

A contract stipulating that the parties would not remove cases to federal court is a valid waiver of the right to remove unless the contract is unreasonable or procured by duress. A state may not require a foreign corporation to waive its right to remove as a condition to doing business within the state.

e. *Separate and Independent Claim*

Whenever a separate and independent federal question claim, which would be removable if sued upon alone, is joined with one or more otherwise nonremovable claims or causes of action, the entire case may be removed and the district court may determine all issues therein. The court may, however, remand the nonremovable claims if state law predominates. 28 U.S.C. §1441(c). This provision prevents a plaintiff from defeating a defendant's right to remove by simply joining a nonremovable claim. The rationale for allowing the court discretion to hear and decide the otherwise nonremovable claim is to promote judicial economy and protect the defendant from having to defend in two suits in different forums (and from therefore not exercising his removal right).

Where there is a single wrong to the plaintiff, for which relief is sought, arising from an interlocked series of transactions, there is no separate and independent claim or cause of action under §1441(c). *American Fire & Casualty Co. v. Finn*, 341 U.S. 6 (1951).

> For example, in Finn, a Texas plaintiff brought an action in Texas state court against two foreign insurance companies and their Texas agent, claiming in the alternative recovery for his fire loss under one of their policies, or that their agent was liable for failure to keep the property insured. The insurers removed to federal court, but the Supreme Court held the removal improper, because the plaintiff's allegations involved substantially the same facts and

> transactions and showed a single incident resulting in a single wrong for which relief was sought. Hence, the claim against the agent was not separate and independent, and because diversity was lacking between the plaintiff and the agent, jurisdiction was lacking. Few cases meet the Finn test.

f.   Venue in Removed Actions

The proper venue for a removed action is the federal district or division embracing the place where the state action is pending. 28 U.S.C. §1441(a). The general venue statutes (see Section VII, *infra*) are irrelevant in removed actions. Thus, it does not matter that the federal court to which an action is properly removed would not have been a place of proper venue under the general venue statutes if the action had been filed there initially.

g.   Removable Actions

In addition to the general removal statute, other statutes authorize removal in particular cases, including a suit against, or prosecution of, a federal officer in state court for any act under color of office (28 U.S.C. §1442); a suit against a federal employee for injury caused by his operation of a motor vehicle within the scope of his employment (28 U.S.C. §2679(d)); certain actions arising out of international or foreign banking (12 U.S.C. §632). Either a civil suit or a criminal prosecution can be removed by a defendant who cannot secure in state court the civil rights guaranteed him by the federal Constitution (28 U.S.C. §1443); however, this is permitted only if those rights will inevitably be denied by the very act of bringing the defendant to trial in the state court. *City of Greenwood, Miss. v. Peacock*, 384 U.S. 808 (1966). These special authorizations of removal do not thereby allow commencement of these suits in federal court originally.

h.   Nonremovable Actions

Statutes prohibit removal in the following cases: actions under the Federal Employers' Liability Act and under the Jones Act (28 U.S.C. §1445(a)); actions against carriers for delay, loss or damage in shipments, where the matter in controversy is $10,000 or less (§1445(b)); workers' compensation proceedings (§1445(c)). Similarly, courts have held nonremovable actions under the Fair Labor Standards Act, or under the Securities Act for recovery for misrepresentation.

i.   Procedure For Removal

The procedure for removal is specified in 28 U.S.C. §1446.

A defendant wishing to remove an action must file a verified petition in the federal district court for the district and division within which the action is pending. The petition must contain a short and plain statement of the facts that entitle him to removal. He must also file (1) a copy of all process, pleadings and orders served upon him, and (2) a bond sufficient to cover costs and disbursements occasioned by removal, in case the suit was improperly removed.

Promptly after filing the petition and bond, the defendant must give written notice to all adverse parties, and must file a copy of the petition with the clerk of the state court. Removal is then effective, and the state court no longer has jurisdiction.

Defendant must file for removal of a civil action within thirty (30) days after (1) receipt of the initial pleading setting forth the claim upon which the action is based, or (2) service of the summons if the initial pleading has then been filed in court and is not required to be served, whichever period is shorter. If the case was not initially removable, defendant must file within thirty days after his receipt of the amended pleading, motion or other paper from which it first appears that the case has become removable. Note that the time runs from the receipt of the pleading by defendant (or his authorized agent), not from the time of its filing in court. However, the 30-day period begins to run when the defendant is formally served the complaint by certified mail, not upon receipt of a faxed courtesy copy of the file-stamped complaint. *Murphy Bros. v. Michetti Pipe Stringing,* 526 U.S. 344 (1999).

j.   *Remand*

If, at any time before final judgment, it appears that the case was removed improvidently and without jurisdiction, the federal court must remand the case to the state court, and may order the payment of just costs. 28 U.S.C. §1447(c). Remand may be upon the motion of either party, or the motion of the court. The removing party bears the burden of proof upon any challenge.

A certified copy of the order of remand must be sent to the clerk of the state court. Upon its receipt, the state court again takes jurisdiction. §1447(c).

An order remanding a case to state court is generally not reviewable on appeal or otherwise. (The one statutory exception is if a civil rights action removed under §1443 is remanded.) 28 U.S.C. §1447(d). However, if the district court remanded a case on grounds not specified in the statute (*e.g.,* federal docket is overcrowded), mandamus will lie to set aside the remand. *Thermtron Products, Inc. v. Hermansdorfer,* 423 U.S. 336 (1976).

E.   PERSONAL JURISDICTION

1.   Federal Personal Jurisdiction

In addition to jurisdiction over the subject matter, a federal court must have jurisdiction over the persons or property involved in the suit. This is sometimes referred to as territorial jurisdiction or personal jurisdiction. Traditionally, such jurisdiction was based upon the presence of the person or property within the state where the court was located; currently, the existence of such jurisdiction turns upon whether there is a constitutionally sufficient connection between the defendant and the forum and whether notice sufficient to satisfy due process has been given to the persons whose interests are at stake in the suit.

Generally, the federal courts are subject to the same limitations on service of process that apply to the state courts.

2. State Personal Jurisdiction

In addition to subject matter jurisdiction - the competence to hear a type of suit - a court must also have the power to bind the parties to the suit (or the property at issue) by its judgment; this jurisdiction over the persons and property is sometimes called personal jurisdiction or territorial jurisdiction.

Historically, the basis for a court's jurisdiction was its power to take custody of persons or property within its own borders. Thus, the traditional bases for jurisdiction included the presence of the person or property in the state. *Pennoyer v. Neff*, 95 U.S. 714 (1877). Domicile of the defendant in the state was an adequate ground for jurisdiction. Consent - express or implied - by the defendant also conferred jurisdiction over him. Property within the state owned by the defendant could provide jurisdiction if attached at the outset of the suit, but the judgment extended only to the defendant's rights and interests in that property. (See Quasi in Rem Jurisdiction, Section (D), infra.)

The current personal jurisdiction analysis focuses more upon due process limitations than territorial limits: (1) Is it fair to require the defendant to defend in the state? (2) Does the state have a reasonable nexus with the dispute? (3) Has the defendant received adequate notice of the action and an opportunity to be heard? Long-arm statutes can extend a state's jurisdiction beyond its own territory if the due process requirements are satisfied.

In personam jurisdiction gives the court power to award a judgment imposing personal liability on the defendant. It is usually the most desirable form of jurisdiction, since, in effect, the judgment attaches to the person of the defendant and follows wherever he goes. Thus, the plaintiff, as a judgment creditor, can execute against any of the defendant's property within the state, and, if that is insufficient, can sue on the state court judgment in other states and execute against property located there.

The current bases for in personam jurisdiction are:

(1)   Personal service within the state;

(2)   Domicile of the defendant in the state;

(3)   Consent of the defendant to be sued in the state (by contract, intentional waiver of objection, or failure to raise the objection in timely fashion);

(4)   Fictional presence of a corporation in the state ("doing business");

(5)   Long-arm jurisdiction.

a.   *Personal Service Within the State*

Personal service upon a natural person within the state subjects him to in personam jurisdiction. In the past, the nature of the plaintiff's cause of action was irrelevant - it need not be related to the state. Thus, in *Grace v. MacArthur*, 170 F. Supp. (E.D. Ark. 1959), in personam jurisdiction was obtained by serving an airline passenger while the plane was flying over the forum state. *Shaffer v. Heitner* (Section XII(D)(3), infra) cast doubt on this particular theory; it required a connection among the defendant, the forum state and the litigation. However, *Shaffer v. Heitner* does not overrule the traditional rule of *Pennoyer v. Neff*; personal service within the state is still sufficient to justify personal jurisdiction over a party. In *Burnham v. Superior Court of California*, 495 U.S. 604, 109 L.Ed.2d 631 (1990), the Court held that a party's temporary but voluntary presence in the state constituted sufficient purposeful availment of the benefits of the state (fire and police protection, for example) so that personal service therein would satisfy the requirements of due process.

Note, though, that many states provide immunity from service of process for a nonresident who is in the state voluntarily to participate in a legal proceeding. Similarly, service may be invalidated if a nonresident is lured into a state under false pretenses.

b.   *Domicile*

Domicile is a basis for jurisdiction even if the service is made outside the state. *Milliken v. Meyer*, 311 U.S. 457 (1940). Domicile requires the maintenance of a residence or physical presence in the state, and the mental intent to make the state one's permanent residence. Residence, on the other hand, means mere physical presence in the state without that intent. A person may be a resident of more than one state, but can be a domiciliary of only one. The defendant must be a domiciliary when process is served for jurisdiction to be acquired; prior or subsequent domicile is ineffective.

A corporation is subject to in personam jurisdiction in the state where it is incorporated. (Its place of incorporation is analogous to a person's domicile.)

c.   *Consent*

Unlike subject matter jurisdiction, personal jurisdiction may be conferred by the consent of the defendant.

i.   Express Consent

If, prior to the action, the defendant has designated an agent in the state to accept process on his behalf (e.g., in a contract), valid service may be made on the agent. *National Equipment Rental,*

Ltd. v. Szukhent, 375 U.S. 311 (1964). However, this rule may not apply if the court is an inappropriate forum or if one party to the contract had disproportionate bargaining power or perpetrated a fraud.

In a cognovit note, a debtor confesses judgment in the event he defaults on his payments and usually also consents to in personam jurisdiction in a specified court. Most states reject such notes as an express consent to jurisdiction.

A defendant can also consent to jurisdiction after a suit has begun by expressly waiving his challenge to personal jurisdiction.

ii.   Implied Consent - By Filing Lawsuit

By filing suit, the plaintiff consents to personal jurisdiction; thus, a defendant may counterclaim and serve the plaintiff's attorney. *Adam v. Saenger*, 303 U.S. 59 (1938).

However, this rule is somewhat modified in regard to class action suits. A plaintiff is held to have consented to the forum state's jurisdiction if she is notified of her option to "opt out" of the class action and fails to do so. *Phillips Petroleum Co. v. Shutts*, 472 U.S. 797 (1985).

iii.   Implied Consent - By Making General Appearance

If the defendant appears and defends on the merits without raising a timely objection to jurisdiction, he has waived his jurisdictional objection, and thus has consented. Usually, waiver occurs unless the defendant raises his jurisdictional objection in either his answer or a pre-answer motion to dismiss for lack of jurisdiction, whichever is filed first.

iv.   Implied Consent - Nonresident Motorist Statute

Most states have a nonresident motorist statute, which provides that a nonresident motorist using the state's highways impliedly appoints the secretary of state or some other designated state official as his agent for accepting process in suits arising from his use of the roads. Such statutes are based on the dubious fiction that a state may exclude a nonresident if he does not consent. The statutes have been upheld on the basis of a state's police power to regulate its roads and its desire to provide an adequate forum for its injured citizens. *Hess v. Pawloski*, 274 U.S. 352 (1927) (Held that driving on a forum state's highways is sufficient minimum contacts with the state to support exercise of personal jurisdiction- state has a right to protect its citizens on the road from out of state drivers). However, the statute must expressly require the state official to give notice of the commencement of the suit to the nonresident. *Wuchter v. Pizzutti*, 276 U.S. 13 (1928). In most states, the nonresident motorist statute has been conceptually superseded by the long-arm statute (infra).

In many states, a foreign corporation is required as a condition of its engaging in business in the state to appoint an agent within the state for receipt of process. Furthermore, a corporation that failed to appoint an agent was deemed to have impliedly designated the secretary of state as its agent for receipt of process; this approach raised questions of restraint on interstate commerce, and the implied consent doctrine was superseded by the "corporate presence" theory.

d.   Corporate "Presence": "Doing Business" in the State

The doctrine of corporate "presence" developed through case law to justify exercising jurisdiction over a foreign corporation. A corporation was deemed to be "present" in the state through the presence of its office, employees and bank accounts there; hence, service could be effected upon its employees or upon the secretary of state. However, if the corporation ceased to have such a "presence" in the state, it could no longer be sued, even for its prior acts. The "presence" theory thus developed into the "doing business" theory: the corporation's transactions within the state were in fact a "presence", so that a corporation could be sued upon its acts within the state even after the corporation had left the state.

The "doing business" basis is still useful if the claim is unrelated to the forum state, i.e., if the event giving rise to the claim occurred outside the state, and the defendant is a foreign corporation "doing business" in the state.

> For example, where a Massachusetts plaintiff was injured in Maine by a defective product manufactured in North Dakota by the defendant, defendant's business activities in Massachusetts were sufficient to satisfy the minimum contacts and fairness requirements of due process, and jurisdiction could be obtained by service upon the Massachusetts secretary of state.

The key factor is the extent of business - the corporation must do business in the state not occasionally or casually, but with a fair measure of permanence and continuity. If several corporations function as basically a single economic unit, having common ownership or interlocking corporate structures, and only one is doing business in the state, jurisdiction probably will be sustained over a sister corporation. However, as long as there is a genuine separation between subsidiary and parent, the subsidiary's activities in the state will not be imputed to the parent.

e.   Long Arm Jurisdiction

International Shoe Co. v. Washington, 326 U.S. 310 (1945) removed the need for the fictions of "consent" and "presence", and laid the basis for long-arm jurisdiction. It declared: "Due process requires only that in order to subject a defendant to a judgment in personam, if he be not present within the territory of the forum, he have certain **minimum contacts** with it such that the maintenance of the suit does not offend 'traditional notions of fair play and substantial justice.'"

Note that under the minimum contacts doctrine there are two bases for the assumption of jurisdiction: (1) if the cause of action arose from the defendant's activities within the state, jurisdiction would be proper; (2) if the cause of action arose from conduct outside the forum state, jurisdiction would be proper if the out-of-state defendant engaged in continuous and systematic business within the state (e.g., a permanent office or regular sales representatives).

i.   Types of Long Arm Statutes

After *International Shoe*, most states enacted long-arm statutes, which are basically of two types.

A.   Broad Scope

Some states (California and Rhode Island) drafted broad long-arm statutes; their reach is coextensive with the Constitution, so that they automatically adjust to new interpretations of the Due Process Clause. Such statutes typically provide that "Persons that shall have the necessary minimum contacts with the state shall be subject to the jurisdiction of the state, and the courts shall hold such foreign corporations and nonresident individuals amenable to suit in every case not contrary to the provisions of the constitution or laws of the United States." In suits under such statutes, the only inquiry is whether the statute as read and applied is constitutional.

B.   Limited Scope

Statutes of a limited scope specify the categories of contacts that will confer jurisdiction, e.g., "a tortious act within the state." Typically, these categories will include defendant's (1) transaction of business in the state; (2) contracting anywhere to supply goods or services in the state; (3) causing tortious injury by an act or omission in the state; (4) causing tortious injury in the state by an act or omission outside the state if he (a) regularly does or solicits business or engages in any other persistent course of conduct, or derives substantial revenue from goods used or consumed, or services rendered, in the state, or (b) expects or reasonably should expect the act to have consequences in the state and derives substantial revenue from interstate or international commerce; (5) having an interest in, using or possessing real property in the state; (6) contracting to insure any person, property or risk within the state; and (7) living as one of the parties to a marriage or former marriage, if the marital domicile of both parties was in the state for at least one year within the two years immediately preceding the commencement of the action, notwithstanding the defendant's subsequent departure from the state.

In suits under these statutes, a two-step inquiry is necessary: (1) Is this case within the statute? (2) Is the statute as read and applied constitutional?

Under a long-arm statute of limited scope, the first question is "Is this case within the statute?"

A.   Tortious Act Within the State

Many long-arm statutes extend jurisdiction over one who commits a "tortious act within the state." Thus, "tortious act" must be defined; not all states have defined it in the same way.

> *For example, in* Gray v. American Radiator & Standard Sanitary Corp., 22 Ill.2d 432 (1961), *a valve, manufactured in Ohio by the defendant, was sold and incorporated into a water heater manufactured in Pennsylvania; the water heater was sold and installed in Illinois where it exploded - allegedly due to a defect in the valve - and injured the plaintiff. The Illinois court held that it had jurisdiction over the defendant because "the place of a wrong is where the last event takes place which is necessary to render the actor liable" - thus, the tortious act was committed in Illinois and the case was within the Illinois statute. Most courts have followed the Illinois interpretation.*
>
> *However, in* Feathers v. McLucas, 15 N.Y.2d 443 (1965), *the New York Court of Appeals interpreted a similar statute more narrowly, holding that a tort and a "tortious act" do not necessarily occur in the same place, and that if the injury occurred within the state, but the negligent act occurred outside the state, New York would not have jurisdiction.*

B.   Tortious Act Outside the State Causing Injury Within The State

In response to *Feathers v. McLucas*, New York, and other states with such limited scope long-arm statutes, added a new section to the statute to extend jurisdiction to a nondomiciliary that commits a tortious act outside the state causing injury to a person or property within the state. To satisfy the "minimum contacts" standard, such provisions apply only if the defendant (a) regularly does or solicits business, or engages in any other persistent course of conduct, or derives substantial revenue from goods used or consumed or services rendered in the state; or (b) expects or reasonably should expect the act to have consequences in the state and derives substantial revenue from interstate or international commerce.

Thus, to determine whether a case is within this section of the statute, you must first be certain that injury occurred within the state; in personal injury actions, this is usually not difficult to establish. However, a plaintiff who is hurt outside the state by a defective product manufactured outside the state cannot satisfy the injury-within-the-state requirement by showing that his medical expenses, loss of earnings, pain and suffering all occurred or were incurred within the state. This provision can also cover commercial injury, which is more difficult to locate. An injury will not be found to have occurred in a state merely because the plaintiff is domiciled or incorporated there; the loss must actually have occurred there.

Next, you must look to the extent of the defendant's business. "Substantial revenue" may be either a large percentage of the defendant's overall revenues, or a large sum of money. The substantial revenue need not be from the product that gave rise to the claim, but may be from other products the defendant sells in the state.

C.   Transaction of Any Business Within The State

Most long-arm statutes specify that if the defendant transacts any business within the state or contracts anywhere to supply goods or services in the state, and the claim arises from this, he is amenable to jurisdiction. The test for a "transaction" is not quantitative, but qualitative; the defendant need not be doing a substantial amount of business in the state, and a single transaction may be sufficient if it is the basis for the claim.

> *In Burger King Corp. v. Rudzewicz, 471 U.S. 462 (1985), the Court determined that a Florida statute which purported to establish personal jurisdiction over any person who "[b]reach[ed] a contract in this state by failing to perform acts required by the contract to be performed in this state" was constitutional and conferred jurisdiction over a Michigan resident who had sought and obtained a franchise from a Florida corporation and then failed to make payments to the Florida corporation.*

Negotiation and execution in the state of a contract that contemplates an ongoing relationship between a domiciliary and a nondomiciliary constitutes a transaction, even if the nondomiciliary works under the contract outside the state. However, the mere execution of a contract in the state does not necessarily constitute a transaction, if it was negotiated outside the state and was for the sale of property outside the state.

A contract to supply goods in the state will confer jurisdiction even if it is negotiated and executed outside the state, provided the claim arises out of the contract. Jurisdiction would not be conferred if the contract provided for delivery of the goods in another state; similarly, supplying goods to others in the state is not enough to grant jurisdiction.

Mail orders probably do not confer jurisdiction, because the contact is so minimal and defense by the buyer in the home state of the mail-order seller would be unduly burdensome.

An agent who transacts business in the state may provide jurisdiction. In *Parke-Bernet v. Franklyn*, 26 N.Y.2d 13 (1970), a California defendant participated in an auction in New York by telephone, using plaintiff's employee as intermediary. Under the "borrowed servant" doctrine, the employee was held to be the defendant's agent and jurisdiction was sustained.

       Multistate Bar Review Book 2

If a tort arises out of the transaction of business in the state, long-arm jurisdiction is available.

> *For example, in Singer v. Walker, 15 N.Y.2d 443 (1965), a geologist's hammer was manufactured in Illinois and shipped to a retailer in New York, where it was purchased by the plaintiff, who was injured in Connecticut when it broke. Although the New York court held that no tortious act had been committed in New York, it upheld jurisdiction on the basis that the defendant had transacted business within the state by soliciting business, printing advertisements and shipping substantial quantities of its products into the state.*

Contracting to insure any person, property or risk within the state is a sufficient contact to confer jurisdiction.

> *For example, In McGee v. International Life Ins. Co., 355 U.S. 220 (1957), a Texas insurance company doing business solely by mail, solicited and sold a policy to a California citizen. The Court held that the company could be sued under the California long-arm statute, even if the defendant sold only one policy in the state. An important consideration here is the forum state's interest in protecting its citizens against insurance companies, which is demonstrated by the state's pervasive regulation of the field.*

### D.	Real Property Actions

In many states, a defendant is subject to long-arm jurisdiction on a claim arising out of his ownership, use or possession of real property in the state. This section would cover a case where a state citizen was injured on the property of a nondomiciliary, or where a nondomiciliary reneged on a contract to sell realty in the state.

### iii.	Long Arm Analysis: Is the Statute Constitutional As Applied

Under a long-arm statute of limited scope, the second step (the first step under a statute of broad scope) is to determine whether the statute as read and applied in this case satisfies due process requirements. The meaning of due process is still evolving, but clearly minimum contacts and some element of purposeful activity by the defendant are necessary to meet its requirements.

### A.	Minimum Contacts

In *International Shoe*, the Supreme Court declared that due process requires that the defendant have certain "minimum contacts" with the forum state "such that the maintenance of the suit does not offend "traditional notions of fair play and substantial justice."" *International Shoe* introduced the

Multistate Bar Review Book 2

notion of "fairness" as the standard for jurisdiction rather than merely territorial concerns. Furthermore, the case declared that "continuous corporate operations within a state" might be sufficiently substantial to justify an exercise of jurisdiction over the firm on matters unrelated to its contacts with the state.

> *In Keeton v. Hustler Magazine, Inc., 465 U.S. 770 (1984), a New York plaintiff sued a magazine publisher, an Ohio corporation with its principal place of business in California, in a libel action filed in New Hampshire, the only state where the suit was not time-barred. The Supreme Court upheld the New Hampshire court's jurisdiction, emphasizing that the plaintiff is not required to have minimum contacts with the forum state. Since the defendant continuously and systematically distributed its magazine in the forum state and the claim arose from that activity, due process was satisfied. The plaintiff could properly seek damages resulting from publication in all states in her action in New Hampshire.*

> *In Helicopteros Nacionales de Colombia, S.A. v. Hall, 466 U.S. 408 (1984), the Supreme Court held that a Texas court could not exercise in personam jurisdiction over a Colombian corporation in a wrongful death action arising out of the crash in Peru of a helicopter operated by the corporation. The action did not arise out of the corporation's activities in Texas, and its contacts with Texas were held insufficient to justify general jurisdiction over it there. The single trip of its chief executive officer to Texas to negotiate the contract under which the corporation provided helicopter transportation to the Peruvian alter ego of a Texas joint venture was not a contact of a "continuous and systematic" nature. Nor did the acceptance of checks drawn on a Texas bank or the purchase of helicopters, parts and training for personnel in Texas satisfy the contact requirements. Mere purchases, even if occurring at regular intervals, are insufficient to ground an assertion of in personam jurisdiction over a nonresident corporation in a cause of action not related to those purchase transactions.*

B.   Purposefulness

The minimum contacts standard was further developed in *Hanson v. Denckla*, 357 U.S. 235 (1958): "It is essential in each case that there be some act by which the defendant purposely avails itself of the privilege of conducting activities within the forum state, thus invoking the benefits and protections of its laws."

> *In Hanson, a Pennsylvania domiciliary established a trust with a Delaware trust company as trustee; she later moved to Florida, where she continued to receive the trust income and where she exercised a power of appointment. In a contest over the disposition of the trust assets after her*

death, the Supreme Court ruled that the trustee had not sufficiently invoked the protection of Florida's laws to render itself subject to Florida jurisdiction, and stated that "the unilateral activity of those who claim some relationship with a nonresident defendant cannot satisfy the requirement of contact with the forum state."

The Court re-emphasized the importance of purposefulness in Kulko v. Superior Court of California, 436 U.S. 84 (1978). In Kulko, a husband and wife domiciled in New York separated after negotiating and signing a separation agreement in New York. The wife moved to California and later obtained a divorce, which incorporated the separation agreement. At the child's request, the father permitted his daughter to move to California to live with her mother; the mother then brought an action in California to modify the separation agreement's provisions for custody and child support. The Court held that the mere presence of the child in a state that was not the marital domicile was not an adequate jurisdictional basis for the action; the defendant had no significant contacts with the forum state and could hardly be said to have "purposely availed himself of" the benefits and protections of California law. Application of the so-called "effects" test to this situation was declared unreasonable and unfair, because the child, unlike a projectile or commercial papers, had not been purposefully or beneficially sent to California by the defendant. California's strong interest in assuring the support of children within the state was protected by the Uniform Reciprocal Enforcement of Support Act, which would permit the wife to obtain a New York judgment on the support petition without her having to leave California.

In World-Wide Volkswagen Corp. v. Woodson, 444 U.S. 286 (1980), the Court recurred to the necessity for the defendant's activity to be purposeful. In Woodson, the plaintiffs had purchased a car in New York and later had an accident in Oklahoma; they sued in Oklahoma, basing jurisdiction on the Oklahoma long-arm statute. The defendants - the retailer and the distributor - were both New York corporations that did no business in Oklahoma and did not ship any products there, or advertise or have agents for service of process in the state. The Supreme Court, in a 6-3 decision, rejected the argument that a car's mobility made injury in Oklahoma foreseeable, and declared that "foreseeability alone has never been a sufficient benchmark for personal jurisdiction under the Due Process Clause." The defendant's conduct and connection with the forum state must be such "that he could reasonably anticipate being haled into court there." However, in dictum the Court said, "The forum state does not exceed its powers under the Due Process Clause if it asserts personal jurisdiction over a corporation that delivers its products into the stream of commerce with the

> *expectation that they will be purchased by consumers in the forum state."*
> *The three dissenting justices would have upheld jurisdiction on the basis that*
> *the defendants had purposefully chosen to become a part of a nationwide -*
> *indeed, a global - network for marketing and servicing automobiles and relied*
> *on the unique mobility of the automobiles as a product.*

> *The California courts could exercise jurisdiction over a reporter and*
> *an editor, who were Florida residents, in a libel action, when the allegedly*
> *libelous magazine article concerned the California activities of a California*
> *resident, the article was drawn from California sources, and the brunt of the*
> *harm was in California. Although employees' contacts with a forum are not*
> *to be judged by those of their employer, their status as employees does not*
> *insulate them from jurisdiction. The defendants acted intentionally and they*
> *knew that the brunt of the injury would occur in California, where the plaintiff*
> *lived and worked and where the magazine had its largest circulation.*
> *Therefore, they could reasonably anticipate being haled into court there,*
> *despite their having no other contacts there. Calder v. Jones, 465 U.S. 783*
> *(1984).*

> *Likewise, in Burger King Corp. v. Rudzewicz, 471 U.S. 462 (1985),*
> *the Court held that Florida had personal jurisdiction over the defendant, a*
> *Michigan resident, where the defendant had initiated contact and signed a*
> *long-term contract with the plaintiff, a Florida corporation, and the contract*
> *had provided that Florida law would apply. Despite the facts that the*
> *defendant had only minimal physical contact with Florida (a brief training*
> *course) and that most of the defendant's contact with the Florida corporation*
> *was through its Michigan branch office, the Court found that the defendant's*
> *knowledgeable and purposeful contacts with a Florida corporation were*
> *enough to establish personal jurisdiction in Florida.*

Supreme Court cases evince an apparent desire to curb the trend in lower courts toward expanding long-arm jurisdiction. Emphasis on territorial limitations, on fairness to the defendant, and on the importance of "purposefulness" indicates that the long arm may not be infinitely extended.

> *Asahi Metal Industry Co. v. Superior Court, 480 U.S. 102 (1987), is a*
> *representative example of these cases. When a Taiwanese tire*
> *manufacturer, Cheng Shin, was sued in California for manufacturing a*
> *defective tire tube that had caused a fatal accident, Cheng Shin sought*
> *indemnification by filing a cross-claim against the Japanese manufacturer of*
> *the tire's valve assembly, Asahi. The Supreme Court unanimously agreed*
> *that California did not have jurisdiction over Asahi, emphasizing that the*
> *contacts Asahi did have with the forum did not evince sufficient*
> *purposefulness. While Asahi sold the assemblies on a regular basis to*

> *Cheng Shin, those sales constituted only a small part of Asahi's business; the Court noted that Asahi had not hired a sales agent, purchased advertising, provided advice to customers nor had it designed the product to target the California market. Since Asahi was an alien corporation whose rights could have been as properly adjudicated in Taiwan as in California and the primary defendant Cheng Shin was also not a California resident, the plurality for the Court concluded that Asahi would face too heavy a burden to have to defend itself in California. Therefore, California could not exercise jurisdiction under its long-arm statute over Asahi.*

Widespread use of the Internet has raised the question as to whether a company can be sued every place that its web site can be accessed. Internet jurisdiction cases are in their infancy, but the heart of the inquiry into personal jurisdiction has always been whether the out-of-state defendant "**purposefully availed**" itself of the privilege of conducting business in the forum state. Long-arm statutes, including New York's, have allowed and disallowed the exercise of personal jurisdiction over defendants who advertise or do business over the Internet.

> *Bensusan Restaurant v. King, 126 F. 3d 25 (2d Cir. 1997), is an Internet jurisdiction case dealing with New York's long-arm statute. The 'acourt in Bensusan held that the fact that a nightclub owner in Missouri advertised over the Internet was insufficient by itself to give rise to a trademark infringement suit brought in New York by a New York nightclub. The court reasoned that because the Missouri nightclub did not have "substantial revenue" from interstate commerce New York's long-arm statute could not be the basis for jurisdiction.*

> *The importance of New York's long-arm statute was further illustrated in American Network v. Access America, 975 F.Supp. 494 (S.D.N.Y. 1997), another Internet jurisdiction case. The plaintiff sued defendant for trademark infringment. The defendant, Access America, offered computer services across the country with 7,500 subscribers worldwide, but only six in New York, constituting .08% of its customer base. Despite the fact that only a very small percentage of the defendant's income was derived from New York, the court found that jurisdiction was proper because of its overall revenue from interstate commerce.*

3.   **In Rem Jurisdiction**

In rem jurisdiction is based upon the physical presence of property in the state. An action in rem is not against any one party, but seeks to settle some question as to the res "against all the world"; by its judgment, the court establishes rights in the property against all potential claimants. However, no personal liability is imposed. The court can dispose of the property or can affect a person's interest in it, but it cannot bind a person beyond that (e.g., it cannot impose damages or an injunction against one not subject to in personam jurisdiction). Examples of in rem actions are those to quiet title against all claimants, to determine ownership of corporate shares, and actions for an accounting of trust assets, for forfeiture of contraband, escheat, and probate actions.

Sometimes, the status of a person domiciled in the state is a res. For example, as long as one spouse is a domiciliary, the marriage itself is deemed a res which is present in the state, and a matrimonial action such as divorce or separation is in rem.

Two things are necessary for a state to have in rem jurisdiction: (1) the presence of the res in the state, and (2) adequate notice to persons with an interest in the res, so that they can participate in any determination.

4. Quasi In Rem Jurisdiction

a. *Definition*

Quasi in rem jurisdiction is of two types: (1) jurisdiction against specific persons to determine rights in property before the court; and (2) jurisdiction over a claim not concerning the property, obtained by the attachment of local assets. The first type resembles in rem jurisdiction because it concerns title to particular property, but differs from in rem because it determines the interest in the property of only particular persons, not of all the world. The second type of quasi in rem resembles in personam jurisdiction because it deals with a claim not related to property - for example, a claim for damages arising from a personal injury - but differs from in personam because the defendant is not personally liable upon the judgment; only the assets attached in the state could be used to satisfy the judgment.

b. *Quasi In Rem - Against Particular Persons*

The court has jurisdiction over an action to determine the title to or interest in property of particular persons if the property is located in the state, even if the court does not have in personam jurisdiction over those persons. Examples of such actions are mortgage foreclosures or quiet title actions. Any person whose interest will be affected by exercise of quasi in rem jurisdiction must be named as a defendant and must have notice and an opportunity to be heard. The court's decree determines the defendant's interest - e.g., a foreclosure extinguishes the mortgagor's interest - but cannot impose personal liability on the defendant - e.g., the court could not hold a nonresident mortgagor liable for the balance of the mortgage debt.

c. *Quasi In Rem - Attachment*

i. Development

Traditionally, a plaintiff who sought money damages from a defendant over whom he could not obtain in personam jurisdiction could attach the defendant's property in the state and use the attachment as a basis for jurisdiction. The judgment in such a quasi in rem case is limited to the value of the property attached; the defendant is not personally liable.

> *When jurisdiction was based upon attaching property other than realty, the situs of the property was problematic. In Harris v. Balk, 198 U.S. 215 (1905), the situs of a debt was deemed to be the state where the debtor was located. Thus, if Deb owed Cred money, and Plain had a claim against Cred, Plain could attach the debt wherever Deb happened to be and thus obtain quasi in rem jurisdiction over Cred.*

> *This principle was taken one step further in Seider v. Roth, 17 N.Y.2d 111 (1966). Seider permitted New York plaintiffs, who were injured in a collision with the Canadian defendant in Vermont, to assert quasi in rem jurisdiction in New York by attaching the insurance company's obligation to defend and indemnify the defendant. The insurer did business in New York, and the duty to defend was considered a "debt" that followed the insurer into the state.*

<u>ii.   Application of Minimum Contacts To Quasi In Rem</u>

Shaffer v. Heitner, 433 U.S. 186 (1977) held that the due process requirement of "minimum contacts" applies also to quasi in rem jurisdiction. To sustain such jurisdiction, there must be a connection among the defendant, the forum and the claim. If the only connection between the defendant and the forum is that his property is in the state, and the claim is unrelated to the property, no jurisdiction exists. In *Shaffer*, the plaintiff brought a shareholder's derivative suit against a Delaware corporation's nonresident officers and directors. Quasi in rem jurisdiction was obtained over the defendants, who had no business contacts with Delaware, by sequestering their stock in the corporation, pursuant to a Delaware statute. The cause of action, which arose in Oregon, was unrelated to the stock. The Supreme Court held that the presence of the property alone would not support jurisdiction in Delaware.

Shaffer explicitly overruled *Harris v. Balk*, and thus left the constitutionality of *Seider* attachments in doubt. In *Rush v. Savchuk*, 444 U.S. 320 (1980), the Court finally invalidated *Seider* attachments. In *Savchuk*, the tort occurred in Indiana, and the defendant's only connection with the forum state, Minnesota, was that his insurer happened to be doing business there. The Court rejected the plaintiff's jurisdictional argument, which it characterized as shifting "the focus of the inquiry from the relationship among the defendant, the forum, the insurer and the litigation to that among the plaintiff, the forum and the litigation." The plaintiff's contacts cannot be determinative of the defendant's due process rights, so the plaintiff's connections, and other questions of fairness and convenience, can only be examined after the defendant has been shown to have "certain judicially cognizable ties" with the forum.

The requirements for quasi in rem jurisdiction are now practically identical to those for in personam jurisdiction. Quasi in rem jurisdiction may still be useful if the defendant has some contacts with the state and yet does not come within a provision of the long-arm statute, but its utility remains to be seen.

Attachment can still be used as a security: for example, if an accident occurred in New York, the defendant would be subject to in personam jurisdiction there and the policy could be attached as a debt to satisfy judgment.

F.   SERVICE OF PROCESS AND NOTICE

1.   Service of Process

Process from federal courts can be served (1) within the state where the district court is located, Fed. R. Civ. P. 4(e); or (2) outside the state, if the state in which it is sitting has a long-arm statute, Fed. R. Civ. P. 4(k). In addition, persons who are impleaded under Rule 14, or who are parties to compulsory counterclaims under Rule 19 may be served outside the state if they live within 100 miles from the place in which the action is commenced or to which it is transferred for trial. Fed. R. Civ. P. 4(k).

Nationwide service of process is available in a few instances, _e.g._, under the Federal Interpleader Act, 28 U.S.C. §2361, and in securities fraud actions, 15 U.S.C. §78a.

A defendant is given notice that an action has been brought against him by the service of process (unless service by publication is appropriate).

a.   *Summons*

Upon the filing of the complaint, the plaintiff may present a summons to the clerk and the clerk shall sign, seal, and issue it to the plaintiff for service on the defendant. Fed. R. Civ. P. 4(b). A summons contains the name of the court, the names of the parties, the name and address of the plaintiff's attorney (or of the plaintiff if he has no attorney). The summons also states the time within which the defendant must appear and that, if he fails to do so, a default judgment will be rendered against the defendant. Fed. R. Civ. P. 4(a). (Because many states have modeled their rules of civil procedure upon the Federal Rules, the Federal Rules will be cited here as typical examples; unless otherwise indicated, cites will be to the Federal Rules.)

Under the Federal Rules and most state rules, the summons and complaint must be served together. Rule 4(c).

b.   *By Whom Served*

In federal courts, a summons and complaint may be served by any person who is not a party and is not less than eighteen years of age. Rule 4(c)(2). However, a party may request that service be made by a United States marshal or a person specially appointed by the court for that purpose, only in (1) in forma pauperis and seamen's suits; or (2) where the court in its discretion orders service by a marshal or special appointee. Rule 4(c)(3). All forms of process other than a summons and complaint or a subpoena (e.g., attachments) must be served by a federal marshal, his deputy, or some person specially appointed by the court. Rule 4.1 (effective in 1993).

In some state courts, service is made by a sheriff or his deputy. Most states permit service to be made by any person over eighteen who is not a party to the suit.

c.   *Methods of Service*

i.   Duty to Waive Service

By amendment to Federal Rule 4 effective in 1993, there is an affirmative duty on the part of competent individuals, corporations, and associations (but not upon governmental entities) who are named as defendants to cooperate in avoiding unnecessary costs of formal service of process by waiving service of process. The plaintiff may request such defendants to waive service of process by a written request sent by first-class mail (or other reliable means) together with a copy of the summons and complaint, a waiver form, and a prepaid means for the defendant to comply with the request for waiver. The request for waiver must allow at least 30 days from the date of sending for the defendant to return the form. If a person does not comply with a request for waiver of service of process, the court will order the person to pay the costs incurred in effecting service unless the defendant can show good cause for the failure. Rule 4(d).

By waiving service of process, a defendant may obtain additional time to answer the plaintiff's complaint. A defendant who waives service is not required to serve an answer until 60 days after the date on which the request for waiver was sent. Rule 4(d)(3).

Where a waiver of service has not been obtained pursuant to the above provisions, service of the summons and complaint must be made in the usual fashion by a nonparty over eighteen or a marshal or special process server (i.e., by service in hand, service on an adult at the last and usual abode, or service on an authorized agent). Rule 4(e).

ii.   Service Upon an Individual

Service may be made upon an individual by (a) delivering the summons and complaint to him personally; or (b) leaving the summons and complaint at his dwelling house or usual place of abode with a person of suitable age and discretion then residing there; or (c) delivering the summons and complaint to an agent authorized to receive service. Rule 4(e). Service that complies with either (b) or (c) is valid even if the defendant never personally receives the papers.

An infant or incompetent person is served by complying with the law of the state in which service is made. Rule 4(g). State law usually requires service upon a parent, guardian or other person having legal custody, and may also require service upon the child or incompetent.

iii.   Service Upon A Corporation

A domestic or foreign corporation may be served by delivering the summons and complaint to an officer, a managing or general agent, or to any other agent authorized to receive process. Some statutes that authorize an agent to receive process also require that a copy be mailed to the defendant. Rule 4(h).

iv.   Service on Federal Officials

Service of process on an officer or employee sued in an official capacity is on the United States attorney. If sued in an individual capacity, whether or not also sued in an official capacity, the officer or employee must be personally served in the usual manner for a private individual. Rule 4(i).

v.   Service by Other Means

Service upon a competent individual or a corporation in a suit in federal court is also valid if it is made in the manner prescribed by the law of the state in which the court is located. Rule 4(e)(1).

Service by publication may be used only if the defendant cannot reasonably be served by any other method.

d.   *Scope of Service*

As amended effective in 1993, Rule 4(e) provides for service of process anywhere in the United States (where a waiver of service has not been obtained, see above), subject only to restraints imposed by statutes and the constitution. Thus, a defendant who resides outside of the state in which the federal court sits may be served anywhere in the United States either pursuant to state law or by the methods specifically contained in Rule 4(e) (service in hand, service on an adult at the last and usual abode, or service on an authorized agent). It should be stressed that service under Rule 4(e) "does not conclusively establish the jurisdiction of the court over the person of the defendant." Committee Notes to 1993 amendments to Rule 4.

e.   *Proof Of Service*

Where service of process is not waived, the process server must file a return of service with the court. If service is made by anyone other than a marshal, an affidavit must be filed, stating the basic facts as to service to prove that the defendant actually has been served properly. If service was by mail, the sender must file with the court the required acknowledgment receipt. Rule 4(l).

Failure to make proof of service does not affect the validity of the service. Rule 4(l). On the other hand, the return is merely presumptive, rather than conclusive, evidence that proper service was made.

f. Time Limit for Service

If service of the summons and complaint is not made upon a defendant within 90 days after the filing of the complaint, the action will be dismissed as to the defendant without prejudice, either upon motion or upon the court's initiative, unless the plaintiff can show good cause why service was not made within that period. However, the time limit may be extended for cause shown. Rule 4(m).

g. Immunity From Process

Parties, witnesses and attorneys who enter a state in order to attend court or to represent a party in connection with one suit are immune from service of process in another suit. The purpose of the rule is to encourage voluntary participation. However, if in personam jurisdiction could be obtained over the nonresident without service in that state (e.g., by service pursuant to the long-arm statute), the purpose of the immunity fails and service may be made in the state.

h. Enticement

Service made after a nonresident is lured into the state under false pretenses can be invalidated. However, if a defendant is already in the state, deception may be used to deliver process (e.g., process server uses false identity to coax defendant out of hotel room).

2. Notice

Due process requires that before jurisdiction can be exercised over a person or his property, he must be given notice and an opportunity to be heard.

a. Reasonableness

The notice must be "reasonably calculated, under all the circumstances, to apprise interested parties of the pendency of the action and afford them an opportunity to present their objections . . . [it] must be of such nature as reasonably to convey the required information . . . and it must afford a reasonable time for those interested to make their appearance." *Mullane v. Central Hanover Bank & Trust Co.*, 339 U.S. 306 (1950).

The means of giving notice must be "such as one desirous of actually informing the absentee might reasonably adopt to accomplish it." Id. The proper means of service are spelled out in the Rules of Civil Procedure of each state (and in the Federal Rules for federal courts). Delivery of the process in person satisfies the due process requirement; other appropriate means generally include service by registered or certified mail, delivery to the agent of a corporation or delivery to the secretary of state if a statute permits (e.g., a nonresident motorist statute.) However, if reasonably diligent investigation fails to disclose the address of an interested party, notice may be given by publication in a newspaper of general circulation. Notice by publication, where proper, is binding on the parties, even if they do not actually see the notice or learn of the action until after it has been concluded. Notice by publication is not proper if the names and addresses of interested parties are available from public records. *Walker v. City of Hutchinson*, 352 U.S. 112 (1956). Generally, the test for whether notice is adequate is its reasonableness under the circumstances.

A mortgagee has a legally protected property interest and is entitled to notice reasonably calculated to apprise him of a pending tax sale; personal service or notice by mail is required where the mortgagee is identified in the public record. *Mennonite Board of Missions v. Adams*, 462 U.S. 791 (1983). Posting a summons on the door of a tenant's apartment is an inadequate means of giving notice of a forcible entry and detainer action. *Greene v. Lindsey*, 456 U.S. 444 (1982).

b. Class Actions

In certain class actions, due process does not require that notice be given individually to class members. (See Section XVII(E), Class Actions, infra). However, in a class action brought under Fed. R. Civ. P. 23(b)(3) (i.e., one where common questions of law or fact predominate over questions affecting only individual members), individual notice must be provided to those members of the class who are identifiable through reasonable effort. Notice by publication in such actions is not permitted even if the cost of individual notice is prohibitive. *Eisen v. Carlisle & Jacquelin*, 417 U.S. 156 (1974) (individual notice required for 2,250,000 class members).

c. Opportunity To Be Heard

Due process requires that a defendant be given an opportunity to be heard before state action deprives him of a property interest.

i. Prior Notice Required

Notice and an opportunity to be heard must be afforded before a wage earner's income may be subjected to prejudgment garnishment. *Sniadach v. Family Finance Corp.*, 395 U.S. 337 (1969). Similarly, a statute that permitted prejudgment replevin upon a writ issued ex parte by a court clerk was held invalid. *Fuentes v. Shevin*, 407 U.S. 67 (1972).

ii. Prior Notice Not Required

In *Mitchell v. W.T. Grant Co.*, 416 U.S. 600 (1974), the Supreme Court held that the issuance of a sequestration writ without notice and a hearing did not violate due process, since the state did allow a prompt hearing after the seizure where the debtor could test its validity. However, in *North Georgia Finishing, Inc. v. Di-Chem, Inc.*, 419 U.S. 601 (1975), the Court invalidated a garnishment proceeding that provided neither prior notice nor a hearing, because it also lacked any opportunity to challenge the garnishment prior to final judgment. Although it is difficult to reconcile all these cases, it appears that prior notice and prior hearing are not required as long as notice and hearing are provided promptly after the taking of property. Factors which have led the court to strike down statutes as violative of due process include the amount of specific detail required to support issuance of the writ; whether the writ is issued by a court clerk, rather than a judge; the time permitted to elapse before a hearing is required; and the complexity of the statute, which may cast doubt on the party's right to take the property.

G.   VENUE, FORUM NON CONVENIENS, AND TRANSFER

1.   Venue

Venue refers to the proper place for trial of an action over which several courts could exercise jurisdiction. In federal courts, the question is in which federal district should the trial be held. The general federal venue statute is 28 U.S.C. §1391.

The purposes of venue requirements are (1) to distribute cases within the court system, and (2) to promote convenience, by ensuring that the place of trial has some relationship with the parties or the cause of action, and it is thus not an undue burden on the parties to try the case there.

Subject matter jurisdiction is the power of the court to adjudicate the controversy presented; it is a question of constitutional dimension, and thus jurisdiction cannot be conferred by consent. A challenge to jurisdiction can be raised at any stage of the proceedings, and if jurisdiction is lacking, an action must be dismissed.

Venue, however, deals with the appropriate place for the exercise of judicial power; it is a question of convenience and is governed by statute. A venue objection can be waived, and thus venue can be conferred by consent. An objection to venue is waived if not timely raised. If venue is improper, the action need not be dismissed, but may be transferred to the proper court if justice would be served thereby.

a.   *Waiver of Venue*

If the defendant fails to object to improper venue at his earliest opportunity, the defense is waived. He must object in a pre-answer motion, or, if none is made, in the answer; otherwise, he has waived. Fed. R. Civ. P. 12(h).

b.   *Venue Rules*

Under the current statute, venue in either a diversity or federal question case is proper in any district in which either

(a)   a defendant resides, if all of the defendants reside in the same state, or

(b)   a "substantial" part of the events or property which are the basis of the claim took place or can be found, respectively.

In diversity cases, venue is also proper in any district in which "the defendants are subject to personal jurisdiction at the time the action is commenced," but only "if there is no district in which the action may be otherwise brought" (*i.e.*, the defendants do not reside in the same state and there is no state in which a "substantial" part of the claim arose).

Similarly, in federal question cases, venue is also proper in any district "in which any defendant may be found" (emphasis added), but only "if there is no district in which the action may be otherwise brought." 28 U.S.C. §1391.

Keep in mind the distinction between venue and jurisdiction.

> *For example, although venue may be proper in the district where a substantial part of the cause of action arose, the court will lack jurisdiction if the defendant is not subject to service of process in that state. Thus, if P, a resident of New York, wants to sue D, a resident of Pennsylvania, in federal court for injuries to P's land in Virginia, venue would be proper in Virginia because the land can be found there, but if D is not doing business in Virginia or is not otherwise subject to the jurisdiction of a Virginia court under its long-arm statute, the federal court sitting in Virginia would lack personal jurisdiction. Venue would be proper only in Pennsylvania, as D would be subject to jurisdiction in his domicile.*

c.   *Residence for Venue Purposes*

i.   Individuals

The venue statute speaks of the residence of the plaintiff and defendant. Are residence and citizenship synonymous? The cases are divided; however, the majority view is that they are synonymous.

> *Thus, if P is domiciled in New York, but has a summer home in Massachusetts, only New York is his residence for venue purposes.*

ii.   Aliens

An alien may be sued in any district. 28 U.S.C. §1391(d). Where an alien is the plaintiff, suit must be in the district in which all defendants reside, or in which the claim arose, regardless of the basis of jurisdiction.

iii.   Corporations

A corporation may be sued in any judicial district in which it is subject to personal jurisdiction. 28 U.S.C. §1391(c). A corporation is subject to personal jurisdiction, not only in the states in which it is incorporated and licensed to do business, but also in any district with which it has sufficient minimum contacts to satisfy the constitutional requirements and the requirements of the state's long-arm statute.

Note that §1391(c) applies only to corporate defendants. For venue purposes, a corporate plaintiff is a resident only of the state and district of its incorporation.

iv.   Unincorporated Associations

For venue purposes, an unincorporated association (*e.g.*, a partnership or labor union) is treated as if it were a corporation, and it may be sued wherever it is doing business.

d.   *Special Venue Statutes*

Many federal statutes specify the proper venue in particular actions, such as patent or copyright cases, or suits against national banks. A statutory interpleader action must be brought in a district where a claimant resides. 28 U.S.C. §1397. A stockholder's derivative action may be brought in any district where the corporation could have sued the same defendants. 28 U.S.C. §1401.

A suit against a federal employee acting under color of legal authority may be brought where (1) the defendant resides; (2) the cause of action arose; (3) any real property involved is situated; or (4) the plaintiff resides if no real property is involved. 28 U.S.C. §1391(e). However, this expanded venue provision does not apply to civil actions for money damages brought against federal officials in their individual capacities. *Stafford v. Briggs*, 444 U.S. 527 (1980). A federal tort claim action may be brought only in the district where the plaintiff resides or where the act or omission occurred. 28 U.S.C. §1402(b).

2.   Forum Non Conveniens

The doctrine of forum non conveniens allows dismissal by a court if it would be an unfair or inconvenient forum. Forum non conveniens has largely been superseded by §1404(a), which permits transfer on a lesser showing of inconvenience; however, an action will be dismissed for forum non conveniens if the appropriate forum is a state court or a court in a foreign country.

Multistate Bar Review Book 2

Dismissal will usually be appropriate where trial in the plaintiff's chosen forum imposes a heavy burden on the defendant or the court, and where the plaintiff is unable to offer any specific reasons of convenience supporting her choice. However, dismissal is not appropriate if the alternative forum does not permit litigation of the subject matter of the dispute. A plaintiff cannot defeat a motion to dismiss by merely showing that the substantive law that would be applied in the alternative forum is less favorable to the plaintiffs than that of the chosen forum. *Piper Aircraft Co. v. Reyno*, 454 U.S. 235 (1981).

3. Transfer

a. *Where Venue Is Improper*

If an action is commenced in the wrong district, the court shall dismiss, or if it is in the interest of justice, the court may transfer the case to any district in which it could have been brought. 28 U.S.C. §1406(a).

Dismissal would be fatal to the cause of action if the statute of limitations had run and would bar any new suit; in that instance, transfer is especially useful.

Transfer can be ordered only if the court in which the action was brought has subject matter jurisdiction; however, a court can transfer an action where it lacks in personam jurisdiction over the defendant. *Goldlawr, Inc. v. Heiman*, 369 U.S. 463 (1962). The case must be transferred to a district in which venue is proper, and in which the defendant is amenable to process.

b. *Where Venue Is Proper: For Convenience*

Even though venue is proper in the district where an action is brought, the court may, in its discretion, transfer the suit to any district "where it might have been brought," "for the convenience of parties and witnesses, in the interest of justice." 28 U.S.C. §1404(a). The policy underlying the statute is the promotion of the convenience of the parties and witnesses.

The phrase "where it might have been brought" limits transfer to a district where the plaintiff could have brought the action at the time the suit was initiated. Thus, consent by the defendant will not permit transfer to a forum where suit could not have been commenced. *Hoffman v. Blaski*, 363 U.S. 355 (1960).

> For example, D, a citizen of New York, moves under §1404(a) to transfer a suit from a federal court in New York to a federal court in Virginia; however, D would not be amenable to process in an action originally brought in a Virginia district court. Transfer is not available.

A motion for transfer may be made by any party at any time. The movant must bring forth evidence that a transfer would promote the convenience of the parties or the witnesses and would be in the interest of justice. When the motion is granted, the papers are transferred to the new forum, and the original forum loses all jurisdiction. The transferee court must apply the law that would have been applied in the original court. *Van Dusen v. Barrack*, 376 U.S. 612 (1964); *Ferens v. John Deere Co.*, 110 S. Ct. 1274 (1990). An order granting or denying a §1404(a) motion is not appealable as a final judgment.

II. LAW APPLIED BY THE FEDERAL COURTS

A. STATE LAW IN FEDERAL COURT

1. The Erie Doctrine

a. *Development of The Doctrine*

Erie Railroad Co. v. Tompkins, 304 U.S. 64 (1938) held that, except in matters governed by the federal Constitution or acts of Congress, the law of the state - whether statute or case law - must be applied by the federal courts. The policies underlying *Erie* are twofold: (1) to discourage forum-shopping, and (2) to avoid inequitable administration of laws.

Erie dealt with an application of state substantive law. In *Guaranty Trust Co. of New York v. York*, 326 U.S. 99 (1945), the issue was whether in a diversity suit in equity the federal court should apply a state statute of limitations or the rule of laches traditionally applied by federal courts in equitable actions. The Court announced an "outcome-determinative" test: if the state statute would make a substantial difference in the outcome, state law must be followed; the court must look to the impact of the choice on the outcome. The most obvious example of such outcome-determinative factors is the statute of limitations; another example is the placement of the burden of proof.

However, *Byrd v. Blue Ridge Rural Electric Cooperative, Inc.*, 356 U.S. 525 (1958) modified York, declaring that impact alone is not the test; instead, the general policy of ensuring the same outcome in state and federal courts must be balanced against any countervailing strong federal policy involved (*e.g.*, federal right to have jury, not judge, pass on a defense). In applying the Byrd balancing test, a court must weigh (1) the state policy underlying its rule, (2) the federal policy underlying its rule, and (3) the likelihood that applying the federal rule will cause a difference in the outcome (*e.g.*, a different outcome will not necessarily result from trying the defense before a jury rather than a judge).

b. *Erie and the Federal Rules*

The doctrine was further limited by *Hanna v. Plumer*, 380 U.S. 460 (1965), which held that *Erie* is not the appropriate test if an issue is covered by one of the Rules of Civil Procedure. The court must decide initially whether the Rule is sufficiently broad to cover the disputed issue. If the Rule does cover the issue, and it is sanctioned by the Rules Enabling Act (none has ever been held invalid), it should be applied, regardless of contrary state law. Likewise, if a Federal Rule of Evidence is valid and applicable, it will be applied rather than contrary state law.

However, when no Rule is directly in point, the court must make "the typical, relatively unguided *Erie* choice"; it must decide on the applicable law in light of the twin goals of *Erie*: discouragement of forum-shopping and avoidance of inequitable administration of laws. If there is no Rule but there is a strong federal policy (*e.g.*, jury trial), you must weigh the federal policy against any state policy and the probability of outcome-determination. If there is no Rule and no strong federal policy, even if the matter is "procedural", the York outcome-determination test would apply. If the matter is clearly substantive, *Erie* governs and state law will be applied.

c.   *Substantive Versus Procedural*

The line between state substantive law and federal procedural rules is not always distinct; for example, should a statute of limitations be deemed substantive or procedural? Does Fed. R. Civ. P. 3, which provides that an action is commenced by filing a complaint with the court, measure the running of the state statute of limitations?

The Supreme Court has construed Rule 3 narrowly, holding that it was not intended to measure the running of a statute of limitations in a diversity action. Thus, where a state statute provides that an action is commenced upon service of the summons, state law, rather than federal Rule, governs as to when and whether the statute has been tolled. *Ragan v. Merchants Transfer & Warehouse Co.*, 337 U.S. 530 (1949); *Walker v. Armco Steel Corp.*, 446 U.S. 740 (1980).

Similarly, a shareholders' derivative action brought in federal court under diversity jurisdiction is governed procedurally by Fed. R. Civ. P. 23.1.

> However, the Supreme Court held that a state statute requiring a security-for-expenses bond had to be enforced in federal court because it was an integral part of the state substantive law authorizing derivative actions. Cohen v. Beneficial Industrial Loan Corp., *337 U.S. 541 (1949)*.

2.   Which State's Law Applies

A federal court must apply the substantive law that would be applied by a state court in the state where the federal court is sitting. Thus, the federal court must also apply that state's conflict-of-laws rules. *Klaxon v. Stentor Elec. Mfg. Co., Inc.*, 313 U.S. 487 (1941).

> For example, if a New Yorker is injured in a collision with a Pennsylvanian in Connecticut, and an action is brought in New York, the federal court in New York will apply New York's choice-of-law rules, whereas if the action is

> *brought in Pennsylvania, the federal court there will apply Pennsylvania's choice-of-law rules.*

If an action is transferred upon either party's motion under 28 U.S.C. §1404 (See Section VII(G)(2), *supra*), the transferee court must apply the law that would have been applied in the transferor court. *Van Dusen v. Barrack*, 376 U.S. 612 (1964) (defendant's motion); *Ferens v. John Deere Co.*, 110 S. Ct. 1274 (1990) (plaintiff's motion).

3. Determining the Applicable State Law

A federal court is bound by the substantive rulings of the state's highest court. Even if a state decision is handed down after the federal trial court decision, a court of appeals must apply the state ruling. *Vandenbark v. Owens-Illinois Glass Co.*, 311 U.S. 538 (1941). If there is no decision on point by the highest state court, the federal court should look to the decisions of lower state courts or, if there are none, to relevant dicta and analogous decisions in that state, and to decisions in other influential or neighboring jurisdictions. The federal court must adopt the rule that it believes the state court would adopt. Alternatively, in some states, the federal court may certify questions of state law to the highest state court for decision.

B. FEDERAL COMMON LAW

Although Justice Brandeis declared in *Erie* that "there is no federal general common law," there is federal common law - decisions that interpret or fill in gaps in federal statutes, treaties or constitutional provisions. In these areas, the *Erie* doctrine does not control, because the application of state law would subject the rights and duties of the United States to "exceptional uncertainty." Areas in which federal common law has been developed include foreign relations, labor law, disputes between states, suits where the United States or its employee is a party, and suits upon federal commercial paper or pollution of interstate waterways.

In instances when federal common law is applicable, it preempts state statutes and case law and must be applied by state courts as well as federal courts. A case "arising under" federal common law is a federal question case.

Sometimes a federal statute will incorporate state law, <u>e.g.</u>, the Federal Torts Claims Act adopts the measure of damages specified by state law. Federal decisions may also incorporate state law, rather than develop federal common law.

> *Thus, for example, if a federal statute fails to include a time limitation on actions, the federal court will adopt the statute of limitations for analogous state actions.*

III. PRETRIAL PROCEDURES

A. PRELIMINARY INJUNCTIONS AND TEMPORARY RESTRAINING ORDERS

1.   Preliminary Injunctions

A court may issue a preliminary injunction only on notice to the adverse party. Under Rule 65, every order granting a preliminary injunction must:

      (1)   state the reasons why it is issued,

      (2)   state its terms with specificity, and

      (3)   describe in reasonable detail, the act or acts restrained or required.

2.   Temporary Restraining Order

Under Rule 65, a court may issue a temporary restraining order without written or oral notice to the adverse party if:

      (A)   specific facts clearly show that immediate or irreparable injury, loss, or injury will result to the movant before the adverse party can be heard; and

      (B)   the movant's attorney certifies any efforts made to provide notice and the reasons why it should not be required.

Every temporary restraining order issued without notice must include the following:

      (A)   date and hour it was issued,

      (B)   describe the injury and state why it is irreparable;

      (C)   state why the order was issued without notice; and

      (D)   be promptly filed in the clerk's office and entered in the record.

The temporary restraining order will expire no later than 14 days after being issued, unless the court for good cause extends it for another 14-day period or longer if the adverse party consents to the longer extension. The motion for a hearing of the temporary restraining order must be set for hearing at the earliest possible time, taking precedence over all other matters. On two-days' notice, the adverse party may move to dissolve or modify the temporary restraining order.

B. PLEADINGS AND AMENDED AND SUPPLEMENTAL PLEADINGS

1. General Rules of Pleadings

The primary purpose of pleadings is to give fair notice to the parties of the claims and defenses in the action. Under this theory of notice pleading adopted by the Federal Rules, liberal discovery procedures, rather than the detailed pleadings of common law, are used to narrow the issues for trial.

The types of pleadings permitted by the Federal Rules are: the plaintiff's complaint, the defendant's answer, the defendant's counterclaim (against the plaintiff), the defendant's cross-claim (against a co-defendant), and the defendant's third-party claim (against a third party who may be liable to defendant if defendant is liable to plaintiff). The additional party can also file an answer. In a few instances, a reply may be permissible.

There are no technical forms of pleading, and the underlying philosophy of the Rules is that "pleadings must be construed so as to do justice." Rule 8(e). Thus, pleadings are not construed against the pleader, but are to be construed liberally. A plaintiff may base his claim on alternative or even inconsistent theories; likewise, the defendant may raise as many defenses as he has, regardless of consistency. Rule 8(d). In federal court, the plaintiff need not elect between alternative theories at trial.

Generally, unless the court orders otherwise, all pleadings, motions, orders, notices and other papers must be served upon a party. However, service (other than of original process) is made upon the party's attorney unless service upon the party himself is ordered, and service can be made by mail or delivery. Rule 5.

In computing any period of time prescribed or allowed by the Rules, the day of the act, event or default from which the designated period of time begins to run is not included. The last day of the period is included, unless it is a Saturday, Sunday or legal holiday, or, when the act to be done is the filing of a paper in court, a day on which weather or other conditions have made the court clerk's office inaccessible, in which case the period runs until the end of the next nonholiday weekday. Rule 6(a).

Whenever a party must do some act within a prescribed period after service of a notice upon him, the court may extend the time for good cause. Rule 6(b).

2. The Complaint

a. Claim for Relief

Each complaint (or other claim for relief, e.g., a counterclaim) must contain: (1) a short and plain statement of the grounds upon which the court's jurisdiction depends; (2) a short and plain statement of the claim showing that the pleader is entitled to relief; and (3) a demand for judgment for the relief to which he deems himself entitled. Rule 8(a).

A party can seek both equitable relief and damages in the same action. The plaintiff is not limited by his demand for judgment. Except in default judgments, every final judgment shall grant the relief to which the party is entitled, even if he has not demanded such relief in his pleadings. Rule 54(c).

The complaint should give the defendant "fair notice of what the plaintiff's claim is and the grounds upon which it rests." A complaint should not be dismissed for failure to state a claim "unless it appears beyond doubt that the plaintiff can prove no set of facts in support of his claim which would entitle him to relief." *Conley v. Gibson*, 355 U.S. 41 (1957).

The burden of pleading an issue is usually on the party who has the burden of producing evidence on that issue at trial. Thus, the plaintiff must plead the matters basic to the action.

For example, in a slander action, the plaintiff must allege that defamatory remarks were published and injured the plaintiff.

Generally, the plaintiff need not plead matters on which the defendant must introduce proof. However, if a defense goes to the heart of the action, the plaintiff must plead that it does not exist - for example, in a suit on an overdue note, payment is considered a defense, but the plaintiff must allege nonpayment in the complaint.

b.   *Form of Complaint*

The complaint (and all other pleadings) must contain a caption setting forth: (1) the name of the court; (2) the title of the action (e.g., *Prynne v. Dimmesdale*); (3) the file number (assigned by the court clerk); and (4) a designation of the pleading (e.g., Complaint, or Counterclaim). Rule 10(a).

The averments of a claim (or defense) are made in numbered paragraphs, each paragraph limited as far as practicable to the statement of a single set of circumstances. Claims founded upon separate transactions or occurrences should be stated in separate counts. Rule 10(b). A party asserting a claim may join with it, either as independent or alternative claims, as many claims - legal or equitable - as he has against an opposing party. Rule 18(a). Each averment should be short and plain. Rule 8(a).

c.   *Allegations on Information and Belief*

Because a party may not be sure of all the underlying facts when he files his pleading, he may make his allegations on "information and belief." Likewise, the defendant may deny on the grounds that she is without knowledge or information sufficient to form a belief as to the truth of the averment. Rule 8(b). However, a pleading cannot be based on information and belief if the party knows or has reason to know the facts or if she has constructive knowledge of the facts because they are a matter of public record.

d. Signature and Verfication

All pleadings, motions and other papers must be signed by the party's attorney, or by the party himself if he has no attorney. The signature certifies that the attorney has read the pleading and that to the best of his knowledge, information or belief formed after reasonable inquiry it is well grounded in fact and is warranted by existing law or a good-faith argument for the extension, modification or reversal of existing law; and that it is not interposed for any improper purpose, such as to harass or to cause unnecessary delay or needless increase in the cost of litigation. If not signed, the pleading or motion will be stricken unless it is signed promptly after the omission is called to the attention of the pleader or movant.

If a pleading, motion or other paper is signed in violation of the Rule, the court, upon motion or its own initiative, may impose upon the attorney, law firm, or parties, an appropriate sanction. Under Rule 11, the purpose of sanctions is generally to deter offending conduct rather than to compensate a party. Thus, sanctions may include directives of a nonmonetary nature (such as reprimanding counsel or requiring attendance at seminars) or fines to be paid into court. An order to pay the expenses incurred because of the filing of the pleading or motion, including attorney's fees, may be entered only where requested by motion and only when it is "warranted for effective deterrence." Where a party by motion seeks to have sanctions under Rule 11 imposed upon another party, the offending party may avoid sanctions by withdrawing or correcting the challenged paper. Rule 11.

A verified pleading is one that is sworn under oath to be true. In federal courts, pleadings need not be verified unless a rule or statute so provides. Rule 11. Verification is required in shareholders' derivative suits, Rule 23.1; suits for injunctive relief, Rule 65; and suits for appointment of a receiver, Rule 66.

e. Pleading Special Matters

Although the general rule is that the pleadings need only give fair notice of the claim, in certain circumstances more detailed allegations are required.

i. Fraud or Mistake

The circumstances underlying a claim of fraud or mistake must be stated "with particularity." Rule 9(b). However, most courts interpret this requirement liberally, ruling that the appropriate remedy if allegations are not sufficiently detailed is a Rule 12(e) motion for a more definite statement, or discovery.

Malice, intent, knowledge and other condition of mind of a person may be averred generally. Rule 9(b).

ii.   Conditions Precedent

In a contract action, the plaintiff must plead the performance or occurrence of all conditions precedent; general averments are sufficient. However, a denial of performance or occurrence must be made specifically and with particularity. Rule 9(c). This rule narrows the issues in dispute, by eliminating the plaintiff's need to prove the performance of any conditions that the defendant admits were met.

iii.   Special Damages

Items of special damage must be specifically stated. Rule 9(g). Special damages are those which do not normally or necessarily flow from the defendant's acts. This rule prevents the defendant from being surprised at trial by the introduction of proof of damages that he had no reason to anticipate.

3.   The Answer

The defendant's answer responds to the plaintiff's complaint by denying its allegations and/or by raising affirmative defenses to the allegations. The requirements as to the form of a complaint, supra, also apply to the answer.

a.   *Time for Filing*

The answer must be served within 21 days after service of the summons and complaint on the defendant. However, if the defendant files a Rule 12 motion, the time for answering is extended: (1) if the court denies the motion or postpones its disposition until trial, the answer must be served within 14 days after notice of the court's action; (2) if the court grants a Rule 12(e) motion for a more definite statement, the answer must be served within 14 days after service of the more definite statement. Rule 12(a). If the defendant fails to answer in timely fashion, a default judgment may be entered.

Furthermore, under Rule 7.1, a nongovernmental corporate party must file along with its response, first appearance, pleading, petition or motion two copies of a statement that identifies any parent corporation, or if there is none, a statement stating that there is no such corporation.

b.   *Denials*

i.   General Denials

A general denial controverts all allegations in the complaint, e.g., "Defendant denies each and every allegation in Plaintiff's complaint." In federal court, a general denial is improper unless the defendant intends in good faith to contest every allegation, including jurisdictional allegations. Rule 8(b).

ii. Specific Denials

In a specific denial, the defendant admits or denies the plaintiff's allegations paragraph by paragraph. If only a part of a paragraph is true, the defendant admits what is true and denies the remainder. Rule 8(b).

If the defendant is without knowledge or information sufficient to form a belief as to the truth of an averment, she may so state in her answer, and this has the effect of a denial. Rule 8(b). However, defendant cannot deny on information and belief if she has knowledge or constructive knowledge of the facts; if a fact is within her knowledge, it will be taken as admitted.

iii. Effect of Failure to Deny

An allegation that is not denied, or that is improperly denied, is deemed to have been admitted, and is binding on the parties. However, allegations of the amount of damages are deemed controverted even if not effectively denied. If no responsive pleading is required or allowed, the allegation is automatically deemed denied. Rule 8(b).

c. *Affirmative Defenses*

Even if the defendant admits the allegations of the complaint, there may be additional facts which, if established, would bar the plaintiff's recovery. These are called affirmative defenses and must be raised by the defendant in the answer. Rule 8(c) lists as affirmative defenses that must be pleaded: accord and satisfaction, arbitration and award, assumption of risk, contributory negligence, duress, estoppel, failure of consideration, fraud, illegality, injury by fellow servant, laches, license, payment, release, res judicata, statute of frauds, statute of limitations, waiver, and any other matter constituting an avoidance or affirmative defense.

An affirmative defense is waived if not raised in the answer. However, an inadvertent omission of a defense may be rectified by amendment if no prejudice would result. Furthermore, if an affirmative defense, although not pleaded, is actually tried, the pleadings may later be amended to conform to the evidence.

4. The Reply

A reply is permitted in only two situations. (1) A reply must be made if the answer contains a counterclaim denominated as such. Rule 7(a). If no reply is made, the allegations of the counterclaim are deemed admitted. Rule 8(b). (2) The court may order a reply to an answer or a third-party answer, either on its own motion or on motion of a party. Rule 7(a). This rarely occurs. No responsive pleadings beyond the reply are permitted in federal court. The allegations in the reply are taken as denied.

5. Counterclaims, Cross-Claims, and Third-Party Claims

a. *Counterclaims*

A counterclaim is a claim for relief against the plaintiff asserted by the defendant in her answer to the complaint. A counterclaim may seek relief exceeding in amount, or different in kind from, that sought by the plaintiff. Rule 13(c).

i. Compulsory Counterclaims

A defendant must assert any claim which he has against the plaintiff at the time of serving the pleading if it "arises out of the transaction or occurrence that is the subject matter of the opposing party's claim and does not require for its adjudication the presence of third parties of whom the court cannot acquire jurisdiction." Rule 13(a). No precise definition of what constitutes a "transaction or occurrence" has been formulated. The most common test is "logical relationship" - if the counterclaim is logically related to the initial claim, it is compulsory. A counterclaim is logically related to the claim if separate trials on each of the claims would involve substantial duplication of effort and time by the parties and the courts.

However, a defendant need not assert an otherwise compulsory counterclaim if: (1) at the time the action was commenced, it was the subject of another pending action; or (2) the plaintiff brought suit by attachment or garnishment, so that the court does not have personal jurisdiction over the defendant. Rule 13(a).

Claims acquired or maturing after service of the counterclaim may - but need not be - added with the permission of the court. Rule 13(e).

If a compulsory counterclaim is not asserted, it cannot be raised in a subsequent action in federal court. This principle is a product of judicial decisions rather than of the Rules, and is characterized by different courts as waiver or as estoppel or as res judicata. Courts also differ as to its effect outside the federal court system; thus, a party who failed to assert a compulsory counterclaim in a federal suit and is therefore barred from raising it in the federal courts may still be able to assert it in some state courts.

ii. Permissive Counterclaims

Any claim that does not arise out of the same transaction or occurrence as the original claim may be pleaded as a permissive counterclaim. Rule 13(b). However, the court may, for convenience, order separate trials for unrelated actions. Rule 42(b). (The court can order separate trial of a compulsory counterclaim, but that is extremely rare.) A permissive counterclaim is not barred if it is not asserted, and may be raised in an independent action.

iii.   Jurisdiction of Counterclaims

A federal court has ancillary jurisdiction of a compulsory counterclaim. However, if the counterclaim is permissive, there must be an independent ground of federal jurisdiction. The one exception is that a permissive counterclaim in the nature of a set-off used only to reduce the plaintiff's judgment does not require an independent jurisdictional ground.

> *For example, if P, a resident of Massachusetts, sues D, also a resident of Massachusetts, for patent infringement the claim comes under federal question jurisdiction. What if D counterclaims against P, claiming that P's action was brought in bad faith to harass D? There is no diversity, but D's claim is a compulsory counterclaim because determination of both claims will involve the same facts; therefore, ancillary jurisdiction will extend to D's claim.*

The plaintiff is deemed to submit to personal jurisdiction by bringing an action; thus, a court will have personal jurisdiction over the plaintiff as to the counterclaim, even if the plaintiff would not have been subject to jurisdiction in an independent action. Similarly, if venue was proper as to the original claim, the defendant may assert his counterclaims even if the venue would not be proper if they were asserted in an independent action.

iv.   Statute of Limitations

If the plaintiff files her claim immediately before the statute of limitations runs out, and the defendant attempts to assert a counterclaim after the statute has run, is the counterclaim barred? This issue is characterized as substantive, and under the Erie Doctrine is determined by state law. The majority view is that the counterclaim will be allowed even if the statutory period expires between the filing of the claim and the assertion of the counterclaim. Furthermore, some states allow a counterclaim that arises out of the same transaction or occurrence to be asserted even if the plaintiff's action was brought after the statute had run on the defendant's counterclaim; however, such a counterclaim usually can only be used as a set-off, and not as an offensive claim.

> *For example, P sues D on a contract claim four years after it arose; D seeks to assert a tort claim against P. However, the statute of limitations for contract actions is six years, but for tort actions is three years. D may assert his counterclaim only if it arose out of the same transaction or occurrence; also D's counterclaim can only be used to reduce any judgment P recovers and cannot be the basis of a positive recovery by D.*

This result is justified by the policies underlying the statute of limitations: preventing the assertion of stale claims and ensuring repose for a potential defendant. The defendant's claim is no more stale than

Multistate Bar Review Book 2

the plaintiff's, and since the plaintiff opened the matter, he must have preserved the evidence and will not be prejudiced by having to defend after the statutory period has expired.

An unrelated (permissive) counterclaim is barred if the statute of limitations has already run on D's claim when P files his action.

b.   Cross-Claims

i.   Requirements

A cross-claim is a claim asserted by one party against a co-party.

> *Thus, if P sues X and Y for injuries suffered in a collision, X may cross-claim against Y for her own injuries in the collision. (Compare a counterclaim, which is between opposing parties, e.g., X counterclaims against P.)*

A cross-claim, like a counterclaim, should be pleaded in the answer, but is not compulsory. The co-party against whom a cross-claim is asserted must file an answer to the cross-claim. Rule 7(a).

A cross-claim must arise out of the transaction or occurrence that is the subject matter either of the original action or of a counterclaim therein, or relate to any property that is the subject matter of the original action. Rule 13(g). In determining the extent of a "transaction or occurrence", the same logical relationship test as is applied in counterclaims is used. A claim against a co-party on an unrelated matter may not be raised as a cross-claim. Unlike a permissive counterclaim, where the plaintiff is interested, an unrelated claim against a co-party would raise a matter in which the plaintiff had no interest and which might prejudice the plaintiff.

A defendant may file a cross-claim against a co-party who "is or may be liable to the cross-claimant for all or part" of the original plaintiff's claim. Rule 13(g).

> *Thus, X can cross-claim against Y for contribution, alleging that both X and Y are jointly liable and that liability should be borne proportionately. Or, if X is only secondarily liable, she may cross-claim for indemnification against Y, who is primarily liable.*

ii.   Cross-Claims Between Co-Plaintiffs

Only parties against whom a claim has been made can cross-claim against each other. Thus, co-plaintiffs can cross-claim against each other only if a defendant has counterclaimed.

> *For example, A and B sue X and Y; X may cross-claim against Y on the same occurrence. If X asserts a compulsory counterclaim against A and B, A could then cross-claim against B for contribution.*

Multistate Bar Review Book 2

iii. Jurisdiction of Cross-Claims

Because cross-claims are related to the transaction or occurrence involved in the main claim, they fall within the ancillary jurisdiction of the court; independent jurisdictional grounds are not required. Likewise, since the parties to the cross-claim are already before the court, personal jurisdiction is satisfied. If the venue of the original action is proper, no venue objection can be raised, even if venue would not exist if the cross-claim were sued upon independently.

c. *Joinder of Additional Parties to Counterclaims and Cross-Claims*

Persons other than those who are parties to the original action may be added as parties to a counterclaim or cross-claim if their joinder is required by Rule 19 or permitted by Rule 20, i.e., they are "indispensable", "necessary" or "proper" parties. (See "Joinder of Parties," infra.)

Ancillary jurisdiction extends to a compulsory counterclaim, or to cross-claims, but a permissive counterclaim requires an independent jurisdictional ground. Likewise, venue is not a problem in compulsory counterclaims or cross-claims, but the venue rules must be independently satisfied as to permissive counterclaims. Whether in a compulsory or permissive counterclaim or a cross-claim, additional parties may be joined only if the court can obtain personal jurisdiction over them.

The statute of limitations runs until an action is commenced against an additional party; it is not tolled by the filing of the original action.

d. *Third-Party Practice (Impleader)*

Third-party practice (or impleader) allows a defendant to assert a claim against a third person not a party to the original action who is or may be liable to the defendant for all or part of the plaintiff's claim against the defendant. Rule 14. Impleader is not mandatory; the defendant may choose to assert his claim in a separate action.

i. When Impleader Is Proper

The claim must be that the third party is or may be liable over to the defendant on the plaintiff's claim. Impleader is improper if the third party's liability to the defendant is direct rather than derivative. Impleader can be used to assert claims for indemnity, subrogation, contribution, or breach of warranty. Whether such a claim is cognizable is a substantive question, and under the Erie Doctrine, a federal court must look to the appropriate state law.

> *For example, if P sues D in a diversity action for injuries suffered in a collision and D seeks to implead X, seeking contribution, the federal court must determine whether state law recognizes a right to contribution. If so, D may implead X even if the state procedural rules do not provide for impleader.*

Impleader is permissible when a third party "may be" liable. Thus, the third person can be made a party to the main action even though his liability to the defendant is contingent upon the defendant being found liable or being required to pay more than her share of liability. This procedure allows the various aspects of the controversy to be resolved in a single lawsuit. However, any party may move to strike the third-party claim, or for its severance or separate trial, and the court may order separate trials of claims or issues to further convenience or avoid prejudice. Rules 14, 42(b).

ii.   Procedure for Impleader

A defendant (third-party plaintiff) may serve a summons and third-party complaint on the third party (third-party defendant) without leave of court not later than 14 days after he serves his original answer. Thereafter, he must obtain leave of court upon notice to all parties. In either situation, the court has discretion whether to permit impleader, and must weigh the Rules' policy disfavoring a multiplicity of suits against any prejudice to the plaintiff from complicating the suit. Rule 14.

A third-party claim can be asserted only against a person not already a party; a counterclaim or a cross-claim is the proper device if the person is already a party.

The third-party defendant must file an answer raising his defenses to the third-party claim and any counterclaims against the third-party plaintiff or cross-claims against other third-party defendants. Furthermore, the third-party defendant may raise any defenses that the third-party plaintiff has against the plaintiff's original claim.

The third-party defendant may also assert against the original plaintiff any claim arising out of the same transaction or occurrence as the main claim.

Impleader is most commonly used by the original defendant. However, when a counterclaim has been asserted against the original plaintiff, he may implead a third party who is or may be liable for all or part of the counterclaim. Rule 14(b). Furthermore, a third-party defendant may implead a person who is or may be liable to him on the third-party claim (this party is known as a fourth-party defendant).

The original plaintiff may assert any claim against the third-party defendant that arises out of the same transaction or occurrence as the original claim, and the third-party defendant must answer, raising his defenses and any counterclaims or cross-claims. The claim may be asserted either by amending the complaint or by a new pleading.

For example, P, a customer, sues D, a retailer, for injuries suffered from the purchased goods. D impleads T, the manufacturer; P may then add a claim

> *against T directly. However, ancillary jurisdiction does not extend to P's claim against T; it requires an independent jurisdictional ground.*

Pursuant to the liberal joinder provisions of Rule 18(a), a party asserting an impleader claim may join with it all of his other claims against the third-party defendant.

iii. Jurisdiction of Impleader

Ancillary jurisdiction extends over third-party claims that arise out of the same "operative core of facts" as the main claim. Neither the diversity requirement nor the jurisdictional amount need be met.

> *Thus, if P, of New York, sues D, of Massachusetts, and D impleads T, also of Massachusetts for indemnification, the third-party action is ancillary and the lack of diversity between D and T does not matter.*

However, ancillary jurisdiction does not apply if the plaintiff asserts a claim against the third-party defendant. Independent subject matter jurisdiction is required.

> *For example, if P, of New York, brings a diversity action against D of Massachusetts, and D impleads T of New York, P may not assert a claim against T because diversity is lacking. Since P could not originally have sued T in federal court, he cannot now use ancillary jurisdiction to evade the diversity requirement. Owen Equipment & Erection Co. v. Kroger, 437 U.S. 365 (1978).*

If the defendant has joined other claims with his third-party claim, ancillary jurisdiction will extend only to those claims that arose out of the same transaction or occurrence as the original claim. Rule 18(a).

> *For example, P, a customer, sues D, a retailer, for injuries from the purchased goods, and D impleads T, the manufacturer for contribution, but also adds a claim for breach of a contract to deliver totally different goods. The contract claim may properly be joined under Rule 18(a), but it requires an independent jurisdictional ground.*

Venue will be ancillary in the same instances where subject matter jurisdiction is ancillary.

Personal jurisdiction must be obtained over parties added by impleader. The territorial limitations on service of process may substantially limit the use of impleader in some actions.

If the main action is dismissed or settled, the third-party action need not be, even though it has no independent jurisdictional ground. However, the court has discretion to dismiss the ancillary action if convenience will be promoted thereby.

6. Amended and Supplemental Pleadings

Amendment of the pleadings is liberally allowed under the Federal Rules. Amendment may be necessary if the other party has successfully challenged the sufficiency of a pleading, or if the party wishes to add claims or defenses that he had not known or had overlooked at the time of filing the original pleading.

a. *Amendment as of Right*

A party may amend his pleading once as a matter of course (1) 21 days after service or (2) if a responsive pleading is required, 21 days after service of such a pleading or 21 days after service of a Rule 12(b), (e), or (f) motion, whichever is earlier. Rule 15(a).

b. *Amendment By Leave Of Court*

After expiration of the period for amendment as of right, a party may amend his pleading only by leave of court or by written consent of the adverse party. Rule 15(a). The rule provides that leave shall be freely given when justice so requires, and refusal to allow amendment is an abuse of discretion, absent some justification such as prejudice. *Foman v. Davis*, 371 U.S. 178 (1962).

Generally, leave to amend will be denied only if amendment would cause actual prejudice to the opposing party. Prejudice does not result merely because the amended pleading raises a new theory of the case or a new claim. The court will primarily consider the timing of the motion. At what stage was the motion made? Was there excusable delay? Will the defendant be hampered in defending because of loss of evidence and witnesses? Is the new cause of action unrelated?

c. *Effect of Amendment*

An amended pleading supersedes the original pleading. If a response to the original pleading was required, then a response to the amended pleading is also required, unless the amendment was very minor. A party must respond to the amended pleading (1) within the time remaining for response to the original pleading; or (2) within 14 days after service of the amended pleading, whichever period is longer. Rule 15(a).

d. *Amendment to Conform to The Evidence*

When issues not raised by the pleadings are tried by the consent - express or implied - of the parties, they are treated as if they had been raised in the pleadings. A party may amend his pleadings upon motion at any time (even after judgment) to conform them to the issues and evidence presented.

However, this is not necessary and failure to amend does not affect the result of the trial on those issues. Rule 15(b).

If a party raises a timely objection at trial that evidence is outside the pleadings, the court may allow the pleadings to be amended. The court must freely allow amendment when the presentation of the merits of the action will be served thereby and the opposing party will not be prejudiced. To enable the objecting party to meet the new evidence, the court may grant a continuance. Rule 15(b).

e. *Relation Back of Amendments*

If a party seeks to assert a new claim in her amended pleading, a problem arises if the statute of limitations has run before the amendment. In some instances, the doctrine of relation back will save the claim.

Where the limitations period had run on the claim before the original pleading was filed, the claim is barred. Amendment cannot be used to circumvent the statute.

However, if the applicable limitations law (e.g., a state limitations law in a diversity action) allows or the new claim arose out of the conduct, transaction, or occurrence set forth in the original pleading, the amendment relates back to the date of original pleading - i.e., it is deemed to have been filed on the date of the original pleading. Rule 15(c). Thus, the claim would not be barred even though the statute had run between the filing of the original pleading and the filing of the amendment. Because the other party had notice within the limitations period of a claim against her arising out of the transaction, she is not prejudiced by the addition of another claim based on the same transaction. Courts are usually liberal in finding that the additional claim arose from the transaction or occurrence.

An amendment changing the party against whom a claim is asserted will relate back if the new defendant: (1) had notice of the institution of the action within the period of time allowed by the Federal Rules for service of process after filing the complaint (within 90 days after filing the complaint), (2) will not be prejudiced by the delay in maintaining a defense on the merits, and (3) knew or should have known that, but for a mistake concerning the identity of the proper party, the action would have been brought against him. Rule 15(c). Therefore, the action must be filed within the statutory limitations period, but a new party may later be brought in if the party had notice of the action within 90 days after the complaint was filed (and the requirements of elements (2) and (3), discussed above, are also satisfied).

> *For example, in* Scarborough v. Principi, Secretary of Veteran Affairs, _____ U.S._____ (2004), *the plaintiff filed an application for attorney fees under the Equal Access to Justice Act (EAJA). The EAJA provides that a prevailing party, in an action against the United States, is entitled to payment of attorney fees provided that party alleges in his application that the "position of the United States was not substantially justified". Plaintiff was the prevailing party in an action for disability benefits against the Secretary of Veteran*

> *Affairs; hence he filed the application for attorney fees. However, counsel failed to make the allegation that the position of the U.S. was not substantially justified, so the Secretary moved to dismiss the application. Scarborough's counsel immediately filed an amended application adding the allegation, however, by this time the 30-day fee application-filing period had expired. The Court held that the timely fee application may be amended after the 30-day filing period has run to cure an initial failure to make the allegation. The allegation does not serve an essential notice-giving function; the Government is aware of the claim and failure to make the allegation is not fatal. Furthermore, the amended application "arose out of the conduct, transaction, or occurrence set forth or attempted to be set forth" in the initial application. Rule 15(c)(2).*

Even though the newly named party was on notice that he might be subjected to liability based on the original pleading, his time to respond starts to run at the time the new pleading naming him is served, and the trial court cannot amend a judgment to impose liability on the new party immediately after the pleadings are amended to include him. *Nelson v. Adams,* 120 S.Ct. 1579 (2000).

f.   *Supplemental Pleadings*

A supplemental pleading deals with events that have occurred after the filing of the original pleading. (Compare to an amended pleading which deals with events that occurred before the filing of the original pleading but that were unknown or overlooked then.) The court has discretion to permit the filing of a supplemental pleading upon motion and reasonable notice. Rule 15(d).

Unlike an amended pleading, a supplemental pleading merely adds to, rather than supersedes, the original pleading. However, under Rule 15(d), a supplemental pleading may cure a defective original pleading, in the court's discretion. The court also has discretion to order a response to a supplemental pleading.

C. RULE 11

1.   Signature

Every pleading, motion and other paper must be signed by at least one attorney of record in the attorney's name or by a party personally if the party is not represented by an attorney. The paper must state the attorney's or party's address, e-mail address, and telephone number.

2.   Representations to the Court

By presenting to the court a pleading, motion, or other paper, whether by signing, filing, submitting, or later advocating it, that attorney or party certifies that to the best of that person's knowledge, information, and belief after an inquiry reasonable under the circumstances:

(1)   It is not being presented for any improper purpose, such as to harass, cause unnecessary delay, or needlessly increase the cost of litigation;

(2)   The claims, defenses, and other legal contentions are warranted by existing law or by a non-frivolous argument for extending, modifying, or reversing existing law or for establishing new law;

(3)   The factual contentions have evidentiary support or, if specifically so identified, will likely have evidentiary support after reasonable opportunity for further investigation or discovery; and

(4)   The denials of factual contentions are warranted on the evidence or, if specifically so identified, are reasonably based on belief or a lack of information.

3.   Sanctions

If, after notice and reasonable opportunity to respond, the court determines that the Rule has been violated, the court may impose an appropriate sanction for the violation. A motion for sanctions must be made separately from any other motion and must describe the specific conduct that violates the rule. Sanctions imposed under this rule must be limited to deter repetition of the conduct or comparable conduct by others. The sanction may include non-monetary directives, an order to pay a penalty, or, if warranted, an order directing payment of part or all of the reasonable attorney's fees and other expenses directly resulting from the violation.

D. JOINDER OF PARTIES AND CLAIMS

1.   Joinder of Parties

To prevent a multiplicity of suits as to the same matter, the Rules provide for bringing in other persons who have claims or who may be liable. If the connection of such a person is so close that the action should be dismissed unless he is joined, he is an "indispensable" party. If he ought to be joined if possible, he is a "necessary" party. If he can be joined or not at the plaintiff's option, he is a "proper" party.

a.   Compulsory Joinder (Rule 19)

In determining a compulsory joinder question, the court must decide (1) whether a person is needed for a just adjudication, (2) whether it is feasible to join that person, and (3) if he cannot be joined, whether the action can proceed in his absence.

Multistate Bar Review Book 2

A person is needed for a just adjudication if (1) in his absence, complete relief cannot be accorded to the existing parties, or (2) he claims an interest in the controversy and is so situated that disposition of the action in his absence may (i) as a practical matter impair or impede his ability to protect that interest or (ii) expose any of the existing parties to a substantial risk of double, multiple or inconsistent obligations by reason of his claimed interest. If a person meets this test, and he is subject to service of process and his joinder will not deprive the court of jurisdiction, he must be joined. Rule 19(a).

Furthermore, under Rule 19(a), if the person should join as a plaintiff, but refuses to do so, the person may be made a defendant, or, an involuntary plaintiff. Additionally, if the joined party objects to venue and joinder of that party would render the venue of the action improper, that party shall be dismissed from the action.

ii.   If Joinder is Not Feasible

If a person is needed for a just adjudication, but cannot be made a party either because he is not subject to process or his joinder would destroy the court's jurisdiction, the court must determine "whether in equity and good conscience the action should proceed" without him, or whether the action should be dismissed. In this determination, the court must consider (1) to what extent a judgment rendered in his absence would prejudice him or the existing parties; (2) whether protective provisions in the judgment decree could lessen or avoid that prejudice; (3) whether a judgment rendered in his absence would be adequate; and (4) whether the plaintiff will have an adequate remedy if the action is dismissed for nonjoinder. Rule 19(b).

If the court determines that the action must be dismissed in the absence of a party, he is regarded as an "indispensable" party. If a party should be joined but the action can continue without him, he is a "necessary" party.

> *For example, P, of Ohio, sues D, of Florida, to force the issuance of stock to P under an alleged agreement whereby P and T, another Ohio citizen, were to jointly purchase shares with the certificates to be issued in T's name. The court held that T must be joined, because, otherwise, the bank could be exposed to double obligation (to P and to T), and issuance to P might also impair T's interest in the stock. T was deemed an indispensable party, and because his joinder destroyed diversity, the action was dismissed. Haas v. Jefferson Nat'l Bank of Miami Beach, 442 F.2d 394 (5th Cir. 1971).*

Note that in the above example, the case was in federal court because of diversity, not because there was a federal question involved. So, if Haas had been a patent or bankruptcy case, then the court would have retained jurisdiction and T could have been joined.

The complaint must state the names of all parties who should be joined and the reasons they were not joined. Rule 19(c). The court then determines whether they are necessary or indispensable parties. A defendant should raise an objection to nonjoinder early, since it may be waived if the delay is too long. However, nonjoinder of an indispensable party can be raised at any time by pleading or motion, or even at the trial. Rule 12(h)(2).

b.   *Permissive Joinder (Rule 20)*

A party who has some relation to the suit, although not close enough to make him necessary for "just adjudication" is a "proper" party and may be joined at the option of one of the existing parties. Two tests must be satisfied: (1) the right to relief arises out of the same transaction, occurrence, or series of transactions or occurrences, and (2) there is a question of law or fact common to all the parties to the action. Rule 20(a).

What constitutes the same transaction or occurrence is determined on a case-by-case basis, but the approach is very similar to the "logical relationship" test applied in the context of a compulsory counterclaim. The court will consider whether there are enough of the same facts involved so that it would be fair to the parties, as well as convenient for the judicial system, to litigate all the claims together.

Not all questions of fact or law need be common - a single common question is sufficient to allow joinder. However, the common question must be of substantial importance. For example, in a collision case the common question may be the defendant's negligence, even though separate questions remain as to each plaintiff's contributory negligence and damages.

Defendants may be joined even if the claims against them are asserted severally or in the alternative.

> *For example, if P is uncertain whether he was injured by D-1 or by D-2, he can claim against each defendant in the alternative, and his or her respective liabilities can be resolved in a single suit.*

Ancillary jurisdiction does not extend to permissive joinder - the diversity and amount-in-controversy requirements must be satisfied as to all the plaintiffs and all the defendants. Likewise, the venue requirements must be met.

The court may order separate trials to minimize delay, expense or other prejudice caused by permissive joinder. Rule 20(b).

c. *Misjoinder and Non-Joinder*

If a party has been improperly joined, the action will not be dismissed, but the party may be dropped upon motion or upon the court's initiative at any stage of the action and on such terms as are just. If a party has not been joined who should have been, he may be added. However, if he is an indispensable party who cannot be joined, the suit will be dismissed. Rule 21.

2. Joinder of Claims

A party asserting a claim (whether an original claim, counterclaim, cross-claim or third-party claim) may join with it as many claims as he has against an opposing party. Legal, equitable and maritime claims may all be joined. Rule 18(a).

Joinder of claims is never required. However, the res judicata doctrine (infra) prohibits splitting a cause of action and will mandate the assertion of all grounds upon which a single cause of action is based.

Each claim must have an independent basis for subject matter jurisdiction.

> *For example, if P has a federal question claim against D, she may not join with it a separate nonfederal claim unless diversity exists. However, if the claims are closely related, pendent or ancillary jurisdiction may apply. Aggregation of claims to achieve the required $75,000 jurisdictional amount is allowed in suits by one plaintiff against one defendant, but not among multiple parties. Personal jurisdiction and venue must be proper as to each claim.*

3. Class Actions

A class action allows suit to be brought by or against a large number of people similarly situated who are represented by one or more class members. The procedure for a class action is governed by Rule 23, but in a diversity action state law governs the substantive rights of class members and the capacity to sue or be sued of class representatives.

a. *Prerequisites to a Class Action*

One or more members of the class may sue or be sued as class representatives if all of the following prerequisites are satisfied: (1) the class is so numerous that joinder of all members is impracticable; (2) there are questions of law or fact common to the class; (3) the claims or defenses of the representatives are typical of those of the class, and (4) the representatives will fairly and adequately protect the interests of the class. Rule 23(a).

i.   Size of Class

No particular number of members is required to constitute a class, but usually minimum class size is thirty to forty. For the class to be large enough impossibility of joinder is not necessary; extreme difficulty or impracticability of joinder will suffice. There is no fixed maximum, but the court will consider the difficulties of management, notice and ascertainment of those contained in the class.

ii.   Common Question

Not all questions of law and fact need be common to all members. For example, damages claims may be separate, but the question of a course of conduct leading to liability may nonetheless be common.

iii.   Typical Claim

The representative's claim need not be substantially identical with those of the other class members. However, it must be sufficiently typical of the class that the representative will act to protect the interests of the class.

iv.   Adequate Representation

Adequacy of representation is essential because a class action judgment binds people who were not before the court. The court will focus on whether representatives have any actual or potential conflict of interest with those represented, and whether the representatives have the incentive, resources and reliability to vigorously prosecute or defend the action. If some class members have divergent interests, the court can divide the class into subclasses and appoint a representative for each subclass. Rule 23(c).

b.   *When Class Actions Are Appropriate*

Under Rule 23(b), a class action may be based on any of three grounds, if the prerequisites of 23(a) (supra) have been satisfied.

i.   To Avoid Adverse Effects from Separate Actions

A class action may be maintained if the prosecution of separate actions would create a risk of (A) inconsistent or varying adjudications that would establish incompatible standards of conduct for the party opposing the class; or (B) judgments that would be dispositive of the interests of nonparty class members or that would substantially impair or impede their ability to protect their interests. Rule 23(b)(1)(A), (B).

Under subsection (A), the court must find that there is a real possibility that separate actions would be filed and that the defendants could be required by them to act inconsistently.

Multistate Bar Review Book 2

> *For example, separate actions to determine the riparian rights of various owners or landowners' rights with respect to a nuisance could result in incompatible adjudications.*

Under subsection (B), the court must find that a separate action would interfere with the interests of other individuals who have similar claims.

> *For example, a suit for distribution of trust assets or for declaration of a corporate dividend would prejudice other individuals, since their rights in the disputed assets would be settled without their being represented.*

ii. Actions for Injunctive Or Declaratory Relief

A class action is authorized where the party opposing the class has acted or refused to act on grounds generally applicable to the class. However, in this type of action the class may seek only final injunctive relief or declaratory judgment. Rule 23(b)(2).

This section is used most commonly in civil rights cases, for example to enjoin racial discrimination in a school system. The action or inaction may have threatened or taken effect as to only a few members of the class as long as the grounds for the action apply generally to the class.

iii. Common Questions Predominate

Finally, a class action is appropriate if the court finds that "the questions of law or fact common to the members of the class predominate over any questions affecting only individual members, and that a class action is superior to other available methods for the fair and efficient adjudication of the controversy." Rule 23(b)(3). This is the most common basis for a class action.

> *For example, where a fraud has been perpetrated on numerous people by similar misrepresentations, that common issue probably predominates over individual issues of damages. However, if fraud were perpetrated through very different techniques of misrepresentation or if the kinds or degrees of reliance of the claimants were very different, a class action probably would be unsuitable.*

In determining whether a class action is superior to individual suits, the court is to consider, among others, the following factors: (1) the interest of class members in individually controlling the prosecution or defense of separate actions; (2) the extent and nature of any litigation concerning the controversy already commenced by or against class members; (3) the desirability of concentrating all the litigation in one forum; and (4) any probable difficulties in managing a class action. Rule 23(b)(3).

c.   *Certification of Class*

As soon as practicable after a suit has been commenced as a class action, the court must determine whether it should proceed as a class action. If the requirements are met and the class action is superior to other available methods, the court will certify the suit as a class action. Rule 23(c)(1). A court's denial of class certification is not a final order and may not be appealed as of right. *Coopers & Lybrand v. Livesay*, 437 U.S. 463 (1978). Instead, the named plaintiffs must try the case as a separate action and on appeal from that judgment may obtain review of the certification order. The separate action has no res judicata effect as to the potential class members not joined.

Alternatively, the court may order that the action be treated as a class action with respect only to particular issues, or that the class be divided into subclasses with their own representatives. Rule 23(c)(4).

Filing of a class action tolls the statute of limitations on each potential member's claim until the decision on certification. The tolling rule is not limited to potential members who make timely motions to intervene in an action after class certification has been denied; the tolling rule also applies to the potential class members who choose to file their own suits after denial of certification, provided the actions are commenced within the time remaining in the limitations period. *Crown, Cork & Seal Co. v. Parker*, 462 U.S. 345 (1983).

d.   *Notice*

i.   Discretionary Notice

In a 23(b)(1) or (b)(2) class action, the court may in its discretion determine the notice to be given class members. Rule 23(c). Individual notice to members is not required by due process if representation is adequate. *Mattern v. Weinberger*, 519 F.2d 150 (3d Cir. 1975).

ii.   Mandatory Notice

In a 23(b)(3) (common-question) class action, the court must direct to class members "the best notice practicable under the circumstances, including individual notice to all members who can be identified through reasonable effort." Rule 23(c)(2). The cost of notifying the class members must be borne by the plaintiffs. *Eisen v. Carlisle & Jacquelin*, 417 U.S. 156 (1974) (individual notice required to 2,250,000 class members). The cost of identifying the class members must also be borne by the plaintiffs; however, in special circumstances, e.g., if the cost were insubstantial or if the information had to be compiled in the ordinary course of the defendant's business, the defendant might be required to identify the class members. *Oppenheimer Fund, Inc. v. Sanders*, 437 U.S. 340 (1978).

iii.   Contents of Mandatory Notice

The notice will describe the suit and the relief sought. The notice must advise each class member that (1) the court will exclude him from the class if he so requests by a specified date; (2) the judgment will bind all members who do not request exclusion; and (3) any member who does not request exclusion may enter an appearance through his counsel. Rule 23(c)(2).

e. *Binding Effect of a Judgment*

In a 23(b)(3) class action, a valid judgment, whether or not favorable to the class, binds all those who have not requested exclusion ("opted out") and who are found to be class members. Rule 23(c)(3). A person who opts out is not bound by the judgment, but on the other hand, she cannot rely on a favorable judgment as collateral estoppel.

Class members in (b)(1) or (b)(2) class actions do not have the right to opt out and are bound by the judgment.

i. Jurisdiction and Venue

Only the citizenship of the named representatives is considered in establishing diversity jurisdiction. Likewise, only the named representatives need meet the venue requirements. However, class members cannot aggregate small individual claims to satisfy the $75,000 jurisdictional amount. *Snyder v. Harris*, 394 U.S. 332 (1969). Furthermore, not only the representatives, but also each class member must have a claim in excess of $75,000. *Zahn v. International Paper Co.*, 414 U.S. 291 (1974). Only if the class members sue to enforce a single right or title in which they have a common and undivided interest may aggregation of claims be allowed. Of course, class actions involving a federal question (e.g., securities fraud) are not limited by an amount in controversy.

f. *Dismissal or Compromise*

A class action cannot be dismissed or compromised without the approval of the court. Notice of the proposed dismissal or compromise must be given to all class members in such manner as the court directs. Rule 23(e). This assures that the class representatives cannot be bought off by a favorable settlement for themselves to the detriment of other class members.

g. *Attorney Fees*

If the suit results in a recovery for the class, the court may award attorneys' fees to the representatives' attorneys out of the sum recovered. *Mills v. Electric Auto-Lite Co.*, 396 U.S. 375 (1970).

h. *Other Representative Actions*

i. Shareholder Derivative Actions

In a shareholders' derivative action, one or more shareholders sue to enforce a claim that belongs to the corporation because the directors or the majority shareholders refuse to bring suit to vindicate the corporation's rights (e.g., suits to redress corporate mismanagement). Derivative actions are similar to class actions, but are governed by Rule 23.1.

The complaint in a derivative action must be verified and must allege that (1) the plaintiff was a shareholder at the time of the alleged wrongdoing; (2) the action is not collusive; and (3) a demand for action was made upon the directors, and, if necessary, upon the shareholders, or why such a demand was futile or excused.

The corporation must be made a defendant, along with those against whom the corporation has a claim. Any recovery belongs to the corporation, so the damage alleged to the corporation is the measure of the jurisdictional amount. A derivative suit may be prosecuted by a shareholder in any district where the corporation could have sued the same defendants. 28 U.S.C. §1401.

A derivative action cannot be maintained if it appears that the plaintiff does not fairly and adequately represent the interests of similarly situated shareholders. Compromise or dismissal must be approved by the court, and notice of a proposed compromise or dismissal must be given to all shareholders. Rule 23.1.

ii.   Unincorporated Associations

Suit by or against members of an unincorporated association as a class is governed by Rule 23.2. The representatives must fairly and adequately represent the class, and the protective provisions of Rule 23(d) and (e) are specifically incorporated (e.g., court approval of dismissal, notice, etc.).

4.   Interpleader

a.   *In General*

Interpleader allows a person who does not know to which of several claimants he is liable (if he is liable at all) to join all the claimants in one action, and require them to litigate among themselves to determine which claim is valid. Interpleader protects the stakeholder from multiple lawsuits and possible multiple liability. Interpleader may be used, for example, where an insurer is uncertain to which of the claimants insurance benefits should be paid.

The stakeholder may initiate an interpleader action, naming all the claimants as defendants, or may interplead in an existing action between the claimants. If he has already been sued, he may interplead by a counterclaim or cross-claim. The stakeholder deposits the disputed property with the court or posts a bond sufficient to insure his compliance with the judgment. If he is disinterested, the court can then dismiss him from the action. If he denies liability or if he has a claim to the property, he remains a party.

The availability of interpleader is determined by federal standards, but the substantive law applied in a diversity action will be that which would be applied by the forum state.

b.   Differences Between Statutory And Rule 22 Interpleader

Interpleader is available either under Federal Rules of Civil Procedure Rule 22 or under 28 U.S.C. §1335; the principal difference is as to jurisdiction.

i.   Statutory Interpleader

Statutory interpleader (28 U.S.C. 1335) may be used where the amount involved exceeds $500, and there are "two or more adverse claimants of diverse citizenship." Thus, only minimal diversity is required: at least one claimant must be a citizen of a state different from that of the other claimants; the citizenship of the stakeholder is immaterial. Nationwide service of process is available in a statutory interpleader action. Venue is proper in the district in which any claimant resides.

ii.   Rule 22 Interpleader

Rule 22 interpleader requires either complete diversity of citizenship between the stakeholder on the one hand and all the claimants on the other, plus more than $75,000 in controversy, or federal question jurisdiction. Thus, Rule 22 interpleader is available where all the claimants are citizens of the same state, as long as the stakeholder is a citizen of another state. Process under Rule 22 interpleader must be served in accord with Rule 4, i.e., within the state where the court sits or pursuant to that state's long-arm statute. Venue lies in the district in which the plaintiff resides, in which all the defendants reside, or in which the claim arose.

5.   Intervention

Intervention provides a procedure whereby a nonparty can enter a lawsuit upon her own initiative to protect her interests. Intervention may be either as a matter of right or permissive.

a.   Intervention of Right (Rule 24(a))

Intervention of right is granted when (1) a federal statute confers an unconditional right to intervene, or (2) when the applicant claims an interest relating to the property or transaction which is the subject of the action and he is so situated that the disposition of the action may as a practical matter impair or impede his ability to protect that interest, unless the applicant's interest is adequately represented by existing parties. Rule 24(a).

No definite standard as to the extent of the potential intervenor's interest has been developed; some courts have required "a direct, substantial, legally protectable interest" while others have allowed intervention on a lesser showing. The requirement of "impairment" has been interpreted broadly; even the stare decisis effect of the judgment in the present action may be sufficient impairment to require intervention of right. Lack of adequate representation "is satisfied if the applicant shows that representation of his interest 'may be' inadequate; and the burden of making that showing should be treated as minimal." *Trbovich v. United Mine Workers of America*, 404 U.S. 528 (1972).

Ancillary jurisdiction extends to intervention as of right, and venue is ancillary as well. However, if the intervenor is a person who would be "indispensable" under Rule 19(a), an independent ground of subject matter jurisdiction must exist to prevent the danger of an evasion of jurisdictional requirements.

b. *Permissive Intervention (Rule 24(b))*

If intervention of right is not available a party may still be permitted to intervene in the court's discretion. Permissive intervention may be granted if (1) a federal statute confers a conditional right to intervene, or (2) an applicant's claim or defense and the main action have a question of law or fact in common. Rule 24(b).

The common question of law or fact need not arise from the same transaction, and the intervenor need not have a direct personal interest in the subject of the litigation. For example, neighbors have been allowed to intervene in an action to set aside a zoning order. In exercising its discretion, the court must consider whether the intervention will unduly delay or prejudice the adjudication of the original parties' rights. Rule 24(b). The court has very broad discretion, and it will rarely be overturned on appeal.

Independent jurisdictional grounds must exist for permissive intervention. Likewise, if intervention will create a venue problem, it should not be permitted.

c. *Procedure for Intervention*

All applications to intervene must be "timely." The court must weigh the possibility of delay and prejudice for the original parties against the harm to the potential intervenor from denial. Particularly in intervention of right, an application should not be denied as untimely.

The applicant must serve upon all parties a motion for leave to intervene, stating the grounds for intervention and accompanied by a pleading setting forth the claim or defense for which intervention is sought. If the constitutionality of a federal or state law affecting the public interest is drawn in question, the court must notify the United States or the state's Attorney General, respectively, if the federal or state government, or an agency, officer, or employee thereof is not already a party. Rule 24(c).

E. DISCOVERY

1. In General

Discovery procedures are methods by which a party can gather information from his opponent and from witnesses to aid in the preparation of his case.

One purpose of discovery is to allow a party to obtain and preserve evidence; testimony of witnesses who are old, or sick or who may leave the jurisdiction can be preserved in a form that can be introduced at trial in the witnesses' absence. Discovery also narrows the issues in dispute prior to trial, thus simplifying both the pleadings and the trial. The use of discovery reduces surprise and delay at trial by apprising the parties of additional evidence, and may substantially aid in establishing claims and defenses through evidence in the other party's possession.

2. Scope of Discovery

Rule 26(b) governs the scope of discovery, and provides in general that parties may obtain discovery regarding any matter not privileged that is relevant to the claim or defense of any party. For good cause, the court may broaden the scope to include any matter relevant to the subject matter involved in the pending action.

a. *Relevance and Admissibility*

"Relevance" is given a very broad interpretation. It does not matter that the information will be inadmissible at trial. Rule 26(b)(1). Discovery may relate to the party's own defense or claim or may extend to the claim or defense of the other party. A party may seek the identity and location of witnesses, and information as to the existence, description, custody and location of any books, documents or other tangible things. Rule 26(b)(1). Even if the party already knows the facts as to which he seeks discovery, his opponent may not object because a party is allowed to discover the position of his opponent on the controverted issues.

b. *Privilege*

Discovery extends only to matters "not privileged." Matter is privileged from discovery if it would be privileged at trial under the applicable rules of evidence. *United States v. Reynolds*, 345 U.S. 1 (1953). On issues governed by state law, the court must apply the state law of privilege as well. The most important privileges are the privilege against self-incrimination, the attorney-client privilege, the physician-patient privilege, and the privileges protecting a confidential communication between spouses and exempting one spouse from testifying against the other.

c. *Insurance Agreements*

A party can discover the existence and contents of a liability insurance agreement. However, information concerning the insurance is not thereby made admissible. Information on the application for insurance is not discoverable. Rule 26(b)(2).

d.   *Trial Preparation Materials*

i.   Qualified Immunity

A qualified immunity protects from discovery materials prepared for litigation. Rule 26(b)(3) states:

> Ordinarily, a party may not discover documents and tangible things that are prepared in anticipation of litigation or for trial by or for another party or its representative (including his attorney, consultant, surety, indemnitor, insurer, or agent)....

However, upon a showing that the party seeking discovery has substantial need of the materials in the preparation of his case and that he is unable without undue hardship to obtain the substantial equivalent of the materials by other means, if the materials would be discoverable under Rule 26(b)(1), they may be discovered.

The policy underlying the "work product" immunity is the necessity for the lawyer to investigate all facets of the case and develop his theories without fear of having to disclose his strategies or information that is unfavorable to his client. *Hickman v. Taylor*, 329 U.S. 425 (1947).

ii.   Extent of Protection

The work-product immunity now extends to persons other than the attorney who are representing a party, e.g., investigators or insurers. However, the document must have been prepared "in anticipation of litigation"; documents prepared in the regular course of business are not within the work-product immunity. The immunity protects only the documents or things themselves; an adversary can use interrogatories or depositions to discover the existence or nonexistence of the documents. Material prepared in anticipation of one suit should also have qualified immunity in a later suit.

iii.   Undue Hardship

Discovery of work product information may be allowed if it is otherwise unobtainable, e.g., if a witness is dead or his memory is faulty. In determining whether "undue hardship" exists, the court will consider the cost of otherwise obtaining the material, the financial resources of the party seeking it, and the likelihood that a "substantial equivalent" cannot be obtained (e.g., a witness who is an employee of the defendant may be hostile toward a discovering party who seeks a statement, and a "substantial equivalent" may therefore be unobtainable, and thus a transcript of his original statement to his employer's attorney might not be immune).

iv. Absolute Immunity

Absolute immunity from discovery protects "the mental impressions, conclusions, opinions or legal theories of a party's attorney or other representative concerning the litigation." Rule 26(b)(3).

v. Statements of a Party or A Witness

A party can obtain a copy of any statement that he had previously made concerning the action or its subject matter. No showing of need is required. Likewise, a nonparty can obtain automatically a copy of any statement that she has made. Rule 26(b)(3). However, a party cannot obtain the statement of a witness except by a showing of necessity sufficient to overcome the qualified immunity.

e. *Expert Information*

i. Experts Who Will Testify

A party may through interrogatories discover the identity of each expert witness his opponent expects to call at trial, the subject matter on which the expert is expected to testify, and the substance of the facts and opinions to which the expert is expected to testify and a summary of the grounds for each opinion. Rule 26(b)(4)(A). Further discovery by other means (e.g., depositions) may be ordered by the court if necessary, but the party seeking discovery generally must pay the expert a reasonable fee for his time. Rule 26(b)(4).

ii. Experts Not Expected to Testify

However, if an expert has been retained by the opponent in anticipation of, or in preparation for, litigation and is not expected to testify at trial, facts known or opinions held by the expert are discoverable only upon a showing of exceptional circumstances under which it is impracticable for the party seeking discovery to obtain facts or opinions on the same subject by other means. Rule 26(b)(4). This exception would apply, for example, if there were only one expert in the field, or if the opponent had hired all the experts in the field. The report of an examining physician or psychologist made pursuant to Rule 35 is not covered by this rule, and may be discovered. If a party is allowed discovery from his opponent's expert, the court may order that the party pay his opponent a fair share of the expert's fees and expenses. Rule 26(b)(4).

f. *Limits on Use of Discovery Methods*

The frequency or extent of use of the discovery methods shall be limited by the court if it determines that: (i) the discovery sought is unreasonably cumulative or duplicative, or is obtainable from some other source that is more convenient, less burdensome, or less expensive; (ii) the party seeking discovery has had ample opportunity by discovery in the action to obtain the information sought; or (iii) the discovery is unduly burdensome or expensive, taking into account the needs of the case, the amount in controversy, limitations on the parties' resources, and the importance of the issues at stake in the litigation. The court may act upon its own initiative after reasonable notice or pursuant to a motion. Rule 26(b)(1).

3. Protective Orders

Because of the wide scope of discovery, the potential exists for abuse of discovery devices in order to harass or oppress the opposing party. Rule 26(c) authorizes the court to "make any order which justice requires to protect a party or person from annoyance, embarrassment, oppression, or undue burden or expense." Such an order may issue upon motion of a party or of the person from whom discovery is sought upon good cause shown. The order will be issued either from the court in which the action is pending, or from the court in the district where a deposition is to be taken.

Protective orders may include: (1) that disclosure or discovery not be had (very unusual); (2) that discovery may be had only on specified terms and conditions, including a designation of the time and place (e.g., if a person is physically or financially unable to attend in the forum state; (3) that discovery be had by a method other than that selected by the discovering party (e.g., interrogatories instead of oral depositions to save travel and time); (4) that certain matters not be inquired into, or that the scope of discovery be limited to certain matters; (5) that discovery be conducted with no one present except persons designated by the court; (6) that a deposition be sealed and opened only by court order; (7) that a trade secret or confidential research or commercial information not be disclosed or be disclosed only in a designated way; (8) that the parties simultaneously file specified documents or information in sealed envelopes to be opened at the court's direction. Rule 26(c). The court may impose such other limitations, as justice requires.

Litigants do not have an absolute right to disseminate information obtained through discovery.

> *For example, a court could properly issue a protective order prohibiting disclosure (other than at trial) of information about the plaintiff religious foundation's financial affairs and identities of its members and donors, where the plaintiff showed that harassment and reprisals would result. Since the order was limited to information acquired through discovery, it did not infringe on the defendant newspaper's First Amendment freedoms. Seattle Times Co. v. Rhinehart, 465 U.S. 1018 (1984).*

4. Sequence Of Discovery, Duty To Supplement And Signing Requirements

Unless the court orders otherwise, methods of discovery may be used in any sequence. Both sides may proceed with discovery simultaneously. Rule 26(d).

A party has a duty to supplement an earlier response in two situations: (1) if there has been a change in the identity and location of witnesses or the name and subject matter of expert witnesses who will testify at trial; and (2) if he discovers that the prior response was incorrect when made, or that it is no longer correct and failure to amend would amount to knowing concealment. Rule 26(e).

Every discovery request, response or objection thereto must be signed by an attorney or an unrepresented party. The signature constitutes a certification that he has read the paper and that, to the best of his knowledge, information and belief formed after a reasonable inquiry, it is consistent with the Rules and warranted by the law or a good-faith argument for changing the law, it is not interposed for any improper purpose, and it is not, in the circumstances, unreasonable or unduly burdensome or expensive. An unsigned discovery paper shall be stricken unless it is signed promptly after the omission is called to his attention. For violation of the Rule, sanctions may be imposed, including the expenses incurred and reasonable attorney's fees. Rule 26(g).

5. Mandatory Disclosure

Rule 26 of the Federal Rules of Civil Procedure imposes upon litigants the affirmative duty to disclose, without awaiting any prior request for discovery, certain information (such as information regarding witnesses, description of documents, identity of persons likely to have discoverable information, computation of damages, and insurance policies which may be available to satisfy the claim) which the disclosing party may use to support its claims or defenses, unless solely for impeachment. Mandatory disclosures are intended to reduce the expense and delay that sometimes is associated with the discovery process.

The requirement of mandatory disclosure is in addition to the current provisions for discovery under the Federal Rules; i.e. a party has an affirmative duty to supplement incomplete or incorrect information. The parties must confer about a discovery schedule and the mandatory disclosures must occur within 14 days of the meeting or conference.

6. Discovery Meeting

Rule 26 imposes a mandatory meeting of the attorneys of record and each unrepresented party to discuss the nature of the claims and the possibilities of settlement, and to make or arrange for mandatory disclosures and develop a proposed discovery plan. The requirement is merely that the attorneys or parties "confer" unless the court orders that they meet in person. The proposed plan must indicate the parties' views and proposals concerning changes which should be made to the ordinary rules for discovery and a statement as to when the mandatory disclosures were or will be made; the subjects on which discovery is needed, when it should be completed, and whether it should be limited to certain issues; and recommendations for scheduling and other orders to be issued.

The meeting should be held as soon as possible and in any event no later than 21 days before the trial scheduling conference or order is due under Rule 16(b). A written report of the proposed discovery plan must be submitted to the court within 14 days after the conference.

Failure to participate in good faith in the development and submission of a proposed discovery plan can lead to a penalty under Rule 37(g) (after hearing, an award of the other party's attorney's fees and expenses caused by the failure).

Apart from the mandatory disclosure time requirements, a party generally may not seek formal discovery before the parties have conferred to develop a discovery plan as required by Rule 26(f).

7.   Methods of Discovery

a.   *Oral Depositions (Rule 30)*

Oral depositions are the most valuable of the discovery tools because they can be taken from any person, whether or not a party, and because they provide for examination and cross-examination of a person face-to-face without time to deliberate carefully and fashion a response. The Rules impose a presumptive limit on depositions; each party is limited to 10 depositions, unless leave of court is otherwise granted or the parties otherwise stipulate. Rule 30(a)(2). Furthermore, a person cannot be deposed more than once without leave of the court. Rule 30(a)(2).

i.   Timing

Generally, leave of court is not necessary to take a deposition, but leave must be obtained if a plaintiff seeks to take a deposition within thirty days after service of a summons and complaint upon a defendant. Rule 30(a). This thirty-day period allows the defendant time to retain counsel. However, leave is not required during the thirty-day period if (1) the defendant has served a deposition notice or otherwise sought discovery or (2) the plaintiff's attorney certifies that the deponent is about to go away and will be unavailable after the thirty-day period. (In the latter case, a deposition cannot be used against a party if he can show that, despite his diligence, he was unable to obtain counsel to represent him at the taking of the deposition.) Rule 30(a).

ii.   Notice and Subpoena

The deposing party must give reasonable notice in writing to all other parties, stating the time and place for the taking of the deposition, and the name and address of the deponent. Rule 30(b)(1).

The notice alone is sufficient to compel attendance by a party. A subpoena must be served on a nonparty, unless he agrees voluntarily to be deposed. The subpoena may also designate documents to be brought to the deposition (subpoena duces tecum). A witness who fails to respond to a subpoena may be cited for contempt. If a deposing party fails to attend, or did not subpoena a witness who then fails to attend, he may be ordered to pay the opposing party's reasonable expenses. Rule 30(g).

Notice and a subpoena may name a corporation or association, describing with reasonable particularity the matters to be examined. The organization must then designate one or more officers, directors or agents to testify on its behalf; they must testify as to matters "known or reasonably available to the organization." Rule 30(b)(6).

iii.   Procedure

Usually, an oral deposition is conducted in a lawyer's office, with all the parties and witnesses represented by counsel. The deposition may be taken before any person authorized to administer oaths who has no disqualifying interest in the case. Rule 28. This is usually a court reporter who also records the testimony, but testimony may be recorded by other means (e.g., video recording) and, if the parties agree or the court orders, the deposition may even be conducted by telephone. Rule 30(b)(4).

The deponent is sworn and then examined and cross-examined by the various parties' counsel. A deposition is limited to one day of seven hours unless otherwise authorized by the court or stipulated by the parties.

If there is objection to a question the reporter notes the objection and the witness answers; if that testimony given at the deposition is used at trial, the judge will rule upon the objection. Rule 30(c).

A stenographic deposition is transcribed, read and signed by the deponent, certified by the officer before whom the deposition was taken, and filed with the court. Rule 30(c), (e), (f).

iv.   Use of Deposition at Trial

A statement in a deposition is generally inadmissible as hearsay. However, it may be admitted in limited circumstances: (1) any deposition may be used by any party for contradicting or impeaching the deponent's testimony as a witness or for any other purpose permitted by the Federal Rules of Evidence (e.g., prior inconsistent statement in a deposition can be used as substantive evidence); (2) the deposition of an adverse party or of an officer, director or other agent of an adverse corporate party may be admitted for any purpose; (3) the deposition of any witness (party or nonparty) may be used for any purpose if the deponent is (a) dead; (b) more than 100 miles from the trial; (c) infirm or imprisoned and unable to testify; (d) not obtainable by subpoena; or if (e) special circumstances make it desirable in the interests of justice to use the deposition. Rule 32(a).

If one party puts into evidence only part of a deposition, an adverse party may require him to introduce any other part that in fairness should be considered with it, and any party may introduce any other parts. Rule 32(a).

### b.	Depositions Upon Written Questions (Rule 31)

Depositions can also be taken upon written questions. Generally, leave of the court is not necessary except when the person being deposed is confined to prison or when the person has already been deposed. A Rule 31 deposition has the advantage that counsel need not spend the time and money to travel to a distant place for the deposition. Instead, a party's lawyer serves upon any person or party written questions she wishes to ask; the opposing party serves cross-questions upon all the parties, and redirect and recross questions may also be served. All the written questions are then sent to the officer who will take the deposition; he puts the questions to the witness, records the oral responses, and transcribes and files the deposition. Because the questioner cannot effectively follow up the answers, this type of deposition is really useful only in establishing formal matters that are not complex.

### c.	Interrogatories to Parties (Rule 33)

Interrogatories are written questions to another party, which must be answered in writing and under oath. Note that while a deposition may be taken of a party or a nonparty, interrogatories can be addressed only to a party. Although interrogatories allow time to formulate careful (or even evasive) answers, they are useful for obtaining details, such as names and addresses of witnesses, or the existence of documents, and for narrowing the issues and obtaining admissions. Oral depositions may then be more effectively used to question a party closely.

The Rules impose a "presumptive numerical limit" on interrogatories; each party is limited to 25 interrogatories, unless leave of court is otherwise granted or the parties otherwise stipulate.

#### i.	Timing

Interrogatories may be served at any time, even with the complaint. A party must answer or object to the interrogatories within thirty days after they are served on him, but not before forty-five days after service of the summons and complaint was served. Rule 33(a).

#### ii.	Scope

Interrogatories may relate to any matters within the scope of discovery defined by Rule 26(b), supra. An interrogatory is not necessarily objectionable merely because an answer to the interrogatory involves an opinion or contention that relates to fact or the application of law to fact. Rule 33(a). Thus, an opinion or contention is not automatically protected by work-product immunity. The court, however, may order that an interrogatory need not be answered until a later time (i.e. after a pre-trial conference).

Interrogatories may not be used to obtain copies of documents, but answers should specifiy the location of the documents and afford the interrogating party the opportunity to inspect and photocopy the documents if discoverable. Rule 33(d).

iii. Duty to Respond

Each interrogatory must be answered separately and fully, unless it is objected to, in which case the reasons for objection must be stated. The answers are signed by the person making them and the objections are signed by the attorney making them. Rule 33(b). If answers are incomplete or evasive, a party may move to compel further answers.

Generally, a party must answer based upon all the information that is within its possession and that can be reasonably obtained without undue labor and cost. Thus, a corporation must examine its employees and records in order to answer fully. However, if the answer can be ascertained from the party's business records and the burden of ascertaining the answer is substantially the same for the propounding party as for the party interrogated, the interrogated party may specify the pertinent records and make them available for inspection and copying by the other party. Rule 33(d).

iv. Use of Interrogatories at Trial

Answers to interrogatories can be used by an adverse party for any purpose. A party is not irrevocably bound by his answers, but the answers may be used to contradict contrary statements or evidence that he introduces at trial.

d. *Production of Documents or Things or Entry on Land (Rule 34)*

A party may serve on any other party a request to produce and permit inspection and copying of any designated documents (e.g., writings, photographs, recordings or data compilations) or things, or to permit entry upon his land or property for the purpose of inspecting, testing, or sampling any tangible things. Rule 34(a).

i. Request

A request for production or entry can be served at any time without leave of court. It must set forth by item or category the things to be inspected and must describe each item and category with reasonable particularity. The request must also specify a reasonable time, place and manner for the inspection. Rule 34(b).

ii. Response

The party upon whom the request was served must serve a written response within thirty days after service of the request (or within forty-five days after service if the request was served with the summons and complaint). The requesting party may seek an order for production if no response is made or if objections are raised.

A party can be forced to produce the documents or things in his "possession, custody or control." Rule 34(a). If the party has a legal right to the document, he must produce it even though it is not currently in his custody. Thus, for example, a party cannot evade a request by giving a document to his out-of-state insurance company.

A party who produces documents for inspection can produce them as they are kept in the usual course of business or can organize and label them to correspond to the categories in the request. Rule 34(b).

iii.   Persons Not Parties

A person who is not a party may be compelled to produce documents or things or submit to an inspection by a subpoena issued under Rule 45. Rule 45's reach as to nonparties is intended to be coextensive with Rule 34's reach regarding parties. Thus, the right to obtain this type of discovery from a nonparty is subject only to the additional technical requirement of a subpoena.

e.   *Physical or Mental Examinations (Rule 35)*

Whenever the physical or mental condition of a party is in controversy, the court may require him to submit to an examination by a physician, psychologist, or other appropriate licensed professional. Rule 35(a).

i.   Court Order Required

Unlike other forms of discovery, a physical or mental examination is available only by court order upon motion by a party. A showing of "good cause" is necessary for the granting of the motion. Rule 35(a).

ii.   Condition Must Be in Controversy

The party's mental or physical condition must be "in controversy." If a plaintiff alleges mental or physical injury or if the defendant asserts his condition as a defense, the condition is clearly in controversy. *Schlagenhauf v. Holder*, 379 U.S. 104 (1964).

iii.   Procedure

Only parties or persons in the custody or under the legal control of a party are subject to examination. (i.e. A parent or guardian suing to recover for injuries to a minor may be ordered to produce the minor for examination.) Rule 35(a). The court usually will appoint the physician or psychologist proposed by the examining party, or an impartial examiner. Its order will specify time, place, manner and scope of the examination; the examination is limited to the matter in controversy.

iv.   Right to Report and Waiver of Privilege

The party examined has an absolute right to a copy of a detailed written report of the physician or psychologist who examined him. After delivery, the examining party is entitled, upon request, to any reports of previous or subsequent examinations of the same condition by the examinee's own doctors. Rule 35(b)(1). By requesting and obtaining a report of the ordered examination, the examinee waives the physician-patient privilege as to any testimony in regard to the same mental or physical condition. Rule 35(b).

f.   *Requests for Admission (Rule 36)*

One party may serve upon another party written requests for the admission of the truth of any discoverable matter. The request may relate to statements or opinions of fact or of the application of law to fact, including the genuineness of any documents described in the request. Each matter must be separately set forth. Rule 36(a).

i.   Response

A matter is deemed admitted unless within thirty days after service of the request the party serves an answer or objection signed by the party or by his attorney. (A defendant has forty-five days after service of the summons and complaint in which to respond.)

Each matter about which an admission is requested must be squarely met by either (1) an admission, or (2) a denial, or (3) a statement of why the party cannot truthfully admit or deny the matter, or (4) an objection, stating the reasons therefor. A party may not give lack of information or knowledge as a reason for failure to admit or deny unless he states that he has made reasonable inquiry and that the information known or readily obtainable by him is insufficient to enable him to admit or deny. Rule 36(a).

The requesting party may move to determine the sufficiency of the answers or objections. Unless the court determines that an objection is justified, it will order an answer to be served. If the court finds that an answer does not comply with Rule 36, it may order that the answer be amended or that the matter is admitted. Rule 36(a).

ii.   Effect Of Admission Or Denial

Any matter admitted is conclusively established at trial. However, the court may permit withdrawal or amendment if presentation of the merits of the action will be subserved thereby and the party who obtained the admission fails to show the court that withdrawal or amendment will prejudice him in maintaining his action or defense on the merits. Rule 36(b).

Multistate Bar Review Book 2

If a party fails to admit the truth of the matter and the requesting party later proves its truth, the court, on application, will order the party who failed to admit to pay the reasonable expenses incurred in proving the matter, including reasonable attorneys' fees, unless (1) the request had been held objectionable, or (2) the admission sought was not of substantial importance, or (3) the party failing to admit had reasonable ground to believe he might prevail on the matter, or (4) there was good reason for the failure to admit. Rule 37(a).

An admission is for the purpose of the pending action only and cannot be used against the party in any other proceeding. Rule 36(b).

8. Sanctions for Failure to Make or Cooperate in Discovery

Rule 37 sets forth the sanctions through which the means of discovery are enforced. Generally, application for sanctions is made by motion to the court where the action is pending (or in the district where a deposition is to be taken).

a. Motion to Compel a Response and Award of Expenses

Upon motion, a court can order a party or witness to answer a question at a deposition or on interrogatories, or to produce a requested document or allow a requested inspection, or to admit or deny a request to admit. If the motion is granted and the court finds that the refusal was without sufficient justification, it will require the refusing party, or the attorney advising the refusal, to pay the reasonable expenses incurred in obtaining the order, including reasonable attorney's fees. If the motion is denied, and the court finds that the motion was made without substantial justification, the court will require the moving party, or the attorney advising the motion, to pay the reasonable expenses incurred in opposing the motion, including reasonable attorney's fees. Rule 37(a), (c). Likewise, costs may be imposed upon a party for failing to attend a deposition that he had scheduled. Rule 37(d).

b. Failure to Comply with Order

Failure to comply with a court order or subpoena may be punished by (1) an order that the matters dealt with in the original order or other designated facts will be taken as established; (2) an order striking designated claims or defenses, or prohibiting introduction of designated evidence; (3) dismissal of an action or claims or defenses, or entering of a default judgment; (4) a contempt order, including a fine, or imprisonment until a proper response is made (refusal to submit to a physical examination cannot be treated as contempt). A party can also be required to pay the expenses incurred in obtaining the sanctions, including reasonable attorney's fees. Rule 37(b).

9.   Filing Discovery with Court

Disclosures under Rule 26(a)(1) or (2) are not filed with the court unless used in the proceeding or the court orders their filing. The same is true of depositions, interrogatories, requests for documents or to permit entry upon land, and requests for admission. Rule 5(d).

10.   E-Discovery

The Rules have expanded all the discovery rules to allow for e-discovery and document production of all electronic media. During conferences on discovery, the parties will agree on a procedure or protocol to govern the e-discovery process. The parties will provide the courts with an e-discovery agreement. E-discovery is expanded from "documents" and "data compilations" to include all electronically stored information, which means you can discover electronic mail, email, word documents, voicemail, instant messages, backup tapes, database files, and more.

F. ADJUDICATION WITHOUT A TRIAL

1.   Voluntary Dismissal

a.   *By Plaintiff Or By Stipulation*

A plaintiff can voluntarily dismiss her action by filing a notice of dismissal at any time before the defendant serves his answer or a motion for summary judgment. Thereafter, the plaintiff can dismiss without leave of court only by filing a stipulation of dismissal signed by all parties who have appeared. Rule 41(a)(1). Likewise, a party may voluntarily dismiss his counterclaim, cross-claim or third-party claim before a responsive pleading is served, or, if there is none allowed, before introduction of evidence at the trial or hearing. Rule 41(c).

b.   *By Leave Of Court*

After the defendant has answered or moved for summary judgment, the plaintiff can dismiss, without a stipulation, only by leave of court and upon such terms and conditions as are just. If a counterclaim has been pleaded before service of the motion to dismiss and defendant objects to dismissal, the court can dismiss only if the counterclaim can remain for independent adjudication. Rule 41(a)(2). Dismissal will be denied only if the defendant would suffer some prejudice other than the prospect of a second lawsuit.

c.   *Effect of Voluntary Dismissal*

Unless otherwise stated in the dismissal notice, the first voluntary dismissal is without prejudice, i.e., the plaintiff can sue again. However, if a plaintiff who has once dismissed again brings suit on the same claim against the same defendant, the court can order the plaintiff to pay the costs of the first action before the second action may proceed. Rule 41(d).

A party's second voluntary dismissal operates as an adjudication on the merits. Rule 41(a)(1). Thus, the plaintiff cannot again bring suit on those claims. This prevents harassment of the defendant and waste of judicial resources.

2. Involuntary Dismissal

The court may order the involuntary dismissal of plaintiff's action for failure to prosecute or for failure to comply with the Rules or court orders. Rule 41(b). However, dismissal is a severe sanction and is not favored.

Generally, an involuntary dismissal is with prejudice and operates as an adjudication on the merits. However, this is not true of a dismissal for lack of jurisdiction, improper venue, or failure to join a Rule 19 indispensable party, or where the court orders that dismissal is without prejudice. Rule 41(b).

3. Default Judgment

If a party against whom a claim has been asserted fails to plead or otherwise to defend, the clerk, upon affidavit or other showing, enters a default. Rule 55(a).

When the plaintiff's claim is for a sum certain, the clerk can enter a default judgment for that amount plus costs, if the plaintiff presents a request and an affidavit of the amount due. No notice to the defendant is necessary. Rule 55(b)(1). In all other cases, the plaintiff must apply to the court for entry of a default judgment and proof is required as to the damages or other relief sought.

If the defaulting party had appeared in the action, he must be given written notice seven days before the hearing on entry of a default judgment. Rule 55(b)(2). A default judgment cannot give relief different in kind or exceeding in amount that prayed for in the complaint. Rule 54(c).

For good cause shown, the court may set aside a default judgment. Usually, the defendant must show not only that he had a valid excuse for his default but also that he has a meritorious defense to the action. A motion to set aside a default judgment should be made within one year after entry of the judgment. Rules 55(c), 60(b).

4. Judgment on The Pleadings

After the pleadings have closed, any party may move for judgment on the pleadings. Rule 12(c). (This motion is analogous to a motion to dismiss for failure to state a claim.) The motion challenges the legal sufficiency of the adversary's pleadings. If matters outside the pleadings are presented, the motion is treated as a motion for summary judgment (infra).

5.   Summary Judgment

The Rule 56 motion for summary judgment allows the court to "look behind" the pleadings to determine whether any genuine issue of fact exists for trial. If not, the movant is entitled to a final judgment as a matter of law without trial.

a.   *Timing*

A party may move for summary judgment at any time before 30 days after the close of all discovery. This deadline can be changed via court order or local rule. Rule 56(b). Parties will often wait until the completion of discovery has allowed them to collect the most information to support the motion.

b.   *Materials Considered*

To support or oppose the motion, the parties submit affidavits, which must set forth facts admissible in evidence, must be made on personal knowledge, and must show affirmatively that the affiant is competent to testify on these matters. The parties may also submit depositions and answers to interrogatories and other papers. Supporting documents must be supported by materials in the record. Rule 56(c). The court may also allow oral testimony. Rule 43(c).

The opposing party, to defeat summary judgment, must introduce affidavits or other proof to show there is a genuine issue for trial; he cannot rely merely upon his pleadings. If he is unable for some stated reason to present affidavits sufficient to justify his opposition, the court may grant him a continuance or may deny the summary judgment motion. Rule 56(d).

If any party presents affidavits in bad faith or solely for the purpose of delay, the court may order him to pay the expenses and attorney's fees for the other party's filing, and may also punish the offending party or his attorney for contempt. Rule 56(h).

c.   *Standard for Summary Judgment*

Summary judgment will be granted only if there is "no genuine dispute as to any material fact." Rule 56(a). Thus, if the only issue at trial would be the legal effect of the facts, summary judgment can be granted. However, if there are disputed material facts, they must be resolved by a trial.

> For example, P moves for summary judgment on a promissory note, presenting the affidavit of a witness who swears he saw D sign the note. If D files no opposing affidavit, no fact question remains and summary judgment is proper. However, if D files an affidavit swearing that his alleged signature was a forgery, a genuine issue as to a material fact is raised, and summary judgment cannot be granted. On a summary judgment motion, the

court cannot decide whether P's witness or D is more believable; it can only decide whether there are issues to be tried.

d. Burden of Proof

The burden is on the moving party to show that there is no genuine issue of fact. *Adickes v. S.H. Kress & Co.*, 398 U.S. 144 (1970). However, the moving party is not required to support its motion with affidavits negating the opponent's claim. *Celotex Corp. v. Catrett,* 91 L. Ed.2d 265 (1986). Under Rule 56(c), a summary judgment may properly be made in reliance solely on the depositions, documents, electrnically stored information, affidavits or declarations, stipulations, answers to interrogatories, and admissions. Summary judgment will be denied if the movant failed to establish the absence of a genuine issue. All doubts will be resolved against the moving party.

If the moving party meets her burden, the burden then shifts to the opposing party to establish that a genuine issue exists. If he fails to do so, summary judgment will be granted.

e. Partial Summary Judgment

If there is controversy as to some material facts but not as to others, the court may enter an order that the uncontroverted facts will be deemed established at the trial. Rule 56(g). Furthermore, if a separate claim has been fully determined, judgment may be entered on that claim if "there is no just reason for delay," leaving the other claims to be tried. Rule 54(b).

f. Appeal

Denial of a motion for summary judgment is an interlocutory order and is not immediately reviewable. The grant of a summary judgment is a disposition on the merits and can be appealed.

G. PRETRIAL CONFERENCE AND ORDER

1. Pretrial Conference

Except in cases exempted by local rule, the judge must enter a scheduling order no later than 90 days after any defendant has been served with the complaint. The order limits the time to join other parties and to amend the pleadings, to file and hear motions, and to complete discovery, and may also deal with any other appropriate matters. Rule 16(b).

The court in its discretion may order counsel to participate in a pre-trial conference. (In some districts, pre-trial conferences are mandatory.) At the conference, the parties may clarify the issues, amend the pleadings, eliminate matters to be proved by agreeing to admissions or stipulations, identify the witnesses, determine whether issues should be referred to a master for findings, and consider the possibility of settlement or use of extrajudicial procedures to resolve the dispute.

The conference is usually held shortly before trial, when parties have made discovery and planned their cases. However, in a complex case, several conferences may be held at various stages. Judges often use the conference to encourage the settlement of the case, once the issues are clearly defined.

The judge prepares a pre-trial order reciting the action taken at the conference, including the amendments to the pleadings, matters agreed upon, and the issues to be tried. The order then controls the subsequent course of the action, unless it is later modified by the judge to prevent manifest injustice.

If a party or his attorney fails to appear at a pre-trial conference, or is substantially unprepared to participate, or fails to participate in good faith, or fails to obey a pre-trial order, the judge may exclude designated claims or evidence, strike pleadings, treat the act as a contempt, or assess the expenses, including attorney's fees, caused by the noncompliance. Rule 16(f).

2. Order

Most cases are settled out of court. Such settlements are often embodied in consent judgments, which are entered on the record and are enforceable like any other judgment.

To encourage settlement, Rule 68 allows a defendant, at any time more than 14 days before trial, to make an offer to the plaintiff to allow judgment against him for a specified sum or property. If the plaintiff accepts within 14 days, the court is notified and judgment is entered. If the plaintiff rejects the offer and fails to receive a more favorable judgment at trial, the plaintiff must pay the costs of the trial from the time of the offer.

IV. JURY TRIALS

A. RIGHT TO JURY TRIAL

1. Source of Right to a Jury Trial

The Seventh Amendment to the United States Constitution provides: "In suits at common law, where the value in controversy shall exceed twenty dollars, the right of trial by jury shall be preserved, and no fact tried by a jury shall be otherwise re-examined in any Court of the United States, than according to the rules of the common law." Rule 38(a) states: "The right of trial by jury as declared by the Seventh Amendment to the Constitution—or as provided by a federal statute—is preserved to the parties inviolate."

2. Availability of Jury Trial

a. In "Suits at Common Law"

The Seventh Amendment guarantee creates a historical test for the right to a jury trial: an action that was "at law" in 1791, when the Seventh Amendment took effect, will be tried to a jury, upon demand; an action that was equitable is not entitled to jury trial. Thus, for example, there would be a right to jury trial in an action seeking damages only, but not in an action seeking specific performance only. Although the Rules of Civil Procedure abolished the procedural distinction between actions at law or in equity, the distinction remains important as to the right to jury trial.

When new causes of action, which were unknown at common law, are created, the right to jury trial applies if the new actions are analogous to actions triable to a jury in 1791. The court will look to the remedy sought in order to characterize the action. Thus, for example, a claim of housing discrimination under the fair housing provisions of the Civil Rights Act of 1968 gives rise to a right to jury trial, because the statute authorizes damages, as well as injunctive relief, and the claim is in the nature of a tort action. *Curtis v. Loether*, 415 U.S. 189 (1974). However, bankruptcy actions have been held to be "inherently proceedings in equity," and hence not entitled to jury trial. *Katchen v. Landy*, 382 U.S. 323 (1966).

b.   *In Statutory and Administrative Proceedings*

Statutes may explicitly grant a right to jury trial or may explicitly deny it. Any action against the United States (except for a suit to recover excess taxes paid) shall be tried without a jury. 28 U.S.C. §2402. An action for a declaratory judgment will be triable to a jury if raised in a lawsuit. *Beacon Theatres v. Westover*, 359 U.S. 500 (1959). The right to jury trial does not extend to administrative proceedings. *Atlas Roofing Co. v. Occupational Safety and Health Review Commission*, 430 U.S. 442 (1977).

Although statutory damages are equitable in nature, a jury trial may still be warranted under some circumstances.

> *For example, in Fetner v. Columbia Pictures TV, Inc., 118 S. Ct. 1279 (1998), the Supreme Court ruled that parties have a right to a jury trial for assessing statutory damages in copyright infringement cases. The Court stated that although the Copyright Act itself does not grant a* per se *right to a jury trial for assessing statutory damages, the Seventh Amendment commands a constitutional right to a jury trial. Thus, the Supreme Court used two tests: (1) whether the Copyright Act itself mandated a right to a jury trial **or** (2) whether the Seventh Amendment sets a constitutional requirment for a jury trial.*

c.   *At Judge's Discretion*

If there is no right to jury trial, the court has discretion to summon an advisory jury (except in actions against the United States); however, its verdict is merely advisory and the judge still must make the findings of fact. In an action not triable of right by a jury, the court, with the consent of both parties, may order a trial with a jury whose verdict has the same effect as if trial by jury had been a matter of right. Rule 39(c).

3. Jury Trial When Legal and Equitable Claims are Involved

Where, through joinder of claims and interposition of counterclaims, the parties are asserting various claims for relief or are seeking various remedies based on the same claim, legal and equitable claims may be intertwined, with issues of fact common to both. In such a case, the order of trying the claims is important, because if the judge rules first on the common fact issue in the equitable claim, his ruling will estop a re-determination of the fact issue in the legal claim, and thus will effectively destroy the right to jury trial on this issue in the legal claim. Therefore, in all such cases, the legal claim should be tried first in order to preserve the right to jury trial. However, if a party would be irreparably harmed by delaying a trial of the equitable claims until after trial of the legal claims, the court can hear the equitable claims first. *Beacon Theatres v. Westover*, 359 U.S. 500 (1959).

a. Where Plaintiff Joins Legal and Equitable Claims

Where the plaintiff has joined a legal claim with an equitable claim (e.g., a claim for damages with a claim for an injunction), he has not thereby waived his right to jury trial on the legal claim. Thus, any issues common to both claims must first be resolved in a jury trial of the legal claim. *Dairy Queen, Inc. v. Wood*, 369 U.S. 469 (1962).

b. Where Defendant Raises a Legal Counterclaim to an Equitable Claim

If the plaintiff brings an equitable action and the defendant asserts a legal counterclaim involving a common issue, the jury must try the issue in the counterclaim first. A typical example is a suit by an insurance company to rescind a policy for fraud in applying for it - an equitable action. If the insured counterclaims to collect the policy benefits, the insured is entitled to a jury trial first as to her right to the benefits, which will necessarily determine the validity of the contract.

c. Where Legal Claim is Raised in an Equitable Proceeding

Proceedings such as class actions, shareholders' derivative actions and interpleader actions are equitable in origin and historically could be tried only in equity regardless of the type of relief sought. However, in *Ross v. Bernhard*, 396 U.S. 531 (1970), the Supreme Court declared that if a legal claim is raised in an historically equitable proceeding, the legal claim must be tried to a jury; the court must look to the underlying cause of action to determine the jury trial right. Thus, in a shareholders' derivative action, there will be a right to jury trial on all the issues that would have been triable to the jury if the corporation had brought the action.

4. Effect of State Law on Right To a Jury Trial

The right to jury trial in the federal court is determined by federal law. Thus, if in a diversity case, state law would deny a jury trial, but the Seventh Amendment would require a jury trial, the federal court must hold a jury trial. *Simler v. Conner*, 372 U.S. 221 (1963). Likewise, if state law would deny a jury trial, but federal courts customarily grant jury trial although not constitutionally required to do so, the federal practice will prevail in a diversity case. *Byrd v. Blue Ridge Rural Electric Cooperative*, 356 U.S. 525 (1958). Finally, if state law would grant a jury trial as to an issue that in federal court would be decided by the judge, the federal practice will be followed in a diversity suit. *Herron v. Southern Pacific Co.*, 283 U.S. 91 (1931).

When a state court adjudicates a federally created cause of action, it must grant a jury trial if there is a strong federal policy favoring jury trial in that type of action (e.g., federal policy of granting jury trial in FELA actions).

5. Demand for A Jury Trial

The right to jury trial is not self-executing; a timely demand must be made.

a. Timing

A written demand for jury trial must be served upon all other parties not later than 14 days after the service of the last pleading directed to the issue on which jury trial is sought. Rule 38(b). The demand can be made in the pleadings or in a separate motion.

If a party has demanded jury trial for only some of the issues, any other party may serve a demand for jury trial as to any other or all fact issues within 14 days after service of the original demand. Rule 38(c).

When amended or supplemental pleadings are filed, a jury demand may be made within 14 days thereafter only as to new issues raised therein. If a general jury trial demand has already been made, no new demand is required. If a new party is joined, she may make a timely demand.

b. Effect

Once a demand for jury trial has been served, other parties can rely upon it and need not individually make demand. However, the plaintiff in an original action may not rely on a demand in a third-party action; he must make a separate demand for jury trial in the main action. If a general demand is made, all issues will be tried to the jury; if the demand specifies only certain issues, the jury will try only those issues, unless another party demands, or the judge orders, jury trial upon other or all issues. Rule 38(c).

A demand cannot be withdrawn without the consent of all parties. Rule 38(d).

If a jury trial was demanded in an action brought in state court, the demand survives its removal to federal court.

c.   Waiver

The right to jury trial is waived by failure to serve a timely demand. Rule 38(d). However, despite the waiver, a court in its discretion may order jury trial upon motion. Rule 39(b). Parties may also agree to waive jury trial, and the court will usually honor such an agreement.

B.   SELECTION AND COMPOSITION OF JURIES

1.   Number of Jurors

Although at common law, twelve jurors were required, the Seventh Amendment guarantees only the right to jury trial "as at common law," not the "incidents" of common-law jury trial. *Colgrove v. Battin*, 413 U.S. 149 (1973). Thus, the court may seat a jury of six to twelve persons. Rule 48.

2.   Selection of Jurors

Jurors are selected from an array, representing a cross-section of the community without systematic exclusion of any racial, economic, political or religious group. A juror must be a United States citizen, at least eighteen years of age, literate and fluent in English, and without a criminal record.

Prospective jurors are questioned at the voir dire to determine if they have any personal interest or opinion in the case or any prejudice that would prevent their exercising impartial judgment. The court may question the prospective jurors or may allow counsel to conduct the questioning. Rule 47(a).

A party may challenge a prospective juror for cause if he has some relationship to a litigant or if he is otherwise biased; each party has an unlimited number of challenges for cause. In addition, each party has three peremptory challenges, which may be exercised to dismiss qualified jurors because a party fears that their occupational or social attitudes may be unfavorable to the party. 28 U.S.C. §1870.

3.   Excuse of Jurors

The court may excuse a juror from service during the trial or deliberations for good cause (e.g., illness or misconduct by the juror which might otherwise result in a mistrial) without resulting in a mistrial. Rule 47(c). However, no verdict can be taken from a jury that numbers less than six persons, unless the parties stipulate to the contrary. Rule 48. Therefore, it is good practice for the court to seat more than six jurors.

4. Unanimity of Jurors

Ordinarily, a jury verdict must be unanimous. However, the parties may stipulate that a verdict of a certain majority of the jurors will be binding. Rule 48.

C. REQUESTS FOR AND OBJECTIONS TO JURY INSTRUCTIONS

After the closing arguments, the judge will orally instruct the jury. He explains to them the substantive law they must apply to the facts and explains which party has the burden of proof on each issue. Federal judges retain the common-law power to comment on the evidence: the judge may impartially summarize and discuss the facts and evidence, but must caution the jury that it is not bound by his discussion of the evidence.

In a diversity case, the substance of the instructions is based on the state substantive law creating the rights and duties. However, the form of instructions and objections is a procedural matter governed by federal law.

The parties may file written requests for proposed instructions at the close of the evidence, or at such earlier time as the judge reasonably directs. The judge informs counsel of its proposed action on their requests before the final arguments, and then instructs the jury after the final arguments. Unless counsel objects to the giving or failing to give any instruction before the jury retires to consider its verdict, he has waived the objection. Counsel must state distinctly the matter to which he objects and the grounds of his objection. Rule 51.

An error in a jury instruction will be deemed harmless and will not result in a reversal on review if it was not misleading when the instructions are considered as a whole. Rule 61. However, if an instruction was plainly erroneous and prejudicial, an appellate court may reverse even if timely objection was not made.

V. MOTIONS

A. PRETRIAL MOTIONS, INCLUDING MOTIONS ON PLEADINGS, MOTIONS TO DISMISS

Instead of filing an answer, a defendant may file a Rule 12 motion, challenging the sufficiency of the pleadings.

1. Motion to Dismiss (Rule 12(b))

a. *Grounds*

The defendant may raise the following seven defenses either in the answer, or at his option, in a pre-answer motion to dismiss under Rule 12(b):

(1)   Lack of jurisdiction over the subject matter;

(2)   Lack of jurisdiction over the person;

(3)   Improper venue;

(4)   Insufficiency of process;

(5)   Insufficiency of service of process;

(6)   Failure to state a claim upon which relief can be granted;

(7)   Failure to join an indispensable party under Rule 19.

b.   *Standard for Granting Rule 12(b)(6) Motion*

Upon a motion to dismiss for failure to state a claim upon which relief can be granted, the court must construe the complaint in the light most favorable to the plaintiff. A Rule 12(b)(6) motion shall be denied unless "it appears beyond doubt that the plaintiff can prove no set of facts in support of his claim which would entitle him to relief." *Conley v. Gibson*, 355 U.S. 41 (1957). Hence, 12(b)(6) motions are rarely granted.

c.   *What Is Considered*

Generally, upon a 12(b) motion only the pleading itself is considered. However, there are two exceptions: (1) the court may take judicial notice of facts universally known and accepted (e.g., matters of public record, historical events, geography and scientific principles); (2) the court may consider whether the movant's own allegations cure any defect in the challenged pleading.

If the movant also presents affidavits or other evidence going to the merits, the court may treat the motion as one for summary judgment under Rule 56 (infra). Rule 12(b).

d.   *Consequences of The Ruling On The Motion*

If the motion to dismiss is granted, the plaintiff usually can amend her complaint, either by filing an amendment to the original complaint or by filing a new amended pleading. If the plaintiff amends, she waives any right to appeal the dismissal of the original pleading.

If the plaintiff wishes to appeal the grant of a motion to dismiss, she must allow a judgment of dismissal to be entered against her, because interlocutory appeal is not available on such orders. If she wins her appeal, the complaint is reinstated and the case proceeds. However, if she loses her appeal, the appellate court still may exercise its discretion to remand to allow her to amend her pleading.

If the motion to dismiss is denied, the defendant must either answer or allow a default judgment to be entered against him.

2. Motion for Judgment on the Pleadings (Rule 12(c))

A motion for judgment on the pleadings is analogous to a motion to dismiss under Rule 12(b)(6); however, it is made after the pleadings are closed but within such time as not to delay the trial. Any party may move for judgment on the pleadings. Again, if supporting affidavits or other material is presented, the court may treat the motion as one for summary judgment. Rule 12(c).

3. Motion for More Definite Statement (Rule 12(e))

If the pleading is so vague and ambiguous that a party cannot reasonably be required to frame a responsive pleading, he may move for a more definite statement before filing his responsive pleading. However, if the pleading is definite enough so that an answer can be made, the court will deny the motion and rely on discovery to alleviate the vagueness. Rule 12(e) motions are rarely granted. A 12(e) motion may not be made if no responsive pleading is permitted. If an order for a more definite statement is entered and it is not obeyed within 14 days after notice, the court may strike the pleading. Rule 12(e).

4. Motion to Strike (Rule 12(f))

A party may move to strike from a pleading "an insufficient defense or any redundant, immaterial, impertinent, or scandalous material." Rule 12(f). A motion to strike must be made before responding to a pleading, or if no responsive pleading is permitted, within 21 days after service of the pleading upon the movant. Motions to strike are not favored and will be granted only if the allegations attacked have no possible relation to the controversy and may prejudice the other party.

5. Procedure

A Rule 12 motion must be in writing (unless made during a hearing or trial), must state with particularity the grounds therefor and must set forth the relief or order sought. Rule 7(b)(1).

A pre-answer motion must be filed within the time allowed for serving the answer (i.e., 21 after service of the summons and complaint). Service of a motion extends the time for answering until 14 days after notice of the court's action upon the motion. Rule 12(a).

Usually, Rule 12(b) and 12(c) motions are heard and determined before trial. However, the court may defer hearing and determination until the trial. Rule 12(d).

Multistate Bar Review Book 2

6.   **Waiver of Defenses**

If a party makes a motion to dismiss based on one of the Rule 12(b) grounds, he must combine in it all the 12(b) grounds then available to him, because certain defenses, if omitted, will thereby be waived. Rule 12(h).

a.   *Defenses Waived if Not Raised in Pre-Answer Motion or Answer*

The defenses of (1) lack of jurisdiction over the person; (2) improper venue; (3) insufficiency of process; or (4) insufficiency of service of process are waived (a) if not raised in a pre-answer motion, or (b) where no pre-answer motion is made, if not raised in the answer or any amendment as of right to the answer. Rule 12(h).

For example, if the defendant, before answering, moves to dismiss because of insufficiency of process (12(b)(4)), he will have waived an objection to improper venue (12(b)(3)) unless he raises it in the same motion. Or, if the defendant makes no pre-answer motion, but fails to raise improper venue in the answer, he has waived that objection unless he adds it to his answer within the 21-day period for amendment as of right.

b.   *Defenses That May Be Raised Before or at Trial*

The defenses of (1) failure to state a claim upon which relief can be granted, (2) failure to join an indispensable party under Rule 19, and (3) an objection of failure to state a legal defense are not waived in the above circumstances. They may be raised in any pleading, in a motion for judgment on the pleadings or at the trial. However, the right to raise these defenses at trial is not absolute, but is in the discretion of the judge. These defenses cannot be raised for the first time on appeal. Rule 12(h)(2).

c.   *Nonwaivable Defense*

The defense of lack of subject matter jurisdiction is never waived. It may be raised at any time by any party or by the court, and may be raised for the first time on appeal. Rule 12(h)(3).

B.   MOTIONS FOR JUDGMENTS AS A MATTER OF LAW

A trial judge enters judgment as a matter of law when a party convinces the judge that there is no evidence upon which the other party can prevail on a given issue or claim - in essence, that there is no basis upon which a jury could find a material fact and so that issue can and should be decided as a matter of law. In essence, the court removes either the whole case or a particular issue from consideration by the jury and determines the outcome or the issue as a matter of law. (In prior practice, this was called a directed verdict when granted during the trial.)

1.   Timing

A party may move for judgment as a matter of law any time after the opposing party has been fully heard with respect to the issue or claim, but before the case has been submitted to the jury. Rule 50(a). Thus, the motion may be made anytime during the trial, but should not be allowed by the court until the opposing party has been apprised of the materiality of the issue and it becomes apparent to the court that the opponent cannot produce any substantial evidence upon which the jury could find for the opponent as to that issue.

A motion for judgment as a matter of law must be made at the close of all the evidence for the party to preserve its right to renew the motion after the jury returns a verdict (discussed, *infra*).

2.   Standard

The motion must state the law and facts which entitle the party to judgment as a matter of law. Rule 50(a)(2). The court must consider the evidence in the light most favorable to the party against whom the motion is made; all legitimate inferences are drawn in the opponent's favor. The court takes into account not only the evidence favorable to the party opposing the motion but also any unfavorable evidence that the jury is required to believe, *i.e.*, uncontradicted and unimpeached evidence supporting the moving party. *Simblest v. Maynard*, 427 F.2d 1 (2d Cir. 1970). The motion must be denied if reasonable men might differ as to the result.

Although the Supreme Court has not spoken to the effect of *Erie* on the standard for judgment as a matter of law, most lower federal courts have held that, in diversity cases, the federal standard, rather than the state standard, should be applied.

An order granting the motion is effective without the assent of the jury. Rule 50(a).

3.   Renewal of the Motion After the Verdict

A judgment as a matter of law may either be granted during the trial or, if renewed, after the jury returns its verdict. Courts will only rarely grant a judgment as a matter of law prior to a jury verdict. If the judge grants a judgment as a matter of law before the jury returns a verdict, but the judgment as a matter of law is reversed on appeal, an entire new trial must be held. However, if the jury decides the case, the judge can then overturn an unsupportable jury verdict by granting a judgment as a matter of law after the verdict; if the judge is then reversed on appeal, the appellate court can simply reinstate the jury verdict and a second trial is unnecessary.

A motion for a judgment as a matter of law must be made at the close of all the evidence for the motion to be renewed and granted after the verdict. Rule 50(b). If no motion for judgment as a matter of law was made at the close of the evidence, the motion cannot later be renewed, and neither the trial nor the appellate court can then order a judgment as a matter of law. See *Oliveras v. American Export Isbrandtsen Lines, Inc.*, 431 F.2d 814 (2d Cir. 1970). Judgment as a matter of law granted after a jury verdict was called a judgment notwithstanding the verdict (or "J.N.O.V.") in prior practice. Judgment as a matter of law after a jury verdict will be discussed further, infra, at "Attacks on a Verdict or Judgment."

In a nonjury trial, the court may enter a judgment on partial findings under Rule 52(c), as discussed *supra*. This is the counterpart of a judgment as a matter of law in a jury trial.

4. Comparison to Summary Judgment

A judgment as a matter of law or a judgment on partial findings differs from a summary judgment under Rule 56 in that a judgment as a matter of law or on partial findings (1) is made only after the court has heard the opposing party's evidence at trial, and (2) can be overturned only if "clearly erroneous." A summary judgment is granted before trial, can be granted on the basis of presumptions and the failure to produce contrary evidence, and is more easily overturned on appeal.

C. POSTTRIAL MOTIONS, INCLUDING MOTIONS FOR RELIEF FROM JUDGMENT AND FOR NEW TRIAL

A verdict may be attacked for insufficiency of the evidence (motion for judgment as a matter of law), or for irregularities and errors in conduct of the trial (motion for new trial). Relief from a judgment may also be sought under Rule 60(b) for mistakes, inadvertence, fraud, newly discovered evidence and other specified reasons.

1. Renewal of a Motion for Judgment as a Matter of Law

A motion for judgment as a matter of law may be granted during a trial (as discussed supra), but is more likely to be granted after the jury returns an unsupportable verdict.

a. *Previous Motion Required*

A motion for judgment as a matter of law must be made at the close of all the evidence to be renewed after the verdict. Rule 50(b). If the original motion for judgment as a matter of law is not granted, the case is deemed to have been submitted to the jury subject to a later determination of those legal questions; thus, if the jury returns a verdict contrary to the law, the court can later enter a judgment as a matter of law without violating the Seventh Amendment guarantee of jury trial.

A renewal of the motion after the verdict is also required; neither the trial court nor the appellate court may enter a judgment as a matter of law on its own initiative.

b.   Timing

Not later than 28 days after entry of judgment, a party who moved for a judgment as a matter of law at the close of the evidence may move to have the verdict and judgment set aside and to have the court enter a judgment as a matter of law. Rule 50(b).

c.   Standard

The motion for judgment as a matter of law raises the question of the legal sufficiency of the evidence, as discussed supra. The court must determine whether, when the evidence is considered in the light most favorable to the party against whom the motion is made, reasonable men could have differed as to the verdict. The court must consider all the evidence favorable to the party opposing the motion as well as any unfavorable evidence that the jury is required to believe, i.e., uncontradicted and unimpeached evidence supporting the moving party. *Simblest v. Maynard*, 427 F.2d 1 (2d Cir. 1970). If there was any substantial evidence supporting the verdict, the motion must be denied.

d.   Joinder with Motion for a New Trial

The renewed motion for judgment as a matter of law may be joined with a motion in the alternative for a new trial.

If the motion for judgment as a matter of law is granted, the trial court must still make a conditional ruling on the motion for a new trial, specifying the grounds for granting or denying the motion. If the judgment as a matter of law is granted but reversed on appeal, and the motion for a new trial was conditionally granted, the new trial will proceed automatically, unless the appellate court orders otherwise. If the judgment as a matter of law is granted but reversed and the motion for a new trial was conditionally denied, the jury verdict is reinstated. Rule 50(c)(1).

The party who won the jury verdict (referred to as P for simplicity) must be careful to preserve her rights. If the trial court grants D's renewed motion for judgment as a matter of law after the verdict, P must serve a motion for new trial within 28 days after entry of the judgment. Rule 50(d). If D's motion for judgment as a matter of law is denied and D appeals the jury verdict, P (as appellee) should assert in the alternative any grounds she may have for a new trial (otherwise, they may not be preserved). Then, if the appellate court reverses the jury verdict, it may determine that appellee is entitled to a new trial, or may order the trial court to determine whether a new trial should be granted. Rule 50(e).

2. Motion for a New Trial

A judge has broad discretion to order a new trial as to all or part of the issues for any of the reasons for which new trials have heretofore (i.e., before the 1938 adoption of the Rules) been granted in actions at law (or in a nonjury action, for the reasons an equity court would have granted a rehearing). Rule 59(a).

a. *Timing*

A motion for a new trial must be served not later than 28 days after entry of the judgment. Rule 59(b). If the motion is based upon affidavits, the affidavits must be served with the motion. Within 14 days after service of the motion, the opposing party must serve any opposing affidavits. The court may further allow reply affidavits. Rule 59(c).

b. *Order for a New Trial on Initiative of Court*

Not later than 28 days after entry of judgment, the court on its own initiative may order a new trial for any reason for which it might have granted a new trial upon motion. Furthermore, the court may grant a timely motion for a new trial for a reason not stated in the motion, after giving the parties notice and opportunity to be heard on the matter. In either case, the court must specify in its order the grounds for granting the new trial. Rule 59(d).

c. *Grounds for a New Trial*

i. In General

In an action tried to a jury, a new trial can be granted as to all or any of the parties on all or some of the issues of fact or law. Rule 59 does not enumerate the grounds for grant of a new trial, but sets as the standard "any of the grounds for which new trials have heretofore been granted in actions at law."

ii. Harmless Error

No error is ground for granting a new trial "unless justice requires otherwise." Thus, any error or defect in the proceeding that does not affect substantial rights of the parties is deemed harmless. Rule 61.

iii. Verdict is Against the Weight of the Evidence

The judge may grant a new trial if the verdict is against the weight of the evidence. The fact that he would have decided the case differently himself is insufficient: he must be convinced that the jury was seriously in error. He must order a new trial if "the verdict is against the clear weight of the evidence, or is based upon evidence which is false, or will result in a miscarriage of justice, even though there may be substantial evidence which would prevent the direction of a verdict." *Aetna Casualty & Surety Co. v. Yeatts*, 122 F.2d 350 (4th Cir. 1941).

iv.   Prejudicial Misconduct

Improper conduct by jurors (e.g., taking a private view of the accident scene, falsely answering a question at voir dire, talking to or accepting a bribe from a party or counsel for a party) is sufficient to require a new trial. Likewise, misconduct by counsel (e.g., improper argument to the jury or inflammatory questions or statements at trial) may necessitate another trial. If the judge acts improperly or prejudicially (e.g., delaying the trial for his own convenience, coercing counsel, witnesses or jurors or making prejudicial comments), he should order a new trial.

To obtain a new trial on the basis of juror bias, a party must first demonstrate that a juror failed to answer honestly a material question on voir dire, and then further show that a correct response would have provided a valid basis for a challenge for cause. Only those reasons for a juror's concealing information that affect his impartiality are sufficient to constitute error affecting the fairness of the trial. *McDonough Power Equipment, Inc. v. Greenwood*, 464 U.S. 548 (1984).

v.   Excusable Lack of Preparation

If a party is unfairly surprised at trial by the introduction of evidence that had a material effect on the outcome, a new trial may be granted. However, this is usually available only if the party was diligent in preparation, but was deceived by the opposing party.

vi.   Newly Discovered Evidence

If evidence is discovered after the trial that is of such a nature as to be likely to affect the result, the motion for a new trial should be granted to avoid injustice. However, the evidence must pertain to facts existing at the time of trial, and the proponent must show that, despite due diligence, he could not have obtained the evidence before trial.

vii.   Errors at Law

If the trial judge is convinced that he made a prejudicial legal error at trial (e.g., in an evidentiary ruling or jury instructions), he can order a new trial.

viii.   Excessive or Inadequate Damages

If the judge finds that the jury's award was excessive or inadequate, he may simply grant a new trial. Alternatively, he may order a new trial subject to a condition: if the plaintiff agrees to reduction in damages to a specified sum, the new trial will not be held (remittitur). Some state courts allow additur - conditional grant of a new trial unless the defendant agrees to a specified increase in damages; however, in federal courts, additur is prohibited by the Seventh Amendment. *Dimick v. Schiedt*, 293 U.S. 274 (1935).

d. *Partial New Trial*

If the error or misconduct taints only one claim or issue, a partial new trial may be ordered. For example, if the court concludes that the jury was reasonable in finding the defendant liable, but that the damages are inadequate, it can order a new trial on damages. The issue must be distinct and separable. *Gasoline Products Co., Inc. v. Champlin Refining Co.*, 283 U.S. 494 (1931).

e. *Nonjury Trial*

A new trial may be granted after a nonjury trial for any of the reasons for which rehearings have heretofore been granted in suits in equity. Rule 59(a)(2). On a motion for a new trial, the court may simply reopen the judgment, take additional testimony, amend or make new findings of fact and conclusions of law, and direct the entry of a new judgment.

3. Motion to Amend Judgment

A motion to amend or alter any judgment (including a default judgment) must be served within 28 days after entry of judgment. Rule 59(e). Thereafter, the judgment may be attacked only by a motion for relief from judgment under Rule 60, or by appeal.

4. Motion for Relief from Judgment

a. *For Clerical Mistakes*

If, through oversight or omission, a clerical mistake is made in entering a judgment, the court may correct the mistake at any time, either upon motion or on its own initiative. If a judgment will be appealed, such mistakes may be corrected before the appeal is docketed in the appellate court, but thereafter may be corrected only with leave of the appellate court. Rule 60(a).

b. *Upon Specific Grounds*

On motion the court may relieve a party from judgment on the following grounds:

(1)   mistake, inadvertence, surprise, or excusable neglect; [negligence of a party or counsel is not sufficient]

(2)   newly discovered evidence which by due diligence could not have been discovered in time to move for a new trial under Rule 59(b); [i.e., within 28 days after entry of judgment]

(3)   fraud (intrinsic or extrinsic), misrepresentation, or other misconduct of an adverse party;

(4)   the judgment is void;

(5)   the judgment has been satisfied, released, or discharged, or a prior judgment on which it is based has been reversed or otherwise vacated, or it is no longer equitable that the judgment should have prospective application; or

(6)   any other reason justifying relief from the operation of the judgment.

A motion for relief from judgment must be made "within a reasonable time" after the entry of judgment, and a motion on ground (1), (2), or (3) must be made within one year. Rule 60(b).

The judge will not grant a Rule 60(b) motion unless the error complained of affects a substantial right of a party. Rule 61.

5.   Independent Suit to Set Aside Judgment

Traditionally, an independent suit could be brought in equity, in certain circumstances, to set aside a judgment; Rule 60 specifically preserves this relief. Generally, equitable relief is available only where a judgment is void (e.g., for a jurisdictional defect), or where it was obtained through fraud (e.g., default or dismissal was obtained by promising not to bring suit in defendant's absence, or by promising plaintiff a settlement). However, an equity court may refuse to act if direct relief is still available in the trial court (e.g., through Rule 60(b) motion).

VI. VERDICTS AND JUDGMENTS

A.   DEFAULTS AND INVOLUNTARY DISMISSALS

1.   Default Judgment

When a party against whom a judgment for affirmative relief is sought has failed to plead or otherwise defend, and that failure is shown by affidavit or otherwise, the clerk must enter the party's default. If the plaintiff's claim is for a sum certain, the clerk must enter judgment for that amount and costs against a defendant who has defaulted for not appearing. In all other cases, the party must apply to the court for a default judgment.

2.   Involuntary Dismissals

If the plaintiff fails to prosecute or to comply with a court order, a defendant may move to dismiss the action or any claim against it. Unless the dismissal order states otherwise, a dismissal under this rule operates as an adjudication on the merits.

B.   JURY VERDICTS

1.   General Verdict

The general verdict is the most commonly used. The jury merely finds for one party or the other and determines the relief to be awarded. This method is simple, but may conceal the jurors' misunderstanding of complex facts or law, or their decision of a case on its emotional appeal rather than on its merits.

2.   General Verdict with Interrogatories

To ensure that jurors correctly considered key elements in a complex case, the judge, in his discretion, may instruct the jury to return a general verdict and may also submit to the jury written interrogatories upon specific facts the decision of which is necessary to a verdict. Rule 49(b).

If the general verdict and the answers to the interrogatories are harmonious, the court enters judgment. If the answers are consistent with each other but one or more is inconsistent with the general verdict, the court may (1) enter judgment in accordance with the answers, notwithstanding the general verdict; or (2) order further jury deliberation; or (3) order a new trial. Rule 49(b). The court cannot enter judgment on the general verdict since that would conflict with the facts found. If he enters judgment based on the answers, he must make every reasonable attempt to reconcile the answers with the general verdict to avoid undercutting the right to a jury determination.

If the answers are inconsistent with each other and one or more is likewise inconsistent with the general verdict, the court must either order further jury deliberation or a new trial. Rule 49(b).

3.   Special Verdict

In a special verdict, the judge submits to the jury written questions susceptible of brief answers on specific factual issues. The jury writes answers to the questions, but renders no general verdict; the court renders the verdict on the basis of the answers. This is a useful device in complex or highly emotional cases, but is still not entirely satisfactory because thorough, unambiguous questions are difficult to draft and because the jury still may render inconsistent answers.

If the judge fails to submit a question on a factual issue raised by the pleadings or the evidence, a party waives his right to trial by jury on that issue unless he objects before the jury retires. If waiver occurs, the judge may make a finding or, if he fails to do so, he is deemed to have made a finding in accord with the judgment on the special verdict. Rule 49(a).

C.   JUDICIAL FINDINGS AND CONCLUSIONS

1.   Judgments

A judgment is the decree or order of the court that finally adjudicates the rights of the parties. Usually, appeal is allowed only from a final judgment.

a. *Judgments Involving Multiple Claims or Parties*

When more than one claim is presented in an action, or when multiple parties are involved, the court may enter final judgment as to fewer than all of the parties or the claims if it expressly determines that there is no just reason for delay and it expressly directs entry of judgment. Rule 54(b).

> *For example, P sues D-1 and D-2 and D-1 successfully moves for summary judgment; unless the express determination is made, D-1's summary judgment is interlocutory and thus not ripe for appellate review until the issues concerning D-2 are resolved at trial.*

b. *Entry of Judgment*

The date of entry of judgment is significant for several reasons; most importantly, it marks the starting point of the time in which to make post-trial motions or to appeal.

Every judgment and amended judgment must be set forth in a separate document. However, a separate document is not required for an order disposing of a motion: (1) for judgement as a matter of law, (2) to amend or make additional finding of fact; (3) for attorney fees; (4) for a new trial, or to alter or amend the judgment; or (5) for relief from judgment or order under Rule 60. Rule 58(a)(1).

Where there has been a general verdict by a jury, or a decision by the court to grant recovery of a sum certain, or a denial of all relief, the clerk must, without awaiting for the court's direction, promptly prepare, sign, and enter the judgment. Rule 58(b).

However, where the court grants some other relief, or where there is a special verdict or a general verdict accompanied by answers to interrogatories, the court must approve the form of the judgment, and the clerk will then enter it. The court must act "promptly" and must set forth the judgment on a separate document. Rule 58(b).

Except as to default judgments, every final judgment shall grant the relief to which the party is entitled, even if the party has not demanded such relief in his pleadings. Rule 54(c). Thus, the court may award damages in excess of those sought, or may order a different type of relief, for example, damages instead of an injunction.

2. Findings and Conclusions

In an action tried on the facts without a jury or with an advisory jury, the court must find the facts specially and state its conclusions of law separately. The findings and conclusions may be stated on the record after the close of the evidence or may appear in an opinion or a memorandum of decision filed by the court.

3. Judgment on Partial Findings

If a party has been fully heard on an issue during a non-jury trial and the court finds against the party on that issue, the court may enter judgment against the party on a claim or defense that, under the controlling law, can be maintained and defeated only with a favorable finding on that issue. The court may, however, decline to render any judgment until the close of the evidence. A judgment on partial findings must be supported by findings of fact and conclusions of law.

D. CLAIM AND ISSUE PRECLUSION

To assure the finality of judicial determinations, to conserve the time of the court and to prevent wasteful relitigation, the doctrines of res judicata and collateral estoppel have evolved. Res judicata, or claim preclusion, prevents a litigant from reasserting a claim that has already been decided on the merits. Collateral estoppel, or issue preclusion, prevents a party from relitigating an issue that has been determined in a prior suit.

1. Claim Preclusion (Res Judicata)

a. *Merger and Bar*

If a final, valid judgment has been rendered on the merits of a claim, the claim cannot be relitigated. If judgment is rendered for the plaintiff, his claim is merged into the judgment and he cannot sue on it again. Similarly, if judgment is rendered for the defendant, the judgment serves as a bar to the plaintiff's suing on the claim again.

For merger or bar to apply, the prior judgment must have been based on the same claim or cause of action that is raised in the second suit, and the judgment must have been valid, final and on the merits. However, the claim (or defense) need not actually have been litigated in the first action: res judicata applies to all claims and defenses that could have been raised as to the cause of action in the original suit.

b. *Scope of a Claim*

The first problem in determining whether res judicata applies is to define the scope of a "claim" or "cause of action." Although no single, definitive test is used, perhaps the most influential is the transactional test: "the claim extinguished includes all rights of the plaintiff to remedies against the defendant with respect to all or any part of the transaction, or series of connected transactions, out of which the action arose." What constitutes a "transaction" or "series" is "to be determined pragmatically, giving weight to such considerations as whether the facts are related in time, space, origin, or motivation, whether they form a convenient trial unit, and whether their treatment as a unit conforms to the parties' expectations or business understanding or usage." Restatement (Second) of Judgments §24.

> *Thus, for example, if P first sues for negligence and later for breach of contract, but each time she is complaining of the same faulty workmanship, the judgment in the first action will bar the second action. Similarly, if D pleaded a counterclaim on which he lost in the first action, he is barred from raising that same cause of action in a second, independent suit.*

c.   *Final Judgment*

Res judicata applies only if the prior judgment was a final determination of the claim. Hence, res judicata does not apply to interlocutory orders.

Summary judgment is entitled to res judicata effect.

A judgment is deemed final even though an appeal is taken; only when the judgment is reversed or modified does its res judicata effect cease.

A judgment must be valid to have res judicata effect - i.e., the rendering court must have had subject matter and personal jurisdiction and the defendant must have had notice and an opportunity to be heard. If the question of jurisdiction is actually litigated, the court's decision on the matter is res judicata.

d.   *Judgment Must Be on the Merits*

The final judgment must also be on the merits. A default judgment is deemed to be on the merits. An involuntary dismissal (e.g., for failure to prosecute, or to comply with a court order) is generally with prejudice and is on the merits. However, a dismissal for lack of jurisdiction, improper venue, or failure to join an indispensable party is not on the merits. Rule 41(b). A second voluntary dismissal is with prejudice and acts as a bar.

A dismissal for failure to state a claim under Rule 12(b)(6) is a judgment on the merits unless the court specifies otherwise. However, usually the court grants leave to amend the complaint.

A consent judgment is given res judicata effect. A settlement will also be treated like a judgment on the merits (although collateral attack may be allowed if fraud in obtaining the settlement is alleged).

e. *Counterclaims*

Failure to raise a compulsory counterclaim bars the defendant from raising it in a later action. However, permissive counterclaims, cross-claims and third-party claims are not required to be raised in the original action and so are not barred.

f. *Change in the Law*

If a final judgment has been rendered, no appeal has been taken and the time for appeal has elapsed, res judicata applies even if the law on which the judgment was based changes. Parties who do not appeal cannot benefit from a reversal simply because their position is "closely interwoven with that of appealing parties."

> *For example, P-1 and P-2 bring an antitrust suit, which is dismissed on a technical ground. P-1 appeals, but P-2 instead files a different complaint, which merely raises the same claim and is therefore barred. While P-1's appeal is pending, the Supreme Court reverses the law on the antitrust technical ground and P-1 reinstitutes his suit. P-2 is still barred from suing again by res judicata. Federated Department Stores, Inc. v. Moitie, 452 U.S. 394 (1981).*

2. Issue Preclusion (Collateral Estoppel)

a. *In General*

If an issue was actually litigated and necessarily determined in an action, the parties to the first action (and nonparties who are in privity with parties) are estopped from relitigating that issue in a later action.

Note an important distinction between res judicata and collateral estoppel: res judicata bars relitigation of an entire cause of action whether or not all its inherent issues were determined in the first suit. Collateral estoppel precludes relitigation only of specific issues that actually were litigated and necessarily determined; the cause of action that raises these issues will be different in the second suit.

> *For example, if Prof sues Dunce for damage to Prof's car in an automobile collision case, Prof must prove that Dunce was negligent in order to win. Later, if a passenger in Prof's car sues Dunce for injuries received in the collision, Dunce cannot raise res judiata because the passenger's cause of action is separate from that of Prof. However, if Dunce lost the case brought by Prof, that means that the issue of Dunce's negligence was litigated and decided against Dunce. Thus, the issue of Dunce's negligence may be taken as proven in any subsequent case brought by the passenger.*

b. Same Issue

Collateral estoppel applies only if the issue raised in the second action is identical to that decided in the first action. However, if the issue arose in two different contexts, estoppel will not apply.

c. Actually Litigated

An issue must have been actually litigated for collateral estoppel to apply to it.

> *For example, L successfully sues T for rent due under a lease, and later sues again for subsequent installments due. In the second suit, D claims that his signature on the lease was forged. Since the validity of the lease was not litigated in the first action, T is not collaterally estopped to raise that issue later.*

Admissions pursuant to Rule 36 are expressly limited to use in the pending action only. Likewise, consent judgments usually cannot be used collaterally. Default judgments are not fully litigated and therefore usually have no collateral effect.

The availability of jury trial in the second action and not in the first has no bearing on whether a matter actually litigated in the first action will raise a collateral estoppel in the second. *Parklane Hosiery Co. v. Shore*, 439 U.S. 322 (1979).

Settlements do not cause issue preclusion unless the parties clearly intend their agreement to have such effect. *Arizona v. California,* 120 S.Ct. 2304 (2000).

d. Necessary to the Determination

To be binding, the issue must have been necessary to the determination in the first suit.

> *For example, Pansy sues Daisy for Pansy's personal injury caused by Daisy's negligence. The court finds Pansy contributorily negligent and therefore judgment is awarded to Daisy, although Daisy is also found negligent. Daisy then sues Pansy. Collateral estoppel does not apply because the finding as to Daisy's negligence was not necessary to the determination in the first action (i.e., because Pansy's claim was barred by her own negligence).*

If two or more issues could have been the basis for the general verdict rendered, none of the issues will have collateral estoppel effect because there is no certainty as to which was necessary to the jury's determination.

e.   *Offensive and Defensive Uses of Collateral Estoppel*

Offensive use of collateral estoppel occurs when a plaintiff seeks to foreclose a defendant from relitigating an issue the defendant has previously litigated unsuccessfully in another action against the same or a different party. Defensive use of collateral estoppel occurs when a defendant seeks to prevent a plaintiff from relitigating an issue the plaintiff has previously litigated unsuccessfully in another action against the same or a different party.

3.   **Persons Bound by Res Judicata and Collateral Estoppel**

a.   *Parties and Persons in Privity*

The parties to a judgment are bound by res judicata and collateral estoppel. A person in privity with a party is also bound. A successor in interest to property is bound by a judgment binding his predecessor. A beneficiary of a trust or an heir to an estate is bound by a judgment binding his representative. A member of the class is bound by the judgment in a class action suit.

b.   *Mutuality of Estoppel*

Due process dictates that a nonparty cannot be bound by a judgment. Traditionally, courts held that a stranger who could not be bound by the judgment should not be allowed to benefit by it either. This rule eroded to a prohibition of using collateral estoppel offensively. However, the Supreme Court has held that, in some instances, offensive use of estoppel by a nonparty is permissible.

> For example, in Parklane Hosiery Co. v. Shore, *439 U.S. 322 (1979)*, shareholders brought suit against the corporate defendant seeking damages resulting from their reliance on an allegedly false proxy statement issued by the corporation in connection with a proposed merger. After commencement of the shareholders' suit but before its trial, the SEC brought suit against the corporation for the same false statements in the same proxy solicitation. The trial court entered a judgment against the corporation in the SEC suit. The Supreme Court allowed the shareholders to use the SEC's judgment offensively to preclude the corporation from relitigating the issue of the falsity of the solicitation.

However, the Court declared that such offensive use would not be allowed if it would be unjust in the circumstances. Factors that would be considered as to its justice include whether the person to be estopped had a reasonable incentive to litigate in the first suit, whether the consequences in the second suit are much more serious than those in the first suit, and whether the nonparty could have joined in the first suit, but "sat out" to gain a tactical advantage.

The doctrine of nonmutual offensive collateral estoppel (under which a nonparty to a prior lawsuit may make offensive use of collateral estoppel against a party to the prior suit) is limited to private litigants and does not apply against the United States government. *United States v. Mendoza*, 464 U.S. 154 (1984). However, the doctrine of mutual defensive collateral estoppel is applicable against the United States government to preclude relitigation of the same issue already litigated against the same party in another case involving virtually identical facts. *United States v. Stauffer Chemical Co.*, 464 U.S. 165 (1984).

VII. APPEALABILITY OF INTERLOCUTORY REVIEW

A. AVAILABILITY OF INTERLOCUTORY REVIEW

1.   Statutory Authorization for Interlocutory Appeal

In equity, the final decision rule did not apply; therefore, by statute certain "equitable" orders can be reviewed prior to a final decision: (1) Interlocutory orders granting, continuing, modifying, refusing or dissolving injunctions; (2) Interlocutory orders appointing receivers; (3) Interlocutory decrees in certain admiralty cases; (4) Judgments in civil actions which are final except for an accounting. 28 U.S.C. §1292(a).

A district judge also has discretion to permit an interlocutory appeal where he certifies that the order "involves a controlling question of law as to which there is substantial ground for difference of opinion and that an immediate appeal from the order may materially advance the ultimate termination of the litigation." An appeal thereupon must be taken within ten days after the order. 28 U.S.C. §1292(b).

By statute, the Supreme Court may prescribe rules providing for appeals of interlocutory decisions from a district court to the Court of Appeals that are not otherwise allowed by statute. 28 U.S.C. §1292(e).

2.   Extraordinary Writs

Interlocutory review may also be available by means of the extraordinary writs of mandamus and prohibition. 28 U.S.C. §1651(a). Issuance of these writs is discretionary and they are used very sparingly; the writs will not issue if adequate review by appeal is available. Mandamus requires a judge to perform an action, while prohibition forbids his taking some action. Mandamus has been used to require jury trial where it had been denied improperly, *Beacon Theatres, Inc. v. Westover*, 359 U.S. 500 (1959); to review a discovery order alleged to constitute "usurpation of judicial power," *Schlagenhauf v. Holder,* 379 U.S. 104 (1964); and to prevent an improper remand of an action removed from state court. *Thermtron Products, Inc. v. Hermansdorfer*, 423 U.S. 336 (1976).

B.   FINAL JUDGMENT RULE

1.   In General

Multistate Bar Review Book 2

The federal courts of appeals have "jurisdiction of appeals from all final decisions of the district courts." 28 U.S.C. §1291. A final decision "generally is one which ends the litigation on the merits and leaves nothing for the court to do but execute the judgment." *Catlin v. United States*, 324 U.S. 229 (1945). This rule minimizes delay and expense because all alleged errors are appealed after the trial rather than in succession during the trial, and because appeal may be unnecessary if the aggrieved party wins a favorable judgment despite the errors.

During trial, most orders are not directly appealable. After trial, an order granting a new trial is not appealable; although an order denying a new trial is not appealable, the judgment itself can be appealed. Although an order may not be appealable in itself, an appeal from the final judgment may raise the erroneous order and it may then be reviewed.

2. Final Decision of Part of Case

Under Rule 54(b), when there is no just reason for delay, the trial court can enter final judgment as to some of the claims or parties in a suit involving multiple claims or parties. Such a final decision of part of a case is immediately appealable and the statutory period for filing an appeal runs from the date of entry of the partial final judgment, not from the date when final judgment is entered as to the remainder of the suit. If there is a court order or decision but no express direction for entry of judgment as to part of a case, there is no immediate right to appeal, and the court may revise the order or decision until there is an entry of judgment.

3. Exceptions

a. Collateral Orders

Orders as to certain collateral matters that are unrelated to the merits of the underlying claims may be immediately appealed even though no final decision has been made in the main case. Only if the issues raised present "a serious and unsettled question" and if some danger of irreparable harm is shown will interlocutory appeal be available. Thus, for example, an order denying a motion to require a plaintiff to post security for defendant's costs in a shareholder's suit is immediately appealable. *Cohen v. Beneficial Loan Corp.*, 337 U.S. 541 (1949). However, an order denying the certification of a suit as a class action is not immediately appealable. *Coopers & Lybrand v. Livesay*, 437 U.S. 463 (1978).

b. Irreparable Injury

Interlocutory appeal will also be granted of "an order, otherwise nonappealable, determining substantial rights of the parties which will be irreparably lost if delayed until final judgment." *United States v. Wood*, 295 F.2d 772 (1961).

4. Procedure for Appeal

To take an appeal, a party files a notice of appeal with the clerk of the district court. The notice need only specify the party appealing, the judgment, order or part appealed from, and the court to which the appeal is taken. Fed. R. App. P. 3. An appeal will not be dismissed for informality of the notice; the court should be liberal in construing the sufficiency of the notice. *Foman v. Davis*, 371 U.S. 178 (1962). Also see *Becker v. Montgomery, Attorney General of Ohio, et al*, 532 U.S. 757 (2001). (When a party files a timely notice of appeal, the failure to sign the notice does not require the court of appeals to dismiss the appeal).

The notice of appeal must be filed within thirty days after entry of judgment (or within sixty days if the United States is a party). However, the time for filing an appeal may be extended an additional thirty days by the court for "excusable neglect or good cause." Fed. R. App. P. 4(a).

The time for filing a notice of appeal will be suspended by the timely filing of any of the following post-trial motions: (1) a renewed motion for judgment as a matter of law (Rule 50(b)); (2) a motion to amend the findings (Rule 52(b)); (3) a motion for a new trial (Rule 59); or (4) a motion to alter or amend the judgment (Rule 59(e)). The thirty-day period for filing notice runs from the grant or denial of the motion. A notice of appeal filed before the disposition of the motion has no effect, and a new notice must be filed within the period after decision on the motion. Fed. R. App. P. 4(a).

If one party files a timely notice of appeal, any other party may file a notice of appeal within fourteen days after the date on which the first notice was filed, or within the remainder of the thirty-day period, whichever is longer. Fed. R. App. P. 4(a).

Usually, the appellant must also file a bond to ensure the payment of his adversary's costs if the judgment is upheld. Fed. R. App. P. 7. He must also file the record on appeal (i.e., the pleadings, motions, orders, verdict and judgment), and any transcript of testimony he wishes to include. The appellant must serve and file his brief within forty days after the record is filed, and the appellee must serve and file his brief within thirty days after the appellant serves his brief. The appellant may serve and file a reply brief within fourteen days after service of the appellee's brief. Oral argument is usually allowed.

C. SCOPE OF REVIEW FOR JUDGE AND JURY

The appellate court reviews only matters that appear on the trial record. Evidence not introduced at trial cannot be presented on appeal. Generally, a party may not appeal from an error at trial unless he made a timely objection at trial (e.g., party cannot appeal erroneous jury instruction unless he objected before the jury retired. Rule 51).

Review of factual determinations at trial is very limited, because the findings of the jury or judge are entitled to deference. An appellate court reviewing a jury verdict will uphold the verdict as long as it is supported by "substantial evidence." If the judge granted a judgment as a matter of law,

Multistate Bar Review Book 2

the appellate court will reverse him only where there was substantial evidence to support a verdict contrary to the judge's. The appellate court may direct entry of judgment as a matter of law under Rule 50 instead of remanding the case for a new trial upon determining that the verdict cannot be sustained. *Weisgram v. Marley Company,* 120 S.Ct. 1011 (2000).

> *For example, in* Weisgram, supra, *the plaintiff brought a diversity suit in federal court seeking wrongful death damages alleging that a defective heater manufactured by defendant caused his mother's death. Plaintiff introduced expert testimony which defendant argued was inadmissible as unreliable. The jury returned a verdict for plaintiff and the defendant's motion for judgment as a matter of law was denied. On appeal, the court found that defendant's motion should have been granted because the experts' testimony was speculative and not scientifically sound. The appeals court did not order a new trial. Hence, the U.S. Supreme Court ruled that an appeals court may order judgement as a matter of law when evidence was erroneously admitted at trial.*

Where the case was tried without a jury, the judge's findings of fact, whether based on oral or documentary evidence, will be set aside only if they were "clearly erroneous" and due regard must be given to the opportunity of the trial court to judge the credibility of the witnesses. Rule 52(a). In areas where a judge has broad discretion, e.g., scope of discovery, the appellate court will overturn his decision only if he was clearly wrong. If the judge has made an error of law, either in instructing a jury or in stating his conclusions in a nonjury trial, the judgment will be reversed, unless the error was harmless.

Made in the USA
Lexington, KY
06 May 2018